Hope's Daughters

Hope's Daughters

A Helping a Day of Wisdom and Hope

R. Wayne Willis

RESOURCE *Publications* · Eugene, Oregon

HOPE'S DAUGHTERS
A Helping a Day of Wisdom and Hope

Resource Publications
An Imprint of Wipf and Stock Publishers
199 W. 8th Ave., Suite 3
Eugene, OR 97401

www.wipfandstock.com

ISBN 13: 978-1-62564-787-0

Manufactured in the U.S.A.

Quotations from the Bible are taken from the Contemporary English Version, 1995, the American Bible Society, 1865 Broadway, New York, New York 10023.

Dedication to Our Grandchildren

Charles Jackson
Anna Gracelynn
Wyatt Blake
Clark Howard
Campbell Scott
Abilene Rose

You must remember this: in the midst of any winter,
there is within you an invincible summer.

Your Adoring Popple

Contents

Preface

When I was twenty-five, I spent the summer working with impoverished children in Brooklyn, New York. I drove the Big Blue Bus. Every Saturday I relocated a load of pre-teens from the asphalt, concrete, and brick jungle of Williams Avenue in Brooklyn to Camp Shiloh, forty-five miles away, where they would experience a week in the verdant, quiet, and cool hills of New Jersey. I can still hear the *oohs* and *aahs* of the kids when they saw their first cow or horse. I can still feel the bus tilt right when they rushed to that side to gawk, point, and marvel.

On my one weekend off that summer, this Tennessee boy walked the sidewalks of Manhattan for the first time, just to see what he could see. I came across a scruffy man wearing the first sandwich board I had ever seen. It read: *I Am a Fool for Christ's Sake.* People approaching him smirked or snickered or rolled their eyes and stepped aside and looked the other way. After I passed him by, my curiosity got the better of me and I looked back to see if there might be something equally provocative on the other side. There I saw giant words that seared my soul for life: *Whose Fool Are You?*

Most of us, as the man in the sandwich board demonstrated, are willing to make fools of ourselves for something—shopping, food, sex, booze, videogames, money, looks, text messaging, status, education, gambling, fame, thrills, pornography, golf—something. If I am going to make a fool of myself, be a dope for something, that summer I decided that it should be for something huge, something helpful, something worthy of the one life I have to spend. My "thing" for the 1960s had been education and degrees, but satisfaction from my professional student identity was wearing thin. Eventually I decided that becoming a *hopeaholic* would be the cause of my life. I decided to concentrate on earning the epitaph *Here Lies a Hope Dope* and maybe take a few others with me.

One year later, I enrolled in a Clinical Pastoral Education program in Memphis, Tennessee, to become a hospital chaplain. For thirty years, most of those in Kosair Children's Hospital in Louisville, Kentucky, I had a ringside seat to the indomitable power of hope. What I learned in those years is that nothing in life is more precious, more life-preserving, than to have someone, when we are teetering on the edge of nothingness, come alongside and help keep our flickering candle of hope from going out. I am indebted to all those patients and their families for almost everything I know—down in the marrow of my bones—about the nature and behavior of hope.

Something I know for sure, because I saw it happen so many times, is that the capacity for hope, like the capacity for growing African violets, reading Greek, riding a horse, saying "I love you," living within means, playing chess, or being assertive, is cultivatable. In the movie *Coal Miner's Daughter*, when Loretta Lynn's husband Mooney gives her a guitar, she objects: "I don't know how to play this!" Mooney barks back: "Well, no one knows before they learn!"

Gloom-and-doom people sometimes learn to become positive people. The Grinch ends up hosting the Christmas feast. Ebenezer Scrooges sometimes morph into philanthropists. Ruthless Chuck Colson, who boasted he would run over his own grandmother to get Richard Nixon re-elected president, became a devout Christian. Larry Trapp, grand dragon of the White Knights of the Ku Klux Klan and a neo-Nazi, largely because of the magnanimous spirit he experienced in Rabbi Michael Weisser and his family, converted to Judaism. Bereaved parents, having lost life's most precious gift, who think for a time they cannot go on and life cannot be worth living, choose—though eviscerated—to soldier on.

It is a cliché, but where there is life, there *is* hope. That is good news. The better news is that hopefulness, like Loretta Lynn's ability to play the guitar, can be acquired. "No one knows before they learn."

Each of these 365 helpings of hope was originally published as "A Hope Note," a column I began writing for *The Corydon Democrat*, a Southern Indiana weekly, in June, 2005. My intent each week is to encourage readers, as Tennyson wrote in "The Ancient Sage," to "cleave ever to the sunnier side of doubt."

Augustine said: "Hope has two lovely daughters. Their names are anger and courage: anger at the way things are but ought not be, and courage to see that they do not remain the way they are." Hope is anything but some passive, vague, wimpy, wispy, cross-your-fingers kind of thing. It is a mighty force that empowers people to make life better. Jesus taught that the denizens of heaven will be those who did something—fed the hungry, cared for the sick, welcomed strangers, clothed the needy, visited prisoners, gave cold water to the parched. Hope moves us to get up and get busy doing something helpful.

Just how important is hope in the grand scheme of things? Jurgen Moltmann in his seminal *Theology of Hope* wrote: "Totally without hope one cannot live. To live without hope is to cease to live. Hell is hopelessness. It is no accident that above the entrance to Dante's hell is the inscription: 'Leave behind all hope, you who enter here.'"

Here is my prescription: Try a helping of hope a day for a year. I hope that, perhaps one day when you may be teetering on the edge of despair, one of these helpings becomes spiritual elixir that enlivens and emboldens your hope.

R. Wayne Willis
Louisville, Kentucky
Father's Day, 2014

Acknowledgments

I feel bounteous gratitude way down in my heart for the help of my two expert readers, the love of my life Dottie Jones Willis, and Carden Michael Willis, our youngest son. They caught poor word choices, subject-verb disagreements, misused semicolons, commas needed, commas unneeded, convoluted thinking, and confusingly-long sentences that needed to be broken down into two or three or more. They make me look, if not good, better.

January

January 1

Most of us who have been knocked down a few times draw strength from some master story, a narrative that urges us to get up and walk on. Our "master" or "super" story might be a scene from a *Rocky* movie, or Robin Roberts fighting her cancer, or a grandparent handling bad news with courage, dignity, and grace.

A friend told me that his latest master story came from an elephant that Dereck and Beverly Joubert, award-winning filmmakers for *National Geographic*, captured on film in Botswana. One night the Jouberts watched a pride of eight lions attack and take down a fully grown elephant. While filming the lions chewing on the downed elephant's back and legs, the Jouberts can be heard rooting for the elephant, "Come on, get up! Get up!" As she watched the elephant accept her fate, Beverly softly whispered this interpretation: "Death begins in the eyes. We've seen this so many times with animals when they give up hope."[1]

Then a mighty miracle occurred. Suddenly the elephant began to swing her body, rocking back and forth. The downed elephant summoned from her depths a mighty surge of strength, enough to explode to her feet, shake off every one of the lions, and charge into the darkness. She said with her body and her whole being: "Enough! I don't have to take this anymore!"

My friend's new master story is really a universal play with four acts:

I. We get brought low.

II. Feeling alone and devoid of hope, we grovel and feel sorry for ourselves.

III. After a time, some voice from somewhere whispers: "Enough! Get off your pity-pot!"

IV. We stand up, dust ourselves off, lift our chins, set our jaws, face forward, and march on.

Happy New Year. Hope on!

January 2

A thirteen-year-old girl, at her church's candlelight Christmas Eve service, rose and gave this testimonial:

> Darkness. Have you ever been in the dark? Did you feel like you would never get out? Have you even gotten out? I've been in the dark. I didn't like it. If you've ever been in the dark, you feel cold, alone, and disconnected from the world. That's how I felt when I was taken away from my birth father. When my birth mom died, my birth dad and I did a lot together. I wanted to be his little shadow. Most of the time when my father was out, you saw me with him. He was the only parent I had left. When I was taken away, I was heartbroken. I now had lost my father and, to make it worse, I went from foster home to foster home. After the second or third foster home, I didn't share my feelings. I still struggle even to this day. I didn't let anyone in my heart. I was tired of being hurt. When the parents I have now took me in, I just thought it was some other couple who would keep me for a little while and then pass me on. But that wasn't the case at all. They put a hand out to me and told me to hold on to it. I grabbed it, and slowly they pulled me out of the dark. They made me a family member. I had a family, and I held onto them. I'm still holding that hand of light today. Neither side is letting go. I found my light.

Oliver Wendell Holmes said that almost all the truth-telling in the world is done by children. I think he spoke truth.

January 3

Most of us have some sound ideas on how we should improve our lives. What we may lack is the courage to take that first step and then the will to follow through.

Money is a great motivator. Heart follows treasure, as in: "Your heart will always be where your treasure is."[2] Really want to give up fried food for your coronary arteries' sake? Promise $25 to family, friends, and work associates if they see you eating any fried food in the next six months. Put the deal in writing, duplicate it, hand it out, post it on your refrigerator, or drop circulars from an airplane.

Many years ago I became aware that I was addicted to caffeine. I raised my right hand and promised my family, my work associates, and my church that if anyone saw me so much as take one sip of coffee over the next six months, I would give that person a $50 bill. I did not slip.

Want to quit saying disparaging things about yourself? Get your family to help you itemize the put-downs that unconsciously pass your lips, such as: "Anything that can go wrong will go wrong for me" or "Just my luck." Then the deal is to drop $5 in a jar, all proceeds going for a good cause like Habitat for Humanity every time your family catches you downing yourself.

I know one recently-bereaved wife who hated identifying herself as a widow. Her grief counselor advised her never to use the word again but to say instead: "My husband died two years ago." The counselor made her (half in jest) promise to give him $10 every time she slipped and used the dreaded "w" word.

Really want to change? Words are too easy. Few things motivate like putting money where your mouth is.

January 4

Ten years after snow-skiing 750 miles to reach the South Pole and one year after becoming the first woman to row solo across the Atlantic Ocean, Tori Murden McClure met Thor Heyerdahl. Heyerdahl had in 1947 crossed the Pacific Ocean, sailing from South America to the Polynesian Islands on a raft made of balsa logs, proving that South Americans had the materials and the ability to reach Polynesia hundreds of years before Columbus sailed to America. Heyerdahl's *Kon-Tiki: Across the Pacific by Raft* became a bestseller in 1950. In 1951 the documentary film of the voyage won an Academy Award.

One day after the two explorers met, eighty-six-year-old Thor asked Tori if she had plans to write a book. After she admitted that she had thought about it, he whispered to her: "Be sure to leave room enough to grow."[3] She knew that he meant something like: "Do not ever let yourself get so totally defined by your past, however great or heroic or inconsequential your life has been."

The day we believe there are no new worlds to conquer is the day something precious in our core begins to wither and die. Lucy once lectured Charlie Brown: "You know, life is like an ocean liner. Some people take their deck chair and put it on the stern, to see where they have been, and some put their deck chair on the bow, to see where they are going. Charlie Brown, tell me, where do you want to put your deck chair?"

Charlie Brown sheepishly confessed, "I can't get my deck chair unfolded."

Some of us, like Charlie Brown, have a deck chair still folded. We can make this year *annus mirabilis*, a year of wonders, a year for exploring new worlds of personal growth.

January 5

Being aware of all good future possibilities is impossible, as impossible as looking at a single apple seed and divining how many apples will come from it. A first grader can count the seeds in an apple, but no genius can count the apples in a seed.

On Saturday, December 18, Louisville meteorologists predicted a heavy snow on the following Wednesday. They described how the storm would begin forming in Texas on Sunday and reach Louisville three days later—on Wednesday morning, at rush hour to be precise.

I saw the satellite view of Texas that Saturday. It showed not one cloud. I laughed and said to my wife: "Give me a break! Forecasting snow even one day in advance in the Ohio valley is tricky. Do they really expect us to believe they can predict a giant snow five days off, before one cloud has formed?"

On Wednesday morning we had a record nine-inch snow. This layman, looking at charts and satellite and radar images with his untrained eye, was unable to see a single sign that a big snow was coming.

We are all a little like that. We have a giant blind spot when it comes to future possibilities, just as my untrained eye was unable to read the meteorological evidence for a giant snow.

What is hope? Hope is the mental and spiritual decision always to keep the door cracked a little, to stay at least a little open to a good possibility even though at the time we may not be able to see it.

Victorian poet Christina Rossetti's prayer says it well: "Lord, grant me eyes to see within the seed a tree, within the glowing egg a bird, within the shroud a butterfly."

January 6

I attended a lecture on Islam by Imam Yahya Hendi, Muslim chaplain at the National Naval Medical Center in Bethesda, Maryland. In his opening remarks he told how often people, when they first see him and hear his accent, inquire: "Where are you from?" He answers: "I am from dust. I am a dustian." Such is his creative attempt to find common ground, to emphasize commonality, to begin with what unites us instead of what divides us, drawing on the words from Genesis: "You were made out of soil, and you will once again turn into soil."[4]

The opposite of dustianism is tribalism, the assumption that one's own tribe is superior to all others. Over forty years ago my wife and I visited London, Paris, and Rome with a tour group. There was a newly-married couple from Connecticut in our group. It soon became clear that their primary agenda was to snap pictures of each other in front of monuments and landmarks to prove to people back home that they had once actually been there. They organized each day around finding a place where they could get *real* food, which to them was American food—specifically, a cheeseburger, fries, and a carbonated drink. They had no interest in understanding, much less appreciating, what to them were vastly inferior cultures.

My high school classmates and I receive at least one e-mail a week from a former classmate whom I barely knew. She forwards articles that either tout her home state or promote noxious (to me) political views. She ends each preachment with multiple exclamation marks!!!!! Each e-mail exudes the attitude: "Pity the poor fool who doesn't believe like me."

Extreme tribalism burns Korans and launches terrorist attacks. The polar opposite of tribalism is a humbler "Come and talk it over"[5] approach that is grounded in the reality that others, just like us, are dustians.

January 7

My grandfather, whom I adored and who adored me, was born in 1892. He was eleven years old when the Wright brothers made their flight at Kitty Hawk.

I remember my grandfather describing the thrill of seeing the first airplane fly over, and how children and adults alike were running and screaming and waving at the godlike man in the incredible flying machine. In early 1969, my parents and I marveled that my grandfather got to experience both the first manned flight and would live to see Neil Armstrong walk on the moon. What unbelievable progress he witnessed in his lifetime!

My grandfather died two months before Apollo 11 made it to the moon.

My father worked as a handyman in a printing office in Manchester, Tennessee. There was one sink in the back of the shop for both washing hands and drinking water. There were dippers hanging on the wall on either side of the sink. The one on the right of the sink we all shared. After we drank from it, we would wash it out by swirling a little water in it and then place it back on the hook. The one on the left was for Henry. He swept the floors and took out the trash. Henry was black. I remember people tittering once when I used Henry's dipper by mistake.

I never knew Henry's last name.

When I saw all the tears streaming down white and black faces the night Barack Obama was elected president the first time, I remembered Henry and his dipper.

What is the greater marvel, that we moved from the Wright brothers to Neil Armstrong in my grandfather's lifetime—a brilliant technological feat—or that we moved from Henry the help to Barack Obama the president in my lifetime?

January 8

It is difficult, yea impossible, to exaggerate the power of hope in the scheme of things.

Think of two giant magnets. One is gravity, beneath us, pulling all things down. The other is hope, before us, drawing all things forward. We cannot stop hope any more than we can stop photosynthesis. That strong-as-gravity magnetic power lures all living things into the future.

Look around. See it in the plant kingdom, as the little acorn's genetic endowment guides it on its way to becoming a majestic oak. See it in March daffodils yellowing the hillside. See it this summer in weeds that thrive in the uncultivated garden. "The violets in the mountains," Tennessee Williams wrote, "break the rocks."

See it in the animal kingdom, in the two-inch-long loggerhead turtle that from the day of its birth on the shores of South Carolina navigates by the earth's magnetic field on an odyssey of eight thousand miles around the Sargasso Sea and back to South Carolina to fulfill the role nature assigned it.

This stupendous force that moves plants and animals forward looks and smells and sounds a lot like what we human animals, when we experience it in ourselves and others, call hope. See it in the sweat of the cardiac rehab patient on the treadmill, in the premature infant exiting the womb squalling and kicking, and in emaciated Sudanese teenagers crossing a desert in search of food.

Rogers Hornsby, one of the best hitters ever in baseball, second only to Ty Cobb, said in an interview: "People ask me what I do in winter when there's no baseball. I'll tell you what I do. I stare out the window and wait for spring."

Hope is what the prospect of spring is for inveterate baseball players or fans in winter—it keeps them going.

January 9

In the last few years, "distracted driving" has become common parlance. We use the term primarily to refer to people irresponsible and inconsiderate enough to read and write electronic messages while driving.

Now some are witnessing "distracted doctoring" in hospitals. Stories are surfacing of neurosurgeons making personal phone calls while operating on a brain, technicians checking airfares or shopping on e-Bay or Amazon while running a heart bypass machine, anesthesiologists using the operating room computer to check basketball scores during surgery, and surgery nurses reading and writing personal e-mails on an operating room computer during a procedure.

Churches are witnessing what could be called "distracted devotion." A cartoon in a religious journal, with no caption, depicts about ten congregants who have just shaken the minister's hand at the end of a service and left the building. There they all are, including the minister, standing on the church lawn, looking not at each other but down at electronic devices, reading and writing text messages and updating Facebook information. No caption was needed.

Thirty years ago in his bestseller *Megatrends*, John Naisbitt predicted that the more high-tech life becomes, the greater will be our need for high-touch (skin-to-skin, face-to-face) antidotes. Naisbitt, a true prophet, foresaw that problem long before Steve Jobs created iPhones, iPads, and iPods, and Mark Zuckerberg friended us with Facebook.

The scene of churchgoers standing on the church lawn making love to words and images in little hand-held boxes stands as a symbol of what has become an addictive, shallow lifestyle for so many.

Should enthusiastically swapping trivia supplant quality time with people on life's lawn, individuals we can physically reach out and touch right here and now?

January 10

She died the way most of us hope to die—full of years, at home, lucid, with family members responding to her every physical and emotional need. One of her sons, when he served her orange juice on her last mornings, said that she would take a sip, smile, and exclaim, "This tastes so good!" When he adjusted the pillow under her feet, she smiled and thanked him, "That feels so good!" When he opened drapes to let in light, she broke into song, channeling John Denver's "Sunshine on my Shoulders."

Survivor of four heart surgeries stemming from rheumatic fever in childhood, this retired kindergarten teacher poured undying devotion and energy into helping the poor. She taught immigrants English as a second language, helped the homeless and ex-convicts find housing, and often invited them into her home for a meal.

When she died, the family discovered a personal manifesto that she had adopted years earlier, typed on red construction paper and taped inside the front opening of her Bible:

> Because the world is poor and starving, go with bread. Because the world is filled with fear, go with courage. Because the world is filled with despair, go with hope. Because the world is filled with lies, go with truth. Because the world is sick with sorrow, go with joy. Because the world is weary of wars, go with peace. Because the world is seldom fair, go with justice. Because the world is under judgment, go with mercy. Because the world will die without it, go with love.[6]

She left her minister a final charge to be read to any who might attend her memorial service: "If, by chance, you wish to remember me, do it with a kind word or deed to someone who needs you."

May we inherit her light.

January 11

Today I passed a (barely) teenage boy in the grocery aisle whose black shirt greeted me in large white letters: "Here I Am. What Are Your Other Two Wishes?" I involuntarily smiled one of those knowing smiles. I remember as an adolescent feeling such exuberant watch-out-world-here-I-come, I-can-be-anything-I-want-to-be grandiosity. Later that day I thought how appropriate it would have been if on the back of the boy's shirt, to add some balance to the front, were the words, "It's Only One Six-Billionth About Me."

Wise people and prophets in every age have advised us to hold our divinity and our mortality, our "I'm king of the world" blessedness and our "We're poor little lambs who have lost our way" frailty, in healthy tension.

When Julius Caesar paraded through the streets of Rome, fresh off victories in Gaul or Germany, a lowly slave stood by his side in the chariot, holding Caesar's crown. As adoring throngs cheered the august one, the slave performed his other role, occasionally whispering in Caesar's ear three Latin words, *sic transit gloria*. In modern English: "All fame is fleeting."

Rabbi Simcha Bunam of Peshischa taught that we should carry two scraps of paper in our pockets. The message on one reads: "The world was created for my sake." The message in the other pocket reads: "You are dust and ashes."[7] When we get to feeling too much the truth of one, we need to remind ourselves of the truth of the other.

In my experience, for every narcissist who needs to hear the dust and ashes message, there are between two and twenty little lost sheep who need to hear the one about being great with divinity.

January 12

She grew up on a tobacco farm in Henrietta, Tennessee. At age twenty four, Pat Summitt stood on a podium in Montreal, having won an Olympic medal. Standing there, she felt imbued with the insight that "if you won enough basketball games, there's no such thing as poor, or backward, or country, or female, or inferior."

This Olympian coached 38 years at the University of Tennessee and won more basketball games (1,098) than anyone, male or female, in NCAA Division I history. Those victories included eight national championships. In her sixties, suffering from Alzheimer's, Summitt has published her memoirs in a book aptly titled *Sum it Up*. Here are some of her summary findings about basketball and life:

Discipline. Over the 38 years Summitt coached the Lady Vols, one hundred percent of her players graduated. She required them to sit in one of the first three rows of every class. Missing class was not permitted or excused for any reason. "If you cut a class, you didn't play in the next game. Period."

Motivation. She considered motivation much harder than teaching because "you have to give more of yourself, constantly rack your brain to think about how to start somebody's engine."

Commitment. While most authorities on commitment emphasize risk-taking, Summitt says it is equally about tedium, "the willingness to persevere through problems without quitting and, more important, without demoralization."

Focus. "If you chase two rabbits, you won't catch one."

Explaining her extraordinary lifetime achievements, Summitt channels Nora Ephron: "Above all, be the heroine of your own life, not the victim."

I have found myself mulling over one of her comments. About Tyler, her only child whom she idolizes, Summitt mentions that "his default disposition is set on thoughtfulness."[8] My troubling take-away from this wise woman's comment is: "On what is my default disposition set?"

January 13

For over thirty years now, in icy January I remember "the man in the water."

On January 13, 1982, less than one minute after taking off in a heavy snowstorm, Air Florida Flight 90 crashed into Washington D. C.'s 14th Street Bridge over the Potomac River. Four of the five crew members and seventy of seventy-four passengers perished.

I have remembered two things from the live television coverage of the crash. One was the temperature—24 degrees. The other was the sight of about a half dozen survivors of the crash clinging to the plane's tail section as it sank below the icy waters. What I have remembered most was the man in the water. For several days, no one knew the middle-aged, balding man's name. But all who watched cannot forget what he did.

As a helicopter crew dropped life vests and flotation devices, he passed lifelines they lowered to him—that could have pulled him to safety—to others. Three times he handed off to strangers his ticket to salvation. By the time the helicopter crew made their last round trip to hoist the one last survivor, the tail section and the man in the water had disappeared.

The coroner determined that the cause of death for only one of the seventy four bodies was drowning. His name was Arland Williams Jr., a balding, forty-six-year-old federal bank examiner and father of two.[9] He had lived his life conservatively until that January day when he magnanimously gave it up for total strangers.

Richard Dawkins discusses in *The Selfish Gene*[10] how in nature red in tooth and claw bees sting (and die) to protect the hive. Birds risk their lives to warn the flock of an approaching hawk. Our species alone, he argues, has the power to choose to rebel against the designs of our selfish gene.

Our species, fully evolved, might look a lot like Arland Williams Jr.

January 14

"IF WE ONLY WANTED TO BE HAPPY, IT WOULD BE EASY, BUT WE WANT
TO BE HAPPIER THAN OTHER PEOPLE, WHICH IS DIFFICULT SINCE WE THINK
THEM HAPPIER THAN THEY ARE"—Baron de Montesquieu

You wonder what Montesquieu, eighteenth century Enlightenment philosopher, would make of the pursuit of happiness in this Facebook age. Today when friends showcase their luxurious cruise and cute puppy, their "What, Me Worry?" faces and accomplished children, we the befriended, with our less-than-luminous lives, may feel just a tad shabby.

I have read "The Story of Ferdinand," a children's story, to my grandchildren several times. It is about a bull in Spain that preferred smelling flowers under his cork tree to snorting and butting heads and fighting other bulls. One day five men came and picked out what looked to them to be the biggest, baddest bull of all, and took him to Madrid to chase and bore a matador. On the day of the bullfight, when Ferdinand the Fiercest got in the ring and saw the flowers in all the lovely ladies' hair, he got as close to them as he could, quietly sat down, and enjoyed sniffing the pleasant smells. Ferdinand would not fight, no matter how many times the Picadores stuck him with spears, so they packed him home to his beloved cork tree. The last page of the story shows Ferdinand smelling flowers, accompanied with these final words: "He is very happy."[11]

Written by Munro Leaf and published in 1936, this story was burned in Nazi Germany because being true to oneself—not conforming to the herd—was not tolerated, much less advocated.

In "Disiderata," Max Ehrman wrote: "If you compare yourself with others, you may become vain and bitter, for always there will be greater and lesser persons than yourself."

Why allow Photoshopped images and spotless profiles spun by Facebook friends get you down?

January 15

Some of the new words in dictionaries are "google" used as a verb and "sexting" for sending sexually explicit pictures over a cell phone. If I could coin one word to become part of our vocabulary, it would be *hopenomics*.

The word economics comes from two Greek words, *oikos* meaning house and *nomos* meaning law. An economist was originally one who "laid down the law" in managing the treasures of a household (or city or nation). The emphasis in the word is on stewardship—distributing assets wisely, responsibly, and resourcefully.

Most of us mean to be conscientious economists. We draw up budgets, pay off credit cards, give children allowances, and diversify investments. We intend to care for our assets wisely and responsibly. What would it look like if we applied commensurate intentionality and acumen to hope?

What if parents majored in keeping a sparkle in their children's eyes over signing them up for everything and setting the bar for parental approval sky-high? What if marriages majored in thoughtfulness and affirmation of each other over acquiring the next thing and rising one more rung on the social ladder? What if teachers were free to fire students' imaginations and encourage critical, creative thinking over teaching them to memorize answers for the next test? What if preachers majored in lifting up parishioners' spirits and fortifying them for Monday struggles and inspiring them to serve suffering humanity over indoctrination on parochial niceties and dissing those who disagree?

Hopenomics, simply put, values people over things, integrity over appearances, goodness over rightness, and lifting others up over pulling them down. Hopenomics also requires us to ask, according to the Great Law of the Iroquois, how our actions today will affect the well-being of children seven generations out.

January 16

A friend and I visited Gethsemani Abbey, down in the heart of Kentucky. A mural at the entrance depicted St. Benedict's face and hands and greeted us with his words: "Let All Guests That Come Be Received Like Christ."

The monk who met us exuded hospitality. We asked if we could take his picture. "Sure." We pushed a little more: "What about taking pictures during the prayer service?" "Sure," he said, "We're used to cameras flashing and clicking. Doesn't bother us at all. Fire at will."

After the prayer service, we walked through the cemetery. There, amidst many white crosses two feet tall, was the grave of Thomas Merton, maybe the most widely read and venerated monk of our times. His white cross was two feet tall. A small brass plaque on the cross simply read: "Fr. Louis Merton, Died Dec. 10, 1968." Visitors had draped two rosaries around his cross.

We learned that the Trappist monks at Gethsemani rise every morning at 3:00 a. m. and have a cup of coffee before the first of seven prayer services interspersed through the work day. Their primary work that supports the Abbey these days is the production and mail-order sale of homemade foods.

Several years ago an eighty-nine-year-old priest leading visitors on a tour there commented: "This place has no practical value. It's about as valuable as ballet. Or opera. Or a rainbow. Or a peacock. Or daffodils. What practical value do they have?"

We value most things because of what they can do for us. They are means to an end. We use them. Some things are valuable to us just for being there. Gethsemane stands as a symbol of hospitality and simplicity, especially for the city slickers among us who are preoccupied with getting and spending.

We bought a box of Trappist bourbon fudge and some Trappist cheese and headed back to the bustling city.

January 17

I was having breakfast with a relative who recently had to move into a nursing home. As we ate, he eagerly gave me, in hushed tones, the lowdown on some of the other residents.

"See that woman in the black dress at the next table? I think she's German, and she finds something critical to say about the food or the service at every meal."

"Hear that man talking real loud? I think he was a preacher, and he loves to hear the sound of his own voice."

"That short woman at the table behind you—she's losing her mind, and at every meal she tells the ladies at her table that her daughter is rummaging through all her papers and that her son dug up her husband and moved him to another place."

For some strange reason, as I scanned the sample of humanity in that dining room, my mind flashed back to a retaining wall I once saw in Delphi, Greece, on the approach to the Temple of Apollo. Every single stone in the fifteen-feet-tall wall that Delphic masons built to support the temple's terrace is a different shape and size. Yet all the stones fit together perfectly, like the pieces of a picture puzzle. You could not insert a piece of paper into any seam. For twenty-five hundred years, earthquakes have not been able to bring down this wall of irregular stones surrounded by regular foundations that have all crumbled.

There is something to be said for being mixed up with irregular stones—people not like us. We learn more from people unlike us, people who don't ditto what we say. Rubber stampers do not enlarge or enrich us; they only reinforce our prejudices.

And sometimes the irregulars among us can help us grow in gratitude, in the awareness that there but for the grace of God go the rest of us.

January 18

Birds do it. Dogs and frogs do it. Snakes and cicadas do it too.

Molting—casting off the outer garment—is more perilous for some animals than for others. Lobsters shed their entire skeleton up to twenty-five times in the first five years of life. Because the lobster's skeleton is on the outside and is so hard that it has no give in it, if it does not shed its shell regularly, it will not grow up; in fact, it cannot grow at all. All through its life cycle, many times the lobster has to lose weight, crack its old shell, and wiggle free.

A just-molted lobster is as soft as a child's rubber toy lobster. With no shell, the lobster is easy prey, very vulnerable. The just-molted lobster has to find a hiding place from predators, like a crevice or cave, until its new body armor arrives.

Shedding is for us humans a major part of "wising up." My wife and I currently are in the process of stuffing many boxes with clothes and books we have decided we will never wear or read again and taking them to Goodwill. We are pulling junk from our storage areas and setting it out for the garbage trucks to haul off. We want to spare our surviving children that unnecessary ordeal.

An essential part of growing up and becoming fully human is shedding masks. Anne Morrow Lindbergh wrote: "I find I am shedding hypocrisy in human relationships. What a rest that will be! The most exhausting thing in life, I have discovered, is being insincere."

It is scary to open the visor of our suit of armor and expose ourselves and, like the lobster, make ourselves vulnerable for a time. But it is necessary if, as the Skin Horse told the Velveteen Rabbit, we are ever to become real.

January 19

"Why do you think people leave their bicycle locks here?" I asked three companions as we walked across the Hohenzollern Bridge in Cologne, Germany. Thousands of padlocks had been attached to the chain-link fence separating the pedestrian walkway from one of the world's busiest train bridges.

A local, standing there reading the inscriptions, explained: "Lovers carve their name on a lock, lock it onto the grille, kiss, and throw the key into the Rhine. It expresses their conviction that their love is a 'lock' for life." One lock read: "Daniel and Nicole 21/12/2009." "Christiana and Willfried" was scratched crudely on another. One creative person had attached with three locks a polished brass ship under full sail, professionally engraved with two words: "Special RelationSHIP."

Many of us did something similar in days of yore when we carved initials into a tree, like "WW + PS."

I like the location. Bridges, like love, connect two separate or isolated entities.

I like the symbolic act of throwing away the key. In our easy-come, easy-go culture, love locks express a desire for something more, a commitment more than a connection, more tenacious than a tryst, more lasting than serial fallings into lust.

I think I can understand the cynicism of those who are disillusioned with love, even those who have taken wire cutters to the padlock. And I can understand those who argue that humans are not wired to be monogamous, or that it is a holy calling to stay celibate, or that it is morally acceptable, even superior, to choose a life devoid of romantic entanglements.

But there is also a place for love-locked souls on the Hohenzollern Bridge who resonate to Shakespeare: "Love is not love / which alters when it alteration finds / or bends with the remover to remove."[12]

January 20

In 1986, The United Church of Canada formally apologized to Canada's aborigines for all the wrongs the church inflicted on them hundreds of years earlier. The United States Senate in 2009 officially apologized for slavery. The apology came 146 years after Lincoln issued the Emancipation Proclamation.

I am trying to understand what good it does to apologize for something someone else did generations ago. Could it be mainly to make ourselves feel and look good for not having done what they did? Let me give it a try.

My grandfather's grandfather, Joseph Willis, in his Tennessee will dated May 9, 1843, bequeathed to his wife "all the land belonging to me with all my negroes, horses, cattle, hogs, sheep, and farming utensils."

The 1810 census showed that Joseph's father, Peter Willis, had thirteen slaves. The slaves were listed right next to "100 yards of homespun fabric made annually by the family (value $50)." In the 1820 census, Peter's plantation was up to sixteen slaves.

In 1833, a slave belonging to Peter's neighbor was hanged. Many slaveholders in the area, including Peter Willis, signed a petition requesting the government to reimburse Peter's neighbor for the value of this slave. The petition does not identify the slave's crime or name or estimated monetary value.

There! I did it. I feel better now, having apologized for the sins of my fathers.

Not really. I assume that my ancestors were just doing what those in their time and culture did, possibly never questioning whether regarding another human being as a piece of property—like a hog or a piece of fabric—was right or wrong.

There is one thing more important than apologizing for the actions of our ancestors. It should move us to ask which people our descendants will wonder how we, in our time and culture, could so blindly and ignorantly mistreat.

January 21

Seated, waiting for the announcement to begin boarding the plane, I noticed for the first time the sign. It had two arrows. One pointed the way for Elite Access, the other for General Boarding. I cracked a slight smile and made a slight groan. I would rather lie down on a bed of nails than stand in a line marked "Elite." I confess that may reveal something deficient about me.

This economy ticket holder, seated in General Boarding three rows behind the plane's Elite, got to observe the pampering going on up there. First, their own private steward whispered with a smile to those of us seated in the cheap seats not to use their bathroom, located just inside the elite section, but to utilize the bathroom in the back of the plane. Then she pulled a thin veil to separate them from us, and latched a rope across the entrance to their section, just in case we forgot. The elite had paid much more for their seats, procuring not just perks of wine and leg room and fluffed pillows, but separation from the riff-raff.

I have since learned that two hundred years ago the French traveled long distances in a covered vehicle called a diligence, which was a glorified stagecoach pulled by five horses. It could carry up to eighteen people. There was room for three elite in the front seat, six middle class in, of course, the middle seat, and six poor people in the back of the coach. An additional two or three— the poorest poor—could be piled on top with the baggage.

Elitism gone to seed is self-righteous arrogance, based on the fiction that money or education or power or bloodline makes us organically different from the proletariat.

I am going to stick with the old proverb that, after the game, the king and the pawn go back into the same box.

January 22

Some of us relish playing a game called "devil's advocate." Over lunch, a friend told me about an epiphany he had many years ago. A mysterious person appeared to him and charged him with a mission, the meaning of which my friend still ponders. Trading on the strength of our relationship, after listening and asking questions for a while, I ventured: "Okay, I'm going to play devil's advocate. Couldn't that very potent, very personal, very real visitation possibly have been a dream fabricated by your unconscious mind?"

A devil's advocate takes a position to test the strength of someone else's position, probing for weaknesses that might help the other person think about it more critically and clarify things more accurately, or at least consider alternative interpretations.

The Roman Catholic Church created the office of devil's advocate in 1587. Pope Sixtus V established the position to question the qualifications of a person being considered for canonization or beatification, so that the process didn't progress carelessly or easily. The job of devil's advocate was to be skeptical, to look for problems in the evidence presented of a candidate's character and saintliness, even to make the case against the miracles attributed to the individual. The office was abolished in 1983 by Pope John Paul II. The number of canonizations and beatifications has soared ever since.[13]

Sometimes we may owe it to our friends, especially those who are unaccustomed to thinking critically about their beliefs—those who are cocksure, dogmatic and intolerant of those who see things differently—opportunity to see things from another point of view. Oliver Cromwell wrote to the Church of Scotland, urging them to repudiate their mule-headed allegiance to King Charles II: "I beseech you, by the bowels of Christ, think it possible you may be mistaken."

January 23

Anabaptists by the thousands were executed by Catholics and Protestants in the sixteenth century. Their crime? They did not believe in infant baptism or war. Holding such unfamiliar, heretical notions on baptism and pacifism, they were punished by death.

Dirk Willems, an Anabaptist awaiting death in a prison near his home in Holland, made a rope from clothes and rappelled down the prison walls. The moat around the prison was covered with ice. Willems dashed across it and made it to the other side. A guard pursuing him fell through the ice. Hearing the guard scream for help, Willems, obeying the commandment of Jesus to love enemies, stopped, turned around, ran back, and pulled the guard to safety. The guard placed Willems under arrest and returned him to prison. On May 16, 1569, Dirk Willems was condemned to death. They burned him at the stake.[14]

Our culture recently finished that once-a-year pageantry where we pivot away from getting ahead, for a few moments, to indulge in a few deferential thoughts and words about a silent baby lying sweetly in a manger. Now done with that, we return to the real world of religious strife and shooting wars of drones, assault rifles, and improvised explosive devices.

The Amish and Mennonites of the sixteenth century, descendants of the Anabaptists, marched to a different drummer. They marched in a dark and bloody time to the disturbing drumming of Jesus's words: "Love your enemies."[15] Many of them like Dirk Willems, because of their peacemaking, lost their lives.

My obedience to Jesus is made of thinner stuff. I am more comfortable with the haloed baby Jesus lying in a manger surrounded by gentle animals making child-friendly sounds than with the grownup Jesus making the centerpiece of his Sermon on the Mount a seemingly absurd mandate to love enemies.

Is loving enemies totally irrelevant and impractical anymore? Twenty-first century middle-earth Christians like me want to know.

January 24

The first convention for women's rights was held in Seneca Falls, New York, in 1848. Men were free to attend but were asked to remain silent.

After conventioneers drafted a document demanding women's right to vote, many newspapers weighed in. A *Lowell* (Massachusetts) *Courier* editorial warned that, with women's equality, "the lords must wash the dishes, scour up, be put to the tub, handle the broom, darn stockings." Philadelphia's *Public Ledger and Daily Transcript* declared: "A woman is nobody. A wife is everything. The ladies of Philadelphia are resolved to maintain their rights as Wives, Belles, Virgins and Mothers." The *Oneida* (New York) *Whig* declared: "This bolt is the most shocking and unnatural incident ever recorded in the history of womanhood. If our ladies will insist on voting and legislating, where, gentlemen, will be our dinners and our elbows? Where our domestic firesides and the holes in our stockings?"

Only one of the more than one hundred signers of the Seneca Falls Declaration of Sentiments was still alive in 1920 when the Nineteenth Amendment giving women the right to vote finally passed.[16]

It is hard to exaggerate how far the movement to include women in the Declaration of Independence's "all men are created equal" dictum has come since the Nineteenth Amendment passed. The female college seniors in a class I teach are unable to appreciate how hard and long the struggle to free women from millennia of patriarchal rule has been. They take with a yawn, as a given, as something obvious to any numbskull, that women are equal to men: "Who would question that?"

Our granddaughter will begin elementary school this year with no doubt in her mind that she is as free as any boy in the class to become a nuclear scientist or a neurosurgeon. Someday she will study history and learn to credit her freedom-fighting foremothers.

January 25

Dr. Kimberly Allison, a young pathologist whose specialty is studying breast cells under a microscope, got breast cancer. The unkindest cut of all was that the diagnosis came while she was still nursing her second child. Dr. Allison wrote the book *Red Sunshine* about her experience. One thing she covers is how becoming a cancer patient changed the way she relates to patients. They can never again be just cells on a slide.

An excellent movie on how becoming the cancer patient can transform the way a physician relates to patients is *The Doctor* starring William Hurt. Hurt plays Dr. Jack McKee, a highly successful, self-absorbed, swashbuckling surgeon who cannot wait to cut into the next patient. He taught one star-struck resident: "Get in. Fix it. Get out. I'd rather you cut straight, and care less. The surgeon's job is to cut."

Then the great physician McKee got a malignant throat tumor. Part of his larynx had to be removed.

Dr. McKee changed the way he trained residents and visited patients. The most influential event in his transformation came after a dying young woman told him a parable about a farmer who kept all the birds and creatures away from his crops with traps and fences. The farmer was very successful, but he was also very lonely. So one day he stood in the middle of his fields from dawn to dusk, his arms outstretched, to welcome the animals. Not a single creature came. They were terrified, you see, of the farmer's new scarecrow.

Then the young woman set the dagger: "Dear Jack, just let down your scarecrow arms and we'll all come to you."[17]

Power may be the great aphrodisiac, but vulnerable love is still life's most effective counter to loneliness and death.

January 26

A goat resides at Kinderdijk in The Netherlands.

Kinderdijk is home to the largest concentration of windmills in the world, some of them 250 years old. Industrious, courageous Dutch men and women created a system of dikes, windmills, and canals that successfully reclaimed land from the North Sea, enabling their families to live safely—of all places—below sea level.

At the entrance to this quaint village now stands a brass goat. It balances on one hoof atop a haystack rising out of a canal. The village people chose that sculpture to symbolize their forebears' victory over the cold and threatening North Sea.

Why a goat? I am told by people who raise sheep and goats that three characteristics of a goat make that symbol make sense. One, goats tend to be independent and headstrong. Goats have a mind of their own while sheep, by contrast, do not like separation from their flock. Two, goats like to take the high ground and move uphill in search of food, while sheep are content to graze, heads down, in a pasture. Three, a goat's tail turns up, while a sheep's tail turns down.

Our time is out of joint. Many Americans have mortgages that are "under water"—they owe more on their house than the house is worth. Hurricanes and storms the last few years have flooded many homes located well above the one-hundred-year flood plain. Those homeowners had no reason to think there was a good reason to carry flood insurance.

When will lifting ourselves out of the economic tsunami that hit this country be over? No one knows.

Remember the indomitable spirits of our foremothers and forefathers who kept overcoming humongous obstacles to improve this country. Remember the Dutch who keep on reclaiming Kinderdijk from the sea.

Remember the hope goat.

January 27

"How can we learn to know ourselves? Never by reflection, but by action. Try to do your duty and you will soon find out what you are. But what is your duty? The demands of each day"— Johann Wolfgang Goethe

Marian Stoltzfus Fisher had no idea what life would demand of her that Monday morning in 2006 when she checked into her little Amish schoolhouse. But when Carl Roberts, a deeply disturbed man, burst into the school and lined the little girls against the blackboard and told them he was going to shoot them all, thirteen-year-old Marian, the oldest, stepped forward and asked him to shoot her first.

Perhaps she thought her sacrifice might sate the gunman's bloodlust so that he would spare the other girls, or that it might buy her classmates opportunity to run, or incentive to run, or enough time for help to arrive. Regardless, five girls beginning with Marian died that day and five were injured. The killer then killed himself.[18]

Marian lived the faith transmitted to her from her Amish mothers and fathers. They had taught her the saying of Jesus: "The greatest way to show love for friends is to die for them."[19]

The Amish grandfather of one of the murdered girls, on the very day of the murders, said of the gunman: "We must not think evil of this man."[20] The Amish set up a charitable fund for the family of the killer. They attended his funeral, explaining: "The Bible teaches us to forgive those who trespass against us, and to mourn with those who mourn."

The Amish tore down the desecrated schoolhouse. Six months later they opened New Hope School, where their children are learning to live in hope, love each other, love their enemies, and forgive those who sin against them.

January 28

I cannot forget the first time I saw the face of William Niehous. He was on the evening network news, having stumbling out of a Venezuelan jungle, looking like warmed-over death. His hair fell down below his shoulders and he had a Rip Van Winkle beard.

More than three years earlier terrorists had kidnapped him, ending the comfortable lifestyle he had enjoyed with his family as the executive of a glass company. The terrorists ripped him from his wife and three kids and held him for millions of dollars ransom. In those three years, living with snakes and mud and the likelihood of execution, Niehous saw not one human face. His captors kept him blindfolded the entire time. Whenever they did remove his blindfold, they were all wearing masks.

One day, in a crude hut, listening to the plaintive cry of a jungle bird, he glanced down and noticed an ant on the floor. It had found a crumb from Niehous's last meal and was carrying it away. He couldn't get out of his mind the enormous weight the insect could carry compared to its size. The ant made him think that God probably had built tremendous resources into all creatures, including himself.[21]

One of the most common comments I have heard from people like William Niehous, whose stable and comfortable lives got suddenly blown apart by an accident or illness, is: "I never would have believed, before it happened, that I could survive a body blow like that."

Ants can move a rubber tree plant. One ant can carry a crumb several times its weight. We, like the ant, have powers within us that we may not know until we are put to the test.

January 29

How realistic is the advice to "forget the past?" Selective amnesia is virtually impossible and I am not convinced—even if we could forget—that it would help much. All our past, for better and worse, got us here. You have to dance, as legendary University of Texas football coach Darrell Royal put it, "with what brung ya."

Charles Dickens, whose past was very painful, at age forty eight went behind his Gad's Hill house with two of his young sons and burned, basketful after basketful, all his private letters. He threw on the bonfire every letter from friends and family—words historians and journalists, then and now, would die for. Dickens wished to be judged on his literature, not on his personal life. He did not want to worry about an unguarded word, privately committed to paper in the heat of the moment years earlier coming back to be held against him or his family.[22]

Frank McCourt, Pulitzer Prize-winning author, begins his book *Teacher Man* with a blanket pardon of those who helped make his childhood in Ireland miserable. He singles out Pope Pius XII, "the English in general and King George VI in particular," bullying schoolmasters who hit him regularly with a stick, his alcoholic father, and assorted others.[23] Let us hope that trumpeting his forgiveness to the world helped him forgive at a deeper level.

Each of us decides how to deal with past emotional pain. One person I know wrote her five worst memories on a paper towel and flushed it. There may be some power in ritualizing a resolution so that we do not allow traumatic events to dominate our lives.

Alice Roosevelt Longfellow advised: "Fill what's empty. Empty what's full. Scratch where it itches." Any time is the right time to burn up coddled grudges and dated emotions, or flush them, and move on.

January 30

Some call it Celtic spirituality. These days the term largely refers to the ancient Irish belief that there are certain places where the curtain separating this world from the other world is very thin, even sheer; places where the membrane separating secular from sacred, the ordinary from the numinous, is porous or permeable; thin places that are thick with the mysterious presence of God. It is as if the door between this world (time) and the next world (eternity) cracks open for a moment, enough to permit us to see the other side.

A friend told me about a trip he and his wife and their children and grandchildren made over the Christmas holidays to an island. At one point the family held something like a tribal council to discuss how they would celebrate Christmas in a tropical paradise. They decided they would send a message, not in a bottle released to the outgoing tide, but written in the sand in big, bold letters.

What message would they send to the universe, to God, to an airplane flying over? They settled on three words: joy, peace, and love. I saw a picture made of the kids standing in the O of JOY. The letters were probably big enough to be read from thirty-thousand feet without glasses.

Methinks when those kids are old and gray they will remember that island and that beach and those grandparents and that Christmas as a thin place where they experienced something bigger than themselves, bigger than life, something mysteriously better felt than told, what Rudolph Otto termed *mysterium tremendum et fascinans*, "the tremendous and fascinating mystery."[24]

One of our primal needs is to spring ourselves occasionally from the humdrum—out of the rat race—and off to a thin place. Taking our little ones to a thin place may be the greatest gift parents and grandparents have to offer, far more precious and lasting than a gift card to an all-you-can-eat pizza place or one more video game.

January 31

The magazine *Mother Jones* made big news in 2012 because it released a surreptitiously recorded and damaging conversation presidential candidate Mitt Romney had with wealthy donors.[25] One hundred years ago, what was newsworthy was Mother Jones herself. Cork, Ireland, even held a three-day festival in 2012 to mark the 175th anniversary of her birth.

When Mary Harris Jones was eighty-seven years old, Teddy Roosevelt called her "the most dangerous woman in America." Carl Sandburg once said that the "she" in "She'll Be Coming 'Round the Mountain" was a reference to Mother Jones's unionizing work with Appalachian miners.

As a teenager, Mary moved with her family to North America. In 1867, yellow fever took the lives of her husband and four children. In 1871, she lost a successful dressmaking business to the Great Chicago Fire.

What do you do when twice you have lost everything? Mary Harris Jones became a passionate crusader on behalf of miners, including young children laboring in the mines. In 1903, she organized a Children's March from Philadelphia to President Theodore Roosevelt's house in Oyster Bay, New York. Hundreds of children carried banners proclaiming: "We Want to Go to School and Not the Mines!"[26]

In a meeting that Mother Jones negotiated with John D. Rockefeller Jr., she described conditions in Colorado mines. Rockefeller, a conservationist, was personally moved enough to visit the mines. Rockefeller proceeded to introduce long-needed reforms.

Mother Jones, tireless, indomitable organizer, once said in a labor union meeting: "I asked a man in prison how he happened to be there and he said he had stolen a pair of shoes. I said if he had stolen a railroad, he would be a United States Senator."

Mother Jones died at age ninety three and is buried at a miners' cemetery in Mt. Olive, Illinois. She earned her epitaph the day she said, "Whatever the fight, don't be ladylike."[27]

January Notes

1. McClellan, "Lion Kings," *CBS 60 Minutes*, no pages.
2. Matthew 6:21.
3. McClure, *Pearl in the Storm*, 289.
4. Genesis 3:19b.
5. Isaiah 1:18.
6. Detterman, "Worshipping the Triune God," no pages.
7. *Our Rabbi Jesus*, "Our Image Stamped," no pages.
8. Summit, *Sum It Up*, 369.
9. McDougall, "Hidden Cost of Heroism," *NBC News*, no pages.
10. Dawkins, *Selfish Gene*, 200.
11. Lawson, *The Story of Ferdinand*, no pages.
12. Shakespeare. *Sonnet 116*.
13. *Unam Sanctam Catholicam*, "History of Devil's Advocate," no pages.
14. Graves, "Dirk Willem Burned," *Christianity*, no pages.
15. Matthew 5:43.
16. *Historynet*, "Seneca Falls Convention," no pages.
17. *The Doctor*, directed by Randa Haines.
18. Blanko, "Carl Charles Roberts IV," *Murderpedia*, no pages.
19. John 15:13.
20. *KLTV*, "Amish Grandfather," no pages.
21. Vitello, "William Niehous Survived," *The Globe and Mail*, no pages.
22. Lewis, "Burning the Evidence," no pages.
23. McCourt, *Teacher Man*, 1–2.
24. Gooch, "The Numinous," 113.
25. *Mother Jones*, "Secret Video," no pages.
26. *America Catholic History Classroom*, "Mother Jones," no pages.
27. *AFL-CIO*, "Mother Jones," no pages.

February

February 1

"Why, what's the matter, / That you have such a February face, / So full of frost, of storm and cloudiness?"—William Shakespeare[1]

Years ago, a part of my job was orienting student chaplains to the hospital world. One thing I did was to have them fill out their own death certificates. That was one way to plunge them into the reality of death in the hospital. Contemplating their own death, they had to fantasize things like how and when it would occur and the name of the next of kin to be notified.

To be a good sport, I also filled out my death certificate. After several years of doing this, it dawned on me that I always chose the first week of February for my death. Why not, I figured, if die I must, die in sync with nature at its coldest, bleakest, and most brutal?

Evidently Februaries across the big pond, at least in Shakespeare's time, were much like Februaries where I live—"full of frost, of storm and cloudiness." A February face is a pale face, deprived of Vitamin D, "full of frost." A February face is a sad face, possibly expressing Seasonal Affective Disorder, sculpted by long nights and cloudy, rainy, icy, or snowy days, and punctuated with too few doses of light. A February face is a long, ground-down face that cries out: "How long, O Lord, how long?"

When we get older, we are more attuned (one would hope) to the impermanence of all things, including Februaries. That may be the hardest part of being young. When we are young and flunk the big test or fail to make the team or get the job or get dropped by the object of our affection or go blank when making a speech and make a total fool of ourselves, it is hard for a while to think we will ever be whole or feel good again. We may even wonder if going on is worth the trouble.

Might you have a February face? If you can hang on just a little longer, change you can believe in—courtesy of Mother Nature—is on the way.

February 2

Diversity in some circles is a dirty word, especially when universities or churches make it the value that dominates all others.

The word stirs positive feelings in me whenever I pass a poster in the foyer of a local elementary school. This is how the poster defines the word: *Different Individuals Valuing Each other Regardless of Skin Intellect Talents Years*. How could people of good will not value diversity defined this way?

I particularly like the four differences the poster singles out not to be de-valued:

Skin. Please do not disparage me because of my extremely pale, sun-damaged skin. I had no control over the skin my parents' English and Irish genes passed to me. And please do not be too critical of me for permanently damaging my skin with sunburns when I was young. I did it out of ignorance, just like those today who ignorantly are damaging their skin in tanning booths.

Intellect. Please do not discount me because of my IQ. Most of my intelligence quotient was determined before I was born. I am responsible only for how I play the finite hand I was dealt.

Talents. Please do not dismiss me for not having the skills of professional athletes or mathematicians, sales persons or politicians, electricians or mechanics, artists or musicians. My DNA did not equip me, constitutionally and temperamentally, for those particular skills.

Years. Please do not disregard me because I am old. Youth could use my experience and wisdom; youth has the vitality and idealism I have lost. We need each other. Together we halves can make a whole.

From Marcus Aurelius comes ancient wisdom on dissing others: "Everything we hear is an opinion, not a fact; everything we see is a perspective, not the truth." Maybe this is why the television show is named "The View" instead of "The Obvious."

February 3

"Options Unlimited—Closed"

That was the message that just crawled across the bottom of my television screen as outside the snow falls. I laughed out loud at the irony in the message. Are we misleading our children and setting them up for discouragement when we tell them their options are unlimited, that they can do anything they set their mind to, that they can be anything they want to be? I like the way Booker T. Washington framed his rise from slavery to becoming a great scientist: "I have been a slave once in my life—a slave in my body. But I have since resolved that no inducement and no influence would ever make me a slave in soul." The fact that Washington did it proves that it can be done; it does not, however, mean that everyone who passionately wants to, can or will.

When another crawl announced *"Dare to Dream—Closed"* I got one more chuckle. I do not know what business that is, but I do know that when our daring to dream shuts down, we are of all people most to be pitied. A few minutes ago I learned that Church of the Open Door was also closed.

I think of Susan Griffin's account of the behavior of poet Robert Desnos in the concentration camp. When guards and other condemned men were marching to the gas chamber in stony silence, Desnos suddenly grabbed the palm of one of the condemned and read the woman's palm. He exuberantly told her that she had a very long lifeline and would have many children, grandchildren, great joy, and long life. He moved down the line reading the palms of fellow prisoners and guards alike and saw a great future for all of them. The guards were so taken aback that they loaded the condemned people back into the trucks and drove them back to their barracks. Desnos ultimately died of typhus shortly after the liberation of the camp.[2]

When churches with names like Resurrection and New Hope and Open Door are marked *Closed*, we may all be in big trouble.

February 4

This love story is true. It is not about young, sexy, tabloid love, but about the "for better for worse, for richer for poorer, in sickness and in health" kind. It is of the marathon, not the sprint, variety

Not that their love story lacked hot-blooded passion. Letters to and from the Pacific theater in World War II yield tender, affectionate pledges of undying devotion. Black and white photos dating back to the early 1940s document hugs and kisses. Several pictures are reminiscent of that iconic shot on *Life* magazine's cover of the nurse being bent over and kissed by the sailor celebrating V-J Day on August 14, 1945, in Times Square.

Fast-forward seventy years. One marriage, two children, five grandchildren, and six great grandchildren later, health issues have necessitated their move into an assisted living home.

The sailor boy died on February 2. On February 4, which would have been their seventieth anniversary, he was laid to rest with military honors.

In removing his things from their room, one of their children came across a sealed, bright-yellow envelope with "To Charlie" scrawled on it. Opening it, they discovered a crudely made card that looks like a piece of red, pink, yellow, and white-striped wallpaper folded in half, with little hearts and kisses glued on the front. On the inside, with a cupid and a heart glued alongside, was scribbled a message and signature: "Happy Valentine's Day! With All My Love, Grace."

Barely able to walk with a walker, unable to leave the facility that had no gift shop, Grace used materials from the art and craft room to construct a from-the-heart gift for her valentine, knowing it might be their last Valentine's Day together, and it was.

Charlie was a world-class grandfather to our three sons. And I could not have had a better father-in-law.

February 5

Yale theologian George Lindbeck coined the intriguing phrase "absorb the universe."[3] I resisted it at first because it sounded so grandiose and ridiculous. Since then, it has grown on me. Now I commend it to you.

Everything—nature, history, philosophy, theology, literature, life—can be so overwhelming that we have to reduce it, simplify it, condense it down to something useable. For many of us that means boiling it down to a few sentences or stories that sum up the essence and meaning of things for us, and in that way we "absorb the universe."

I offer one example. A friend was going through the hardest time of his life. He had flown to New York City to appear before a committee to be examined for a certification that he had spent years and a small fortune seeking—and they turned him down. Rejected and humiliated, he felt like the world's biggest loser. He spent forty-eight hours walking the streets of Manhattan, distraught over what he was going to do.

Many years later, nearing the end of a successful career, as he told me this story he said that only one thing back then kept him from jumping off a bridge. It was a verse that his high school English teacher made him memorize, sentences from "Invictus" by William Ernest Henley: "It matters not how strait the gate, / how charged with punishments the scroll. / I am the master of my fate: / I am the captain of my soul." He remembers muttering that sentence hundreds of times as he stumbled up and down the island of Manhattan processing his failure and even questioning whether he had a future.

I hope you have a strong default sentence or two to fall back on—to absorb the universe—when the going gets toughest.

February 6

If you can remember when drivers dimmed car lights by stomping the dimmer with their left foot, then you could be a dinosaur like me.

Dr. Martin Luther King Jr. and his brother were driving one evening in the mid-1950s from Atlanta to Chattanooga. The oncoming drivers evidently didn't know to dim their lights when meeting a car, and A.D. King, who was driving, became furious. At one point A.D. said, "The next driver who refuses to dim his lights, I'm going to give it right back to him; I'll leave mine on bright and blind him and we'll see how he likes it." Dr. King said, "Oh no, don't do that. There'd be too much light on this highway, and it will end up in mutual destruction for all. Somebody's got to have some sense on this highway."[4]

Someone has got to have sense enough to dim the lights.

I teach college seniors the Socratic method of group discussion. They learn to listen respectfully when someone speaks and then respond with civility. Cutting off or drowning out or ridiculing a person with whom they disagree earns an "F" in participation. To see how *not* to have a group discussion, I tell them to turn on particular television shows where panel members yell at, shout down, and put down each other.

Dr. King also said in the same sermon to his Dexter Avenue Baptist Church in Montgomery:

> Force begets force, hate begets hate, toughness begets toughness. And it is all a descending spiral, ultimately ending in destruction for all and everybody. Somebody must have sense enough and morality enough to cut off the chain of hate and the chain of evil in the universe. And you do that by love.

Another Valentine's Day can remind us, on this dark, narrow, rancorous highway of life, to lower our voices, dim the lights, and try a little love.

February 7

Last week I thought of Daniel Boone and Jeremiah Johnson. I also thought of George Washington's shoeless army trudging through the snow at Valley Forge. "How," I thought, "when they were so cold and so wet so much of the time, did they ever make it?"

I was roughing it, farm-sitting for my organic-farmer son and daughter-in-law while they were out of state at a sustainability conference. In the depths of January, in their tiny farmhouse with its wood-burning stove, composting toilet, and no television, a cold, steady rain beating down, I toughed it out. With unmitigated respect for their simple, no-frills, anti-materialistic lifestyle, this city slicker was missing the comforts of home.

Then I thought of Haiti. And I thought of our next-door neighbor who will live every day for the rest of her life wondering if and when her cancer will return. Suddenly I thought: "What a spoiled ingrate I am, with Haitians having gone from poor to destitute or from alive to dead, and my neighbor from healthy to full of cancer, and here I sit feeling deprived, and for only three days. How pathetic!"

Rabbi Arthur Waskow writes about the Jewish Feast of Sukkot (Tabernacles), when observant Jews build fragile huts (sukkah) with leaky roofs and live in them a week to remind themselves of the flimsy, temporary shelters their ancestors erected while wandering for forty years through the wilderness. Rabbi Waskow suggests than in our time, when we put our faith in steel-and-concrete structures like Pentagon buildings and World Trade Centers, Sukkot can remind us: "We are in truth all vulnerable. We all live in a sukkah. There are only wispy walls and leaky roofs between us."[5] And I would add, fault lines beneath us.

Earthquake, tornado, or flood victims could have the effect of making us more grateful for the common treasures we take for granted, like clean water, food, or a roof.

February 8

It is easy for us near the bottom or in the middle of the food chain to scapegoat "rot at the top" for the country's ills. We shake fingers at the leaders of Enron, or Ponzi operators who squander the life savings of many, or hedge fund managers or banks that lose billions and then get bailed out by Congress and become richer than ever. Some who have broken laws and get caught may even serve time in a prison for very important people.

Journalist Michael Kinsley insists that the real scandal is not as much what is illegal up there in rarefied air, as what is legal; meaning, CEOs and CFOs who, breaking no laws, after doing a mediocre to catastrophic job get showered by the company's directors with tens of millions of bonus dollars—sometimes to keep them on, sometimes to dispatch them post haste. Some of those people at the top do nothing illegal, but lie to or stomp on anyone to advance themselves another rung up the success ladder and make their fortune.[6]

Port Royal's naturalist, Wendell Berry, drawing on nature makes this point: "Rats and roaches live by competition under the law of supply and demand; it is the privilege of human beings to live under the laws of justice and mercy."[7]

Is there anything that has a greater claim on us than consuming, than getting ahead? Is there any law higher than the law of supply and demand? If what moves us most—wherever we find ourselves in the social hierarchy—is out-competing others, and that instinct is decoupled from duties of justice and mercy, we just may have made our bed with the rats and the roaches.

February 9

A friend of mine described a profound insight he had while driving from Louisville to Nashville. It was February, and a major ice storm had struck the area the night before. For many miles, both sides of I-65 were strewn with broken and damaged trees.

As my friend looked over the debris, he observed a pattern. Many of the trees were leaning. All those trees were situated in a grove where the trees around them had caught the tilting trees and held them. The grove kept them from snapping and falling.

All the trees that had snapped and broken off at the trunk, and all the ones that were lying on the ground uprooted, had one thing in common—they had either been standing on the perimeter of the forest or they had been standing alone.

He mentioned this to me and another person over lunch. The other person, who was a biologist, told him that if he could only have seen beneath the surface, he would know that the roots were also connected. The interlaced trees were bracing each other below as well as above ground. When the rains came down and turned to ice and the winds beat upon the forest, the intertwined trees were able to stand.

Several weeks after that lunch conversation, I serendipitously came across these words from psychologist and philosopher William James: "Our lives are like islands in the sea, or like trees in the forest. The maple and the pine may whisper to each other with their leaves, but the trees also commingle their roots in the darkness underground, and the islands also hang together through the ocean's bottom."

Going it alone is high-risk, perilous behavior. Interdependence—not dependence, not co-dependence, and not independence—steels us for the ice storms of life. Being in community enables us to stand. Sometimes community alone saves us from being uprooted, breaking, or crashing to the ground.

February 10

"HOPE IS ROOTED IN THE SPIRIT"—Mark Hertsgaard [8]

The ground was so saturated from rain that, when I pulled on the dandelion plant, the entire taproot slid out. The slender white root was eleven inches long! Human hope, like the dandelion, has deep roots. Hope reaches down to our core. It is our nature, as is the nature of every living thing—from bacteria to whales, from the sequoia to the dandelion—to do everything it can to live and thrive. Albert Schweitzer summed up his reverence for life philosophy in one sentence: "I am life that wants to live, surrounded by life that wants to live." We are hardwired for hope.

"HOPE IS CHOSEN BY THE HEART"—Mark Hertsgaard

Unlike the dandelion, we humans vote daily, consciously or unconsciously, for or against hope. Every year around fifty thousand Americans, in a population of over three hundred million, complete suicide. Many more of us choose risky behaviors—poor eating habits, under-exercising, tobacco use, alcohol abuse, road rage, tanning booths, distracted driving—that fight our innate hopefulness. Scripture says: "I set before you life and death, blessings and curses: choose life."[9] Hope is a choice.

"HOPE IS GUIDED BY THE MIND"—Mark Hertsgaard

A dandelion does not lie awake at night strategizing how it should behave tomorrow, but we do use our minds to choose whether to fly off the handle or extend a hand of friendship, to care only about number one or jump in the water and rescue the perishing, to spoil the land or plant an orchard that we will not live long enough to harvest. Milton wrote: "The mind is its own place and in itself can make a heaven of hell or a hell of heaven.

February 11

Robert wrote to Elizabeth in January of 1845 to praise her poetry: "I love your verses with all my heart."

Elizabeth Barrett, one of England's most prominent poets, was an invalid. In her mid-teens she had been struck down by a mysterious illness that rendered her reclusive and bedridden. A cousin of Elizabeth, John Kenyon, arranged for Robert Browning, six years her junior, to visit in her room. There began one of the most famous love stories immortalized in writing.

In one of Robert's early visits, Elizabeth was able to lift her head off the pillow for the first time in a long time. Between visits, they exchanged nearly six hundred letters. Robert kept her room populated with flowers. Elizabeth eventually became able to sit up in bed. Twenty months after their first meeting, they eloped, permanently leaving the polluted air of London for the warmer, cleaner, therapeutic air of Italy.

Elizabeth never saw her father again. He disinherited her, as he did all of his eleven children who married. Letters from Elizabeth to her father were returned unopened. Elizabeth's health improved remarkably in Italy. At age forty-three, she was able to give birth to a son. The family of three lived happily there for fifteen years. Elizabeth died in Robert's arms.[10]

Out of that relationship came some of history's greatest expressions of romantic love. One of her "Sonnets from the Portuguese" begins: "How do I love thee? Let me count the ways. / I love thee to the depth and breadth and height / My soul can reach."

The poem ends: "I love thee with the breath, / Smiles, tears, of all my life!—and, if God choose, / I shall but love thee better after death."[11]

I hope you aspire to make this a romantic Valentine's Day.

February 12

"WHEN YOU WIN, BRAG GENTLY. WHEN YOU LOSE, WEEP SOFTLY"— James Clyburn

When I first read those words, I remembered what legendary Notre Dame Coach Lou Holtz said about football: "You're never as good as everyone tells you when you win, and you're never as bad as they say when you lose."

Why not get cocky over a big victory, or dejected over a big defeat? Because one day does not a lifetime make. No one event, short of death, is the final word. We are all unfinished symphonies. All things are in flux. Scarlett O'Hara got it right in the final line of *Gone with the Wind*: "Tomorrow is another day."

So who is James Clyburn? When he was only twelve, Clyburn helped organize civil rights marches. In college, he helped organize demonstrations. In 1970, when he won a primary race for the South Carolina House of Representatives, his wife Emily left him a little note in the sink that read: "When you win, brag gently. When you lose, weep softly." He put her wisdom on his mirror. It came in handy several months later when he lost in the general election.

Clyburn also lost, twice, running for South Carolina secretary of state. Finally, in 1992 he ran to represent South Carolina's Sixth Congressional District and won. Today he is the highest-ranking African-American in Congress. When interviewed by StoryCorps, he gave this interpretation of his long journey: "We have a state seal in South Carolina. The Latin phrase on the seal says *dum spiro spero* — 'While I breathe, I hope.' And I've always felt that there's hope. And so I have never given up."[12]

Since 1976, America's bicentennial, February has been designated by every American president as Black History Month. Actor Morgan Freeman demurred then, saying: "I don't want a black history month. Black history is American history."

James Clyburn's story is one all-American story of equanimity, persistence, and hope.

February 13

Two things I know for sure this Valentine's Day. When you are up, nothing beats having someone special to celebrate it with you; when you are down, nothing is finer than having someone special to hold your hand and halve your misery.

Several Saturdays ago my wife, who probably never took a sick day in her life, was taken down by a mighty bug. Saturday afternoon she lay on the sofa bundled up, chilling, and virtually immobilized, moaning, "What a wasted day" and "I don't have time for this."

I did what any red-blooded, thoroughly-modern husband would do. I grabbed the remote and started flicking. We ended up spending the next six hours watching parts or all of the best romantic movies—some call them "chick flicks"—we could find on cable, including *Pretty Woman, Sleepless in Seattle, 27 Dresses,* and *Hope Floats.* It was an afternoon of pure, warm, unadulterated escapism.

Flu symptoms did not disappear, but the victim got a six-hour reprieve and partially redeemed a lost day.

The most memorable line we took from the movies that afternoon came at the happy ending of *Hope Floats.* It was Birdee's summation: "Momma says that beginnings are scary, endings are usually sad, but it's the middle that counts the most. Just give hope a chance to float up, and it will."

It is the middle—the children and bills and disagreements, the mountains climbed and valleys traversed together—that counts most. Down in those valleys, counting on hope to float up makes even the nastiest parts of the journey bearable.

There was nothing meritorious about my being there for my life companion the day she was struck down. I was but returning the favor. "Love," James Thurber said, "is what you've been through with somebody."

February 14

Why do people get married anyway?

In the movie *Shall We Dance?* the character played by Susan Sarandon asks that rhetorical question over dinner and then gives her answer: "Because we need a witness to our lives."

She elaborates:

> There are billions of people on the planet. What does any one life really mean? But in a marriage, you're promising to care about everything—the good things, the bad things, the terrible things, the mundane things. All of it, all the time, every day. You're saying, 'Your life will not go unnoticed, because I will notice it. Your life will not go unwitnessed, because I will be your witness.'

I came across a story that illustrated for me the truth of Sarandon's words. It was about the *Guinness' Book of World Records* marriage champs. He was one hundred and she was one year older. John and Amelia Roccio had been married eighty-two years. Asked by a reporter the secret of their marriage, the 101-year-old woman thought for a moment and answered: "He never put me down. He liked everything I did."[13] He served admirably—according to the one who knew him best—as her advocate.

Drs. John and Julia Gottman, perhaps the world's foremost marriage scientists, for thirty years scientifically and mathematically studied over three thousand married couples. They became expert enough that they could analyze a fifteen-minute slice of conversation between a couple and with over 90 percent accuracy predict whether that relationship would last another fifteen years. One of their most important findings was that in marriages that last, the ratio of positive to negative emotion expressed is at least five to one.[14]

What we crave most—whether married or single—is someone to notice us. And care. And say so.

February 15

Religions are hardly united on how to regard the self. Jesus commanded his disciples both to love and deny self. Jesus himself once went without food for forty days. He urged his followers to take up a cross. St. Paul wrote: "I keep my body under control and make it my slave."[15]

Some religions lean to the left, majoring in self-actualization and love of neighbor; some lean to the right, advocating mortification of the flesh.

The season of Lent is a time of denial and sacrifice for many Christians; a time to discipline self by giving up Twitter, nail-biting, bottled water, *The Bachelor*, vanilla-spice latte, or something.

Pope John Paul II occasionally flagellated himself with a belt and slept on bare floors to draw himself closer to the sufferings of Christ. For Shiites in Iraq, Muharram is the month of the year to cut themselves with knives and flog themselves with whips made of knotted cords as they mourn the seventh-century death of Prophet Mohammed's grandson, Imam Hussein. Ignatius Loyola, founder of the Jesuits, slept in a thin shirt on the floor of an unheated room, stood barefoot in the snow, and for meals took only a handful of nuts, a piece of bread, and a cup of water.

I am personally all for self-control, disciplining desires, and eliminating impediments on our way to higher ground. What raises a red flag for me is what Gautama Buddha, in his search for enlightenment, learned from his extreme austerity measures. He lived on fruit, roots, and leaves for six years until only skin and bone remained.[16] Excessive self-mortification, he concluded, merely wore out his body and brought a pride and self-righteousness that poisoned any gain he might have got from it.

St. Paul, who disciplined his body, wrote: "What if I gave away all that I owned and let myself be burned alive? I would gain nothing, unless I loved others."[17]

February 16

"PIGS GET FAT, HOGS GET SLAUGHTERED."

An economics professor uses this saying to teach his students a lesson. The words have several layers of meaning. The most obvious is that there is nothing wrong with wanting more and providing well for our families, so long as that drive does not lead to "cooking the books," insider trading, pyramid schemes, or other illegal activities. That could land you in prison, provided you get caught.

Another meaning goes one layer deeper than the fear of getting caught. "Getting fat"—making a good income, acquiring many things, having the accoutrements of success—does not bring personal contentment. The good life in our day, Edwin Searcy writes, has become a matter of "securing the bottom line, building up a good portfolio, bolting the door against trouble, and playing your part as a consumer."[18] We know people who have done all that but lead lives of quiet desperation.

There is another interpretation. Maybe the good life is neither about getting fat nor about getting slaughtered. Maybe it is more about relationships. Alexander Solzhenitsyn, Russian historian, novelist, and Pulitzer Prize winner, spent almost a dozen years in labor camps and in exile because he spoke out against Joseph Stalin. He advised: "Own what you can always carry with you; know languages, know countries, know people. Let your memory be your bag."[19]

"Own what you can always carry with you." Solzhenitsyn does not mean what we can carry in a wallet or backpack or wheelbarrow or U-Haul. He means the bag of memories we have made and always carry in our hearts and minds. If we get slaughtered—swindled out of our life savings or sentenced to a concentration camp or diagnosed with terminal cancer—that bag of memories is the one thing that cannot be taken from us.

February 17

Last fall, on his third birthday, one of our grandsons spent the night with us. We gave him his birthday gift just before bedtime—superhero rubber boots. He quickly put them on and was not easily persuaded to remove them before going to bed.

He and I "camped out" in a tent in our basement that night. Twice as I slept I was aware of a presence looming above me. When I opened my eyes each time there stood a grinning Clark. He spoke not a word. He just stood there smiling, proudly displaying one new boot in each hand.

Yesterday I spent the day grandparenting Clark on his parents' farm. The day was cloudy and chilly and the ground saturated from recent snows. At one point he asked and I granted him permission to put on his coat and boots to go outside and play.

He came inside less than ten minutes later, clearly a contented boy. I thought nothing more about his time outside until I opened my car door to go home and saw the record of Clark's whereabouts—muddy boot prints, half a dozen on the driver's black leather seat and half a dozen on the passenger's side and another dozen on the back seat.

No, I do not think I would have been amused if his father had done that when he was three. And no, I would not have been happy if it had been our other car with beige fabric instead of easy-to-clean leather seats.

Yes, the thought has crossed my mind that the next time I go to the farm I should lock the car. No, I have not removed the boot prints yet. Maybe this afternoon I will. Or maybe I will not.

I understand why Gore Vidal said, "Never have children, only grandchildren."

February 18

Candy Lightner, realtor, mother of three, had her world shattered in one second on May 3, 1980. Her thirteen-year-old-daughter Cari, walking down a quiet street, was struck from behind by a car. The impact threw Cari 125 feet, killing her. Clarence Busch, the driver of the car, did not stop. He had been arrested for another hit-and-run accident just two days before hitting Cari. For his four earlier drunk-driving convictions, he had served less than forty-eight hours in jail.

When Lightner learned later that Busch would probably serve little or no jail time, she was furious. In her book *Giving Sorrow Words* she said that she felt enraged and helpless. Her fury drove her to action. She promised her friends: "I'm going to start an organization, because people need to know about this."

From her personal tragedy came the birth of MADD, "Mothers Against Drunk Driving." Within months of Cari's death, Lightner was testifying before legislatures. Using money from Cari's insurance and her own savings, she quit her job and began traveling the country giving speeches, rallying volunteers, and lobbying for tougher drunk driving laws. She said, "You kick a few pebbles, you turn a few stones, and eventually you have an avalanche."[20]

In 1984, she stood next to President Ronald Reagan as he signed the bill that changed the drinking age from eighteen to twenty-one. There were twenty-six thousand alcohol-related automobile fatalities in 1982. In 2010, the number was twelve thousand.

Anger is a natural, predictable part of grief. After being furious for a time after a personal tragedy, some, like Candy Lightner, throw that fury into constructive action.

Augustine said that hope has two lovely daughters, anger and courage.[21] Anger, instead of immobilizing and depressing us, in time can become the fuel that lights a fire within us to stand up and work to make something constructive come for others out of our sorrow.

February 19

"I'VE NEVER HAD A HUMBLE OPINION. IF YOU'VE GOT AN OPINION,
WHY BE HUMBLE ABOUT IT?" —Joan Baez

I find this statement disturbing, not because I disliked Joan Baez or her music, but because those words represent how so many people these days, celebrities and common folk alike, think. If you have a strong opinion, you should shout it from the housetops and ridicule any position that differs. Humility is for wishy-washy, weaker, lesser souls. What need is there for a spirit of meekness or compromise when you have truth all figured out?

One reviewer of Jonathan Haidt's *The Righteous Mind: Why Good People Are Divided by Politics and Religion* wrote:

> Whatever favored position you have politically, try to always question what else it is you are missing. After all, very smart and good people are conservatives, liberals, Buddhists, Christians, atheists, and many other things. Is it more likely that your positions are right and everyone else is just missing it (the position of the righteous mind), or that you probably have a grain of truth in a field that contains many other grains? [22]

Other great thinkers over the centuries have said as much. Mechthild of Magdeburg, a thirteenth-century mystic, said that our understanding of the workings of the universe is the same as the amount of honey a honeybee can carry away on one foot from an overflowing jar—not much.

Sir Isaac Newton, after discovering the law of gravity, wrote: "I do not know what I may appear to the world, but to myself I seem to have been only like a boy playing on the sea-shore, and diverting myself in now and then finding a smoother pebble or a prettier shell than ordinary, whilst the great ocean of truth lay all undiscovered before me."

Albert Einstein said: "We still do not know one thousandth of one percent of what nature has revealed to us." Maybe we should begin more discussions with a soft "In my humble opinion" and mean it, and then concentrate on understanding the other person's point of view.

February 20

Kurt Vonnegut was at a party with his friend Joseph Heller, the writer of bestseller *Catch-22*. The party was being given by a billionaire hedge-fund manager. Vonnegut whispered to Heller: "Joe, how does it make you feel to realize that our host probably makes more money in a single day than you've earned in forty years from writing *Catch-22*?"

"I have something," Heller said, "that he will never have—the knowledge that I've got enough."[23]

One study on happiness sought to ascertain if and how happiness is tied to money. An interviewee was heir to an enormous fortune. He testified that what mattered most to him in life was his faith, and that his greatest aspiration was "to love the Lord, my family, and my friends." As to how much money was enough, he admitted that he personally could never feel truly secure until he had $1 billion in the bank.[24]

John Bogle, retired CEO of The Vanguard Group, in his book titled *Enough*, gives his views on this country's financial system. Bogle says that we have gone from an agricultural economy to a manufacturing one to a service one to what is now a financial one. "We have pinned so much of our collective fortune on extracting value from trading paper," he insists, "that we are losing our grip on what it means to actually build anything of value, let alone how to serve others."[25]

Joseph Heller said that the question he was addressing in *Catch-22* was: "What does a sane person do in an insane society?" Einstein gave this as his answer: "There are some things that count that can't be counted, and some things that can be counted that don't count."

How much money do we need? Wendell Berry's answer is: "To make a living is not to make a killing; it's to have enough."

February 21

Decades ago Randy Newman recorded a song named "Short People" that ended up on many greatest-hits albums. The song was a sarcastic poke at all people whose prejudice against others is based on external things like gender or race or size.

A "eureka" moment on the importance of height came early in my professional life. I was invited to participate on a panel with three cancer research scientists and physicians of renown. I had good reason to feel more than a little insecure. As we mounted the stage and prepared to sit in our chairs, in a split second I couldn't help but make the observation that I was the tallest of the four! Something clicked inside me that day: bigger, faster, and stronger may have ruled in Neanderthal times, but in our day what is between the ears counts more.

Oliver Wendell Holmes Sr., great intellectual, medical reformer, and poet stood "five feet three inches when standing in a pair of substantial boots." The story is told that once he attended a meeting in which he was the shortest man present. "Dr. Holmes," one man quipped, "I should think you'd feel rather small among us big fellows." "I do," retorted Holmes. "I feel like a dime among a bunch of pennies."

Lloyd George, orator, champion of the underdog and British Prime Minister during World War I, was once introduced with the remark: "I had expected to find Mr. Lloyd George a big man in every sense, but you see he is quite small in stature." "In North Wales," Lloyd George countered at the beginning of his speech, "we measure a man from his chin up. You evidently measure from his chin down."

Height matters. Experiments show that taller men, like women of beauty, have some advantages in life, especially in making good first impressions. Over the long term, however, thoughts and deeds wear better.

February 22

Where I attend church, there are prayer request cards in the pew racks. Worshipers are invited to write a few words about someone "for whom we are praying" and to sign their own name.

A little seven-year-old girl has filled out three cards over the last few weeks. The first one reads: "Please help the people that need your love and gidens."

The second: "People whom are in the hospitel and whom are about to die and the ones whom are hurt."

The third: "Please help the people that do not have any food or something to drink please help the people who are poor! Please help them be safe and helthy."

That third one ends with the salutation "Love," followed by her name, followed by her drawing of a heart. On the other side of the card she drew a girl with long hair and a smile on her face who is being followed by a little dog. They are walking toward a body of water with a slide or a ladder going down into it.

Some Sundays she is the only one in church who fills out a prayer request. I suspect that she may be closer to the angels, closer to pure religion than the adults on her pew and in the pulpit. One thing all the great religions of the world teach is compassion for the poor and needy. At the tender age of seven she already has got it—sensitivity to the needs of the dying, the hospitalized, the hungry, and the poor. Her parents should be very proud of her, and they are.

Jesus told the adults, "If you don't change and become like a child, you will never get into the kingdom of heaven."[26] You wonder what he might have meant.

February 23

Humility gets a bad rap in our day. We associate it with low self-esteem, passivity, weakness, Caspar Milquetoast, and humble pie.

Humility and humus come from the same root word. Humus is the good, rich earth beneath us. We buy big bags of it to enrich our gardens. What binds us humans together, the high and the low, as last rites and funerals remind us, is that we all come from humus and to humus we shall return.

When we forget that we are humus, we run the risk of committing what the ancient Greeks considered the greatest sin, the sin of hubris. They defined hubris with stories of individuals who were feeling their oats so much that they forgot they were humus.

Sometimes hubris happens to people who come into political power. If you are the president or a senator, and millions have cast their vote for you and smile at you and applaud you and are deferential toward you, it must be hard not to feel that you, as king of the world, can do as you please. That is hubris.

One of the most poignant moments in the movie *Schindler's List* is the one when a drunken Nazi is sitting with Schindler on a balcony. The Nazi, Amon Goeth, is picking off Jews with his high-power rifle, just for sport; gleefully shooting them—they're just fish in a barrel to him. When Amon comments about the power he has to kill arbitrarily, Schindler corrects him:

> Power is when we have every justification to kill, and we don't . . . . A man steals something, he's brought in before the Emperor, he throws himself down on the ground. He begs for his life, he knows he's going to die. And the Emperor pardons him. This worthless man, he lets him go . . . That's power, Amon. That is power."[27]

Hubris uses power to promote self and exploit others. Humility is virtuous because it helps us identify with and stand in solidarity with those who we know, like us, are really humus.

February 24

Two men in a hospital for the incurably ill shared a room. The man in the bed next to the window sat in a chair each afternoon for one hour to keep fluid from building in his lungs. The other man, whose spinal column was fused, had to spend all day flat on his back.

During the hour each day he was sitting up, the man next to the window shared with his roommate the interesting things he saw going on outside. There was a park out there and in the middle of the park a small lake where swans swam, parents and their children sailed toy boats, and visitors fed ducks. From day to day he would paint in vivid detail scenes of teenagers throwing a Frisbee, lovers walking arm in arm, or children flying multicolored kites. The patient in the other bed would just close his eyes and enjoy imagining those scenes in his mind.

One night the man next to the window died. As soon as it seemed appropriate, the other man asked the nurse if he could be switched over to the bed by the window. She moved him, and soon after she left the room he managed to raise himself on one elbow high enough to peek over the window sill and get his first look at the park. What he was startled to see was a blank wall.

That afternoon he learned from the nurse that the man who had described such wonderful things outside was blind and could not see even the wall. She suggested: "Perhaps he was just trying to help you not get too discouraged."[28]

Logic without imagination can be cold and sterile. Take it from a genius named Einstein: "Logic will get you from A to B. Imagination will take you everywhere."

February 25

"Humans are born soft and supple. When dead,
they are stiff and hard. Plants are born tender and pliant.
When dead, they are brittle and dry"—Lao Tzu

The great Chinese philosopher urges us to take a critical look now and then at our routines. As familiar and comfortable as they are, they can become deadly, as someone suggested by calling habits "graves with the ends knocked out."

That is certainly true in marriage. Many years ago my wife and I enjoyed a play in which the wife blindsided her husband on their twenty-first anniversary with the confession that two things about him had over the years come to irritate her to no end.

First irritation: "You seem so much smaller." She meant by that how he had fallen off her pedestal. Early on he had been her hero who could do no wrong, but after twenty-one years together she had come to see him as ordinary, hardly bigger than life, and with no surprises left in him.

Second: "I don't like your nose." She meant the never-varying way he blew his nose; specifically, one blast followed by three short puffs, followed by folding his handkerchief the same way every time. The wife was chaffing in a marriage that had become a victim of stagnation, monotony, and humdrum.

When my favorite uncle came for a visit, as he rode in my car several times he commented on what an extraordinarily smooth ride it was. I was a bit mystified as to what was going on. Come to find out, his car had gradually drifted out of alignment, but he didn't notice it until he rode in someone else's "aligned" car.

To avoid becoming brittle and dry, it might be good sometimes to take a different route home, answer the phone with a different greeting or inflection, or vary the way we blow our nose.

February 26

I'm incapable of watching the conclusion of *Mr. Holland's Opus* without choking. Maybe principals should make it required viewing for everyone on the faculty at the beginning of the school year.

In the movie Richard Dreyfus plays Glenn Holland, a gifted musician and composer who believes his destiny in life is to compose one great symphony. He takes a high school teaching job only to pay the bills.

Over the next thirty years, he fails to become famous as a composer. But he does endear himself, through great caring and competence, to hundreds of students.

At the end of the film, an auditorium of adoring former students surprise Mr. Holland with a "This Is Your Life" kind of tribute. One former student who went on to become the state governor delivered this living eulogy:

> Mr. Holland isn't rich and he isn't famous, at least not outside of our little town. So it might be easy for him to think himself a failure. But he would be wrong, because I think that he's achieved a success far beyond riches and fame. Look around you. There is not a life in this room that you have not touched, and each of us is a better person because of you. We are your symphony, Mr. Holland. We are the melodies and the notes of your opus. We are the music of your life.

In Camelot, every good teacher at career's end would get fifteen minutes of fame. Grateful former students would return home, fill the auditorium, use some ruse to lure the teacher there, rise when she enters the room, and give her a standing ovation.

Back in our real world, an "I'm a better person because of you" letter will have to do.

February 27

My first brush with celebrity was Senator Estes Kefauver of Tennessee, who twice sought and twice failed to win the Democrat Party's nomination for president. When I was fourteen, he and his entourage came into the drug store where I worked as a soda jerk. I remember how tall he was and how long the holder for his cigarette was. He ordered a small coke. His bodyguard gave me a nickel. I rang it up, and that was that. After he left, the pharmacist came over and told me the identity of the distinguished-looking gentleman.

The second celebrity I saw and heard up close was Pat Boone. His little sister Judy and I were freshmen in the same college when, the first week we were there, Pat, at the height of his popularity, came and gave the school a free concert in her honor.

In 1965, Harvey Lavan "Van" Cliburn came to Abilene, Texas, to give a concert. My girlfriend, far more cultured than her hayseed boyfriend from Tennessee, persuaded me to go. Taking with me no appreciation for classical music, I was mesmerized. For the first time in my life, I was aware of being in the presence of true greatness.

In 1958, Cliburn, twenty-three years old, had won the first International Tchaikovsky Piano Competition in Moscow. Six months earlier the Soviets had launched Sputnik, scaring Americans into believing Russia could destroy us with intercontinental missiles loaded with atomic bombs.

Cliburn captivated the Russians with his performance. Premier Nikita Khrushchev personally approved the judges awarding the prize to an American, saying, "Is Cliburn the best? Then give him first prize." *Time* magazine proclaimed Cliburn, "The Texan Who Conquered Russia."[29] Cliburn helped bridge the gap between two mortal enemies. Immaculately expressed music did what fifty thousand nuclear-tipped missiles did not and could not do.

Van Cliburn died February 27, 2013. He taught me the difference between celebrity and greatness.

February 28

Matthew Henry, famous Presbyterian minister in the British Isles three centuries ago, got mugged and robbed. That very night he recorded this prayer of thanksgiving in his journal: "I thank Thee first because I was never robbed before; second, because although they took my purse they did not take my life; third, because although they took my all, it was not much; and fourth because it was I who was robbed, and not I who robbed."

Hope does not deny facts. Hope construes facts. It puts the facts in perspective.

Patricia Neal, Academy Award-winning actress, finally in her eighties got her star on the Hollywood Walk of Fame. Her life had some great setbacks—the death of her oldest child at an early age, three massive strokes, a car accident that almost killed her, a philandering husband, and a divorce. When she got her star, she said: "In the past year I received two very good parts: a new shoulder and a new knee. They both are working beautifully. I am an actress, and I will take any good part as long as I can stand up. And when I can no longer do that, I will take them lying down."[30]

Neal illustrates how hope has a pinch of defiance, a Snoopy-like "curse you Red Baron!" pluck and swagger in it. Hope, she also illustrates, employs humor to laugh in spite of and at the facts.

Some of the facts, like economic ones and natural disasters and human cruelty, are grim. But what Matthew Henry and Patricia Neal demonstrate is that facts do not have the last word. Spiritual realities like hope and gratitude do. They trump facts.

Dorothy L. Sayers wrote: "Facts are like cows: if you look them in the face hard enough, they generally run away."

February 29

I accompanied my wife, in April, 2009, to Denver, Colorado, where "Great Teachers for Urban Schools" had invited her to speak at their annual conference. While she presented and networked, I photographed gorgeous Colorado.

When we arrived on Tuesday, the meteorologists' forecasts were grim. They warned from Tuesday all the way to midnight Friday: "If you thought our surprise fifteen-inch spring snowfall last week was something, wait till Saturday!" For four days they did everything but guarantee a three to six-inch snow Friday night followed by several inches more on Saturday.

Our flight home departed at 6:20 a.m. Saturday. I lost three hours sleep Thursday night strategizing, sweating (literally) how I would cope with a foot of snow. What if we get stuck in Denver for days? What if I wreck the rental car driving through a foot of ice and snow? What if the car gets stuck and we miss our flight? What if the rental car employees cannot make it to work and shuttle us to the airport? What if the alarm clock fails to go off at 3:30 a.m.?

The apocalyptic forecasts were greatly exaggerated. Denver got a dusting. "Man!" I heard one red-faced weather expert report early Saturday morning, "If that storm hadn't gone one hundred miles north of where we expected it to go, Denver would be in really big trouble this morning."

That experience reinforced a life lesson: never put all your eggs in the basket of experts. My wife had said as much all week: "You know, they could all be wrong."

Concentrating on undesirable possibilities or even probabilities fuels endless worries. The snowstorm-that-never-was taught me what Mark Twain learned: "I am an old man and have known a great many troubles, but most of them never happened."

February Notes

1. Shakespeare. *Much Ado about Nothing*. Act 5. Scene 4.
2. Griffin, "Love the Marigold," 66–67.
3. Lindbeck, *Nature of Doctrine*, 117.
4. King, "Loving Your Enemies," no pages.
5. Waskow, "Sukkah of Shalom," 107.
6. Toobin, "Real I.R.S. Scandal," no pages.
7. Peters, *Wendell Berry*, 8.
8. Hertsgaard, "Green Dream," 254.
9. Deuteronomy 30:19.
10. Everett, "Life of Elizabeth Barrett Browning," no pages.
11. Browning, *Sonnets From the Portuguese*, 43.
12. Reed, "James Clyburn," no pages.
13. Holguin, "Happily Married," no pages.
14. *Gottman Institute*, "Research FAQs," no pages.
15. I Corinthians 9:27.
16. *Sakya*, "Life of Buddha," no pages.
17. I Corinthians 13:3.
18. Hyde, "Choose Life," no pages.
19. Solzhenitsyn, *Gulag Archipelago*, 516-517.
20. *Biography*, "Candy Lightner," no pages.
21. All writers who use this quotation attribute it to Augustine. I have not been able to find it in Augustine's body of work. The earliest I find the quotation is in a book written in 1988 by eminent American theologian, the late Robert McAfee Brown. In his *Spirituality and Liberation: Overcoming the Great Fallacy*, Brown introduces a chapter with the quotation, but does not give his source. Allan Aubrey Boesak in *Dare We Speak of Hope: Searching for a Language of Life in Faith and Politics* comments on page 43 that the quotation "seems to have come to us via Anselm of Canterbury, who attributes it to Augustine." Boesak does not give his source for that assertion. Whether Augustine ever said or wrote it is largely immaterial and irrelevant to me. What does matter is that this characterization of hope speaks truth, and I believe it does.
22. Curry-Knight, *Top 500 Reviewer*, no pages.
23. Popova, "Kurt Vonnegut," no pages.
24. Wood, "Secret Fears," 1.
25. Roc, "Enough," no pages.
26. Matthew 18:3.
27. *IMDb*, "Schindler's List Quotes," no pages.
28. Warner, "Man Behind the Window," no pages.
29. *The Economist*, "Van Cliburn," no pages.
30. Shearer, *An Unquiet Life*, 346.

March

March 1

I once received a lovely gift from someone in or around Leavenworth, Indiana. It is a framed piece of embroidery that has one of my favorite Bible verses sewn on it. I only wish I could find out who made it (or had it made) so I could thank her (or him).

Some of life's greatest gifts—the ones that mean the most—are the anonymous ones.

Last weekend I listened to two different couples tell of their recent experience in a restaurant. When they asked for the check they were informed by the waiter that someone had already picked up the tab. I have also heard of people at a drive-through restaurant, or in a grocery check-out line, or at a gas station who had a similar experience—some anonymous donor, for whatever reason, had already paid their bill.

My favorite "anonymous gift" story comes from Chilean poet Pablo Neruda. He tells of a time as a child, playing in his back yard, when he saw the hand of a little boy or girl come through a hole in the fence. The next time he looked, the hand was gone, but in its place was a little white sheep. Little Pablo spontaneously ran in his house and brought out his own treasure, a pine cone he loved, left it in the same spot, and took the sheep. The two children never met. Years later, in a house fire, the little white sheep perished. Pablo Neruda said that even as a grown man, whenever he passed a toyshop he looked in the window for a little white toy sheep to replace the one he lost.[1]

To feel the affection of someone whose identity is unknown enlarges our souls, tenderizes our hearts, and binds us to a not-all-bad human race.

March 2

I have lived, by my account, a charmed life—definitely not in the eyes of the rich and famous, and probably not to those up close and personal who know my deficiencies and heartbreaks. But as one who for three decades saw some of the worst things that befall individuals and families, I have become something of an expert at putting things in perspective.

My charmed life? I grew up a much-loved son. I won that lottery. It could have been different.

In 1969 I became a husband. I know now I could not have done better. I won that lottery. It could have been very different.

In 1972 I became a father. Our three sons have grown up to be responsible, interesting, respectable human beings. I could not be prouder. I won that lottery. It could have been very, very different.

Thanks to our sons and their wives, I acquired a fourth title-for-life in 2008. Six grandchildren for as long as they live will refer to me as Popple.

On the birth of our first grandchild on February 24, 2006, a picture and a quotation came to me. I am sure they will never leave my mind. The picture came from the 1977 television miniseries *Roots*. It is the scene where Omoro, Kunta Kinte's father, took his eight-day-old baby boy into the jungle. On a beautiful, starlit night he reverently lifted his eyes and his newborn to the heavens and solemnly proclaimed: "Behold, the only thing greater than yourself."

That blessing brings to mind words from Wordsworth: "A child, more than all other gifts that earth can offer to declining man, brings hope with it, and forward-looking thoughts."

This is the story of my charmed life and I am sticking with it: the world should go on.

March 3

Two professions vie for top spot on my most-respected list. One is teaching.

Yes, I know that some teachers are flat-out incompetent. I had a few doofuses. All of our children, unfortunately, also had a few.

For decades now I have lived with a woman who is both a career teacher and my wife. I have seen her donate everything but her spleen to motivate students. I have witnessed nights up until 4:00 a.m. grading papers, weekends spent preparing for the next week, and out-of-pocket small fortunes spent on supplies, gifts, decorations, and rewards.

Good teachers get satisfaction from knowing they gave it their best. Their "hallelujah" payoff, however, is when a former student surfaces years later to say something like: "You were simply the best—thanks forever."

In his autobiography, world-class journalist David Brinkley tells of the profound disappointment he was to his mother from the day he was born. When he first showed her some of his fledgling attempts to write, she wadded them up and threw them in the trash and told him not to waste his time on "such foolishness." But one day in English class, Mrs. Barrows Smith pronounced: "David, I think you ought to be a journalist." Brinkley writes that at that moment "a world turned for me."[2]

Educator Horace Mann wrote: "If you attempt to teach without inspiring, you're hammering a cold iron."

Is there a teacher living who significantly inspired and encouraged you or nudged you at a critical moment in your life in the right direction? It might mean the world to put that into words and pass it along to your Mrs. Smith. Someday it will be too late.

March 4

Physicians see their hospitalized patients for five to ten minutes a day. Nurses assume life-and-death responsibility for those same patients for eight or ten or twelve hours straight.

Many times I have visited in the homes of parents whose child died. As I heard them relive that awful loss, they often singled out a competent and compassionate nurse as their only positive memory on the worst day of their lives:

"I saw the nurse wipe a tear from her eye."

"The nurse mopped our child's brow and held his hand until he took his last breath."

"The nurses taped messages above our child's bed like, 'I prefer to be called Cookie' and 'Yes, I would love a foot massage' and 'Please wind my music box.'"

"The nurses stayed with us long after their shift was over."

"Except for the way the nurses took care of our emotional needs, I don't know how we would have made it through."

"Six of those nurses took a day off without pay and drove all the way down here for the funeral."

One woman whose grandbaby was born premature and spent three months in the neonatal intensive care unit addressed this poem to the nurses of the unit and tacked it on their bulletin board: "*To My Nurses.* Tiny / Fragile / Born too soon / Surrounded by machines / Invaded by tubes / You—you saw underneath it all—Me! / And because you / Worked and hoped / Worked and cried / Worked and prayed / And worked / *I am!*"

Good nurses do much more than tend to physical needs. They dispense tender, loving care to patients and their families. That alone sometimes keeps hope alive.

March 5

I grew up in a church that did not recognize Christmas and Easter as special religious days. Every Easter we heard a paragraph at the beginning of the sermon if not an entire sermon on "Why We Do Not Keep Easter."

As an adult, I have come to appreciate some of the pageantry and symbolism of Holy Week. My favorite day is the Saturday between Good Friday and Easter.

Some early Christians believed that on "Holy Saturday" Jesus went throughout the hadean realm and announced to all souls residing there, beginning with Abel, the good news of what God was getting ready to do on Easter.

My personal reason for appreciating Saturday is far less esoteric—I can identify more readily and more often with the disciples of Jesus on that day than I can on the Friday before or the Sunday after.

On Friday the disciples were totally disillusioned and dejected, their leader having died a shameful death. I have known very few times of despair in my life. I am fortunate every year to have only a few situational depressions that last a couple of days at most. Some people I know live much of their lives in a deep, dark, Good-Friday funk of depression.

On Sunday, by contrast, the disciples were euphoric, ecstatic—running and jumping and shouting for joy. I am grateful to have about a dozen of those as-good-as-it-gets resurrection days every year, days on which I yell "Yippee!" or croon a few bars of "What a Wonderful World."

But the other 350 days of my year are more like Saturday of Holy Week. I plod along, old griefs and losses still percolating on the back burner of my memory. But also in the mix is hope for one more mountaintop experience, one more new beginning, one more Easter morning. I believe that yearning will carry me all the way home.

March 6

During an ice storm, I found myself observing trees; more precisely, three neighborhood trees. My next door neighbor has a row of twelve-year-old Bradford pear trees on our property line. He had seven until a storm took one out. An ice storm split scores of limbs off the surviving six. Bradford pears have beautiful white flowers for ten days in the spring, but their limbs grow fast and at a steep angle and they are, consequently, brittle trees. After Bradford pear trees reach the age of twelve or so, a stiff wind or ice storm can snap big branches off or smack down the whole tree.

Another neighbor has a magnificent willow tree. Every limb, covered with half an inch of ice, moved and swayed—danced with the winds—but lost not a limb.

In my yard are five Thuja green giant trees, evergreens between eight and twelve feet tall. Covered with ice, the tops of all five bent over and kissed the ground. They looked more like chuppahs than trees. Now a week later and the ice melted, three are perfectly straight, one is almost straight, and the fifth—the oldest and tallest—leans a lot, like a stooped old man bending forward at a forty-five-degree angle.

I can identify with the Bradford pear. Sometimes I am rigid. When I become aware of it, Theognis of Megara's words may come to me: "Wisdom is supple, but folly keeps in a groove." I can identify with the willow. I do not break easily. My life work has helped me put things in perspective and shrug off many things as "just" inconveniences that are incidental.

The older I get the more I identify with old Thuja. We get partly bowed by winter storms, but not broken. And it takes us longer to straighten up.

March 7

John Wooden grew up in Hall, Centerton, and Martinsville, Indiana. He led his high school basketball team to the state championship game three years in a row. He made the all-state team each of those years. At Purdue he was a consensus All-American basketball player for three years and led Purdue to the National Championship in 1932.

Wooden went on to become arguably the greatest college basketball coach of all time, leading UCLA to four perfect seasons and ten NCAA championships. What was the magic of the great leader? He credits the seven-point creed his father gave him when he graduated from grammar school for his deep, strong rooting:

1. Be true to yourself.

2. Make each day your masterpiece.

3. Help others.

4. Drink deeply from good books, especially the Bible.

5. Make friendship a fine art.

6. Build a shelter against a rainy day.

7. Pray for guidance and give thanks for your blessings every day.[3]

Wooden gave his players—and offers us—wings. These are some of my favorite words of wisdom, collected from the greatest coach that I wing to you:

"You can't live a perfect day without doing something for someone who will never be able to repay you."

"Talent is God-given. Be humble. Fame is man-given. Be grateful. Conceit is self-given. Be careful."

"Consider the rights of others before your own feelings, and the feelings of others before your own rights."

"If you don't have time to do it *right*, when will you have time to do it *over*?"

March 8

"Angry Loner"

Newspaper headlines chose those two words to describe Cho Seung Hui, the mass murderer at Virginia Tech. I recall that the acquaintances of Lee Harvey Oswald described him with the same two words. The two boys who ravaged Columbine had earned the same epitaph. Going it alone is risky business. The first thing the Bible pronounces "not good" is aloneness.

There was a popular book published in 1961 titled *A Nation of Sheep*. It criticized those who swallow uncritically whatever the authorities—presidents, parents, and preachers—feed them.

Our pride revolts at being called a sheep. Sheep are not known for being smart. They just go with the flock. Sheep-like passivity and docility in humans lead to wars and all manner of ills. Americans value independence and self-sufficiency. We imagine ourselves tigers and lions and eagles and such—almost anything but sheep. But one day, sooner or later, life puts us in touch with, like it or not, our essential sheepness. It may come in the form of a diagnosis, a marriage crisis, a parenting crisis, a job loss, or a death. Then we suddenly realize how frail, weak, defenseless, shorn—sheeplike—we really are.

Support groups like Alcoholics Anonymous have grasped the importance of being in a flock. The first step in their twelve-step program is to admit powerlessness to control or fix or manage their lives on their own.

We need a flock to include and enfold us, to accept us as we are, to draw us out of our autonomy. We need a flock that can allow us to ventilate our self-loathing and dissipate our anger. As the Yale boys put it in their Whiffenpoof Song: "We're poor little lambs who have lost our way."

Do I hear a *baa*?

March 9

How does suffering shape us? There are two leading theories.

One is represented by Somerset Maugham, British author, writing about what he witnessed as a medical student: "Suffering did not ennoble; it degraded. It made men selfish, mean, petty and suspicious. It absorbed them in small things. It made them less than men."

The other point of view can be summed up in three succinct sentences from three experts on suffering:

Friedrich Nietzsche: "What doesn't kill us makes us stronger."

Ernest Hemingway: "The world breaks everyone, and afterwards many are strong at the broken places."

Helen Keller: "Although the world is full of suffering, it is full also of the overcoming of it."

Think of Patrick Henry Hughes, born with multiple anomalies—scoliosis, no eyes, inability to walk, and arms that cannot be straightened. Patrick began playing piano at nine months. He played trumpet in the University of Louisville marching band and became a virtuoso pianist and vocalist. He was a "straight A" student in his college classes.

How do we understand a Patrick Henry Hughes and his response to suffering? First, Patrick chose his family well! His mother, father, and two brothers have an earned "A" in family. They bathed Patrick in affirmation, support, and encouragement all the way. What if Patrick Henry Hughes had been born into another family, a family that for whatever reason did not believe in him or did not know how to help him? We do not want to go there.

And then there is Patrick's indomitable spirit. Smiling, he insists that he is "just an ordinary guy living my life." He prefers to think and talk about "abilities" instead of "disabilities."[4] No family, however wonderful, can dictate spirit. The child alone holds those controls.

Suffering is no match for the dynamic duo of "A plus" community and "A plus" attitude.

March 10

On his sixty-first birthday, trial lawyer Clarence Darrow wrote:

> I once thought that when the time should come that I could no longer play
> ball there would be nothing left in life . . . I used to wonder what people could
> do to have fun after they were twenty years old; then I raised it to twenty-five;
> then I raised it to thirty. I have been raising it ever since, and still wondering
> what people can do for pleasure when they are old. But we are there with the
> same old illusions and the same old delusions, with fantasies promising us
> and beckoning us; with castles that we begin to build, never stopping to think
> whether these castles will be finished; we get our satisfaction and we kill our
> time listening to the voices and building the castles.[5]

In Sara Gruen's *Water for Elephants* a man in his nineties says: "Age is a terrible
thief. Just when you're getting the hang of life, it knocks your legs out from under you
and stoops your back."[6]

He elaborates:

> You start to forget words—they're on the tip of your tongue, but instead of
> eventually dislodging, they stay there. You go upstairs to fetch something, and
> by the time you get there you can't remember what it was you were after. You
> call your child by the names of all your other children and finally the dog
> before you get to his.

I think both the aging Clarence Darrow and the fictitious man in *Water for El-
ephants* speak truth. Age is a terrible thief "just when we're getting the hang of life."
But we had best go into life's final chapter "with fantasies promising us and beckoning
us." It is better not to stop building those castles—whether we finish them or not is
outside our control and largely irrelevant.

I am all for being realistic about old age. Notwithstanding, season reality with
a little hope. Getting old is like eating cabbage—it goes down better with a little salt.

March 11

The ten-point scale.

It has become a common measurement in our time. Medical people ask: "How would you describe your pain on a ten-point scale?" If I assign my pain ten points, that means it is unbearable, the worst pain I have ever felt. The aim of the scale is to quantify a subjective experience.

That may be a fair way to speak of how much we enjoy or dislike a movie or how delectable or disgusting we find a casserole. Maybe the ten-point scale is also useful in putting life's experiences, especially negative ones, in perspective.

Several days ago a little old lady backed into our new car and left a big dent in the driver's side. She was at fault, her insurance will fix it, no one was hurt, and we are left with an unsightly car door for a week or so before I drop it off at a body shop to be repaired. I assign that a two. In the course of human events, it was so minor—a minuscule annoyance, an inconvenience, a flea bite—a one or a two.

I think I would give ten points only to a situation of utter devastation and hopelessness. Seeing my family herded into a gas chamber to be exterminated would be a ten. I think I would give a nine to a member of my family being raped or murdered or completing suicide. I might survive it, but I would go forward broken, nursing an almost unbearable wound in my heart forever.

My point is that many of us overreact to life's stressors. We "catastrophize" (psychotherapist Albert Ellis liked to say) over life's dented doors.

And yes, my family tires of hearing me ask: "On a ten-point scale, how many points should you give that?"

March 12

Whatever we think of Tiger Woods's philandering and his public confession of guilt or Paula Dean's public apology for using racial slurs, one thing on which we can agree is the one thing their business associates had foremost on their minds: "How is this performance going to affect the Tiger Woods (or Paula Dean) brand?"

Gatorade, AT&T, Nike and other companies once bet over $100 million annually that the Tiger Woods brand—greatest golfer in world history plus all-around nice guy—would make them more bucks.

Brand, when I was growing up, was something a cowboy put on a cow. Cowboys seared their unique mark into the hide of their property. Today the word refers to the image cultivated by a person or a business. The advertising industry aims to sear a brand (more than a product) into consumers' brains. Tiger Woods's business partners are hoping his confession will help pull his weakened brand out of the fire.

I was discussing Albert Schweitzer with a class of college seniors and used a sentence often spoken of Schweitzer: "He made his life his argument." With three earned doctorates, Schweitzer decided that instead of spending his life ensconced in a European university talking up Christian love and service, he would give his life to putting into practice love and service as a jungle doctor in Africa.

One student in my class had an epiphany that she put in writing and gave to me: "Schweitzer definitely has caused me to wonder whether or not I am making my life my argument. It's also made me wonder what my argument really is."

Each one of us—whether we are aware of it or not—is building a brand. Our life is an argument for something. A sobering question is, to quote one tenderhearted college senior, "what my argument really is."

March 13

"Amazing Grace"

Probably no one ever called her that in her first one hundred years. Orphaned at twelve, taken in by family and friends until she was adopted, Grace Groner worked as a secretary for forty-three years. She bought her clothes at rummage sales, never owned a car, and lived alone in a one-bedroom cottage. These days thirteen hundred Lake Forest (Illinois) College students have scholarships, internships, and studies abroad because of her. They call her "Amazing Grace."

When she died in January, 2000, at age one hundred, Grace Groner left $7 million to her alma mater, Lake Forest College. She never sold the three shares of Abbott Laboratories stock she bought in 1935 for $180. When she died, after many stock splits and dividends reinvested, her initial investment had grown into a $7 million fortune.[7]

I recently listened to a professor sound off about "this generation," in particular how they make no provision for the future. He stereotyped them as addicts to "instant gratification and instant communication." His caricature was of a student wolfing down a Big Mac (instant food paid for with plastic money), text-messaging with the other hand (im chewing bm now), while steering the car with his knees. He would not expect any of them, like a Grace Groner, to set aside anything for old age.

Most of us admire the plodding, intentional game plan of a John McPhee, Pulitzer Prize-winning writer, Princeton professor, and author of twenty five books. He says he hardly ever has cranked out more than one single-spaced page a day. "You know, you put an ounce in a bucket every day," he explains, "before you know it you have a quart."

Aesop's ancient story about the turtle and the hare may be truer in our time than ever before. There is still something to be said for eschewing immediate pleasure for taking the long view; something to be said for the discipline and perseverance of the turtle, or John McPhee, or "Amazing Grace" Groner.

March 14

Three women who met each other almost half a century ago on the campus of George Peabody College in Nashville reunited, this time bringing their spouses with them to a Turkish restaurant. Together their three marriages represented 128 years of lasting love. Joining them was one couple's daughter and the daughter's fiancé.

At one point one of the old married men quipped: "It would be a shame to deny this young couple the benefit of all the wisdom assembled here. Let's each of us put into one word the secret of our marriage."

The first to volunteer said "forgiveness." Holding grudges, nursing old wounds, is malignancy in a marriage. His wife offered her one word, "sensitivity." Stay attuned to what your beloved is thinking and feeling and needing.

A second married woman said "compromise." Her husband contributed "devotion." Total commitment to protecting and nurturing the relationship trumps everything else.

The third married man said "mutual-respect." He hyphenated the word to conform to the game's one word rule. His wife agreed: "respect." She said, "We admire each other's talent, knowledge, creativity, and pursuit of excellence. We are equally yoked in our own little mutual admiration society."

The young unmarried couple was invited to participate: "Surely you don't want to just be voyeurs—what do you two value most in your relationship?" She said "support." They encourage each other and give each other a soft place to fall when life gets messy. He volunteered "awareness." Pick up on the vibrations, the heart-sounds, of your beloved.

The eight values overlap. Taken as a whole they may give a pretty clear profile of real love—not the feeling of love, or the idea of love, but the dogged practice, day in and day out, of the behaviors that make love last.

March 15

Some of my friends e-mail me stories, corny jokes, or political commentaries that are just not my cup of tea, but I cannot bring myself to tell them to stop so I just grimace and touch the delete button. For some reason I opened one today. I am glad I did. It made me smile and think.

It seems a volunteer greeter who worked in the registration area of a large hospital sometimes showed up ten to fifteen minutes late for his shift. However, when on duty, he greeted everyone with a friendly, bright-eyed, hospitable smile. Everyone agreed he was a tremendous asset. One day the director of volunteers invited Sparky to join her for a cup of coffee. After praising his work ethic and chipper spirit, the manager asked: "I'm just a little curious. About half the time you show up a little late. I know you retired from the military. What did they say to you there when you came in late?"

Sparky answered: "They said, 'Good morning, Admiral. Can I get your coffee, sir?'"

Some of the people I admire most are the rich and famous who have a servant heart. I think of Bill Gates and Warren Buffet, some of the richest people in the world, who now are giving much energy and much of their fortunes to bless the world's poorest and sickest. I think of Jimmy Carter who for over thirty years after finishing his presidential term has been volunteering for Habitat for Humanity, building houses for people who otherwise could never be homeowners.

Two quotations come to mind, the first from philosopher and Rabbi Abraham Heschel: "When I was young, I admired clever people. Now that I am old, I admire kind people."

The other comes from Indian poet and philosopher Rabindranath Tagore: "I slept and dreamt that life was joy. I awoke and saw that life was service. I acted, and behold, service was joy."

March 16

A little over a century ago, the National American Woman Suffrage Association held its national convention at Louisville's Seelbach Hotel. It would be another decade, though, before the Nineteenth Amendment granted all women the right to vote.

Did anyone then foresee that in less than a century more than half the students in many seminaries, medical schools, and law schools would be women? Who foresaw that three United States Supreme Court justices would be women? The "Rules for Teachers" one hundred years ago illustrate how far women have come:

1. You may not marry during the term of your contract.

2. You may not keep company with men.

3. You must be home between the hours of 8:00 p.m. and 6:00 a.m. unless at a school function.

4. You may not loiter downtown in any of the ice cream stores.

5. You may not travel beyond the city limits unless you have permission of the chairman of the school board.

6. You may not ride in carriages or automobiles with any man except your father or brother.

7. You may not smoke cigarettes.

8. You may not dress in bright colors.

9. You may under no circumstances dye your hair.

10. You must wear at least two petticoats.

11. Your dresses may not be any shorter than two inches above the ankles.

12. You must sweep the floor once a day, scrub the floor with hot soapy water once a week, clean the blackboards once a day, and start the fire at 7:00 a.m. to have the school warm by 8:00 a.m.[8]

How much freedom for women is going to be enough? As the grandfather of two little girls, I only want for them what I want for our four grandsons—the freedom to become all they desire and all they have the ability to become.

March 17

When thirty-three Chilean miners were entombed in 2010, one of the first stories leaked about them was a light, funny moment. One miner, not knowing whether he or any of them would survive, created a makeshift blond wig and pretended to be a well-known Chilean philanthropist handing out $10,000 to each miner on the day they all got rescued.[9]

I thought of what Randall Patrick McMurphy, imprisoned like the miners but in a mental hospital, said in *One Flew Over the Cookoo's Nest*: "I haven't heard a real laugh since I came through that door. Man, when you lose your laugh, you lose your footing."

We could call it McMurphy's law: humor keeps us from losing our footing. Humor, when life gets as dark as a cave or a mine or a mental hospital, helps keep hope alive. If we are serious to a fault, life can get to us, even drive us crazy, especially when the odds are overwhelmingly against us.

Norman Cousins, admitted to the hospital with a potentially terminal diagnosis of ankylosing spondylitis, watched Marx Brothers videos and Candid Camera videos as part of his effort to mobilize his salutary emotions. He believed that he could enhance his body chemistry's healing work. He "made the joyous discovery that ten minutes of genuine belly laughter had an anesthetic affect" and gave him at least two hours of pain-free sleep. Cousins survived his illness. One thing he said he discovered from it was that "hearty laughter is a good way to jog internally without having to go outdoors."[10]

Hope and humor act like a tonic, releasing endorphins, our body's own pain-reducing, immunity-building substance. Someone said: "You have two legs and one sense of humor. If you're forced with the choice, it's better to lose a leg."

March 18

The number of centenarians in the United States was under forty thousand in 1990. In 2014, more than one hundred thousand of us have lived one hundred years or more.

I enjoyed reading a *New York Times* article: "Secrets of the Centenarians"[11] on how some centenarians answer the question they get asked most: "What is your secret to a long life?"

Mae Anderson, 103, of Great Neck, New York, said:

> I think not looking into the past and just living in the present is a very good thing, because picking up certain things from the past—what you should have done or could have done—is not going to help you. We're always grateful for what we can do, and we try to forget what we didn't do or shouldn't have done.

Esther Tuttle will not reach one hundred till next July, but she is bound and determined to get there. At ninety two she wrote her memoir and titled it *No Rocking Chair for Me*. She told the reporter her secret: "Being conscious of your body. Your body is your instrument. So I always did exercises, did a lot of yoga, stretching exercises, and walking. Eat in moderation and drink in moderation."

One-hundred-year-old Travilla Demming of Tucson said: "I always put anything disagreeable or bad out of the way. That's the secret of life. Don't emphasize anything that is evil or bad, but just get rid of it or rise above it." She concluded: "I'm having a fun old age, except I'm getting rustier and rustier by the day."

Most longevity researchers agree that 20–30 percent of longevity is genetically determined. That leaves lifestyle (think Esther Tuttle) and attitude (think Mae Anderson and Travilla Demming) as dominant factors. Although not in control of our genes, we do control our lifestyle and attitude.

Maybe old Jonathan Swift had it right: "The best doctors are Dr. Diet, Dr. Quiet, and Dr. Merryman."

March 19

"ALL WE HAVE IN LIFE IS WHAT WE NOTICE."

Leonard Pitts, columnist for the Miami Herald, tells about an eighteen-mile hike he took to raise money against breast cancer. That day he saw things on the hike that he drove by daily on his commute but had never seen—a lake not quite visible from the road; a sidewalk curving gracefully beneath an overhang of trees; a quaint little wooden footbridge over a hollow. He surmised: "We're all going to the same destination. The only difference is in what we choose to see along the way."

Victor Frankl saw Nazis strip concentration camp prisoners of everything that symbolized their previous lives. Families and friends got separated, clothing got ripped off and thrown away, possessions got taken away, and bodily hair got shorn. But Frankl noticed something else. He saw a few people, in the face of certain doom, walking through the huts comforting others, even giving away their last morsel of bread.

Frankl survived the Holocaust and went on to write one of the great books of the twentieth century, *Man's Search for Meaning*, in which he said of those he had noticed giving away their last piece of bread: "They offer sufficient proof that everything can be taken away from a man but one thing, the last of the human freedoms—to choose one's attitude in any given set of circumstances, to choose one's own way." [12]

What we bring to life is more potent than what life brings to us. I believe Zen master Richard Baker Roshi was right when he said that all we have in life is what we notice. Or as Marcus Aurelius, the Roman philosopher-king put it over eighteen centuries ago: "The color of our thought dyes our world."

March 20

I saw advertised on the internet a "eulogy pack" for the sudden death of a stepfather.

The company was running a half-price special: six speeches and six poems for only $24.99 (regularly $49.98). Each eulogy articulates the sadness and disbelief of a stepson or stepdaughter at the death of a beloved stepfather. It speaks of what your stepfather meant to you in your life, his many talents and skills, and how much he will be missed, especially because he had a sudden, unexpected death. The eulogy ends with a poem that the stepchild is instructed to read quietly and sincerely. A different pack, also half-price, is offered if the stepfather's death followed a long illness. And there are other eulogy six-packs for sale, tailored to the death of a stepmother, grandfather, or almost any other relationship.

Emotionally-constipated people through the ages have hired others to do their mourning or cheering for them. Dickens's Oliver Twist had a job as a professional mourner. The undertaker hired him to attend funerals and look sad, weep, and model grief, and so give permission to others attending the funeral to do the same. Today, for $49.98, he might be able to hire out as a reader of eulogies composed by professionals.

Late-night talk shows and political rallies and other entertainment venues have been known to place a "plant" in the audience to laugh at jokes or applaud, hoping the plant's emoting will be contagious, in much the same way cheerleaders are planted at ballgames.

In the 1936 presidential campaign, Roosevelt defended any mistakes he might be making in his efforts to be a compassionate leader by quoting "the immortal Dante" who said that "divine justice weighs the sins of the cold-blooded and the sins of the warm-blooded on different scales.[13]

Fish swim, birds fly, flowers bloom, and humans emote. When all is said and done, may we be found among the warm-blooded ones who rejoice with those who rejoice and weep with those who weep.

March 21

James Anthony, many years ago at Washington University Medical School in St. Louis, conducted a study of "superkids"—kids who adapt to terrible circumstances with extraordinary coping skills and keep finding ways to overcome. One family he studied featured a schizophrenic mother who believed someone was poisoning their food. Her twelve-year-old shared the mother's fears and would eat only restaurant food. The middle child, age ten, would eat at home but only when her father was there. The seven-year-old who ate at home every day explained, "Well, I ain't dead yet."

Anthony explained that children are like dolls. One is made of glass, another of plastic, another of steel. Hit by a hammer, the first one breaks, the second gets a dent, and the third gives off a fine, metallic sound.[14]

My reigning poster child for superkids is Jeannette Walls. Walls is a successful writer, author of bestseller *The Glass Castle*. She lived her childhood in cardboard boxes, broken cars, and abandoned houses, driven from pillar to post with eccentric parents, her father forever pursuing an imaginary glass castle.

One day in the Mojave Desert her mother pointed out to Jeannette a scraggly, freakish Joshua tree that had been so whipped by the wind over centuries that it existed in a permanent state of wind-blown-ness (like Jeannette and her family).

Months later, Jeannette saw a little Joshua tree sapling growing close to the old tree. She told her mother that she wanted to dig it up and replant it near the two-room house they were renting, promising to water it and care for it every day so it could grow straight and tall. Her mother frowned and said: "You would destroy what makes it special. It's the Joshua tree's struggle that gives it its beauty."[15]

And thereby hangs a tale.

March 22

Recognizing his lifetime of service as a jungle doctor, *Life* magazine in October, 1947, titled an article about Albert Schweitzer "The Greatest Man in the World."

Schweitzer, who earned doctorates in philosophy, theology, and medicine before he moved to Africa, came to America only once, in 1949. When he was to arrive by train in Chicago, where he would receive an honorary doctorate of laws, a committee of dignitaries from the university stood at the depot, waiting to greet him. They knew what he looked like—the whole world knew what Schweitzer looked like—but Schweitzer had never met or seen a picture of any of the welcoming committee. When Schweitzer disembarked, the committee observed something they could not forget.

Dr. Schweitzer noticed a bent old woman carrying her bags with great difficulty. Spontaneously dropping his grip to the depot floor, the seventy-four-year-old doctor picked up her bags and carried them to a cab. After helping her into the cab, he returned to his grip and began to look for someone to chauffeur him to his speaking engagement.

That afternoon the dean of the University of Chicago Divinity School, introducing Dr. Schweitzer, set aside Schweitzer's massive curriculum vitae and spoke straight from the heart: "This morning Albert Schweitzer carried a feeble little old lady's bags. As long as we live we will never again see a person in need and be able to pass on by. Ladies and gentlemen, Dr. Albert Schweitzer."[16]

Schweitzer once wrote of his decision to leave his prestigious, comfortable life in Europe: "I wanted to be a doctor so that I might be able to work without having to talk. For years I had been giving of myself in words . . . but this new form of activity would consist not in preaching the religion of love, but in practicing it."[17]

He meant to make his life his argument. Mission accomplished.

March 23

If you asked for the world's foremost therapist for desperate, suicidal people, that might be Aaron Beck, psychiatrist emeritus of the University of Pennsylvania Medical School. Beck has spent much of his professional life studying and treating despondent people. Beck found defective thinking patterns that all the suicidal people had in common. Faulty thinking, what another cognitive therapist Albert Ellis called "stinking thinking," took them down and kept them there.

A common flaw he found in their thinking was a sense that they were basically inadequate persons, defective goods, life's failures who just could not get it right. As in Murphy's Law, they had convinced themselves that "anything that can go wrong will go wrong for me." Their low opinion of themselves contaminated most everything they touched.

They also saw the prevailing state of things as permanent—fixed, static, frozen. They could see no exit. Believing that they are losers, and unable to imagine things ever getting better, they concluded that the future was hopeless.[18] That surely was what Mark Twain had in mind when he said, "There is no sadder sight than a young pessimist."

We all know on our better days when we are not depressed that life hardly works that way. We know that things are constantly changing and we know how ignorant we are of the way things are going to be one week off, much less a year away.

I sometimes think of life like the four quarters of a football game, or four trips around the track in the mile run. By those measures, I am most likely in the last quarter of the game or on my last lap around the track.

But this time of year I find myself thinking of life in terms of four seasons: spring is childhood, summer is adolescence, fall is maturity, and winter is death. I hope you will think of this spring as a gift—another chance for one more birth. Fuchsia and chartreuse, pink and green, are overwhelming brown and gray. It is spring again, and once more all things seem possible.

March 24

Do you hear what I hear? The shrieking, I mean. That is the sound of winter giving up. The dull, brown earth is surrendering its oppressive hold on us, giving up to buttercup and crocus, dandelion, forsythia, and redbud, to robins stalking and spearing earthworms in the yard, to geese piercing the sky.

Fortunate to live in a four-seasons part of the world, annually I get to cheer on the new birth. Let us raise glasses! Let us toast those deep yellows and pinks and purples, for they mean we have made it through another winter. It could have been different. Let the shrieking begin.

Russian novelist Leo Tolstoy in April of 1858, having survived another brutal winter just south of Moscow, could not contain his jubilation in a letter to his aunt and confidant Alexandra:

> It's spring! It is so good to be alive on this earth, for all good people and even for such as I. Nature, the air, everything is drenched in hope, future, a wonderful future. The springtime has such a powerful effect on me that I sometimes catch myself imagining I am a plant that has just opened and spread its leaves among all the other plants and is going to grow up simply, peacefully and joyfully on the good Lord's earth. When this happens, such a fermentation, purification, and orchestration goes on inside me that anyone that has not experienced it himself could not imagine it himself. Away with all the old worn-out things . . . to the devil with them all! Make way for this wonderful plant that is filling out its buds and growing in the spring.[19]

"Everything is drenched in hope." Or, in the words of scripture: "Winter is past . . . flowers cover the earth, it's time to sing."[20]

Hallelujah! Amen!

March 25

"A child, any child, is a garden, and a garden without a wall." So wrote novelist and Presbyterian clergyman Frederick Buechner. Staying with the garden metaphor, Buechner wrote:

> Anything can enter there . . . and anything can depart, quite at will, as long as the wall-lessness lasts: birds and friends, secrets, hates, games, fear, and magic of all sorts. But then . . . a wall appears, and then . . . the garden is enclosed. Whatever is there is there to stay.[21]

Buechner's metaphor helped me connect with an event in the life of Jesse Stuart. In 1954, Kentucky named him poet laureate. He wrote thirty-two books, four hundred short stories, and gave five thousand lectures all around the world.

As a schoolboy, Stuart had a remarkably undistinguished career. However, in Mrs. Hamilton's history class, one day he spoke a few words that moved Mrs. Hamilton to tell the class that "Jesse sounded just like a future Patrick Henry in this room." Mrs. Hamilton may not have remembered a week later even speaking those words. She surely never imagined how formative that one sentence would become in Jesse's life. But Jesse never forgot, and decades later he singled out that moment in Mrs. Hamilton's history class as a moment of recognition he sorely needed at that point in his life.[22]

I hope people who go into teaching these days aspire to become a Mrs. Hamilton. I hope their greater aim as they instruct is to inspire children to believe in themselves, to put an "I *am* able" thought in their minds before those walls start going up and the garden becomes enclosed.

Lee Iacocca, I believe, tells it right: "In a completely rational society, the best of us would be teachers and the rest of us would have to settle for something less, because passing civilization along from one generation to the next ought to be the highest honor and the highest responsibility anyone could have."

March 26

Once upon a time there was an old sea captain who for decades sailed his vessel flaw-lessly, earning the devotion and admiration of all his crew. The venerable captain had one peculiarity. Every day before sailing he went to his cabin for a few moments alone. The crew thought perhaps he was saying prayers for himself and his men. Whatever he was doing, they assumed it was the key to his sailing prowess.

One day a crew member followed him on his morning routine and watched through the keyhole. He saw the captain go to a locked box, unlock it, take out a scrap of paper, read it, return it to the box, and lock it in. After that ritual he left the cabin with a smile on his face and confidently sailed another day.

When the old captain died, the crew could not wait to get to that locked box and see what was on the paper. After they reverently buried him at sea, they reverently tip-toed down to his cabin, unlocked the door, unlocked the box, opened it, and unfolded the creased, yellowed paper, which read: "The right side is the starboard side."

We need regularly to peek outside our rut and ask the really big one: "What is this thing called life all about? Where is it going? Am I being true to myself? Am I on course, or has my vessel run aground?"

"Now and then we all need to take our mind out and dance on it," Mark Twain wrote, "because it's getting all caked up."

For those of the Judeo-Christian tradition, the right side—whether the Repub-licans, the Democrats, or the Independents are in—is incontrovertible. Micah's sen-tence in scripture sums up what the right side is: "See that justice is done, let mercy be your first concern, and humbly obey your God."[23]

March 27

Last night I had the strangest dream. I dreamt I had one day to live. I awoke from the dream to plan my final day.

Morning breaks with a large glass of fresh-squeezed orange juice, chased with a bowl of muselix and strawberry yogurt, the way they mix them in Switzerland.

For weather, I enjoy a bright blue sky with a few white puffy clouds and a constant temperature of seventy-six degrees. After breakfast my wife and I take a walk in the woods reminiscing about the night we met in 1966 and the night in 1968 she accepted my proposal.

We come back to the house and lie out in lounge chairs, absorbing some rays. I have missed the feel of sun on my skin ever since 1977 when I had the first of many surgeries for sun-caused skin cancers.

Our three sons and their families come over in the afternoon. I ask the boys to come prepared to share one favorite memory of me. Then we throw a football around, the way we used to do when we were young. Our last meal together is a picnic that includes a few of my favorite things—ripe watermelon, honey-roasted peanuts, a pimento cheese sandwich with tomato and pickle on it, and dark chocolate with almonds.

As the sun begins to set we listen to Louie Armstrong sing, "What a Wonderful World," watch *Forrest Gump*, and then for the hundredth time spend several hours reviewing pictures of the children and grandchildren as they evolve from babes to children to adults. After memory-sharing time, I hug each person for a minute or two and whisper to each a final, private, carefully-composed blessing (choking up, characteristically, each time).

Through the mist of tears I thank them for making my life complete. After singing together, with piano and guitar, some golden oldies like "Goodnight, Irene," "House of the Rising Sun," and "Softly and Tenderly Jesus Is Calling," I bid them *bon voyage*, blow them a kiss, and, all done, lay me down to sleep and pleasant dreams.

March 28

"You can tell a lot about people by the way they handle three things: a rainy day, lost luggage, and tangled Christmas tree lights."

Maya Angelou's words came to my mind as I read a publication that arrived in the mail from my alma mater. In the obituary for the best English professor the school had in my years there, I saw—say it isn't so—a grammatical error! What poetic injustice for a professor who spoke and wrote only impeccable English. The mistake came in the sentence about a Performing Arts Center "named in honor of he and his wife." My wife's reaction was: "Your professor must be trying to get out of his grave right now."

Did the writer not know that the object of a preposition is him instead of he? Surely she would not say, "I thought a lot of he." The editor fell asleep at the wheel. Kids today do not know the nominative from the objective case. They would not know how to diagram a sentence if their life depended on it. This is what happens when students are not required to take Latin.

After a half minute of righteous, unforgiving indignation, I remembered what Maya Angelou said. I also remembered a college friend who turned against any teacher who pronounced recognize "rec-ig-nize" or who wore socks a shade lighter than his slacks.

I remembered the time I gave a speech and credited Matthew Arnold for a line that was William Ernest Henley's. A smiling stranger came up afterwards, delighted to set me straight.

The gospel message for people like me is: "Lighten up just a little. Chill out. Don't major in minors. Get indignant over child abuse or prejudice, not a preposition. Get a life."

Or so it seems to I.

March 29

I hear that this summer honey bees and other pollinators are going to be scarce. They were hard to find last summer. I saw only a precious few bumbling and stumbling over each other as I cautiously picked my way through the flower garden, creating our next arrangement of zinnias, yarrow, purple coneflowers, and Shasta daisies.

In the garden I feel great awe as I watch the bees cooperating with Mother Nature. I feel a healthy respect for their stingers. Now I also have this fear that we humans are doing something that threatens their very existence.

My favorite flowers are those that double the pleasure—the ones with sweet aromas that equal their beauty. It is hard to pass Russian sage or lavender without stroking the leaves or flowers. The clean, sweet smell lingers on my hands long after I have gone indoors. I understand that flowers served this utilitarian purpose in the olden days. In sixteenth-century London, raw sewage flowed through the streets. To combat the stench when traveling from one place to another, some Londoners would pin to their lapels a little arrangement of flowers they called a nosegay. The flowers helped to neutralize the noxious smells and make the trip more tolerable. They make the nose gay.

Frances DeSales, sixteenth-century theologian and educator, coined the term "spiritual nosegays," meaning thoughts of faith and hope that help us wind our way around and through the garbage on the streets of life.

Currently I am wearing two spiritual nosegays. They go off in my brain several times every day. One is from Augustine: "Do not despair, one of the thieves was saved. Do not presume, one of the thieves was damned." The other is Bret Hart's: "A bird in the hand is a certainty, but a bird in the bush may sing for you."

To travel more hopefully through life's polluted streets, wear a good nosegay.

March 30

The Golden Gate Bridge in San Francisco is the most popular place in the United States for people to end their lives. Since the bridge was finished in 1937, over twelve hundred have jumped to their deaths.

A study was published in 1978 entitled "Where Are They Now?" The study followed 515 people who had perched themselves on the bridge between 1937 and 1971, prepared to jump, but had been talked down or got grabbed before they jumped. Years or decades later, 94 percent were still alive or had died of natural causes.[24]

Having been saved from themselves in their darkest hour, like George Bailey on the bridge in *It's a Wonderful Life*, they went on to discover a life worth living, a future they could not imagine when they were depressed out of their minds and prepared to jump. That is why therapists say that we should never make a big decision when we are depressed.

I think of so many people I came to know over the years I was a hospital chaplain. Our paths intersected at their most desolate, God-forsaken hour. How many times I heard them say, "I just want to die" or if their child had died, "I just want to die too." Sometimes I run into these people years later. They are alive! They carried on, rebuilt their lives out of the rubble and decided—however crippled and scarred—that life was worth living after all. It was impossible for them to foresee a future back then when they were mired in a deep, dark, cold, muddy hole.

There is an old Chinese proverb: "Always keep a green branch in your heart. Someday a bird will perch on it and sing for you."

March 31

"SPRING IS NATURE'S WAY OF SAYING, 'LET'S PARTY!'"—Robin Williams

This time every year I exult in the fecundity of planet earth. I also find myself wondering how many springs I have left. Then wisdom reminds me that the ultimate matter is not how many more springs I will have but how many more I will enjoy.

There is a huge difference. An ancient story tells me so. Aurora, the Roman goddess of dawn, fell in love with a mortal youth named Tithonus. Aurora was beautiful and blond, with rose-colored skin like the dawn. Zeus, the chief of the gods, offered Aurora any wedding gift she might desire for her beloved. She asked that Tithonus might live forever, that he might never die: "Give him immortality—everlasting life."

But Aurora forgot to ask that her lover might stay forever young. Poor Tithonus got everlasting life. He grew older and older, more and more decrepit. His limbs got feeble, his hair became snow white, his voice grew weak, and he babbled incessantly—but he did not die. The gift of everlasting life became a Frankenstein-like, never-ending curse. Aurora eventually, pitying Tithonus, turned him into a grasshopper to end his suffering.

Geneticist David Sinclair, an expert at Harvard on the subject of aging, has shown that resveratrol, a plant compound found in red wine, can extend the lifespan of yeast, worms, fruit flies, and fat mice by activating proteins called SIRT1. Professor Sinclair said: "Our bodies have an extraordinary ability to repair themselves. We're seeing the beginning of technology that could one day allow us to reach 150."[25]

Some predict that the anti-aging pill will be ready in about five years. Thanks, but I think I will pass.

March Notes

1. Neruda, "Childhood and Poverty," 12–13.
2. Brinkley, *David Brinkley*, 24.
3. Litsky, "John Wooden," no pages.
4. Cartwright, "Seeing," no pages.
5. Darrow, "Reflections," no pages.
6. Gruen, *Water for Elephants*, 12.
7. Frank, "Secretary," no pages.
8. *New Hampshire Historical Society*, "Rules for Teachers —1915," 1.
9. Barrioneuvo, "Stories of Hope," no pages.
10. Cousins, *Anatomy of an Illness*, 43.
11. Brody, "Secrets of Centenarians," no pages.
12. Frankl, "Man's Search,"104.
13. Burns, *The Three Roosevelts*, 325.
14. Flaste, "Superkids," 12.
15. Walls, *Glass Castle*, 38.
16. Meyer, *Love Out Loud*, January 8, 2013. This story may or may not have happened. It has enjoyed wide circulation and is consistent with Schweitzer's life.
17. Schweitzer, *Out of My Life and Thought*, 92.
18. Nemade, "Cognitive Theories of Major Depression," no pages.
19. Troyat, *Tolstoy*, 185.
20. Song of Songs 2:11–12.
21. Buechner, *The Seasons' Difference*, 31–32.
22. Richardson, *Jesse*, 35.
23. Micah 6:8b.
24. Seiden, *"Where Are They Now?"* 203–214.
25. Humphries, "Healthy Life Extended," no pages.

April

April 1

A photography trip to the southwest with three middle-aged men brought home to me how set in our ways we can become with the years.

Upon arrival at our condominium in Pagosa Springs, Colorado, we went shopping for breakfast groceries to last us one week. One of us, it became clear as we strolled the aisles of the grocery, believed that every day should begin with a "full monty" breakfast—sausage, eggs, gravy and biscuits. Another of us, at breakfast and at all other meals, required junk food. At every gas stop he bought and devoured a candy bar. He went to bed at night anticipating breakfast, which meant scarfing down decadently-delicious doughnuts. A third member of our expedition was accustomed to two brands of cereal mixed in a large bowl with whole milk. The fourth required a small bowl of high-fiber, low-fat cereal with skim milk.

The four men had two things in common—a love for photography and a set-in-stone breakfast routine. Eating habits became chains in the grocery store that exposed us as rigid and resistant to compromise. It also made our grocery shopping much more expensive.

Jose Ortega y Gasset defined the hero as one who is supple, who can break out of ruts: "His life is a perpetual resistance to what is habitual and customary. Each movement that he makes has first had to overcome custom . . . Such a life is a constant tearing oneself away from that part which is given over to habit and is a prisoner to matter."[1]

One morning on our great adventure, toward the end of the week, throwing caution to the wind I indulged in the fat-laden, cholesterol-loaded, full-monty breakfast.

It was delicious. It has been more than a decade now. I think I will be okay.

April 2

It was in April about a decade ago that I asked the building and grounds man at church why he had not cut down a particular tree. With dogwood, redbud, and other flowering trees bursting forth, this one small tree showed no sign of life. All its brown leaves from the previous fall held fast. The groundskeeper agreed with me, cut it down, and hauled it off.

I learned two things too late about that tree. It had been planted three years earlier by a church member as a memorial to his beloved brother. And it was not dead. It was a pin oak, and pin oaks are one of two trees in this part of the world that do not drop their dead leaves before spring.

I could not have been a more contrite sinner. I made an apologetic phone call, made an apologetic home visit, wrote an apologetic letter, and offered apologetically to pay for a replacement tree.

Three things I have learned from that humiliating experience.

One, I have developed a deep appreciation for those little beech trees with off-white leaves that hang on all winter. In a forest, unlike the evergreens and the barren deciduous trees, beech trees keep their translucent, pale leaves until April. Holding pale-white leaves in a forest of barren trees in the depths of winter, they are a dream come true for photographers and nature lovers.

Two, I have a new fondness for pin oaks. A large pin oak grows one hundred feet from our front door. New growth just this week has pushed last year's dead leaves off the twigs, and wind has splattered brown all over a greening neighborhood. There are several theories, but no one knows for sure why the pin oak waits until April to drop its dead leaves. It is a mystery, and I love mysteries.

Three, I have learned that when we mess up royally, sometimes the best we can do is genuinely repent and chalk it up as one of life's many precious learning experiences.

April 3

Gail Godwin, in a book simply titled *Heart,* relates a true story about a couple who, for one of their many involvements, maintained a greenhouse so they could grow flowers that bloomed all winter.

One cold winter night, driving to their chamber orchestra rehearsal and having a little time to kill on the way, they decided to take the long route down by the river. They came upon an old woman walking on the road that followed the river. They barely knew her, but it was bitter cold so they stopped and asked if they could give her a lift. She hesitated initially, but then accepted. When they dropped her off at her house, they spontaneously gave her the jar of nasturtiums they had planned to give to "someone or other" at the orchestra rehearsal.

Weeks went by and then one day they received a note from the woman saying that she had been so depressed all winter that she was on the way to drown herself in the river the night they stopped and offered her a ride and gave her some flowers. She said she took the gift of bright flowers in the dead of winter as a sign that she was supposed to live.

Saved—not by a bouquet of nasturtiums but by two hearts that were human, hospitable, compassionate, welcoming, and warm. This story holds no high drama. It does not have what it takes to make the evening news or the morning paper. To the media it is not like rescuing someone from a burning building or a shark or a pit bull attack.

There is undeniable safety in staying in our comfort zone, cool and detached; there is undeniable danger in opening ourselves to another and risking rejection or making a fool of ourselves. Rod McKuen, who ran away from home at age eleven after his alcoholic stepfather broke his arms and ribs, offers this wisdom gleaned from personal experience: "Be sentimental. Don't stay cool, stay warm."

McKuen's sage advice echoes Dag Hammerskjold's journaled ambition: "If only I may grow—firmer, simpler, quieter, warmer."

April 4

I know several people who have come down with a bad case of shingles. For many, shingles runs its course in a few weeks or months. Some victims, however, have what unfortunately appears after several years to be a life sentence. Shingles will not kill them. They will eventually die of something else. But they will itch and burn almost every day.

Shingles strikes me as being a lot like the grief process. Some people, after a significant loss, grieve for a few weeks and then start putting life back together. Others get stuck in grief, as with shingles, chronically.

A sudden and unexpected human tragedy, like the school shootings in Columbine, Colorado, or Newtown, Connecticut, quickly brings calls from ministers and other community leaders for healing and closure. But premature closing of an open wound can set up enormous trouble later. Medical personnel clean the gravel or glass or grass out of a wound and thoroughly irrigate the wound before they stitch it shut. If they sew it up prematurely it will look good on the outside but bad things will be going on inside. It will fester and set up big trouble later.

How long should a grief wound stay open? The correct answer is: as long as it takes.

But what about people who appear to be stuck? We can do two things that may help. We can occasionally mention their loved one by name: "I've been thinking about Jesse a lot lately and about you. Can we talk? I've got the time. How are you doing?" The ultimate insult for the bereaved is that their loved one has been forgotten by everyone else.

Then we should cut them some slack, knowing that healing requires tincture of time.

April 5

"What you do," Emerson said, "speaks so loud that I cannot hear what you say."

Some estimate that "body English"—non-verbal gestures, facial expressions, posture, and tone of voice—accounts for 70-90 percent of human communication.

Presidential campaigns bear witness. Those of us who watched the first presidential debate of the television era, Nixon versus Kennedy in 1960, thought Kennedy won, while those who listened on radio believed Nixon won. Kennedy had a nice suntan; Nixon looked pale and his "five o'clock shadow" showed. Kennedy appeared relaxed, while Nixon looked sweaty and uneasy.

Edmund Muskie was the frontrunner for the Democratic nomination for president in 1972. But in New Hampshire he voiced his anger at a newspaper publisher for printing attacks on Mrs. Muskie and he appeared to have tears running down his cheek as he spoke. The public interpreted his anger and tears as instability, vulnerability, and weakness. Looking un-presidential, he lost the nomination.

In 1980, at the end of the only Reagan-Carter debate, Reagan took the initiative to walk across the stage to shake hands with Carter. To the public, that gesture seemed warm, magnanimous, and hospitable, contrasted with Carter's rigidity.

Who can forget Al Gore sighing into the microphone throughout his debate with George Bush in 2000? Some observers believe the condescending sigh more than any one thing handed the debate—and ultimately the presidency—to Bush.

Do Americans value style more than substance in their president? Appearance is terribly important in human relationships just as is the presentation of food in a restaurant. When I am seated before I get up to give a speech, my wife tells me that I have a tight, cold, serious-to-grim expression on my face. I need to work on that.

April 6

Eunice and Bessie were sisters. When their father died they came into a considerable sum of money. Bessie, who was younger, let Eunice know that she wanted to do some traveling, but Eunice balked: "Dad was a saver. He would roll over in his grave if he knew we squandered his hard-earned money."

The sisters purchased a small department store and over the next few years made the store very profitable. One day Bessie suggested: "Let's close the store for a month next January and visit a resort. It might be fun using some of those cosmetics and clothes we sell. We might even meet some gentlemen." Eunice nixed the idea, explaining that they would lose loyal customers who would take their business elsewhere.

After many years, the sisters had made enough money to put themselves on easy street. "Come on," said Bessie, "let's sell the store. Let's visit Mexico and Bermuda." Eunice explained: "We can't sell now. In this economy, no one would pay us what the store is worth."

One day Bessie had a stroke and died. Eunice never entered the store again. She gave Bessie the most expensive funeral the town had ever seen, sold the store, and went into seclusion.

Several months later she asked and was granted permission to dig Bessie's casket up and fly her to Mexico. After personally supervising the reburial, she rented a little cottage not far from the grave. Three weeks later Eunice obtained another disinterment permit and had Bessie's body dug up and flown to Bermuda. She bought a little bungalow on the beach. She hired engravers to etch on Bessie's tombstone two rosebuds that bracketed six words: "Gather Ye Rosebuds While Ye May."

Eunice and Bessie finally made it to the places they had longed to see.[2]

April 7

To understand hope, we do not go sit at the feet of people who have never known defeat. Nor do we look to those who skim over life's surface and live superficial lives. The most poignant snapshots of hope emerge from the depths of human experience, from those who have managed to keep their hope alive in the bleakest and most desperate conditions.

Mary Tyler Moore said it well: "You can't be brave if you've only had wonderful things happen to you."

Think of Senator John McCain of Arizona, who was shot down over Hanoi in the Vietnam War and survived five years of torture and solitary confinement. Of his and other American prisoners' struggle to survive in the Hanoi Hilton, McCain wrote in his autobiography, *Faith of My Fathers*: "We possessed a divine spark that our enemies could not extinguish—hope."

Think of Max Cleland, who returned from Vietnam in 1968 a triple amputee, having lost both legs and his right arm to a grenade. "Bitterness raged in me," he wrote in his autobiography *Strong at the Broken Places*.

> As I lay there alone, the futility of my life bore in on me. What was I living for? To get myself together every morning to go through the pain, anguish, and humiliation of therapy just to do it again the following day? I sank into dark depression. In a deep wrenching of the soul, I lay in bed, convulsed with agonizing, gut-wracking sobs. I was bitter over the past. I was afraid of the future. And the torturous present seemed unbearable.

Cleland eventually rose from his slough of despond to become the head of the Veterans Administration. Georgia elected him to the United States Senate. He summed up his personal struggle in these words: "I knew I either had to get bitter or get better."

Mary Tyler Moore and John McCain would surely agree.

April 8

Eugene Peterson, pastor, scholar and poet, watched three baby swallows that were perched side-by-side on a branch above a lake in Montana. One of the parents came alongside the chicks on the branch and started shoving them to the end of the branch until the one on the end fell off. Somewhere between the branch and the water, four feet below, the chick's wings started working and it became airborne. The same thing happened with the second one. It got shoved off the end and suddenly found its wings and flew away. The third chick was different. Not to be forced off, yet at the end of the branch, this little one loosened its grip just enough that it swung downward until it was hanging upside down. But it refused to let go.

The parent was unsympathetic. It pecked at the desperately clinging talons of the little chick until finally it was more painful for the poor chick to hang on than risk flying. The parent knew what the chick did not; namely, that the chick could fly and that there was no good reason not to do what it was designed to do. Peterson concluded: "Birds have feet and can walk. Birds have talons with which they can grasp a branch and cling tightly. Birds can walk and they can cling. But flying is what they were meant to do, and it is not until they are flying that they are at their best."[3]

In us humans, two voices compete. One advises: "Stay put. Play it safe. If you leave your toxic relationship or dead-end job, the ocean will swallow you whole."

Higher angels whisper: "You are never going to be content to cling when you are made to soar."

April 9

It will not be much longer until we will see the first monarch butterflies of this year. Having wintered in central Mexico, they wind their way northward toward Canada, a three thousand mile trip as the butterfly flies. Some of them fly hundreds of miles non-stop over the Gulf of Mexico.

None of them will make it to Canada. They will lay eggs when they get to the southern United States. Then they will die. It will be up to their children and grand-children to complete the next legs of the journey. Then late this summer the Monarchs in Canada will begin their trip south toward the trees in Mexico from which their grandparents and great grandparents launched their odyssey months earlier. Some of their grandchildren will return to the very same tree where great-great-great grand-mother began the round trip.

Is there a more gorgeous creature in all of nature? Sometimes scores of Monarchs take a short break on their odyssey to enjoy the nectar of my butterfly bushes and pose for my camera. I have noticed that birds leave them alone. Some chemical that the butterflies ingest as they feast on milkweed renders them nasty to birds' sense of smell and taste.

How do the Monarchs navigate? Scientists think a combination of 250 million pairs of DNA in their genome, plus a biochemical protein process, plus reading the position of the sun accurately, plus an inbuilt magnetic compass navigates the less-than-one-ounce creatures on their way.[4]

How ironic that we humans marvel at the satellites and Global Positioning Systems we have created, congratulate ourselves on how big our brains are, and put down others by saying they must have a brain the size of an insect.

April 10

One of Afghanistan's gifts to the world was the thirteenth-century mystic and poet Rumi.

My favorite wisdom from Rumi: "Be a lamp, or a lifeboat, or a ladder. Help someone's soul heal. Walk out of your house like a shepherd." The lamp, lifeboat, ladder, healer, and shepherd metaphors mean nothing to the wolves of Wall Street or the rats racing down Main Street who, like Willy Loman in Arthur Miller's *Death of a Salesman*, are preoccupied with "coming out number one."

Rumi's metaphors speak to those who agree with the Dalai Lama's alternative philosophy that "our prime purpose in this life is to help others, and if you can't help them, at least don't hurt them."

This world needs more people to serve as *lamps* for those who are bewildered, confused, or lost; who desperately wait for someone to shine a little light to help them find their path.

This world needs more people to serve as *lifeboats* for those who are sinking, desperately waiting and hoping for someone to throw out a lifeline.

This world needs more people to serve as *ladders* for those who one day find themselves down deep in a ditch, desperately unable to get out on their own.

This world needs more *shepherds* who will take up a staff and start acting as if they care about the scattered, scared sheep around them.

Ludwig Wittgenstein the philosopher wrote: "I don't know why we are here, but I'm pretty sure it is not in order to enjoy ourselves." This world needs more of us who, in addition to enjoying ourselves, reach out to souls that have been bruised and beaten down by life and are starving for a little of the balm of human kindness.

April 11

You may have noticed that friend is now a verb. On Facebook, you "friend" people—you select those you want for a pen pal or correspondent. If at any time that is not working, you can change your mind and de-friend or un-friend those you earlier friended, and the swapping of verbiage with that person ends.

Many years ago I was un-friended by someone I considered a good old friend. A one-page, single-spaced letter arrived in the mail, charging that our friendship had been one-sided ever since we met in college. He cited, among other things, all the times he had driven out of his way to see me and my family while I had never once been to Miami to visit him. He ended by saying he never wanted to see or hear from me again.

I moved from shock, through anger and defensiveness, to hurt. Ignoring his wish never to hear from me again, I hand-wrote him a letter of apology. My one confrontational sentence was that I wish he had not squirreled away his grievances over the years and then unleashed them in a torrent.

His "You're fired!" letter with my name on it arrived over thirty years ago. It still hurts when I think there is a person out there somewhere who remembers me as a miserable excuse for a human being, much less a friend.

Last time I checked, Facebook limits subscribers to several thousand friends. Most all those thousands have to be acquaintances or contacts or names more than friends. True friends are those who come to you when you are going through a divorce or lose your job or get diagnosed with a terminal illness. Real friendship implies a depth of honesty, intimacy, vulnerability, and empathy. Friendship needs face-to-face time spent reading each other's body language and hearing nuances of inflection and tone in each other's voice.

Friendship might even mean hopping a plane to Miami.

April 12

"The time will come when men such as I will look upon the murder of animals as they now look upon the murder of men"—Leonardo da Vinci

"I do feel that spiritual progress does demand at some stage that we should cease to kill our fellow creatures for the satisfaction of our bodily wants"—Mohandas Gandhi

"Non-violence leads to the highest ethics, which is the goal of all evolution. Until we stop harming all other living beings, we are still savages"—Thomas Edison

The first Earth Day, over four decades ago, was the brainchild of Senator Gaylord Nelson of Wisconsin. He assumed it would be a one-time "nationwide demonstration of concern for the environment so large that it would shake the political establishment out of its lethargy." The environmentalist who most motivated Gaylord Nelson was the mother of modern environmentalism, biologist Rachel Carson. Her book *Silent Spring* argued that blanket spraying of the pesticide DDT was polluting the water supply and destroying wildlife. The person who struck the match that raised Rachel Carson's consciousness, fathering the modern environmental movement, was Albert Schweitzer and his "reverence for life" philosophy. Schweitzer taught and practiced respect for all living creatures, not just humans. Rachel Carson dedicated *Silent Spring* to him.[5]

I have not spiritually evolved like Edison, Gandhi, Schweitzer, and da Vinci to the point of not eating cows and pigs and birds. I do believe that in a less barbaric, kinder, and gentler world, that would be the rule. Factory farming of animals in that advanced civilization would be considered as abhorrent as dog-fighting and cock-fighting are among civilized people today. My job until "the peaceable kingdom" comes is to put into practice better the reverence for life philosophy I now hold dear in my heart.

April 13

My favorite pediatrician wrote in an e-mail: "A friend of mine is an aspiring writer. He has a PhD in English. But his childhood was so happy, so perfect, that I don't see how he can become a success as a writer. Do you know many or even one successful writer who had a happy childhood?"

Alexander Pope, twisted by childhood tuberculosis, was a hunchback four and one-half feet tall. He is the third most-quoted English writer. When John Keats, beloved English Romantic poet, was eight, his father was killed in an accident. Keats's mother died of tuberculosis when he was fourteen. Alfred Tennyson's father was disinherited in favor of a younger brother. Alfred's father became an alcoholic and died an early death. Tennyson is the second most-quoted English writer.

Would we have *And Still I Rise* and *I Know Why the Caged Bird Sings* but for the poverty and abuse Maya Angelou knew in childhood?

Nathaniel Hawthorne, author of *The Scarlet Letter*, whose father died of yellow fever when Nathaniel was four years old, saw the same truth my pediatrician friend saw and wrote: "The world owes all its onward impulses to people ill at ease."

The pediatrician had a mother who was mentally ill and bought booze whenever she could save up a little money. He wrote: "I had no guidance, and had to learn everything by myself—trial and error, usually error." He is one of the most respected, kindest pediatricians in this part of the country—and a published writer.

April 14

Several years ago a Southwest Airlines plane had to make an emergency landing when, at thirty-four thousand feet, a five-foot-long piece of metal suddenly exploded from the roof of the cabin. Investigators say that after tens of thousands of takeoffs and landings, the plane's aluminum skin—thin as a nickel—cracked under all the stress.

I think the Southwest fleet has the smartest exteriors of all the airlines—shiny, glossy red, blue, and orange. The plane that cracked from fatigue had skin that looked good as new. Just goes to show that you can't judge a plane by its cover.

On the same page as that story was the story of Cindy Jackson. Cindy then held the world record for cosmetic surgeries. Others may be in first place now. She had had fifty-two procedures, financing those efforts to improve her appearance with $100,000 of inheritance from her father. She explained that, going back to early childhood, she suffered from poor self-esteem.

"Money," Norwegian playwright Henry Ibsen mused, "can buy the husk of things but not the kernel."

I originally intended to say something at this point about caring for our kernel (our soul) as much as we care for our husk (our appearance). All that changed this afternoon. When I paid for two crimson azalea bushes at the local nursery, a twenty-year-old (give or take a couple of years) asked for the last four digits on my credit card. I told him 1909 and then made the mistake of quipping: "It was a very good year—the year I was born." I smiled. I was not prepared for his response. He looked up, politely smiled, and exclaimed: "Really! I had a great aunt who made it to 102. Congratulations!"

I got in my car, glanced at myself in the rear view mirror, and drove home vowing to pay more attention to my husk.

April 15

"WE SHOULD TRY TO BE THE PARENTS OF OUR FUTURE RATHER THAN
THE OFFSPRING OF OUR PAST"— Miguel de Unamuno

I think of two times in my life when that think-outside-the-box, imagine-a-different-future philosophy worked wonders.

For much of my adult life, Belfast, Northern Ireland, seemed to be the most hopeless place on earth. Catholic and Protestant communities were armed camps. Sniper fire, riots, and terrorist attacks over thirty years took more than three thousand lives. But after twenty-two often-deadlocked months of negotiations, a major breakthrough, largely engineered by U. S. Senator George Mitchell and British Prime Minister Tony Blair, occurred. An accord was reached May 23, 1998. Since then, Belfast citizens have acted like parents of their future instead of offspring of their past.

Then there is the animosity of Egypt and Israel that goes back to the exodus of the Hebrew slaves from the land of the Pharaohs three thousand years ago. I remember the Six-Day War of 1967 and the Yom Kippur War of 1973. Not many people then guessed that Israel and Egypt might ever be able to live together in peace, much less for decades. But in 1978 President Jimmy Carter, following two weeks of intense negotiations at Camp David, motivated Egyptian President Anwar Sadat and Israeli Prime Minister Menachem Begin to sign a peace treaty. The peace has been uneasy at times, but for over forty years now the two ancient enemies have behaved like parents of their future instead of offspring of their past.

Desmond Morris in *The Naked Ape* wrote convincingly of the aggressive, warmongering aspect of the human animal. But another part of our nature accomplishes extraordinary feats of restraint, dialogue, humility, forgiveness, and peace. Bravo for leaders who transcend a biological penchant for war long enough to give peace a chance.

April 16

Two stories, one fiction and one true, buttress my belief that there may be hope for us all, after all.

In *The Music Man* Robert Preston plays Professor Harold Hill, a con artist. He moves from one little town to another selling band instruments and uniforms. Harold himself cannot play one note. As soon as he collects the parents' money, he skips town.

In one little town in Iowa he meets his match. Marian the librarian discovers soon after Hill arrives that he is a fraud. But as he brings hope to Marian's little brother, discovering gifts in a shy little boy with a lisp, Marian sees something redeemable in the music man. While the rest of the town is getting wise to him and preparing to tar and feather him, Marian jumps to his defense. Fully expecting him to skip town, Marian cannot help falling in love with him. She values his gift for bringing out the best in others. She eventually convinces him of his own goodness. Her tender heart turns around not only his life but hers as well.

Then there is H. L. Menchen, who was one of America's most influential social critics in the early twentieth century. A confirmed bachelor, his writings ridiculed the whole idea of love. "Marriage is a wonderful institution," he wrote, "but who wants to live in an institution?" In the 1930s, when Menchen was in his fifties, he fell in love and married a twenty-four-year-old college instructor. Newspaper headlines read: "Mighty Menchen Falls," "Menchen, Arch Cynic, Capitulates to Cupid," and "Et Tu, H.L.?" His popularity with the public plummeted. Menchen gave this explanation to his earlier admirers: "I formerly was not as wise as I am now."[6]

Each of us is a work in progress. Until we breathe our last we are unfinished symphonies. Like Harold Hill and Mighty Menchen, we have opportunity to become warmer and wiser until our work on Earth is done.

April 17

A Native American described his inner struggles: "Inside of me there are two dogs. One dog is mean and evil. The other dog is good. The mean dog fights the good dog all the time." A young brave asked, "Which dog wins?" The old man paused a moment and then said, "The one I feed the most."

I saw this truth illustrated in a hospital. I came upon two ladies, each pulling a red wagon overflowing with toothpaste, phone cards, candy, comic books, and many other things. They were giving it away. The ladies informed me that they had over one hundred items that people in the hospital might need. Room to room they went with the question: "Anything we have here that you could use?"

They came once a month with over $100 of items bought and given by their little church in a community eighty miles away. One of the ladies once worked in a pediatric oncology unit and had developed enormous sympathy for families who have to make an unplanned visit to the hospital and find themselves a long way from home missing all the comforts of home. "It's a thrill seeing their eyes light up," she explained. "We often see a smile. Our visit may be the only time they'll smile that whole day."

A little act of kindness stirs embers of hope in troubled hearts. The act is twice blessed, according to Shakespeare: "It blesseth him that gives and him that takes."[7]

That is the same truth to which the Dalai Lama pointed when he said: "To make others happy, practice compassion; to make yourself happy, practice compassion."

Or, feed the good dog more.

April 18

To celebrate their one-thousandth issue, *Reader's Digest* in October, 2009, added a ninety-page supplement entitled, "It's All About You," explaining that "the power of the individual grows every day." They identified fourteen trends that they predicted would change lives over the next decade. The first three trends were "Re-Engineering Your Body," "Do-It-Yourself Doctoring," and "Me Me Media." Coming in last, barely making the list at number fourteen was "The Power of We."[8]

The same day that this *Reader's Digest* arrived, I saw a television commercial for a brand of jeans. In the commercial half a dozen campers were being chased by a bear. The voiceover said something like this: "You don't have to outrun everyone; just one," meaning that the bear will be content with mauling only one so just make sure you are not the slowest one.

Is life really "all about you"—your wellness, your job, your rights, your opinions, your security, your net worth, your feelings, your individuality?

The images from a natural disaster like Hurricane Katrina that will linger longest in my mind are not those of individuals stealing things and fending for self. The images I will remember are of people moving heaven and earth to rescue one person: a Coast Guard officer chopping a hole in a roof to rescue a child, someone carrying an elderly lady to a boat, someone hoisting the weakest or slowest or youngest or oldest or sickest into a helicopter.

Maybe, truth be told, we are not so much like amoebas, single-celled and independent, as we are like coral, interrelated and interdependent. Maybe one of the enduring lessons from natural as well as man-made disasters is that our caring for each other is superior to the everyone-for-self, it's-all-about-you principle which is the old law of the jungle recycled. Maybe the last trend identified by *Reader's Digest*, "The Power of We," is the last, best hope for an "It's all about me" culture.

April 19

Roger Ebert and Annette Funicello died four days apart, he on April 4 and she on April 8. Their deaths affected me personally, mainly because both of them were my age.

Ebert, the first film critic to win a Pulitzer Prize, fought with cancer of the thyroid and salivary glands for his last decade. Surgeries on his face and neck radically altered his appearance and cost him the ability to speak, eat, or drink. I think, "Why not me? That could have been me."

Funicello was discovered at age twelve by Walt Disney. Becoming the most popular Mouseketeer, she went on to a successful singing and movie career. In 1987 the girl-next-door was diagnosed with multiple sclerosis. She suffered from this degenerative and debilitating neurological disorder for her last quarter century, unable even to walk or talk her last few years. I think, "That could have been my life for the past quarter century."

Almost thirty years ago one of our best friends was diagnosed with a terminal brain tumor. A thoroughgoing wife and mother of two young daughters, Janet chose to be a stay-at-home mom. She meticulously kept house and prepared her family three nutritious meals every day. She died young. My wife and I occasionally comment on all Janet missed, usually adding, "That could have been your fate or mine."

I began school with a boy named Jerry who sat through twelve grades with us. He had suffered brain damage at birth. Through no fault of his own, he talked funny, walked funny, and could not do his schoolwork. His grandmother reared him. I don't know whatever became of Jerry. That could have been me or my child.

When the sky falls on us, it is normal to ask, "Why me?" Those of us who are spared probably should pause to wonder, "Why not me?"

April 20

Phil Jackson did what no other professional basketball coach has done and what may never be replicated. He won ten NBA championships. The first six were with the Chicago Bulls and the last four with the Los Angeles Lakers. His autobiographical book *Sacred Hoops* gives big clues as to how he did it. Jackson takes a holistic approach to coaching, blending the selflessness and compassion he learned from his Pentecostal parents with the sacred principles of Native Americans and Zen Buddhism. Players and sports writers refer to Jackson reverentially as the "Zen Master" of sports.

Sacred Hoops unpacks three aspects of his coaching magic. One is akin to what televangelist Robert H. Schuller popularized as "possibility thinking." Jackson calls it "mindfulness." He teaches his players to cultivate "beginner's mind." Whatever it is called, it references this truth: "In the beginner's mind there are many possibilities; in the expert's mind there are few."[9] Always assume, he might say, that there are good possibilities out there that we at the present moment are unable to see.

A second insight comes from the Native American saying: "One finger cannot lift a pebble."[10] Jackson teaches "communal" basketball which means substituting "we" for "me" and learning how to flow together the way the five fingers of the hand work together. There are implications of this principle not just for basketball but for families, churches, and businesses.

A third has to do with living fully in the moment. He quotes a story from a Laotian Zen master: "You see this glass?" the master asked. "For me it is already broken. I enjoy it. I drink out of it. When my elbow accidentally brushes it off the table and it falls to the floor and shatters, I say, 'Of course.' When I understand that this glass is already broken, every moment I spend with it is precious."[11]

This is the Buddhist teaching of impermanence, similar to the Latin *carpe diem*, "pluck the day." Tomorrow, for better or for worse, will not be the same as today. Phil Jackson might add: "Just think about it."

April 21

Goats desperately need a good public relations campaign. When the kicker misses the game-winning field goal in the last seconds of the Super Bowl, he is forever more termed the game's goat. Jesus referred to the heaven-bound people on judgment day "sheep" and the hell-bound people "goats." A scruffy or grumpy old man is an "old goat." When people irritate you they "get your goat." Why are we so hard on the goats?

I had the opportunity to visit the Naval Academy in Annapolis. At the entrance stands a sculpture of a bigger-than-life goat. The goat is springing at a forty-five-degree angle, head down, its fierce horns clearly on the way to a collision with some thing or some body.

For the Naval Academy's mascot, why not a dolphin or a barracuda or a great white shark? Why a goat? I can think of two possible reasons. One is those horns. I am told that most male goats get dehorned as kids because "they know what to do with them"—sometimes the goatherd gets the butt. Perhaps the Navy is thinking of their submarine's torpedo butting a boat, or a Navy linebacker butting an Army fullback.

There is at least one more possibility. In the eighteenth century, the Navy sometimes carried goats on their vessels crossing the ocean. Goats ate the garbage and the spoiled food. The goats also provided milk and butter for the crew.[12] And if things got desperate enough, the goat could be the dinner entree. But of course in that time of wooden ships there was always the danger that the goats would get hungry enough to chomp a hole in the side of the ship.

Some of us can identify with the lowly goat. Jesus promised that, when his regime comes, "Everyone who is now first will be last, and everyone who is last will be first."[13]

April 22

If the deceased have passed to another dimension where they are able to observe their own funerals, surely Mr. Lynn enjoyed his. He had run a little business for half a century. When he opened there were seven other drug stores in that part of town. But the area depreciated and all the stores but his failed or moved away. Mr. Lynn stayed. "People can pay their telephone bills here, buy stamps and money orders, and drop off their mail for the postman to pick up," Mr. Lynn told a newspaper reporter. "We are here to offer neighborhood service and don't claim to be anything else."

At Mr. Lynn's funeral, a grandson stood to tell how he had always thought of the drug store as a lighthouse and his grandfather as the lighthouse keeper. Another grandson played a jazzy, original version of "Amazing Grace" on the piano. A grand-daughter stood to say that her grandfather was so highly regarded by so many that she failed to realize that he was not a famous person until she was eight years old. An old friend sang "Thanks for the Memories," using original lyrics composed by Mr. Lynn's youngest son.

A neighborhood resident stood to testify about all the tabs Mr. Lynn forgave and all the medicines he gave away to poor people he knew would never be able to pay. The minister described Mr. Lynn as the consummate people-person who asked caring, open-ended questions, listened attentively, remembered what you told him, and always opened with a follow-up question the next time he saw you.

After the funeral my wife and I drove by his store. All you could see was a hand-written sign on the door explaining that the store was closed for a funeral. Nineteen wreaths the neighborhood poor had purchased to honor him were attached or leaning against the storefront to decorate his—and their—store.

April 23

She is the unofficial spiritual leader in her school. She rarely is seen because she works behind the scenes. She is the janitor who comes in late at night to clean the offices. Her *modus operandi* is to leave personal notes, handwritten on poster paper, on the chairs of professors and administrators. Each one is titled "Thought for the Day" followed by a happy face and her name. Each one is different, written with a different color of pen and on a different color of paper. Each one is personal, tailored to what she intuits to be the needs of that individual that day.

These unsolicited gifts sometimes contain a misspelling or imperfect syntax, punctuation, or grammar, but the message is unmistakable:

"Relationship is hard work—work hard"

"Abilities aren't given just to make a living"

"Satan say I won't finish this. God say Oh yes you will!!! Which one are you listening to"

"Helping yourself is great but helping others is grand"

"What a privilege to be able to walk and talk. Everyone don't have that privilege"

"Don't let go"

"You are custom design a one of a kind"

"Take a licking get back up kicking"

Highly educated in the school of hard knocks, she has found a Joanie Appleseed kind of calling, broadcasting seeds of faith, hope, and love wherever she roams. Joanie Appleseed was recently presented the school's first ever Rooster Award for unbridled contributions to school morale. Even though she may not have an office or a desk on which to put the rooster, her school wants her to know she is something to crow about.

April 24

Which name should be used in an obituary? Should it read James Earl Carter or James Earl "Jimmy" Carter? Should it be Paul William Bryant or Paul William "Bear" Bryant? More and more nicknames, I notice, are making the title. Some are shortenings of a long name like "Beth" for Elizabeth or "Dot" for Dorothy or "L. A." for Lawrence Allen. Some are descriptive like "Tiny" or "Red" or "Curly." I assume all, or most all, are affectionate terms of endearment appreciated by the nominee. You would not expect "Four Eyes" or "Thunder Thighs" or "Know It All" to make the obituaries.

Over a matter of several weeks I have seen these nicknames inserted in quotation marks between the names their parents gave them: "Hoss," "Cookie," "Sweet Pea," "Buddy," "Sonny," "Bo," "Ice Man," "Stretch," "Kitty," Cheese Cake," "Tootie," "Squeaky," "Fuzzy," "Junior," "Tex," "Lucky," "Spanky," "Smiley," "Chicken," and "Boo."

I went through twelve years of school with a good friend named Donald. But none of his friends ever called him Donald. He was and still is "Duck" to us. Duck went on to become a successful dentist. Since he was called "Duck" for life, should "Duck" make the title over his obituary?

Our sons called their maternal grandfather "Gay Gay." Our firstborn, in his fledgling attempts to say "granddad" made sounds like "gay gay." We laughed. It took. Our sons, now in their thirties and forties along with their wives and their own children will forever know him only as "Gay Gay." No, we did not include "Gay Gay" in his obituary.

I did not have a nickname growing up. Now I guess I do. Our first grandson, trying to say something like "Papa" came out one day with "Popple." I liked that and encouraged it. Our five other grandchildren are following suit.

Your next of kin gets to decide what name will introduce your obituary. Sometimes nicknames follow us through life and beyond. I think they should survive us. I hope mine does.

April 25

Town hall meetings and television panel discussions in many cases generate more heat than light.

History offers some good models for positive, civil public discourse. Ancient Athens, generally regarded as the world's first great democracy, pioneered public debating of issues. Every male citizen was expected to spend a part of his day in the agora down the hill from the Parthenon listening to ideas being promulgated by anyone who believed he had something worth saying. The democratic assumption was that everyone probably has some idea that could contribute to the good of Athens.

Every Sunday at Marble Arch in Hyde Park, beginning in the mid-nineteenth century, Londoners and tourists have gathered at what is called Speakers Corner. Anyone who stands on a soapbox stands to draw a crowd. If you do not like what the speaker is saying, there is no need to stand there and take it. You do not need to boo or hiss or try to shout the person down. Either you dialogue with the speaker, or you move on and listen to someone else.

For thirteen years, my wife and I and four other couples have been members of a book club. There have been many strong exchanges in our discussions but we have never cut each other off or raised our voices. The person in the group who is my polar opposite politically has probably taught me the most. I respect his views as well-reasoned, consistent and highly moral, even though I often disagree with his conclusions. I am always eager to hear and process his points of view. He returns the courtesy.

The Romans were fond of the Latin word *civis* from which our words civility and civilization derive. They believed that there was no place in a civilized society for rude, crude, "in your face" conversation. Good citizens keep a civil tongue and exercise civic pride. They would consider a Jerry Springer-like brouhaha not only uncouth, cruel, and crude, but uncivilized.

April 26

Queen for a Day had an almost twenty-year run, beginning on radio in 1945 and then switching to television in 1956.

The show featured two or three women who told a sad story about hard times they were facing, maybe involving a handicapped child or disabled husband or not having enough money to afford a washing machine or a wheelchair or to pay the utility bill. Then the studio audience determined by their applause which tale of woe would win the title *Queen for a Day*. The winner got draped in a regal robe, crowned with a tiara, presented with a dozen red roses, and set on a throne. There she watched curtains open, revealing the gift she had named as her heart's desire plus additional prizes like a vacation or a new vacuum cleaner.

The host of the show signed off each show with the words: "This is Jack Bailey, wishing we could make every woman a queen for every single day!"

As demeaning to women as that contest may seem today, it touched a tender nerve for the millions of us who tuned in. It tapped into the recognition or support we all crave as represented in Andy Warhol's comment: "In the future, everyone will be famous for fifteen minutes."

Today is my mother's birthday. My brother and I gave our mother a ninetieth birthday banquet. On a cloudless, warm, April day, her sixteen best friends, her two sons, her four grandsons, and their families gathered in a restored Victorian mansion. After a dinner fit for a queen, words of tribute flowed, us to her and her to us. Tears of love flowed down cheeks. My brother and I gave our mother, according to her, the best day of her life.

Gentle reader, is it not far better to speak the words and show the love now than over lifeless remains?

April 27

In 2012, the United States government issued 138 patents with the word "toothbrush" in the title. Interesting, because one century ago very few Americans brushed their teeth.

Two things changed all that. American soldiers, fighting wars in Europe and Asia, brought "toothbrushing," a military-mandated habit, home and advertising executive Claude Hopkins made a fortune marketing something to Americans called Pepsodent. One of the earliest radio commercials I can remember had us children chanting: "You'll wonder where the yellow went when you brush your teeth with Pepsodent."

Charles Duhigg, in his book *The Power of Habit,* explains how Claude Hopkins made a fortune selling Pepsodent. A marketing genius, Hopkins understood that three things are necessary to establish a habit: a cue, a behavior, and a reward.

In toothbrushing, the cue is the yellow, grainy buildup of plaque. You can see it in the mirror. You can feel it by passing your tongue or finger over it. Only one thing stands between you and the reward of gleaming, pearly-white teeth, clean, tingly feelings in your mouth, and a winning smile—the habitual behavior of brushing with Pepsodent. Or that is what Hopkins persuaded Americans to believe.[14]

A good friend of mine successfully utilized this cue-behavior-reward principle to improve his life and health. Chagrined when he looked in the mirror and saw his paunch, he devised a plan. The *reward* he sought was to become twenty pounds lighter. The *cue* was sitting down with his wife for the evening meal. The *behavior* to make the desirable a reality was substituting for the big dessert at the end of the meal one bite—one delectable, postage-stamp-size rectangle of a Hershey candy bar.

Now every evening they anticipate and then partake of their one small bite of chocolate. Savoring it, they look in each other's eyes and smile, celebrating their reward of svelte, smaller shapes.

April 28

Several years ago John Bale, left-handed pitcher for the Kansas City Royals, broke his pitching hand. He had to miss two months of the baseball season. He did not break his hand pitching, or batting, or colliding with another player. In a moment of frustration, he punched a door.

Working in a hospital, I more than once saw a patient's family member with his hand in a cast. Each time I learned that he (it was always a male) in a moment of anger had punched a wall or the door of the room or a car.

A man was visiting a cactus garden just outside Phoenix, Arizona. At one point he threw himself into the cacti, rolled around in the patch for a few minutes, and came out a bloody mess. A witness called 911 and then, in disbelief, asked the man: "What on earth were you thinking?" The man sheepishly confessed: "At the time it seemed like a good idea."

Sometimes our impulsive actions are about as foolhardy and harmful as taking a roll in a cactus patch. That is often true of knee-jerk, short-fuse anger.

Warren Christopher, who successfully negotiated the Iranian hostage crisis of 1980, commented about his unflappability under the most trying conditions: "You should never get angry except on purpose."

We need the anger arrow in our quiver, but not for "going off" or terrorizing others or punishing ourselves or escalating tensions or in general raising the misery index around us. We must make sure that our anger, as Christopher said, is purposeful. We use our anger to bring about constructive, productive change. I like Thomas Jefferson's advice on not "popping off." He wrote: "When angry, count to ten before you speak or act. If very angry, count to one hundred."

April 29

I have three sons and no daughters. I am one of two sons and have no sister. My father was one of two sons and had no sister.

The last Willis man in my paternal line to have a daughter was my grandfather's father, Thomas Henderson Willis who fathered a girl (along with three sons). It has been 121 years—five generations—since a girl swimming against the tide made it through the Willis-male gene pool to us.

On April 29, 2008, family history changed. At long last a Willis male (our middle son) and his wife brought forth an eight-pound, seven-ounce living doll. We were and are shocked and smitten.

Some of us cried tears of joy. In the waiting room was another woman also shedding tears. When I struck up a conversation with her she explained that hers were tears of joy for her only grandson born three months ago. She had just learned that he may get to go home for the first time next week. He was born several months premature. After weeks in the neonatal intensive care unit, he developed an infection. Surgeons had to remove part of his intestine.

That family lives sixty miles from the hospital. The practice of kindness for strangers, performed in this case by the Ronald McDonald House, has made their three-month dislocation bearable. The parents of this only child and his grandmother glowed with pride as they described their boy to us: "He's our miracle baby." Now up to five pounds, he is "a born fighter."

With babies—male or female, born well or born ill—come shrieks of delight, tears of joy, and sometimes tears of sorrow. May little ones, thrust into a world they never sought, find in parents and grandparents a warm, welcoming, safe place to land.

April 30

QUESTION: What do Charles Shultz, Sebastian Thrun, and Steve Jobs have in common?

ANSWER: All three successfully challenged the traditional model of higher education.

The late Charlie Shultz, creator of *Peanuts*, arguably the greatest cartoonist in history, failed at least one subject every year of high school. When it came time to go to college, he took a correspondence course from an art school instead, since all he really wanted to do was draw and he did not want to have instructors looking over his shoulder while he drew.

Sebastian Thrun, one of the top professors at Stanford University, has put his popular "Introduction to Artificial Intelligence" course online. Those who are getting educated by him online get for free what costs Stanford students $60,000 a year. Thrun's criticism of traditional college education is that it is based on exclusivity. It serves only a privileged few, and Thrun thinks not very well and quite inefficiently.

Steve Jobs dropped out of expensive Reed College his freshman year and audited a calligraphy class. The genius who created the Apple II, the first highly-successful personal computer, followed by the iPhone, iPad and iTunes, credited much of his success to the calligraphy class. Without that class, the personal computer would not have had the varied and enchanting fonts that we beneficiaries know and love and take for granted.

These men are incontrovertible proof that traditional university education is not for everyone. Life's most important truths often are not learned sitting in a college classroom. Some of our most successful citizens did not take the college route, much less complete a degree.

Steve Jobs summarized his wisdom in a moving 2005 commencement address at Stanford. Here are two enduring insights from that speech:[15]

"Your time is limited, so don't waste it living someone else's life. Don't settle."

"You've got to find what you love. If you haven't found it yet, keep looking. Don't settle. As with all matters of the heart, you'll know when you find it."

April Notes

1. Gasset, "The Hero," 144.

2. The earliest version of this story I can find comes from Robert L. Peterson's *New Life Begins at Forty* on page 135. The book consists of columns Peterson wrote five days a week for the *New York Journal American* that were picked up by almost one hundred other newspapers. He titled this story, "Don't Put Pleasure in Cold Storage."

3. Peterson, *Run with the Horses*, 43–44.

4. Gray, "Monarch Butterflies," no pages.

5. *Albert Schweitzer Fellowship*, "On Earth Day," no pages.

6. *Yahoo Voices*, "Top Curmudgeon Writers," no pages.

7. Shakespeare. *The Merchant of Venice*. Act 4. Scene 1.

8. *PR Newswire*, "Reader's Digest Celebrates," no pages.

9. Jackson, *Sacred Hoops*, 118.

10. Ibid., 91.

11. Ibid. 185–186.

12. *Goatlocker*, "Navy Terms," no pages.

13. Matthew 20:16.

14. Duhigg, "Power of Habit," 1.

15. *Network World*, "Apple's Steve Jobs," 1–2.

May

May 1

The over-planned, goal-dominated life is, in my humble opinion, overrated.

John Grisham, successful-lawyer-turned-writer, whose books have now sold over three hundred million copies, never planned to write books. He told college graduates:

> If you are sitting out there now with a nice, neat little outline for the next ten years, you'd better be careful . . . Life has a way of presenting opportunities that you don't really notice at first. Success a lot of times depends on whether you make a change and try something that you hadn't planned, something new.[1]

In high school, I was preparing myself to become an aeronautical engineer because I wanted to help America win the space race with Russia. Then a new minister came to town who knew Greek. His brilliant interpretations of the scriptures based on the original language moved me to make a sea change. I enrolled at the same college he had attended and majored in Greek. What I would eventually do for a job never crossed my mind. I only knew that I enjoyed translating the New Testament from the original Greek.

When I was one month away from completing my third degree, another student crossed my path on campus one day and asked, as we chatted, "What are you going to do next?" This professional student laughed, "I have no idea." Before we parted he suggested: "You might want to consider hospital chaplaincy." Having no other good options, I looked into it. I ended up making a career of it. I do not remember the name of the man whose suggestion changed the course of my life.

Golda Meir, Israel's first woman Prime Minister, told the children of Fourth Street Grade School in Milwaukee in 1969:

> It isn't really important to decide when you are very young just exactly what you want to become when you grow up. It is much more important to decide on the way you want to live . . . If you are going to get involved with causes that are good for others, not only for yourselves, then it seems to me that that is sufficient."[2]

May 2

"More is never enough," some sage said. Those with obsessive-compulsive disorder know that too well. Someone asked Nelson Rockefeller, at that time one of the richest men in America, "How much is enough?" He smiled and gave an honest answer, "Just a little bit more."

Do you have enough?

To Johann von Goethe, thought by many to be Germany's greatest philosopher ever, are attributed these nine requisites for contentment:

> Enough health to make work a pleasure. Enough wealth to support your needs. Enough strength to battle with difficulties and overcome them. Enough grace to confess your sins and forsake them. Enough patience to toil until some good is accomplished. Enough charity to see some good in your neighbor. Enough love to move you to be useful and helpful to others. Enough faith to make real the things of God. Enough hope to remove anxious fears concerning the future.

I like Benjamin Franklin's contribution to the contentment discussion:

> There are two ways of being happy. We may either diminish our wants, or augment our means. If you are idle or sick or poor, however hard it may be to diminish your wants, it will be harder to augment your means. If you are active and prosperous or young and in good health, it may be easier for you to augment your means than to diminish your wants. But if you are wise, you will do both at the same time, young or old, rich or poor, sick or well; and if you are very wise you will do both in such a way as to augment the general happiness of society.[3]

Would it not be excellent to find in our depths both the will to discipline our desires and the compassion to apply some of our bounty to lightening the loads of others?

May 3

After Michael Carneal shot and killed three students at Heath High School in Paducah, Kentucky, in 1997, Timir Banerjee, Louisville neurosurgeon, felt moved to do something. He founded SPAVA, "The Society for the Prevention of Aggressiveness and Violence among Adolescents." His organization has gone into elementary, middle, and high schools across the nation and successfully taught anger management skills and impulse control. "We want our children to learn to negotiate and arbitrate and discuss and think first," Banerjee said, "rather than pull out a gun."[4]

At the 2000 Olympics in Sydney, Marion Jones established herself as the fastest female runner in the world. She became America's new hero, decisively winning three gold medals. By 2008, however, for lying to federal investigators about using performance-enhancing drugs, she was making twelve cents an hour sweeping floors in a federal prison. For years, as part of her community service, Marion Jones delivered her "Take a Break" speech to high school students. She urged them to do what she wishes she had done—take a break and do some hard, critical thinking before making any big decision.[5]

A close personal friend who was the medical director of an intensive care unit had a practice of occasionally stepping back from a patient he was tending and silently standing alongside her bed with his forefinger to his lips or against his temple. His team waited respectfully in silence. Then, after maybe thirty seconds, he returned to work. I once asked him about it. He explained: "It's my pregnant pause. Instead of full speed ahead, I've found it helpful often to hesitate. You need to stop at times and question what you're doing."

Spontaneity and the "Ready-Fire-Aim" approach have their place. Many times, however, "Don't just do something—stand there" serves us and others better.

May 4

How do you know when it is time to hang it up, to call it quits? For some time now I have had two models, one for how to do it and another for how not to do it.

Harper Lee walked away elegantly. She wrote the Pulitzer Prize winning *To Kill a Mockingbird* in 1960. A 1999 American Library Journal poll found it the best novel of the twentieth century. It has been translated into more than forty different languages. More than forty million copies have sold. Harper Lee chose not to write a *To Kill a Mockingbird* sequel or any other novel. She lives with her centenarian sister in Monroeville, Alabama, their hometown. The world-famous novelist is an extremely private person and has rarely given an interview.

She is proud, however, of her one book. She once declined an invitation to speak with the explanation: "It's better to remain silent than to be a fool."[6] Harper Lee quit while she was ahead and went out on top.

Y. A. Tittle, born the same year as Harper Lee, misjudged when to hang it up. In 1963, Yelberton Abraham Tittle, future Hall of Fame quarterback, set an NFL record by throwing thirty-six touchdown passes. But he is most famous for a photograph of him made the very next year—helmet knocked off, bald, bloodied, kneeling in the end zone after a tackle that gave him a concussion and a cracked sternum. His team, the New York Giants, won only two games that season. Ancient (by football standards) at thirty-eight, Tittle retired at the end of that devastating season. About the iconic picture he later said: "Heck of a way to get famous. That was the end of the road, the end of my dream. It was over."[7]

In jobs as well as relationships, discerning the right time to walk away is critical.

May 5

"Don't be evil" is Google's corporate slogan. Unlike the core-values statement of most companies, this one does not mince words or put you to sleep.

The positive translation might be "Do unto others as you would have them do unto you," but Google's slogan has more bite. It is a catchy way to express Immanuel Kant's categorical imperative not to do anything that you would not bind on all humanity or, put positively, do only what would be good if the whole human race did the same. "Don't be evil" assumes as Kant did that most people mean to be decent and that there is some universal sense of what is right and what is wrong.

It is inevitable that a company as big as Google is going to make mistakes and at times compromise values. The leaders are, after all, fallible human beings. But having "Don't Be Evil" as a central pillar of their identity does, according to those who work there and those who have investigated and written about Google, significantly influence behavior.

On their website and on their bulletin boards they have statements like:

> Trust and mutual respect among employees and users are the foundation of our success, and they are something we need to earn every day . . . If you have a question or ever think that one of your fellow Googlers or the company as a whole may be falling short of our commitment, don't be silent. We want—and need—to hear from you . . . We expect all Googlers to be guided by both the letter and the spirit of this Code . . . Don't be evil, and if you see something that you think isn't right—speak up![8]

What difference would it make if your workplace espoused and groomed a culture genuinely based on trust and transparency and invited you to blow the whistle on the organization when it fails to practice what it preaches?

May 6

This spring I am sitting in the catbird's seat observing the circle of life. It is my good fortune that robins are again attracted to our yard and house. A couple is begetting the next generation on our bathroom window ledge. Robin redbreast has laid a turquoise egg each of the last three days. I am hoping for one more egg tomorrow.

Mom will incubate the eggs for two weeks. With the incubation patch on her belly she will keep the eggs the perfect temperature. She will rotate the eggs with her beak several times a day to keep them from sticking to their eggshells. She will leave the nest for only a few minutes in a twenty-four hour period to find herself a few worms to eat.

When the babies are born they will require many worms. Mom and dad will deliver each baby over one hundred worms a day for two weeks. When the babies are about fourteen days old the food deliveries stop. The fledglings will get the message that mom and dad expect them to fend for themselves. Fledglings reluctantly and awkwardly leave the nest. For two weeks the parents give them a crash course in flying and harvesting their own worms. After those two weeks of schooling, the little ones are on their own.

Maybe we humans should take a note or two from the robins. After a period of high attachment, maybe we also are meant to set our children free. Nature's formula is good nurturing followed by good weaning, serious engagement followed by serious disengagement, intentional bonding followed by intentional relinquishment.

All our parental love aims at our children's individuation—their ability to find their own way, stand on their own two feet, and take wing. Parents are ultimately not for dependence, but to make dependence on them unnecessary.

May 7

The greatest of all Greek heroes was Heracles. Wandering aimlessly at eighteen, wondering how he should live his life, Heracles came to a fork in the road. The road to his right was hilly, rough, and ugly, but he could see beautiful mountains in the distance. The road to his left was wide and smooth, lined with shade trees and flowers and benches on which to stop and rest, with beautiful mountains beyond it.

While Heracles pondered his choice, two lovely women appeared, one approaching him from each road. The woman on the road to his left spoke first: "Follow me down this pleasant path and you'll find music and mirth, wine and food, all the way to the beautiful mountains. On this road your every comfort will be provided."

Then the other woman spoke: "Let me warn you: this road is crooked, with many potholes. It leads you through deep, dark valleys. If you want fruits and flowers, you'll have to plant and tend them yourself. If you want people's respect, you'll have to earn it. All this road offers is what you win by your determination."

"Could I have your name?" Heracles asked. "My name is Struggle," she replied. Heracles turned to the other woman: "And you?" "My name is Ease," she said with a seductive smile. That day Heracles put his hand into the hand of the beautiful woman named Struggle and set foot onto the difficult road that led to the beautiful, blue mountains.

Excellent living, Greeks believed, came only one way—through rigorous self-discipline and personal struggle. Aristotle summed up the excellent way: "We are what we repeatedly do. Excellence in life is not an act, but a habit. Sow a thought, reap an action; sow an action, reap a habit; sow a habit, reap a character; sow a character, reap a life."

May 8

Over one millennium ago an Ethiopian noblewoman wrote:

> The day when a woman enjoys her first love cuts her in two. A man spends a night by a woman and goes away. His life and body are the same. But the woman conceives. She carries the fruit of the night nine months long in her body. Something grows into her life that never again departs from it. She is a mother. She is and remains a mother even though her child dies, though all her children die. For at one time she carried the child under her heart. And it does not go out of her heart ever again. All this a man does not know. He does not know the difference between before love and after love, before motherhood and after motherhood. Only a woman can know that and speak of that.[9]

I thought of that nameless mother's declaration when I read about an exhibition in 2013 at London's Foundling Museum. Charles Dickens lived next door to Foundling Hospital. He wrote about it in his novels and supported it financially. It was a children's home founded in 1741 by a philanthropic sea captain for the "education and maintenance of exposed and deserted young children."

Unwed mothers and mothers too poor to rear their newborns gave them up to the Foundling Hospital, hoping the child might find there a better life. The exhibition, called *Fate, Hope and Charity,* consisted of small tokens mothers left with their babies as identification should they one day return to claim their child. Each coin, trinket, patch of cloth, playing card, key, button, medal, nut, poem, or note bears witness to the grief of one mother separated from her child.[10]

At one time she carried the child under her heart, and dead or alive, that child does not go out of her heart ever again.

May 9

How do we decide right from wrong? We generally work out two sets of answers. One path is represented by The Ten Commandments. Some things we deem just plain right or plain wrong. Different people in different times and cultures sort issues as diverse as artificial insemination, racial segregation, gambling, war, spanking children, women's suffrage, and eating pork chops into right or wrong categories. The other path is consequences. Judge any act solely on where it leads. Calculate benefits against burdens, the way you choose between colleges or decide whether to treat a cancer with radiation, chemotherapy, surgery, or some combination—go with what brings the best results for the most people. To tweak Shakespeare: "There is nothing either good or bad but consequences make it so."

Thomas Merton hints at another ingredient of ethical decision-making. In a 1966 letter to an idealistic young man, Jim Forest, he wrote:

> Do not depend on the hope of results. You may have to face the fact that your work will be apparently worthless and even achieve no result at all. Concentrate not on the results, but on the value, the truth of the work itself. And there too a great deal has to be gone through, as gradually you struggle less and less for an idea and more and more for specific people . . . In the end, it is the reality of personal relationships that saves everything."[11]

Merton refers to the two paths, but adds a proviso: select your companions carefully for the decision-making process.

Some churches major in marching to that drummer. One local church promotes itself as a "thinking, feeling, healing" community. What a grand, utopian ideal—to make life's journey accompanied and supported by such company! Many hospitals march to that drummer. They appoint multidisciplinary ethics committees to address their medical dilemmas, apportioning a mix of good-hearted people who are expected to bring multiple perspectives.

To challenge and guide each other through moral briar patches, birds of a feather—individuals reputed to be responsible, just, rational, and kind—need to flock together. In the end it is that cross-pollination of relationships and viewpoints that, as Merton said, saves everything.

May 10

One day a bird's nest appeared on our deck. The engineer turned out to be a robin. When she flew off to pull worms out of the grass, I tiptoed out on the deck and slyly sneaked a peek. Three Carolina-blue eggs lay in her nest. Two weeks later she had triplets. Two more weeks later, mother and fledges flew away.

One act of that drama I will not forget. Before the chicks were hatched, late one afternoon the winds kicked up, the sky turned black, and a mighty storm with thunder, lightning, and hail beat upon our deck. Mama bird opened her wings and wrapped them around the nest, forming a cone-shaped umbrella. Torrents of water bombed the tent formed by her wings and bounced or rolled off. Hail hammered her body and bounced off. The mama robin waterproofed everything—the whole nest and the three eggs—with her wings. Only her head and wings were exposed.

She closed her eyes and took the hail's best punches. Pea-sized hail pounding her quarter-pound body must be the equivalent of grapefruit-size hail hitting a human head. If the hailstones had been much larger or lasted much longer she could not have survived. She did not budge until the rain stopped. She knew that her purpose in the grand scheme of things was to bring her little ones safely through the storm.

I think of all the mothers (and fathers) who sacrifice body and soul—whatever it takes—to protect and sustain their young.

Emily Dickinson's lines are apropos: "Hope is the thing with feathers / That perches in the soul / And sings the tune without the words / And never stops / at all / And sweetest / in the gale / is heard / And sore must be the storm / That could abash the little bird / That kept so many warm."

May 11

When I went off to college, the first day there I met a boy who had never spent one night away from home. His mother stayed in the motel nearest campus for his first nine days at college. She appointed me—hardly Mr. Maturity at the ripe age of seventeen—to be Don's protector, advocate, and mentor. The first clue I got that I might be in big trouble was when I observed her combing his hair. He later told me that he had never once combed his own hair. After she went home, I taught him how to apply the Brylcreem, hold the comb, look in the mirror, and part his hair.

Before our freshman year was over Don was in prison, having fallen in with the wrong crowd. He had been the proverbial fish out of water.

Erma Bombeck, mother of one daughter and two sons, wrote these wise words in her column for May 15, 1977:

> I see children as kites. You spend a lifetime trying to get them off the ground.
> You run with them until you're both breathless . . . They crash . . . You add a
> longer tail . . . They hit the rooftop. You pluck them out of the spout . . . You
> patch and comfort, adjust and teach. You watch them lifted by the wind and
> assure them that someday they'll fly. Finally they are airborne. They need more
> string so you keep letting it out. But with each twist of the ball of twine there is
> a sadness that goes with joy. The kite becomes more distant, and somehow you
> know it won't be long before that beautiful creature will snap the lifeline that
> bound you together and will soar as it is meant to soar, free and alone. Only
> then do you know that you did your job.[12]

My mother loved me with all her might. Then she let me go. I am forever grateful that she followed that script.

May 12

Some of us carry terrible scars that are invisible. I think of the convicts who were on death row for many years before DNA proved them innocent and set them free. I think of innocent little children who were sexually abused by a relative or clergy. I think most of bereaved parents. How most manage to soldier on, critically wounded for life, I do not know. But I think what Nelson Mandela said about his experience may be one key.

Mandela spent eighteen of his twenty-seven years as a political prisoner breaking rocks on Robben Island, located close to Cape Town, South Africa. In his autobiography *My Life*, Bill Clinton tells of his visit with Mandela at the rock quarry years after Mandela was released. At one point in the tour Clinton asked him: "I know you did a great thing in inviting your jailers to your inauguration [as president of South Africa], but didn't you really hate them?"

Mandela answered:

> Of course I did, for many years. They took the best years of my life. They abused me physically and mentally. I didn't get to see my children grow up. Then one day when I was working in the quarry, hammering the rocks, I realized that they had already taken everything from me except my mind and my heart. Those they could not take without my permission. I decided not to give them away.

Clinton later had a follow-up question: "When you were walking out of prison for the last time, didn't you feel the hatred rise up in you again?"

"Yes," Mandela said, "for a moment I did. Then I thought to myself, 'They have had me for twenty-seven years. If I keep hating them, they will still have me.' I wanted to be free, so I let it go."[13]

The bad news is that muddling through loss and grief is horrendous. Mandela said it took him years to work through his. The good news is that it beats the alternative—letting resentment and bitterness, self-pity and rage, have their way with us.

As Elsa implores in Disney's movie *Frozen*: "Let It Go!"

May 13

My first e-mail of the day, from a friend, proclaimed: "When people say something is 'done' rather than 'finished' it drives me nuts. People are finished and turkeys are done!!!!!!!"

I had two visceral reactions. One was, "You really need to get out more." Funny how we can let minuscule things drive us nuts. One of my mentors used to say: "It's not the sharks in life you have to worry about; it's the minnows." My second response, I have to confess, was, "I hate it when people use more than one exclamation mark!" If your word choice is adequate, there is no need to hold your finger down on the exclamation key.

Grammar nuances and niceties, I admit, are overly important to me. My wife in another room heard me groan recently when an anchor person on the local evening news said: "They should have consulted with *he* and *I.*" Frequently I hear people with several college degrees say things like, "I should have went home" or "I shouldn't have drank so much" or "Her and me had a great time," and I cringe.

I wrote a column several years ago that spelled the word "peek," p-e-a-k. A reader wrote a letter to the editor that sarcastically exposed my error. I am still smarting. Yes, I wished a pox on her house.

Back in 1837, two University of Paris law professors dueled with swords. The issue was a semicolon. The London Times reported: "The one who contended that the passage in question ought to be concluded by a semicolon was wounded in the arm. His adversary maintained that it should be a colon."[14]

In mellow old age I am determined to strike a compromise within myself neither to slaughter the King's English nor draw my sword over a semicolon.

May 14

In the summer of 1968, shortly after the assassinations of Martin Luther King Jr. and Robert Kennedy, I sojourned in the slums of Brooklyn, New York. I was an idealistic graduate student off to help poor kids. A former occupant of the apartment, another bleeding-heart do-gooder, had scribbled these lines on the wall above my mattress:

> Love is dead. Peace is beyond our reach. There's no point in pursuing our course. All hope is lost. And we? What's to become of us? This is the question that plagues my mind and destroys my sleep. We too are lost, with all our hopes, for this wicked world is closing in for the kill. The kill. What is to become of us when we die? We'll be forgotten along with all the others who were losers.

Several years ago my wife and I spent a night, not in a slum, but in a swanky hotel. A poem on the wall titled "Last Summer in Kentucky" was nicely matted and framed: "The road down to Harlen's a rocky old road, / and the road up to heaven is steep. / The road down to hell is as slick as a grease pit. / I've traveled on each."

Many of us have slid down some slippery, road-to-Harlen-like slopes. Many of life's misfortunes are outside our control. What we make of them, however—how we spin them—is our doing.

Some nameless Jew scratched the star of David and this confession on a basement wall in Germany during World War II: "I believe in the sun even when it is not shining. I believe in love even when I do not feel it. I believe in God even when He is silent."[15]

What happens to us in life is not the final word. The interpretation that we put on it is.

May 15

I begin this writing with a lump in my throat. On this the anniversary of my proposing, I write to praise my wife. I know her better than anyone, but everyone who knows her will agree with three things I say about her.

She is the quintessential worker bee. She recalls saying to herself back in elementary school, "Others may be smarter or faster or more popular or stronger or prettier, but no one will ever out-work me." She is a driven, super-achieving workaholic. Whether involved in an individual or a team task, she gives no less than 110 percent.

Her favorite word is the Latin *excelsior*, which translates into English as "always improving" or "ever higher." She stops at nothing short of excellence. More than forty years of evaluations by administrators and students grade her teaching performance in superlatives. When you find highest quantity (productivity) and highest quality (excellence) homogenized in one person, the end product is a work of art.

She is a hugger, a touchy-feely, warm, vulnerable, transparent, affectionate soul. It is her nature to be loving toward others, and I—lucky me—am the primary recipient.

Neither of us knew what we were doing on May 15, 1968, when I proposed on the great lawn of George Peabody College for Teachers and she responded with an enthusiastic yes. Now, through the retrospectroscope, I fully know what I was doing. For my life-companion, I was getting simply the best.

May 16

"It is what it is."

We keep hearing that expression a lot. Coaches say it when asked about their sorry won-lost record. CEOs say it when asked about their company's bankruptcy. It means something like: "What it is, is reality. I don't like it, and you don't have to like it, but it can't be changed. The issue now becomes what to do next." It is a modern rendition of George Eliot's wisdom: "It's but little good you'll do a-watering last year's crop."

Someone once told me that he had a delete button in his brain. Most of us do not. We spend a lot of energy and time revisiting, replaying, and regretting portions of our past. In Lewis Carroll's *Through the Looking Glass* the King says: "The horror of that moment I shall never, never forget!" The Queen rejoins: "You will though if you don't make a memorandum of it." What can we do with memoranda in our brains of the times people hurt us or neglected us?

Sometimes dying people can instruct us. I knew a thirteen-year-old girl who was on a ventilator. With a tube down her throat, she could not talk but she could write. I invited her to write a prayer that I would leave in the hospital chapel. She handwrote much, but these are the first sentences of her prayer: "I hope I live to be very old. If I don't, Lord, please take care of my mother. Help my father who has hurt me, but I have forgiven him."

I knew some of the unspeakable things her father did to her. The girl died two days after writing the prayer.

Yes, whatever happened "is what it is." But we can re-frame and re-image it. We can make it less a white-knuckled fist clutching a memorandum and more a fist loosening its grip on the painful memory, and so let it—with time—go.

May 17

Several summers ago our church held Vacation Bible School at night and offered, for the first time, a class for adults. My wife and I volunteered to teach the class. On opening night we gave those who showed up a piece of paper shaped like a bumper sticker and a magic marker. Their instructions were to write on the bumper sticker the main theological message they took from their religious upbringing.

One burly, hairy guy, when it came his turn stood up, beamed a great smile, and unfurled this bumper sticker across his broad chest: "Sunbeam, Sunbeam, Jesus Wants Me for a Sunbeam." We all laughed at the sight. I doubt that his teacher ever knew the bright, sunny message that she successfully implanted on the heart of an impressionable little boy, a boy who brought nothing to Vacation Bible School but a mind as open and receptive as a sponge or a new-plowed field. What she offered "took." Forty years later, he remembered.

Thomas Carlyle as a young boy had a beggar come to his door. His parents were gone. On boyish impulse, Carlyle broke open his piggy bank and gave the beggar all he had. Many years later he wrote that never before or after did he know such sheer, unadulterated joy as he felt that day.

All of us are constructing with our lives either a bridge or a pier. A pier stands alone, goes nowhere, and connects to nothing. A bridge extends us beyond our own little island and connects us to another island or to the mainland. A bridge liberates us from the prison of our aloneness, our preoccupation with self, and opens us to others—like Thomas Carlyle to the beggar or the Vacation Bible School teacher to the little boy.

May 18

At many universities it is traditional for retiring professors to give a "last lecture," their thirty-minute manifesto on whatever they deem most important.

When Randy Pausch, forty-six, professor of Computer Science at Carnegie Mellon University gave his last lecture in September of 2007, most people, including Pausch, assumed it would literally be his last lecture. The husband and father of three small children had been diagnosed a year earlier with pancreatic cancer. Tests a month before the last lecture showed that the cancer had spread to his liver and spleen.

His last lecture and a book with that title, along with interviews by Oprah Winfrey and Diane Sawyer, squeezed the heartstrings of a nation. I saw a short clip of a portion of the commencement address Pausch delivered at Carnegie Mellon. Here is the essence of his advice to the class of 2008:

> Find your passion, and if there's anything I've learned it's that you're not going to find it in things or in money, because you'll always be able to look around and find others who have more, and then you'll feel bad. You must find your passion in people, in relationships.[16]

His wisdom reminded me of something that self-made billionaire Ross Perot said when he spoke to Harvard Business School students years ago:

> Guys, just remember, if you get real lucky, if you make a lot of money, if you go out and buy a lot of stuff it's gonna break. You got your biggest, fanciest mansion in the world. It has air conditioning. It's got a pool. Just think of all the pumps that are going to go out. Or go to a yacht basin any place in the world. Nobody is smiling, and I'll tell you why: Something broke that morning . . . Things just don't mean happiness.'[17]

Isn't it too bad that it usually takes a serious illness or the specter of death to drive some of life's gigantic truths home?

May 19

The college graduation ceremony was being held in the school's basketball arena. The arena held thousands and was filled to capacity.

A number of family members within earshot of me talked on their cell phones throughout the program. I could see that some of the graduating seniors were also talking on their cell phones. Suddenly it dawned on me that the parents seated close to me and their graduating children down on the floor of the arena were talking to each other! What I have learned since is that many parents and children, whether in the same city or thousands of miles apart, talk to each other several-to-many times a day. One parent calls her son every morning to make sure he's awake and getting ready for class.

A stamp cost three cents when I went off to college. I wrote home fairly often. Then about once a month, when long-distance rates were low late at night or on a weekend, I scraped together a dozen quarters and found a pay phone and called home. I talked with my parents for about three minutes (the amount of time $3 bought), just enough for us to assure each other that everything was okay and to hear each other say the three magic words.

Some college administrators refer to parents enmeshed in their offspring's life, partly through the miracle of cell phones, as "hovering" or "helicopter" parents. Sometimes they describe the student-children of these parents as tethered or on a leash or with an uncut umbilical cord, unable to make decisions about almost anything without talking to home.

Maybe it is a delayed adolescence thing. It is fairly common nowadays, I have heard, for adolescence to extend to age thirty and beyond. I am sure it is healthy now, with life expectancies of eighty or ninety, not to hurry adulthood. I just hope these well-rooted kids, when it comes time to individuate, will find out that they also have wings strong enough for flying.

May 20

A resident in a local nursing home developed a rash that itched. Word got around that she had scabies. Before too long, many staff and residents who had been around her started itching and scratching. Skeptical that the rash was scabies, her physician called in a dermatologist. Sure enough, the patient had a non-contagious type of dermatitis and as soon as the word got out that her rash was not scabies, everyone's itch went away. "Belief," William James said, "helps create the fact."

Just as negative beliefs can help create negative facts (itching from presumed scabies), positive beliefs can help create positive facts (itching ends). Consider the placebo. When a trusted physician prescribes a placebo, 30 percent of the time the patient gets good results. A placebo or "sugar pill" has nothing medicinal in it. Drug companies may choose not even to manufacture a medication that gets less than 30 percent satisfactory results because they know a sugar pill can accomplish that. The classic placebo study was conducted by anesthesiologist Henry Knowles Beecher. In his 1955 paper "The Powerful Placebo" he examined fifteen studies involving 1,082 patients and concluded that 35 percent who were given a placebo got "satisfactory relief" for everything from post-surgery pain to headaches to anxiety.[18] Belief helps create the fact.

The great teacher, Sir William Osler, was wont to tell his medical students: "What happens to a patient with tuberculosis depends more on what he has in his head than what he has in his chest."

"One of the very first things I figured out about life," novelist Barbara Kingsolver ruminates, "is that it's better to be a grateful person than a grumpy one because you have to live in the same world either way, and if you're grateful, you have more fun."

You may be healthier too.

May 21

"How are you?"

"Fine. Yourself?"

A wise man taught me years ago that we should calibrate our response to the common greeting "How are you?" to the depth of the relationship we think we have with the asker. "Fine. Yourself?" is a good enough reply for a stranger or a casual acquaintance. The speaker is most likely not really wanting information. It is an innocuous, friendly convention that simply acknowledges seeing or hearing the other person, like saying "hi" or "hello." "Fine. Yourself?" completes the transaction.

But sometimes we sense that the other person might be open to, or even wanting, a little more authenticity. When I worked in a children's hospital and heard staff ask "How are you?" I sometimes found myself giving a slightly more nuanced response: "Not bad." It was an attempt with fellow workers in a great cause to model a little more truthfulness. In a world where children had had the worst befall them, "fine" felt insensitive and out of touch. How can you feel fine when you personally know little children who are dying from child abuse or brain cancer? Sometimes I responded: "Could be a lot worse." Those working with sick and dying children know exactly what those code words mean.

Once a co-worker who knew I was having a bad day, after we exchanged pleasantries said to me, "I can tell you're hurting. Let's go talk. I've got the time."

We ducked in an empty patient's room and I spilled the beans. I hope you have someone sensitive enough to do that for you. Regardless, you can *be* that someone to some Wayne or Jane who is having a "horrible, terrible, no good, very bad day." Just say, "Tell me how you're doing. I've got the time."

May 22

Yehuda Bauer, professor of Holocaust studies at the Hebrew University of Jerusalem, delivered a speech to the German Bundestag in which he said: "I come from a people who gave the Ten Commandments to the world. Time has come to strengthen them by three additional ones, which we ought to adopt and commit ourselves to: thou shall not be a perpetrator; thou shall not be a victim; and thou shall never, but never, be a bystander."[19]

I thought of that quotation when I read that Augusta Thomas, eighty-seven-year-old member of Grace-Hope Presbyterian Church in Louisville, Kentucky, was moving to Washington, DC, to accept a national labor union office for which she had campaigned hard and which she won at the union's convention last year. Many wondered if she had lost her mind, leaving behind nine children, eleven grandchildren, and twenty-two great-grandchildren for a job out of town.

But those who wondered did not know the trail of activism Augusta Thomas has left behind. In 1960, she joined Woolworth's lunch counter sit-ins in Greensboro, North Carolina, an action that became a pivotal moment in the civil rights movement. "They spat on me and knocked me off the stool," she remembers. They arrested her twice.

One of her prize possessions is a picture frame with her photo that was made when she received the 2007 "Rosie the Riveter" Award from her Kentucky union. It has inscribed on it: "A woman's place is in her union."[20]

I hope, if I live into my late eighties like Augusta, that I am speaking up and standing up for causes that help the less fortunate. As long as I am mentally and physically able, may I fail at becoming a rocking chair potato who watches boob tube drivel all the live-long day.

I once discovered two sentences on a note someone left in the hospital that continue to haunt and inspire me: "What if life's final exam consists of only one question: have you loved the ones you were given to love? It's not too late to change your answer."

May 23

Seinfeld star Jason Alexander, once a spokesman for a fast-food chain, lost thirty pounds in eighteen weeks and became a spokesman for Jenny Craig. His incentive for the weight loss came when he turned fifty and his youngest child asked him, "Dad, when I'm fifty, how old will you be?" When chubby Alexander added up the numbers and came up with eighty six, his son looked at him mournfully and directed a zinger of a follow-up: "Are you going to be here?"[21]

When Michelle Obama visited a Maryland elementary school, a second grader asked her an immigration question: "My mom says that Barack Obama is going to take everyone away who doesn't have papers." The First Lady answered: "Yes, we do have to make sure that people can be here with the right kind of papers, right?" The innocent little girl sadly reported: "My mom doesn't have papers."[22]

A mother shared with me two weeks ago, in the context of a group discussion about eating factory-farmed animals, a comment that her grown son made when he was three. When the family sat down for the Thanksgiving dinner, the three-year-old began to cry. "What's wrong, honey?"

The child sobbed: "I can't eat a turkey!" At three, awareness that the turkey set before him had once been alive but had been beheaded and roasted, troubled his tender heart and made his parents think twice about the origins of the foods they offered their only child.

As President Obama was shaving one morning, he said he was greeted with these words from his daughter Malia: "Dad, have you plugged the oil hole [the one caused by British Petroleum in the Gulf of Mexico] yet?"

Art Linkletter illustrated over several decades hosting "House Party" that kids say the darndest (and often truest) things.

May 24

The day before I graduated from college, I observed alumni gathering for their half-a-century-after-graduation reunion. I studied them for a minute—bent, slow afoot, wheelchair-bound, wrinkled, overweight, gray—and felt a rush of pity. At age twenty-one, fired up and ready to go forth and conquer, I commented to a friend, "Wouldn't you hate to be one of those old geezers?"

In 2010, I re-united with classmates who graduated in 1960 from high school in Tennessee. Many of us had not seen each other for fifty years. At sixty-seven, many of us bore little or no resemblance to our seventeen-year-old selves. Nametags were a necessity.

Two themes of the weekend—after the "You're looking good!" re-introductions—emerged. One was a sobering response to a display of thirty-four deceased classmates' pictures. We felt both our "It could have been me" and our "I may be next" mortality. We realized that at the reunion five years off, our picture could make that big board.

A second theme was extraordinary courage displayed by classmates. One came with a catheter bag pinned to a pant leg. One who had suffered a catastrophic stroke walked and talked with great difficulty, and fell once. Another had had colon cancer surgery a month earlier and had begun chemotherapy two days before the reunion. Another wore shorts, exposing an artificial leg. One was slumped in a wheelchair, debilitated and balded by cancer treatments. One came fresh from the death of both his only child and his only brother.

The take-back-home message for many of us was, in Tennyson's words: "Tho' much is taken, much abides; and tho' / We are not now that strength which in old days / Moved earth and heaven; that which we are, we are; / One equal temper of heroic hearts, / Made weak by time and fate but strong in will / To strive, to seek, to find, and not to yield."[23]

May 25

Just before one of our sons was born, a grandfather told me that parents should never name a child until they hold him and look him over—take his measure—for a few days. Only then are they prepared to choose a name that fits the baby's temperament or appearance. Most of us do not do that. We read a naming-your-baby book to find a name with a good meaning, or we already have a name that we have been waiting years to use, or we choose a name that sounds pretty or cute or regal.

I performed a wedding for a couple who named their first child Alexander Everest. Who doubts that they have sky-high hopes for that boy, scripting him with the name of the man who conquered the world coupled with the name of earth's highest mountain?

People in Africa's Uruba tribe, who believe they are the descendants of biblical Ham, re-name their children throughout their lives based on their child's characteristics or experiences.[24]

I think of how that might have worked in our family's history. In our salad days, different ones of us would have been Fleet Feet, Still Waters, Fat Brain, Workaholic, or Silver Tongue. There were other periods when we would have earned the name Desperately Seeking Somebody, Rebel without a Cause, Must Have Last Word, He Who Lost His Airplane Ticket in Atlanta, or She Who Trips and Falls a Lot.

I wrote my memoirs several years ago and divided my life into four parts, with a different title for each segment. Part one covered my first twenty years. My name then was Happy Fella. Although it is not politically correct to say so, I admitted that I had a happy childhood. Names for subsequent eras became more serious and complex and far less carefree.

What names should you have had, or should you have now, based on temperament, experience, and reputation?

May 26

The cast of characters numbered around ninety. First was the line of sixty-one old, white veterans, seated in wheelchairs at the World War II Memorial in our nation's capital. Seventy years earlier, mere lads, they had left home and family, risked life and limb, in far-away places they had never seen or heard of, to stop tyrants hell-bent on ruling the world.

Accompanying these sixty-one were about twenty-five men wearing blue shirts that identified them as members of Honor Flight New England. They were men who had volunteered to raise the money to fly old soldiers from Boston to see for the first time the memorial honoring them for their sacrifices.

One man dressed in a black leather suit with bright orange chaps slowly worked his way down that row of men, extending his hand and saying to each soldier the same words: "Thank you for your service." On the back of his jacket were embroidered the words: "Old Glory Chapter, Laurel, Maryland, Harley-Davidson Motorcycles."

It was one week before Memorial Day. My wife and I were there for the funeral and burial of a dear aunt in Arlington National Cemetery the next day. My wife's uncle is a three-star general. How right it seemed to us to learn that the spouse of a general, having endured separation over many dangerous tours of duty and having largely raised the kids, is also entitled to a plot in Arlington National Cemetery.

I made a photograph of the man from Old Glory Chapter shaking the veterans' hands. It is now the screensaver on my computer. I will never live another Memorial Day without thinking of those old soldiers. And I will remember a black granite wall at the Korean War Memorial not far away on the National Mall. Inlaid in silver are four words writ large: *Freedom Is Not Free.*

May 27

Robert Heinlein wrote:

> A human being should be able to change a diaper, plan an invasion, butcher a
> hog, conn [control] a ship, design a building, write a sonnet, balance accounts,
> build a wall, set a bone, comfort the dying, take orders, give orders, cooperate,
> act alone, solve equations, analyze a new problem, pitch manure, program
> a computer, cook a tasty meal, fight efficiently, die gallantly. Specialization
> is for insects.[25]

Heinlein is considered one of the top three science fiction writers of the twen-
tieth century, alongside Isaac Asimov and Arthur Clark. I am not a science fiction
fan, admittedly a deficiency of mine, but I have come to value many of Heinlein's
commentaries on life. See if there is a Ben Franklinish piece of wisdom here for you:

"You have to trust people. Otherwise you are a hermit in a cave, sleeping with
one eye open."

"Between being right and being kind, I know which way I vote."

"When you're rich, you don't have friends; you just have endless acquaintances."

"A motion to adjourn is always in order."

"All men are created unequal."

"Do not handicap your children by making their lives easy."

"A society that gets rid of all its troublemakers goes downhill."

"Always listen to experts. They'll tell you what can't be done, and why. Then do it."

"Courage is the complement of fear. A man who is fearless cannot be courageous.
He is also a fool."

"A man who marries at my age isn't taking a wife, he's indenturing a nurse."

"Touch is the most fundamental sense. A baby experiences it, all over, before he
is born and long before he learns to use sight, hearing, or taste, and no human ever
ceases to need it. Keep your children short on pocket money — but long on hugs."

May 28

The unspeakable carnage from the 2010 earthquake in Haiti calls to mind Albert Schweitzer's phrase "the fellowship of those who bear the mark of pain."

"Who are the members of this fellowship?" wrote the physician who gave his life to serving the sick of Africa, many of them members of the same tribes whose seventeenth and eighteenth-century ancestors were shipped off to Hispaniola (now Haiti) in slave ships. The fellowship is "all those who have learned by experience what physical pain and bodily anguish mean."

> They belong together all the world over; they are united by a secret bond. He who has been delivered from pain must not think he is now free again, and at liberty to take life up just as it was before, entirely forgetful of the past . . . He must help . . . bring to others the deliverance which he has himself enjoyed."[26]

Standing in the earthquake's rubble with two grieving mothers, Father Hans Alexander, a Haitian priest whose Catholic church had been reduced to a hollowed-out shell, said to a journalist: "Catholics and Protestants and other religions are praying together now." The journalist noted that the priest "doesn't ask them about their religion; he asks them about their pain."[27]

I do not understand the callous statements of some radio and television personalities who cynically comment on the Haitian earthquake, one of the greatest natural disasters of modern times that maimed and orphaned and killed hundreds of thousands. These commentators remind me of bombardiers who drop their load from thirty-thousand feet, from comfortable, hermetically-sealed offices far removed from the about-to-perish humanity below, or technicians who, like playing video games, cause drones to rain down destruction halfway around the world. Maybe those media personalities have lived privileged lives and cannot begin to identify with the wretched poor. About those like himself who grew up living a charmed life, Schweitzer wrote: "Whoever is spared personal pain must feel called to help in diminishing the pain of others. We must all carry our share of the misery which lies upon the world."

May 29

This is a true tale of two fathers and two children.

I once worked with a highly-moral, highly-successful woman who for more than thirty years had sought her father's approval. He had never molested or abused her. He had provided well for her material needs. He was a good citizen and an active church member. But he had never found it within him to say directly to his daughter, in any arrangement of words, "You're a good daughter and I'm proud of you."

The night before he underwent a high-risk, potentially-lethal surgery, sitting on the side of his bed holding his hand she summoned up the courage to ask: "Dad, do we have any unfinished business? Is there anything you'd like to say to me?" She waited— the yearning of her soul etched on her face—and after a long pause heard these words: "You know where my insurance papers are. And you know where my will is. And you know I love my family." Dad missed the prompt; daughter missed the craved blessing.

Sam Keene, highly successful philosopher and author, gave this tribute to his father as his father lay dying: "Dad, you have always been there whenever any of us children needed you. And across the years you have given us the best single gift that any parent could give—you took delight in us! In all sorts of ways you let us know that you were glad we were here, that we had value in your eyes, that our presence was a joy and not a burden to you."[28]

If you have trouble articulating love for a child or a parent, I have a game plan for you:

One, memorize nine words: "Have I Told You Lately That I Love You?"

Two, go deliver.

May 30

An old Hasidic story tells about a man who went around town slandering the rabbi. One day the man came to himself and went to the rabbi to ask forgiveness. The rabbi responded: "I'll forgive on one condition—if you'll go home, cut up a feather pillow, and scatter the feathers to the four winds. Then come back to see me." The man did as told. When he returned, the rabbi said: "One more thing. Now go and gather all the feathers."[29]

It is impossible to undo the wrongs we have done to others. I shudder whenever I think back to the twenty worst things I have said or done that hurt others.

Alfred Nobel invented dynamite in 1867. When his brother Ludvig died, a French newspaper published Alfred's obituary by mistake. It called Alfred "the merchant of death," saying he "became rich by finding ways to kill more people faster than ever before." Because of his invention of dynamite and many other inventions and investments, Alfred Nobel had become extremely wealthy. Concerned about his "merchant of death" legacy, in his will Alfred Nobel designated most of his estate to establishing Nobel prizes. The fifth prize was for "the person or society that renders the greatest service to the cause of international fraternity and the establishment or furtherance of peace."[30]

Csanad Szegedi, a rising political star in Hungary who is known for his anti-semitic comments, was shocked several years ago to learn that his grandmother was Jewish. An Auschwitz survivor, she had chosen to hide her heritage and ordeal from her grandchildren. Szegedi has been for some time now, according to a rabbi who meets with him, "in the middle of a difficult process of reparation, self-knowledge, re-evaluation, and learning."

We wish him Godspeed as he, like Alfred Nobel and the rest of us, attempts to gather up the feathers.

May 31

My anniversary is one week from today.

Poster boys for the Marriage Hall of Shame like John Edwards, Tiger Woods, Mark Sanford, and Arnold Schwarzenegger model for us how not to build trust and respect in a marriage. Then there are the serial marriage poster children like Larry King and Elizabeth Taylor who were married eight or more times. While they can serve as models of marriage failure, they also underscore an irrepressible human drive—the desire to belong intimately to another person, a drive that makes us try again and again, whether we are married or unmarried, to get intimacy right.

My favorite parable of getting intimacy right comes from philosopher Arthur Schopenhauer. He tells a story of porcupines trying to huddle together on a cold night to keep warm. Whenever they tried to get close they needled each other with their quills, so they backed off and shivered some more. They continued to shuffle back and forth—moving toward each other and then withdrawing—until they found the optimal spacing, the position where they could comfortably warm each other without getting punctured.

We are like the porcupines. Love hurts. Getting close and becoming vulnerable to another gives that person enormous power over us, including the power to injure us.

Why keep trying? In *Annie Hall*, Woody Allen jokes about a man who tells his psychiatrist: "Doc, my brother's crazy—he thinks he's a chicken."

The doctor says: "Why don't you turn him in?"

The man explains: "I need the eggs."

Relationships are messy and painful, but we need the eggs. We huddle up—although we are prickly like porcupines—because we need warmth.

May Notes

1. *Academy of Achievement*, "John Grisham, 2–3.
2. Nichols, "Ensuring the Legacy," no pages.
3. Franklin, *Poor Richard*, 46.
4. Carter, "Program Targets Adolescent Violence," no pages.
5. Turnbull, "Last Oprah Confession," no pages.
6. Singh, "Harper Lee," no pages.
7. Crowe, "The Biggest Snap," no pages.
8. *Google*, "Code of Conduct," no pages.
9. May, *Love and Will*, 116.
10. *Foundling Museum*, "Faith, Hope and Charity," no pages.
11. Shannon, *Hidden Ground of Love*, 294–297.
12. *Toledo Blade*, May 15, 1977, E, 3.
13. Clinton, *My Life*, 782–783.
14. Collins, "Has Modern Life Killed the Semicolon?" 1.
15. *Australian Memories*, no pages.
16. Pausch, "Graduation Speech," no pages.
17. Farnham, "How to Live with a Billion," no pages.
18. Beecher, "The Powerful Placebo," 1602–1606.
19. *USHMM*, "Frequently Asked Questions," no pages.
20. Davidson, "Augusta Thomas," 1–2.
21. *Jenny Craig*, "Jason Alexander," no pages.
22. Witt, "Elementary School Student," no pages.
23. Tennyson, *Ulysses*.
24. *Tribe*, "Yorba Culture," no pages.
25. *Robert Heinlein Quotes*, no pages.
26. Schweitzer, *On the Edge*, 173.
27. Meacham, "Lives and Houses Shattered," 1.
28. Claypool, "Art of Living," 23.
29. *Judaism 101*, "Speech and Lashon," no pages.
30. *Trigo*, "Alfred Nobel," no pages.

June

June 1

'Tis the season for commencement speeches. Most are unremarkable—clichéd, superficial, boring, and forgettable.

The last time I attended a commencement service was more than a decade ago when my niece graduated from college in Tennessee. The speaker was a congressman. One-third of his speech heaped praise on the dignitaries present, one-third recited his "stump" speech that touched on all his favorite political issues, and one-third was a litany touting the many favors he had done for his constituents. He used no notes. He could not have given the speech ten minutes of forethought. I noticed how many of the thousands in the sports arena began talking on their cell phones as he droned on. Several times when I rolled my eyes or sighed my wife elbowed me and whispered, "Behave!"

History professor Charles Beard, who was born in Indiana and taught most of his career at Columbia University in New York City, was approached by a publisher late in his career about writing a book on "The Lessons of History." Dr. Beard said: "I don't need to write a book. I can tell you everything I know about history in four sentences":

"The bee that robs the flower also fertilizes it."

"Whom the gods would destroy, they first make mad with power."

"When it's dark enough, you can see the stars."

"The wheels of justice grind slowly, but they grind exceeding fine."[1]

That was not a commencement address, but it would have been a memorable, unforgettable one. Few of us are capable of saying things so profoundly and so provocatively with such an economy of words. If more preachers, politicians, and other public speakers made those three standards theirs, more of their listeners who come craving a pearl will go away satisfied.

June 2

I have heard of people doing without for a week or a month just to see how the experience felt. One family experimented doing without for one whole year.

Last week my wife and I "unplugged"—we did without radio, television, internet, and e-mail for three days and three nights. We were in the house of a couple who had moved into an assisted-living home, busily going through everything they had accumulated during sixty-five years of marriage, deciding which things to toss and which to sell. Because electricity to the house had been cut off, we were virtually out of touch with the outside world for seventy-two hours.

I read about one journalism professor who asked two hundred students in her media literacy class to avoid all media for one day—no text messaging, no phone, no television, no radio, no computer, no e-mail, and no internet. She was shocked to hear her students' reports about experiencing extreme isolation, depression, and boredom. One mentioned being "fidgety" all day. A few said they felt miserable or depressed or empty.[2]

Some observers believe that college students these days are so addicted to technology that they have the same withdrawal symptoms as drug addicts do when their "drug of choice"—social networking—gets taken away. Some fear that youth are losing their desire and ability to talk to others in person.

When my wife and I re-connected with the world, the first thing we learned from the car radio was that Arnold Schwarzenegger had a ten-year-old love child and Lady Gaga was scheduled to appear on "The David Letterman Show." No new war or peace broke out in our three days unplugged. We concluded that we could do much worse than talking only with each other for several days.

June 3

On Memorial Day I joined a small army of volunteers on an organic vegetable farm. Our mission: to search out thistle and destroy it. Opposed to spraying chemicals on their fields, organic farmers pull or cut one weed at a time. Armed with shovels to dig weeds up and machetes to chop them down, we sallied forth. My weapon was a machete. For half a day I was Ramar of the Jungle, my favorite action hero when we got our first television set in 1953. Wearing knee-high mud boots and slogging my way through waist-high wheat and oats, I hacked thistle.

Thistle does have some redeeming value. Goldfinches love its seeds. After prickles are removed at a mill, the leaves make good fodder for livestock. Herbalists use thistle seeds to treat liver problems. Some of my favorite photographs are of butterflies lunching on their purple flowers. The problem with thistles is that when they are allowed to seed, the air spreads their silky, dandelion-like hairs everywhere. Thistle competes very well with vegetables planted around them—choking them out, robbing them of sunlight, water, and nutrients.

There is a second problem. If you touch one, you get tattooed with a hole that will not soon be forgotten.

Thistle has been the pariah of plants since the opening pages of the Bible when Adam and Eve, having fallen from grace, are told that the earth would ever after, as part of punishment for their sin, grow "thorns and thistles."[3] It is tempting to divide the human race into good and evil, wheat and weeds. Jesus cautioned against doing that, but rather to let weeds and grain grow together and leave it to God at the end of time to judge which is which.[4] As one bumper sticker reads: "Love 'em all; let God sort 'em out."

That is good advice for self-righteous, self-appointed judges of others, but not for farmers hoping to make a crop.

June 4

Our family has our own living legend—my wife's father. When our sons face a personal crisis, they get inspiration thinking of their grandfather and how he would rise to the occasion. He had to grub and scrape and fight for everything he got in life. His mother abandoned him and his father abused him. He made a salutary marriage choice and worked as many jobs as necessary to support the two children they begat.

In his eighty-seventh year he had to deal with several physical losses. Both legs, due to two bad knees and one broken bone, went out of commission. Then a torn bicep rendered his right arm useless. With each loss he amped up his workout routine with whatever limb(s) he had left, preparing to climb the next mountain.

His only son (my brother-in-law) compared him to the Black Knight in a Monty Python movie. When the Black Knight refused to let King Arthur cross over a bridge, King Arthur cut off his left arm. The Black Knight insisted, "It's only a scratch." When the king cut off his right arm, the Black Knight remarked, "Just a flesh wound." After King Arthur cut off both his legs, the Black Knight conceded, "All right—we'll call it a draw." As the king crossed the bridge and rode away, the indomitable Black Knight, a quadruple amputee, yelled at him: "Come back here and take what's coming to you. I'll bite your legs off!"[5]

My father-in-law had one consistent strategy through life—hurdle, go around, go under, or go through whatever stone life rolls in your way. If they made a movie of his life, it would be titled *True Grit*. Yes, he was up late many nights watching John Wayne movies.

June 5

I wish we could clone Mrs. Brown.

Our oldest grandchild just graduated from first grade. Mrs. Brown was his teacher. Her public school classroom looked just like America—female and male; red and yellow, black and white; laid back and spirited; stocky and skinny; dressed up and dressed down; precocious and struggling; Catholic, Protestant, Jew, and None.

My wife, an educator of teachers, and I observed Mrs. Brown working her magic on Grandparents Day and then again on Awards Day, the next-to-last day of school. Both times she was clearly the maestro who had earned the love and respect of her twenty-four students. After presenting a video that celebrated activities of the class through the school year, Mrs. Brown called each student, one by one, to the front of the room. She shook the child's hand, presented a large manila envelope with the student's name printed in large letters on it, and then publicized one special achievement distinguishing that child.

There was a Future Author award and a Kind Heart award; a Helping Hands and a Future Inventor and a Magnificent Manners Award; a Hardest Worker and a Most Improved and a Neatness and a Most Focused and a Future Researcher and a Book Nook and a Future Storyteller award. When my grandson was called forward, Mrs. Brown deemed him Most Outgoing. Then she added this explanation: "Jackson worked hard to befriend everyone in this class."

I have several opinions of that little ceremony. One, probably all the children went home believing that they have at least one special gift that put them at the head of their class. Two, when they are as old as their grandparents, they will remember the identity they earned in Mrs. Brown's first-grade class. Three, there are some Mrs. Browns out there working magic. They earn all the respect and support we can give.

June 6

Long before the "Arab Spring" of 2011, there was the "Prague Spring" of 1968. Czecho-slovakia, ripe for throwing off the communist yoke on their back, watched as thousands of tanks and hundreds of thousands of Soviet troops rolled into their country and squashed their Prague Spring.

For the next two decades poet Vaclav Havel, both underground and above ground, led the resistance. He was imprisoned multiple times for his opposition, once for four years. After the Soviet Union collapsed in 1989, the people of the new Czech Republic elected Havel their president.

In his dissident days Havel wrote a piece titled "An Orientation of the Heart." In it he discussed how to keep hope alive in a hopeless time.

Hope he defined as "an orientation of the spirit, an orientation of the heart." Hope, instead of being found in the way things are, is "anchored somewhere beyond [the world's] horizons."

Hope, he continued, "is not the same as joy that things are going well." With little or no indication that a cause is headed for success, hope is the ability to stay the course because the cause is right. Whether it succeeds or not, after all, is beyond our control. The bad guys sometimes will win.

Hope also "is definitely not the same thing as optimism." It is totally unrelated to evidence or events that portend things turning out well. Rather, hope gives courage and strength "to live and continually to try new things, even in conditions that seem as hopeless as ours do."[6]

Sometimes those doing the grunt work of justice and peace can see no evidence that they are making headway. Then hope, "an orientation of the heart," kicks in, enabling the grunts to keep the faith and go the distance.

June 7

Today my wife and I celebrate our wedding anniversary. I am disappointed that no one has ever asked us the secret of our success. So here and now, before God and everyone, I tell all.

We complement each other. She is a type A+ personality; I would call my personality, relative to hers, a B+. She is a Secretariat thoroughbred; I am more like Roy Rogers's reliable Trigger or Robert E. Lee's steady Traveller. She values my stoicism and penchant for stopping to smell roses; I value her passion to climb every mountain and ford every stream to slay the next dragon.

We are both Virgos. We are hard on ourselves, and we also hold others to high standards. We grew up in the same cultural and ethical stew. Our old-fogey core values—duty, honor, integrity, truthfulness, self-discipline—have served us well, carrying us, so far, through life's white waters. You could say we are equally yoked.

We could write a book on mutual respect. I honestly think she is the greatest—the best human being I could have landed for a life companion. I have occasionally heard her say similar things about me. We are thrilled each time the other succeeds; we are proud of whatever the other accomplishes.

Our communication system purrs. Discussions in the home we built are frequent, free-ranging, and thorough—just ask our kids. We are open and honest, sometimes to a fault. We do not spend much energy wondering where we stand with each other. Instead of wondering, we simply ask.

These four cylinders, humming together, make our little marriage vehicle run right well. No two relationships work exactly alike. Nothing feels worse than having one that is broken; nothing feels finer than having one that runs well—most of the time.

June 8

You wonder what advice Davy Crockett might have for members of Congress today.

Before he moved to Texas and died fighting at the Alamo, he was The Honorable David Crockett, sent to Washington in 1826 by Tennesseans to represent them in the United States House of Representatives. It was a heady time for Tennesseans and especially for those in Congress since "Old Hickory"— President Andrew Jackson—was a Tennessean.

At President Jackson's urging, Congress passed the Indian Removal Act which gave the federal government authority to relocate Native Americans in the east to territory west of the Mississippi River. The Act led to the infamous "Trail of Tears" where tens of thousands of Cherokees were herded to Oklahoma. Up to four thousand died of starvation and disease along the way.

Congressman Crockett believed the Indian Removal Act was "wicked" and "unjust." Colleagues warned him that he was going to ruin himself politically, but as a matter of conscience he voted against it. He became persona non grata with Tennesseans and with the president. His constituents voted him out of office. He departed Tennessee with the words: "You may all go to hell, and I will go to Texas."[7]

Crockett was not enthralled to the president, to his political party, or to Tennessee constituents. He was in thrall to justice and mercy. The word "thrall" is a word the Vikings used in reference to the lowest members of their society. Today we would call them slaves.

What if members of Congress today were enthralled (enslaved) not to donors or political party or the president or to getting re-elected, but to conscience? What if they were enthralled not to one issue, be it "No New Taxes" or "No Change to Entitlements," but to the future wellbeing of the country? Imagine that.

June 9

In 1914 Woodrow Wilson declared Mother's Day a national holiday. Another half century went by before a president got around to making Father's Day a national holiday.

Fathers historically have been for fearing and obeying but not much for loving. Fathers ruled. Many of them feared that any show of tenderness might be interpreted as a sign of weakness.

Small wonder that Martin Luther all his life had trouble praying "Our Father, who art in heaven." Father, in his mind, out of his own childhood experience, stood for severity, punishment, judgment, harshness, and cruelty. John Newton, the slave ship captain who wrote "Amazing Grace," also wrote: "I knew that my father loved me, but he did not seem to wish me to see it."

Some think the most toxic of all father-child relationships is one of "proximity without intimacy" where the dad is physically but not emotionally present. As playwright Arthur Miller said of his father: "I had no animosity toward my father, simply no great relationship. It was like two searchlights on different islands."

Of his efforts to be a less exasperating father to his own children, Martin Luther wrote: "Spare the rod and spoil the child—true, but beside the rod keep an apple to give him when he does well." I question the rod part of Luther's advice, but I know the apple part is true.

We dads do not owe our kids Hummers or trips to Cancun. Any old fat cat can do that. We do owe them an apple when they do well, a "You are good stuff and I believe in you."

If you have a living father, I hope this Father's Day you will give him a call. Say whatever needs to be said. I wish I could call mine.

June 10

In *The Conversion of Chaplain Cohen*, Rabbi Herbert Tarr tells the story of David, an orphaned boy raised by a loving aunt and uncle. As David goes off to enter the American army as a chaplain and they are saying their farewells at the train station, David grabbed their rough working hands in his smooth student ones and said: 'How can I ever begin to repay you for what you've done for me!"

Uncle Asher spoke gently: "There's a saying that the love of parents goes to their children, but the love of these children goes to their children."

"That's not so!" David protested, "I'll always be trying to . . ."

David's aunt interrupted: "David, what your uncle means is that a parent's love isn't to be paid back; it can only be passed on."[8]

While the Bible mandates love for neighbor, the stranger, and God, it does not command us to love our parents. What it requires instead is a measure of respect that stays in force even through times of tension or estrangement.

The Greeks had a word for everything, and they had a word just for "family love." The word was *storge*. *Storge* is a fairly cool word. It does not have in it the heat of *eros*, the Greek word for passionate love. It does not have the warmth of *philos*, the Greek word for a friendship kind of love. It does have a little *agape* in it, the Christian word for treating people right regardless of how we feel about them. But s*torge* is primarily about acceptance, tolerance, even "putting up" with family members we find difficult.

Fathers are a Whitman's Sampler. Some we lionize. Some we enjoy. Some we tolerate. Some we fire.

Sometimes we thank them; sometimes we forgive them.

June 11

A marathoner runs twenty-six miles. The course at Badwater, the "baddest" of all the ultramarathons, is 135 miles. It is the most extreme footrace in the world. This grueling, life-endangering contest begins in Death Valley, 280 feet below sea level. The race is run in July when the temperature hovers around 120 degrees. The pavement beneath the runners' feet gets up to two hundred degrees. Badwater ends by having the participants run halfway up Mount Whitney, the highest point in the contiguous United States.

The first time Scott Jurek ran the Badwater in 2005, he won the race in record time, twenty-four hours and thirty-six minutes. Even before that race, many thought of Jurek as the greatest ultraracer of all time. But how he won Badwater is the stuff of which legends are made.

At about the sixty-mile mark, the heat overcame Jurek and he collapsed. Lying in the dirt with some other runners more than ten miles ahead of him, Jurek told himself that it was hopeless, that he was toast. Then, as reported by Christopher McDougall in the greatest of all running books *Born to Run*, Jurek said to himself: "You're just going to have to do something totally outside the box, like start all over again. Pretend you're just waking up from a good night's sleep and the race hasn't started yet. Then run the next eighty miles faster than you've ever run before."[9]

After cogitating in the dust for ten minutes, appearing to everyone else to be finished or even dead, Jurek got up, passed everyone ahead of him, and shattered the course record.

One thing I think I am beginning to learn is that the way we talk to ourselves in the ultramarathon of life more often than not makes the difference between victory and defeat.

June 12

He was adopted when he was six weeks old. At age two he came down with a mysterious mal-absorption syndrome that caused him to stop growing for several years.

Scott Hamilton's life took a turn for the better when he discovered ice skating. He loved hockey but preferred figure skating. Compensating for his small frame (five feet, two inches tall), he competed with Herculean energy and determination. He won four consecutive national and world titles and then, in 1984, the Olympic gold medal.

In 1997 Hamilton was diagnosed with testicular cancer. Years after recovering from that, he came down with a brain tumor that was surgically removed. An artery was nicked during that procedure and physicians had to use another procedure to remove an aneurysm. One side effect of the whole ordeal was the loss of two-thirds of the vision in his right eye.[10]

At fifty-seven, Scott Hamilton lives in Franklin, Tennessee, with his wife and two children. He runs the Scott Hamilton CARES program that shares online information about chemotherapy and provides one-on-one mentorship for cancer patients. He works as a volunteer with Special Olympics. In 2009 he published *The Great Eight: How to Be Happy (Even When You Have Every Reason to Be Miserable)*. The "eight" are his eight principles of living positively.

Two things that I heard him say in interviews I wrote down and memorized as soon as I heard them. Coming from him, I believed, made them keepers. Once, when he was being interviewed, someone used the cliché about seeing the glass half empty or half full, and Hamilton interrupted: "As long as you are alive and kicking, as long as you have another day, you have a *full* glass."

The second insight is like the first: "The only disability in life is a bad attitude."

June 13

My father and his father and I had a peculiar tradition. Whenever we saw each other after a long absence, say when I came home from college, we kissed on the lips, and that in a culture and at a time when real men were not supposed to fear or grieve or cry or demonstrate affection in public—especially with other males.

Our society is still not sure what to make of politicians who shed a tear. Corporate officers do not want peers or subordinates or board members to see them sweat because feelings, except those associated with aggression, are still equated with vulnerability and weakness—leaving yourself open.

Psychiatrist Will Gaylin gave his book *Feelings* the sub-title *Our Vital Signs.* Our enormous capacity for feelings distinguishes us from rocks and Rambos and robots. Guilt, embarrassment, and grief are "vital signs." To exult and shout for joy and kiss on the lips are signs that our humanity may still be intact.

Keats wrote in *Endymion*: "But this is human life: the war, the deeds, / the disappointment, the anxiety, / imagination's struggles, far and nigh, / all human; bearing in themselves this good, / that they are still the air, the subtle food / to make us feel existence."

What it means to be human is not to guard ourselves against entanglements, not to immunize ourselves against disappointment or narcotize ourselves against pain, and not to hug affectionate feelings close to our vest. Part of what it is to be fully human is to feel existence and express it.

If you have a living father, I hope this Father's Day you will get in touch with him. Give him a hug. Oh, go ahead and give him a kiss, on the forehead or cheek if not on the lips. Night is coming.

June 14

My father died in 1991, when he was seventy-five, of leukemia. His father died at age seventy- seven of leukemia. I have wondered for many years if biology is destiny and I will follow suit.

I had a good father. He did not have an alcohol problem and did not abuse my mother or me. He hugged and kissed and encouraged me. He told me he loved me. I would bet that two hundred million Americans wish they could say that.

With Father's Day approaching, three warm memories of my father spring to mind.

When I was sixteen, my father and I spent an afternoon swimming in a saltwater swimming pool in San Antonio, Texas. He taught me how to jackknife off the small diving board that day. One-to-one attention like fishing or throwing a football or learning to jackknife is a big part of fathering. I hope our three sons remember such times with me.

When I came home from college after my sophomore year, thinking I knew it all (sophomore means "wise fool"), I gave my parents a little lecture on how things are either right or wrong, with no in-between. "Name one thing you are sure of," my father said. I shot back: "Well, that tomato over there is red." He said: "From over here, it looks a little pink to me." He helped me become a nuanced, critical thinker. I hope my sons will always be nuanced, critical thinkers.

The last time I saw him alive, his parting words were: "If there's ever any way I can be of help to you, just let me know." I knew my father meant that. He died the next day. I hope my sons believe that I would lay down my life for them or their children because I know that I would.

If you have a good, living father, you are truly blessed. I hope Sunday he receives from you a verbal bouquet.

June 15

I will not soon forget the year one of our sons celebrated his first Father's Day. It was for him a proud, mellow experience having, as he put it, "joined the club." He penned some tender from-the-heart sentences in the card he gave me introduced with: "Most of what I know about being a father to a little child is what I learned at home as a boy." Here are a few of the "rules" he said he learned from me:

"Spend one-on-one time with your child. Go out for a burger and fries. Give undivided attention."

"Enjoy time at home with your family. Grill out dinner. Have a picnic on the patio."

"When given silly Father's Day-related tee shirts, wear them proudly throughout the year for many, many years."

"Be occasionally sweet and sentimental. Express your love with words and with actions. Let your child see you cry and laugh and experience emotions."

He ended his ruminating by giving me the best-of-all Father's Day gift in one crisp sentence: "Thanks for getting me off to a strong start."

I am well aware that he could have written a book on rules I broke or mistakes I made or times I failed him. He was kind, for Father's Day, to concentrate on the positive.

My wife and I occasionally marvel at how our sons have found it within them to forgive us our parenting trespasses. Maybe they figured out they were only hurting themselves to nurse the sins of omission and commission we committed against them. I am happy for both them and us that they found a way not to contaminate their futures by clutching that baggage.

June 16

I am an infrequent flyer. My wife and I hop on a plane once or twice a year. When we do, at some point we comment that flying is no fun anymore: security checks are a hassle, the food is not good (or simply is not), and we are crammed in like sardines.

Several years ago we flew to Switzerland. The non-stop flight from Washington, DC, to the heart of Europe took eight hours. When our forebears came to these shores, there was only one way to get here: sailboat. The trip took three to four weeks, often with days or weeks of gale-force winds that made sleep almost impossible and motion sickness a constant companion and death appear imminent.

Nathaniel Willis, who came over in the fall of 1831, wrote an article about it for the *New York Mirror*, in which was this sentence: "In rough weather, it is as much as one person can do to keep his place at the table at all; and to guard the dishes, bottles and castors from a general slide in the direction of the lurch requires a dexterity and coolness reserved only for a sailor."[11]

With the invention of the steamboat, travel across the Atlantic became much smoother and quicker: two weeks. Passengers surely thought the Age of Aquarius was dawning. They could not have imagined ever making the trip, as we did from America to Switzerland, in a matter of hours.

We give lip service to "all we take for granted," meaning that we accept as a given—without thinking about it, without appreciating it, or feeling an ounce of gratitude—comforts inconceivable to our ancestors. Maybe our children's children will be able to wrinkle their noses like Jeannie and instantly materialize across the sea. They will not have lack of leg room or bad food to complain about. But unless human nature fundamentally changes, I am confident that they will think of something.

June 17

I just read another article about how being rich is overrated. "Secret Fears of the Super Rich" in the April, 2011, issue of *Atlantic Monthly* argues that there are significant downsides to being rich. Most of the responses to that article were unsympathetic. A common theme: "Poor little rich crybabies! I'd swap my money problems with theirs in a heartbeat."

The article covers three categories of wealth:

Inherited wealth. Heirs and their children may have little incentive to work or ever to postpone gratification.

Earned wealth. Even with tens of earned millions, many still feel financially insecure, thinking it would take on average at least one-quarter more than their current worth to have enough.

Sudden wealth. Sometimes called "accidental" or "lucky" wealth, these are people who won the lottery or bought a little Microsoft stock before it began to appreciate or sold their high-flying stock before the bubble burst.

All three categories of rich people are apt to question whether family and friends really love them or just love them for their money. Freud taught that love and work are the most important things in life. As F. Scott Fitzgerald illustrated in *The Great Gatsby* and Tom Wolfe in *The Bonfire of the Vanities*, riches threaten both.

Mark Twain described an untroubled family in *The Gilded Age* that had found a happy medium:

> . . . having only riches enough to be able to gratify reasonable desires, and yet
> make their gratifications always a novelty and a pleasure. Not so poor that they
> have to worry much about food and shelter, they are not so well off that they
> cannot thrill over a new outfit or a trip to the fair.[12]

Those who are neither filthy rich nor dirt poor may be best positioned to achieve happiness. I am grateful and content to be blessed with that kind of wealth.

June 18

He is an American original. When his wealth surpassed $100 billion, the world's youngest self-made billionaire had a new term invented for him—centibillionaire. Bill Gates is the co-founder of Microsoft. His fame and fortune came from developing software for the personal computer.

Now in his fifties, he and his wife Melinda are majoring in making a life instead of making a living. They operate the world's largest transparent charitable foundation. Their foundation focuses on improving health and education in the world's poorest places.

One key to understanding how one man could achieve so much and now be so committed to improving the human condition is to look at his father, Bill Gates Sr. For Father's Day my wife gave me a book that the senior Bill Gates wrote, *Showing Up for Life*. In the last chapter the senior Gates, an activist for humanitarian causes all his life, repeats his contention that "everything begins with showing up." On the book's last page he quotes words that inspired him from physician Rachel Naomi Remen's *Kitchen Table Wisdom*:

> We are all here for a single purpose: to grow in wisdom and learn to love. We can do this through losing as well as through winning, by having and by not having, by succeeding or by failing. All we need to do is to show up open-hearted for class. Fulfilling life's purpose may depend more on how we play than what we are dealt. You have to be present to win.[13]

The younger Bill Gates wrote the foreword to his father's book: "Dad, the next time somebody asks you if you're the real Bill Gates, I hope you say, 'Yes.' I hope you tell them that you're all the things the other one strives to be."

For a father or a mother, that is the supreme compliment.

June 19

I literally scratched my head and groaned after watching the first ten minutes of the evening news. Earlier in the day I had read national crime statistics showing that murder, rape, armed robbery, and other violent crimes in the United States nosedived over the past twenty years. The homicide rate fell a whopping 50 percent. Property crimes dropped 64 percent.

Back in 1994 the Gallup survey found that more than 50 percent of Americans said crime was the nation's biggest problem. In a recent Gallup survey, that number had plummeted to 2 percent.[14] Why is violent crime way down? Is it because more police are on the streets or more bad guys are in prison? We do not fully know. Historians a generation from now will be better positioned to analyze why.

Notwithstanding, why were the first four reports on the evening news about brutal, ghastly things local humans had done to each other? Is this region an aberration, with violence rampant only around here? Is violent crime so rare now that reporters have to seek it out? Do companies anxious about ratings and their own extinction seek out the grisliest stories they can find to keep viewers and beat the competition and save their jobs?

If an alien landed on Earth and watched the evening news, it surely would conclude that at this time at this dot on this planet the human race has evolved very slowly and loves torturing and killing other humans.

Does watching exclusive, breaking news of one more blood-splattered wall and wailing relatives do something deleterious, even irrevocable, to our psyches? Are we like our ancestors who packed coliseums to enjoy blood sports? Is media feeding us a distorted view of the human race?

Might our time be better spent gardening, taking a brisk walk, playing with a child, or writing a memoir?

June 20

You may have seen the piece on television about a man on a city street in Wales who threw ten thousand dollars of bills up in the air and shouted, "Free money!" A security camera revealed what happened next. Half a dozen stunned, excited people began scooping up as much money as they could. What got my attention was one person who only got a few bills because he was using only his left hand because his right hand was holding a cell phone that appeared to be permanently attached to his hand and right ear.

One can only imagine the ultimate kinds of matters being discussed on that cell phone call, concerns more valuable and urgent than picking up hundreds or thousands of free dollars. My guess is that the gravitas of the conversation was at best equal to: "What do you think of the price of eggs in Japan?" or "Have you heard the latest on George Clooney?"

The double-mindedness of the man in Wales reminded me of a program I watched years ago on educational television. Natives were demonstrating how to catch a monkey. They made a hole in a log and put some bait inside. A monkey came along and put its hand in the hole and grasped the bait. When it tried to get its closed fist out of the hole, it could not. Determined not to lose what it had, the monkey was easily captured by the natives. All the monkey had to do to go free was to let go.

It is dangerous in humans as in monkeys to be double-minded—to have divided loyalties. Being clear on who we are and what we value most can make a world of difference in a moment of crisis or, like the man on the street in Wales, in a moment of opportunity.

June 21

I would estimate that first-time visitors to the Grand Canyon spend an average of fifteen minutes on the rim. They have a look, snap a few pictures, make a "selfie" or two, hand their camera to a stranger who makes a photograph of them with the canyon in the background, let out one "Wow! It's really deep," buy some souvenirs, and leave. Their mission was to be able to go home and boast: "Yeah, we were there, and it was magnificent. Let me show you my pictures."

Some of us are, like them, dabblers. We are a Jack or Jill of all trades but master of none. We believe life is too complex, too many-splendored to specialize too much. We are the fox in the old Greek saying: "The fox knows many things but the hedgehog knows one big thing."

Some of us are more like the hedgehog. We want to simplify and focus. We might take a day or two riding a mule or hiking down the Grand Canyon to the Colorado River and back. We want to experience the place, not just glimpse it. We aspire, as Thoreau said, to "live deep and suck out all the marrow of life."

I want to be more of a hedgehog. There are a couple of areas where I want to major, take the plunge, go the distance. I collect "all things hope." I have pillows and candles, figurines and Christmas tree ornaments, greeting cards and stepping stones, shirts and rocks tattooed with that word. Last year one of our daughters-in-law gave me a bottle of Australian wine named Hope. This past Father's Day one of our sons gave me a sweatshirt he had ordered from a small college in Michigan emblazoned with four letters: *Hope.*

My hope is that someday when hard times come, some of those words and thoughts and symbols I have surrounded myself with for years will come into my mind's view and help get me through.

June 22

Is philanthropy breaking out all over? First there was the news that the world's richest man, Bill Gates, was stepping back from his Microsoft responsibilities to concentrate fully on spending his billions combating malaria, AIDS, and other global health problems. Then multi-billionaire Warren Buffett announced that he would donate most of his $44 billion fortune to Bill and Melinda Gates's foundation and leave only a few hundred thousand dollars to each of his children.

Rick Warren, minister of Saddleback Church, seventy thousand people strong, has announced what he did with the proceeds from his bestseller *The Purpose-Driven Life*. He decided not to take any more salary for his church work. Warren has repaid all the money the church paid him over the past quarter century. He explains, "I gave it all back because I didn't want anyone to think that I do what I do because of money."[15] He has set up a number of foundations to help the poor and the sick. He drives a twelve-year-old Ford, has lived in the same house for the last twenty-two years, and doesn't own a boat or a jet.

I know what cynics say about Gates, Buffett, and Warren: "If I had billions, I'd gladly give all but one billion away!" or make a snide remark about "guilt money" or a tax write-off. But the fact remains that they did it and they did not have to. They could easily be like most movie stars and CEOs who keep on grubbing for their next million or billion. Whether we are affluent or poor or somewhere in-between, more is hardly ever enough.

What would life on this planet be like if we, in our little circles of influence, with our little piggy banks, did what Gates and Buffett and Warren are doing on a world stage with their fortunes?

June 23

We do not have to look far to find heroes. We have no need to conjure up a distant warrior or athlete, movie star or world leader, to move and inspire us. Furthermore, if we knew them up close and personal they might lose some of their luster.

I like the way Edward Abbey, once referred to by Larry McMurtry as "the Thoreau of the American West," said it:

> Yes, there are plenty of heroes and heroines everywhere you look. They are not famous people. They are generally obscure and modest people doing useful work, keeping their families together, and taking an active part in the health of their communities, opposing what is evil (in one way or another) and defending what is good. Heroes do not want power over others. There are more heroic people in the public school system than there are in the world of politics, military, big business, the arts and the sciences combined.[16]

I spoke with a father who regularly takes his young daughters on nature walks. As they walk he points out flowers and leaves and wildlife, calling each by name. That daddy is giving his girls a gift that will keep on giving, a gift good for a lifetime, a gift that will outlive him, a gift superior to a trip to Disney World. Those girls will be telling their grandchildren someday about magic walks they enjoyed with their dad.

Keats was right: "A thing of beauty is a joy forever. / Its loveliness increases; it will never / pass into nothingness." The best news is this: you and I, ordinary people, have a chance to become some child's hero.

June 24

I am ugly. I am unattractive. I know that my skin is awful, my hair is greasy, and society simply does not permit women to weigh as much as I do. But, mind you, this is not the same as having low self-esteem. Because when I look in the mirror, I hate my *body*, not *myself*. I simply shake my head and think, "This isn't me. This mediocre sack of meat isn't me. I'm just renting it out, driving it around. It's a tool. It's a vehicle. I use it to take myself places that I need to go, and that's all there is to it. I decided a while back that everyone has his or her own strengths and weaknesses, and I would do well to focus on my strengths instead of my weaknesses. Even people who are bad at everything are less bad at some things than they are at others. I concluded that I was less bad at learning things than I was at looking pretty, so I would ultimately benefit far more from sharpening my skills than from trying in vain to undo the effects of losing the genetic lottery. It would be far more useful to promote the idea that people can contribute to the world in a variety of interesting and fulfilling ways besides making others salivate over their bodies.[17]

These words were written by Stephanie, an undergraduate at a prestigious university. One day she may discover a cure for cancer or pilot a rocket to Mars. She makes me question my values. I say that I value others' insides over their surface, but in reality I am way too external.

Those of the Judeo-Christian tradition believe this about the messiah: "He wasn't some handsome king. Nothing about the way he looked made him attractive to us"[18] Appearance may have been the sole reason some rejected him.

June 25

She was the last surviving child in a family of three boys and three girls. She lived well into her nineties. Her only child, a daughter, jotted down some memories and gave them to the preacher to make sure he got her life right at the funeral.

The daughter wanted the preacher to remember Nell as an excellent seamstress. One year in elementary school three dresses made by Nell were on stage the night of the talent show—one on her daughter and two on her daughter's classmates whose parents could not afford a new dress for them to wear.

Nell loved "anything green and growing—brown or half-dead for that matter." No leaf or twig or sprout was too small for her to rescue to a glass of water or a pot. And almost without fail that sickly sprig not only survived but flourished. Nell often greeted people with, "What do you have blooming?"

She was proud of her son-in-law. She told him: "I never had a son, but if I had, I would want him to be just like you."

Nell had worn out one Bible and not long before she died bought a new one. It contained several dried and pressed four-leaf clovers. She carried the largest one she ever found in her wallet. She was constantly on the lookout for another one, and could spot a four-leaf clover that other seekers would walk right past.

Two days before Nell died she got to hold her newborn great-granddaughter for the first and last time. The family interpreted that cradling as something like the passing of a torch to a new generation, a sign of hope in the midst of grief and loss as well as great-grandmother's blessing on the newborn.

The graveside service ended with everyone singing "God Be with You Till We Meet Again." The forty in attendance agreed that Nell's was a life well lived.

June 26

As we age we need to keep finding new heroes who are older than we are—old people who still dream, whose example calls to us in Tennyson's words: "Come, my friends, / 'Tis not too late to seek a newer world."

One of those heroes for me is Kozo Haraguchi of Japan. Early in 2005, in the rain, he set a new world speed record in the ninety-five to one hundred age category. He ran one hundred meters in 22.04 seconds.[19] What do I find hopeful about that? Haraguchi did not begin running competitively until age sixty-five. He thought at the time that it might help him stay healthy. He gave as the secret of his success taking an hour-long daily walk around his neighborhood.

Then there is Billy Graham. Over a sixty-year span he spoke to 210 million people in 185 countries. At age eighty-six, despite stultifying afternoon heat, he spoke flawlessly to a crowd of ninety thousand in New York City for twenty-three minutes. Suffering from prostate cancer, Parkinson's disease, and hydrocephalus, healing from a broken hip and pelvis, asked if this was the end of his career Graham replied: "I never say never."[20]

Closer to home there is my mother. For twenty-five years she led a brigade of volunteers who shampooed hair once a week at the local nursing home. She regularly listened to women residents—sometimes ten and twenty years her junior—complain about how they could not do much anymore because of their age. Healing from heart surgery and several cancer surgeries herself, she smiled and spoke an encouraging word to them. Then she finished rinsing and drying their hair.

One other day a week she delivered Meals On Wheels, often to people much younger than she.

"It's sad to grow old," Brigitte Bardot once reflected, "but nice to ripen."

June 27

The quality of some children's programing on educational television these days is, I think, superb. While caring for our two-year-old granddaughter so both her parents can work, I noticed her correctly using words like "imitate," "frail," and "obliterate." Come to find out she was picking up good vocabulary from programs like "WordGirl" and "Sid the Science Kid."

WordGirl is a ten-year-old caped crusader who bravely advocates a better vocabulary for children. The creators of the show, believing that we have been dumbing down children's programming too long, designed a show to instill in children a love for language. With at least some children it is working famously.

One day I came across an old Tom and Jerry cartoon on cable television's Cartoon channel. I invited my granddaughter to watch. At the end I asked her if she enjoyed watching Tom and Jerry, the cartoon characters I had enjoyed as a boy. With a frown and great drama she reported, "Oh, no. The big guy's always chasing the little guy and trying to harm him. It's way too violent."

"The soul is healed," Dostoevksy wrote, "by being with children."

My soul was touched, if not completely healed, by a story a mother shared with me this past week about her three-year-old daughter. The little girl for several weeks had enjoyed picking fresh berries from the raspberry bush in their backyard, stuffing them in her mouth as soon as she picked them. About a week after the bush quit bearing, the little girl joyfully discovered one last raspberry. She reached deep into the bush to harvest and eat it. That night her mother heard her end her bedtime prayers by thanking God for "the wast waspberry."

Do I hear an amen?

June 28

Three words currently perch atop my anathema list. Excellent words, they have been so overused in our day that their once excellent meaning has been lost. Whenever I hear one of them, those around me hear an involuntary sigh.

One is *awesome*. I once heard a minister use it in a sermon over a dozen times (I quit counting at twelve), referring to everything from God to a movie to a super-sized portion of fast food. When everything is awesome, nothing is awesome.

A second is *amazing*. I heard an interview with Katie Holmes when she used the word at least five times in less than two minutes to describe husband Tom Cruise. This was several weeks before she divorced him. When everything is amazing, nothing is amazing. And the speaker displays a limited vocabulary.

Triggering my loudest protest is *absolutely*. It has insidiously in our time replaced simple "yes." How many times have those caught lying peppered their lie liberally with "absolutely." It is as if the school of lying coached them: when telling a small lie, raise your voice; a big lie, wave your hands and pound on the table; a whopper, say several times with great feeling, "Absolutely!" Whatever happened to simple "yes" and simple "no"?

Superlatives should be saved for rare and extraordinary occasions, like observing the formation of a new galaxy thirteen billion light years ago courtesy of the Hubble telescope, or experiencing a red dawn from the southeastern rim of the Grand Canyon.

My favorite word now is *magnanimous*. From two Latin words, *magna* meaning great and *animus* meaning spirit, magnanimity is about having a big-hearted attitude that extends us beyond our little, narrow, selfish pursuits to care about other human beings and the planet. I will find it hard not to overuse a word that has such gorgeous meaning.

June 29

"Fred Snodgrass, 86, Dead. Ballplayer Muffed 1912 Fly." So proclaimed a headline in *The New York Times* on October 16, 1974, sixty-two years after Snodgrass, centerfielder for the New York Giants, dropped a routine fly ball. That drop resulted in the Boston Red Sox winning the World Series. One imperfect moment branded Fred Snodgrass for life and carved an ignominious niche for him in the annals of American sports history, a burden that he carried for six decades.

Last weekend while I was changing planes in the Baltimore airport, I picked up a discarded *Washington Post* newspaper and perused it. I was a little surprised when I got to the obituaries to see that under the name of each person "of note" was a title: "Self-Taught Fossil Hunter"; "Battled Castro with Bazookas and Sabotage"; "Bluegrass Pioneer Who Sang of Miners and the Downtrodden." And then the rest—little-known commoners who had died the day before—were also dignified with a descriptive title: "Teacher's Assistant"; "Volunteer Coordinator"; "Cub Scout Leader."

Robert Frost thought of his poem "Stopping by Woods on a Snowy Evening" as his "best bid for remembrance."[21] In our serious, more reflective moments, we may wonder what our best bid for remembrance—restricted to a sound bite, a caption of only a few words—might be. It might be an academic degree, the job we held the longest, the number of grandchildren we leave, a fondness for fly fishing or embroidery or the New York Jets.

My favorite epitaph I discovered on a New Mexico tombstone: "Ever she sought the best; ever she found it." That those who know us best might choose a magnanimous spirit over a job we worked or a title we earned to sum up our life would be the highest praise.

June 30

Who are these people and why have they traveled hundreds of miles—some of them thousands of miles—to spend a few days or a week at the beach? Some are obviously determined to wear home the ultimate tan. They keep their bodies slathered not with sunscreen but with suntan oil or baby oil. They meticulously turn themselves every twenty-three minutes. They like their bodies as they like their steaks—well done. Their well-done skin will enable their dermatologists and plastic surgeons to retire early and well.

For some, frivolity—mindless, carefree play—is the order of the day. If not on a boogie board, they are flying a kite or building a sand castle or throwing a Frisbee. For a day or a week they are kids again. Some are clearly there because they want to be good parents and make good memories for their children.

Some come primarily to ogle nearly-nude bodies, some to run twice a day in preparation for cross-country season, some for the fishing, some to collect shells, some to photograph sunrises and sunsets, some to eat fresh seafood at fine restaurants every evening, some to polish off best-selling, escapist novels. A few of the most ambitious may accomplish several or all of the above.

My favorite people to watch are the ones who set a folding chair in the surf, facing the ocean, where the waves lap around their feet and ankles. They just sit there, staring into infinity, oblivious and indifferent to what those around them may be doing. When the incoming tide rises to the seat of the chair, they just stand up, move the chair a few feet back from the ocean, and sit back down and stare some more.

I assume they are restoring their souls. Maybe they are thinking deep thoughts about the mystery of it all—why we are here, where we came from, where we are going. I like to think they are dreaming big, oceanic dreams. I hope they find what they came seeking. I am glad they can afford to do whatever it is they are doing. I hope all their finest dreams come true.

June Notes

1. *Encyclopedia Britannica*, "Charles A. Beard," no pages.
2. Bart, "College Students Unplugged," no pages.
3. Genesis 3:18.
4. Matthew 13: 24–30.
5. *Monty Python*, "Scene 4: Arthur Meets a Brave Knight," no pages.
6. Havel, "Orientation of the Heart," 82–83.
7. *Teach American History*, "Davy Crockett," no pages.
8. Tarr, *The Conversion*, 27–28.
9. McDougall, *Born to Run*, 128–129.
10. Tresniowski, "Not Again," no pages.
11. McCullough, *The Greater Journey*, 14–15.
12. Twain, *Gilded Age*, 197.
13. Remen, *Kitchen Table Wisdom*, 80.
14. *Gallup*, "Most Important Problem," no pages.
15. *Forbes*, Pastor Rick Warren," no pages.
16. Abbey, *Postcards from Ed*, 158.
17. *Quora Digest*, "What Does It Feel Like to Be Unattractive?" 145.
18. Isaiah 53: 2b
19. *BBC News*, "Japanese," no pages.
20. Benjamin, "Billy Graham," no pages.
21. Parini, *Robert Frost*, 212.

July

July 1

If you happen to be a patriot composing a speech or a prayer for an Independence Day rally, do I have a quotation for you:

> I now pray to God that he will bless in the years to come our work, our deeds, our foresight, our resolve; that the almighty may protect us from both arrogance and cowardly servility, that he may help us find the right way . . . and that he may always give us courage to do the right thing and never to falter or weaken before any power or any danger.[1]

The speaker did everything but end, as all recent presidents have, with "and God bless America."

The speaker was not George Washington or Abraham Lincoln. The year was 1938. The speech ended with: "Long live Germany and the German people!" The speaker was Adolf Hitler. At the time of the speech Nazis were issuing belt buckles to soldiers engraved with three words: *Gott Mit Uns*. God is with us.

We should be suspicious when leaders slather their speeches and promote their policies with manipulative God-of-course-is-on-our-side rhetoric. That popular bumper sticker from the Vietnam War era, "My Country Right or Wrong," originated from Republican senator Carl Schurz of Wisconsin. But the bumper sticker truncated the quotation and impugned Schurz's meaning. His complete sentence was: "Our country right or wrong; when right to be kept right, when wrong to put it right."[2]

Almost everyone I know is a patriot. Patriot simply means "lover of country." I will lift up a grateful heart on July 4 and proudly sing of love for my country. But when our country starts down the wrong path, whether the leader is George Bush or Barack Obama or the next White House occupant, our patriotic and moral duty is to join the loyal opposition.

July 2

When our country was born, the constitution counted slaves as three-fifths of a human. When my mother was born, women only one year earlier had been given the right to vote. When I was born, lynching was acceptable among many "respectable" Americans. White church-going ladies and gentlemen even posed for photographs in front of black men being burned or hanged.

We should never think that the present condition of things is going to stay the same. As historian Howard Zinn in his chapter "The Optimism of Uncertainty" writes:

> There is a tendency to think that what we see in the present moment will continue. We forget how often in this century we have been astonished by the sudden crumbling of institutions, by extraordinary changes in people's thoughts, by unexpected eruptions of rebellion against tyrannies, by the quick collapse of systems of power that seem invincible. The struggle for justice should never be abandoned because of the apparent overwhelming power of those who have the guns and the money and who seem invincible in their determination to hold on to it. That apparent power has, again and again, proved vulnerable to human qualities less measurable than bombs and dollars: moral fervor, determination, unity, organization, sacrifice, ingenuity, courage, patience.[3]

Lest we forget, at the beginning of the eighteenth century no one in her right mind would have thought than the colonies in the new world could chase the supposedly invincible British empire, tail between its legs, home.

Anthropologist Margaret Mead said as much: "Never doubt that a small group of thoughtful, committed, citizens can change the world. Indeed, it is the only thing that ever has."

July 3

Rarely, maybe three or four times a year, someone comes to our front door and rings the bell. Usually it is a child raising funds for a school project, or Scouts selling candy, fruit, or magazines.

This time I opened the door to a stranger and a sheepish-looking little boy by his side who was holding a plastic bag with something in it. The man extended his hand and politely introduced himself. I awaited the sales pitch.

He announced, "My son has something to say to you." The boy, about seven years old, softly apologized for watching an older boy steal tomatoes from my garden. His father commented, "I've taught him that when you see someone else do wrong and you do nothing about it, you are as guilty as he." Then the boy handed me two little tomatoes, the stolen property he confessed to receiving from the other boy. I shook the little thief's hand, took the bag of two tomatoes, and told him I accepted his apology. I moralized about it being a very important day in his life, a precious learning experience that he will remember when he is as old as I.

The next morning the doorbell rang again. It was the older thief himself with his mother. When she said that her son was there to apologize, he gave a knee-jerk protest: "But I wasn't the only one!" The boy was holding a bowl of crushed ripe and green tomatoes that he had stomped or beaten into pulp. We went through the "I apologize" and "I accept your apology" routine and I received his mashed tomatoes.

After I closed the door, I smiled. Something timeless had just transpired. Boys were caught being mischievous boys, testing the boundaries. Parents were caught teaching their children right from wrong. Is this not the stuff of which morality and civility are made?

July 4

It is staggering to think that of the millions of experiences we have in our early years, as adults most of us can recall only a precious few. My children tend to remember things like the time their dad failed to have the luggage carrier secured on top of the station wagon and it flew off during morning rush hour on a busy interstate in Washington, DC, destroying some of their clothes and toys and creating a traffic jam and much horn-honking. Many good things happened on that vacation, but that may be the one thing they remember and possibly the only specific thing they can recall from that entire year.

A formative event I remember well happened when I was in fourth grade. It is the only event I can remember from fourth grade. The teacher asked me to step outside the classroom (uh oh!). There she told me that the next day a poor boy named Wallace would be joining our class and that he would not have any friends or any change of clothing and would smell bad. The desks in that classroom were two-seaters. You shared your desk all day, every day, with another student of the same gender. My teacher told me that she wanted me to share my desk for the rest of the year with Wallace. She explained that she chose me because she knew I had been reared right and she thought I would be up to the challenge. I remember not feeling very lucky or grateful to be the chosen one, but at some deeper level I think it helped solidify in me a belief that part of my being a good person and part of being my parents' son was to treat poor people right.

When you think of "the poor," I hope you will picture a little fourth-grader named Wallace. I hope you will think of people like him, who through no fault of their own are dependent on people like you and me—Americans pledged to back "freedom and justice for all"—to treat them right.

Happy Independence Day!

July 5

At age sixteen, Elizabeth Jane Cochran felt so demeaned when she read a column in the newspaper titled "What Girls Are Good For" that she wrote an aggressive reply. The editor was so impressed with her arguments that he offered her a job.

Instead of writing articles about cooking or fashion, Cochran wrote about the poor, especially the way women were being exploited in sweatshops. Demoted for those reports when companies pulled their advertising, she talked her way into a job with Joseph Pulitzer's *New York World* where she was given an assignment to cover the Women's Lunatic Asylum on Blackwell's Island. Going undercover, posing as a mentally ill person, she got herself committed to the asylum. Following discharge, Cochran wrote an exposé. It became a book titled *Ten Days in a Madhouse*. A grand jury investigated and recommended all the changes Elizabeth Jane Cochran, innovator in investigative reporting, had proposed.[4]

When she proposed journaling a record-setting, round-the-world trip to her editor, he told her that only a man should attempt it, since a woman would have to carry too much luggage. He changed his mind after Cochran designed a dress that could withstand three months of travel and promised to carry everything else she needed in a purse sixteen inches long and seven inches high.[5] She set the world record, traveling 24,900 miles in seventy two days and instantly became an American folk hero. One newspaper deemed her feat "a tribute to American pluck, American womanhood and American perseverance."[6]

Elizabeth Jane Cochran later became America's first female war correspondent, writing from the front lines of World War I for almost five years. As a teenager, she had adopted the pen name Nellie Bly. All Nellie Bly's accomplishments came years before American women were even allowed to vote.

Is this a great country or what?

July 6

Our age obsesses over *the bottom line*, by which usually is meant a number of dollars. But many with impressive bottom lines and huge portfolios live lives of quiet desperation. Balance sheets and annual reports, as demonstrated by Enron and WorldCom and Lehman Brothers, can lie. Books can be cooked and statistics can be massaged to look grand and, in the day of reckoning, implode.

There is a bottom line bigger than the financial one. Dag Hammerskjold, legendary Secretary General of the United Nations who died in a plane crash, pointed to it in an entry he made on Pentecost, 1961, in his journal:

> I don't know who—or what—put the question. I don't know when it was put. I don't even remember answering. But at some moment I did answer 'Yes' to someone or something, and from that hour I was certain that existence is meaningful and therefore, in self surrender, my life had a goal.[7]

That other bottom line which he addresses is how we each embrace, or refrain from embracing, the dance of life.

Tab Hunter, sex symbol of the late 1950s, ends his autobiography with this paragraph: "If you happen to spot me, in the middle of some seemingly insignificant place, lifting my face to the sky and mumbling something—don't worry. I'm only saying 'Thank You.' That's what life is all about."[8]

Maybe the ultimate bottom line is whether at the end of this day's hullabaloo or this life's hullabaloo we can lift a grateful face to the sky and say with Hunter and Hammerskjold, "Yes! Thank you!"

July 7

One of our family traditions is a vacation on the beach in South Carolina the second week in July.

While the rest of my family is out in the sun having fun (and damaging their skin), I am in the condominium reading books or babysitting. Having had many sun-caused cancers on my Irish skin, I cannot afford any more exposure between 8:00 a.m. and 6:00 p.m. So every day I hit the beach at 6:20 a.m. with my camera and tripod, expecting a glorious sunrise at 6:32 a.m. Two out of three mornings I am not disappointed, and I go a little crazy trying to make an Ansel Adams masterpiece.

I have loved the dawn ever since I saw the movie *Shane* as a little boy. I remember most the final scene when Shane rode off, not into the sunset, but into the sunrise. Sunsets on the other hand bear a certain melancholy for me, as in Tennyson's "Crossing the Bar": "Sunset and evening star, / and one clear call for me! / and may there be no moaning at the bar, / when I put out to sea." Sunsets for me are too much about endings, too much like grief and loss and death.

Two of the most inspirational personalities of the twentieth century were Franklin Roosevelt and Ronald Reagan. Nothing was more characteristic of FDR than his optimism; nothing cartoonists used more than his smile; no word applied more by journalists than "sunny." The Reagan slogan, "I believe it's morning in America," revealed his basic disposition and set a tone for his eight years.

Whenever someone comes out with a list of the most beautiful words in the English language, "dawn" almost always comes out near the top. I know the reason why.

July 8

Love hurts. I know it, and if you are a few years old, I suspect you know it. French philosopher Montaigne wrote it: "Love is not love without arrows and fire." Divorcees know it. The eleven-year-old spurned by her heartthrob knows it. Bereaved parents most of all know it. All of us who have given our heart to someone know this: Arrows pierce. Fire burns. Love hurts.

Maybe the best we can say in defense of loving is that it beats the alternative. C. S. Lewis said it well in *The Four Loves*:

> To love at all is to be vulnerable. Love anything, and your heart will certainly be wrung and possibly be broken. If you want to make sure of keeping it intact, you must give your heart to no one, not even to an animal. Wrap it carefully round with hobbies and little luxuries; avoid all entanglements; lock it up safe in the casket or coffin of your selfishness. But in that casket — safe, dark, motionless, airless — it will change. It will not be broken; it will become unbreakable, impenetrable, irredeemable. The alternative to tragedy, or at least to the risk of tragedy, is damnation. The only place outside of Heaven where you can be perfectly safe from all the dangers and perturbations of love is Hell.[9]

I hope you can find the courage within yourself to give your heart to someone one more time. Take a risk. Remove your mask. Like the lobster, shed your shell and become vulnerable again.

The heart you save may be your own.

July 9

Jasmine Roberts, twelve years old, won her Science Fair with a project that proved that the toilet water in some restaurants is cleaner than the ice they serve in their cold drinks. When asked on *Good Morning America* where she got the idea to conduct the weird experiment, Jasmine replied: "People always expect the expected; I wanted to expect the unexpected."[10]

The problem that comes with age for many of us is that we outgrow the wonder and curiosity of childhood. Something like *imaginationsclerosis*, hardening of the imagination, sets in. Our eyes no longer dance with hope. We settle for what Jasmine called "the expected."

Who would ever have dreamed that a little girl growing up in Stamps, Arkansas, back in the Depression, so traumatized by sexual abuse at age eight that she spoke not a word for over a year, would grow up to be one of our great writers? Maya Angelou was only the second poet ever invited to compose and deliver a poem at a presidential inauguration.

Who would ever have dreamed when Tom Dempsey was born with half of one of his arms missing and half of one foot missing that he would grow up to kick a sixty-three-yard field goal in 1970 for the New Orleans Saints, the longest at that time in National Football League history, and do it with his half-foot?

Vachel Lindsay in "The Leaden-Eyed," his most famous poem, wrote: "Let not young souls be smothered out before / They do quaint deeds and fully flaunt their pride. / It is the world's one crime its babes grow dull / Its poor are ox-like, limp and leaden-eyed. / Not that they starve; but starve so dreamlessly, / Not that they sow, but that they seldom reap, / Not that they serve, but have no gods to serve, / Not that they die, but that they die like sheep."

Oh to have the eyes of a child again—eyes like Jasmine's that are not leaden, eyes that still have a sparkle, eyes that still expect the unexpected.

July 10

Woody Allen imagined himself saying to an audience of college graduates: "More than any other time in history, mankind faces a crossroads. One path leads to despair and utter hopelessness, the other to total extinction. Let us pray we have the wisdom to choose correctly."[11]

Looking down the road, like Woody Allen, sometimes we can see no good possibilities.

It is relatively easy to make educated guesses and go with probabilities. But occasionally a far-out possibility trumps the odds. How many football fans expected before the 2014 Super Bowl game began that the iconic Peyton Manning and the Denver Broncos would be routed by the Seattle Seahawks by thirty-five points, 43–8? Who looked at Teddy Roosevelt the child—asthmatic, nearsighted, tutored at home because he was too sickly to attend school—and entertained for one minute the thought that he would grow up to be a war hero, a president, and entitle his most famous speech "The Strenuous Life"?

First-century Roman engineer Sextus Julius Frontinus, when the empire was at its peak, wrote: "Inventions have reached their limit, and I see no hope for further progress." In 1899, President McKinley was advised to close the U.S. Patent Office because, according to the commissioner of patents Charles Duell: "Everything that can be invented has been invented." Thomas Watson, chairman of IBM, said in 1943: "I think there is a world market for maybe five computers."

Remember Sextus Julius Frontinus or Tom Watson or Teddy Roosevelt or the Seattle Seahawks the next time you think the future is a lock.

July 11

Jesse Stuart grew up in a hollow in Greenup, Kentucky, so deep in the woods that according to Stuart: "The hoot owls holler in the daytime. They mistake daytime for night." Stuart's father could hardly write his own name. But by the time he retired, Jesse Stuart had written thirty-two books and four hundred short stories. Kentucky named him poet laureate in 1954.

Jesse Stuart made it out of W Hollow to Vanderbilt University with little more than the clothes on his back. Hunger was an ever-present companion. He got by on eleven meals a week—one on Sunday, two on Monday, one on Tuesday, two on Wednesday and Thursday, one on Friday, and two on Saturday. Ever-hungry, the large-framed man filled up on water before class so his stomach would not growl and make the rich girls sitting around him giggle.

Early in life Jesse Stuart determined the role that physical hunger would play in his life. In his autobiography *To Teach, To Love* he wrote:

> I have known hunger on a Kentucky hill plowing. I always felt sorry for the mule. He pulled the plow, and I only guided it through the roots and drove the mule. He knew as much about plowing as I did. I didn't have to drive him. A mule knows right where to step. But he can't tell his driver whether he is hungry or not. And food, for the mule, is all he lives for. Give it to him. I don't live for food alone. I live on food and dreams. Give me mostly dreams. Cramp your guts when they growl. Push them against your backbone with your hand flat against your stomach. But don't cramp your dreams.[12]

Some of us out of necessity live our lives on the mule level. We must concentrate almost all our energies on chasing basic things—house, car, food, clothes—while our spirits go hungry.

Jesse had it right. We live on dreams as well as food. Chase dreams. We have to eat, but we miss something huge if we deny our spirit's hunger. As Jesus said, "No one can live only on food."[13]

July 12

Some have humongous emotional trauma to overcome. While some of us struggle to forgive an insult or a slight, others are dealing with rape or murder or terminal illness.

In 1994, a twenty-two-year-old Rwandan native named Ilibagiza was home from university spending Easter with her family. While she was home, Rwanda's Hutu president was killed when his plane was shot down. That incident sparked a three-month slaughter of almost one million ethnic Tutsis. Most Americans never heard about the genocide because at the time O.J. Simpson was dominating our television news.

Ilibagiza's father arranged for her to hide in the home of a local minister, an ethnic Hutu. She hid in his tiny bathroom, seven feet long and three feet wide, with seven other starving women. They hardly moved, out of fear of being discovered, and wore the same clothes for ninety-one terrifying days. Ilibagiza's father was shot and killed by soldiers soon after she went into hiding. Her mother Rose was killed with machetes. Her two brothers and four grandparents also were killed.[14]

Eventually Ilibagiza went to work in New York City for the United Nations. She spoke to groups about understanding and forgiveness. "I don't want just to hate somebody," this courageous young woman whose entire family was mercilessly slaughtered tells her audiences. "I felt bad enough that I don't want just to hold this kind of bad feeling in my heart for long, if I can help it."[15]

The Buddha taught that holding on to hatred and hostility is like spitting at heaven—much of the spittle falls back in the spitter's face. Most of us have much less to forgive than Ilibagiza. May we find the grace to stop spitting into the wind and, like Ilibagiza, find something more constructive to do with our pain than spit.

July 13

For half a day I toiled on an organic vegetable farm. "I have four hours to volunteer," I said, "What do you want me to do?" The farmer assigned me four rows of young corn to weed.

Organic vegetable farmers, to produce food free of chemicals and to respect the environment, use no pesticides or artificial fertilizers. Because my assigned corn rows had not been mulched, the weeds were thriving. There were two or more of them for every corn stalk. For over three hours I inched along on my hands and knees, engaging one weed at a time in hand-to-weed combat. When I reached the end of one row I made a 180-degree turn, moved over one row, and started down that one. The temperature was above ninety.

Homer's story of Sisyphus leapt into my hot brain. Sisyphus was sentenced by the gods to roll a boulder up a hill. Every time he almost reached the top, it rolled back down. Sisyphus would walk to the bottom of the hill and push it to the top again. It rolled back down again. That cycle was his endless fate. I found myself feeling for all those people who do repetitive jobs day after day—altering hemlines, changing tires, stocking shelves, hoeing weeds, filling prescriptions, filling potholes, filling teeth. How do they cope with the boredom? How do they keep their spirits alive and well?

Several things (beyond knowing that after four hours I would finish and return to my air-conditioned life) helped my attitude. A cool breeze occasionally refreshed me. A pair of red-wing blackbirds dazzled me with their beauty and cheery oak-a-lee songs. I imagined the beneficiaries of my weeding in just a few weeks sinking their teeth into the sweet corn, wiping their mouths, and feeling delight.

And I discovered that the repetitive nature of the task freed the right side of my brain to compose a newspaper column.

July 14

In Louisville, Kentucky, two home invaders forced a mother and her fourteen-year-old daughter and twelve-year-old son into a bedroom and wrapped them in duct tape. An eight-year-old had hidden herself in the kitchen pantry. She calmly dialed 911 and whispered that two robbers with guns were in her house. When police arrived she quietly ran from the pantry to the front door and let them in. The robbers—two convicted felons—were arrested. No one was injured. Detectives praised the little girl's presence of mind and credited her with saving the lives of her family. No adult could have done better; many adults would have done far worse.

In Philadelphia, Pennsylvania, Steve Montforto took his wife Kathleen, three-year-old Emily and fifteen-month-old Cecilia to a Phillies ballgame. In all of his years holding season tickets, Steve had never caught a foul ball. This Tuesday would be different, fulfilling one of his lifelong dreams. Bursting with manly, fatherly pride, he presented the ball to Emily. Emily, three years old, dressed in a pink Phillies hat and shirt, spontaneously tossed the ball toward the field.

When gasps and groans went up from the crowd, Emily's dad—fearing his daughter might think she had done something bad—gave her a bear hug and a big smile. Mother Kathleen's main concern was that the ball Emily innocently and playfully threw away might have hit someone in the lower deck.[16]

If these are not two snapshots of humanity at its best—an eight-year-old whose grace under fire saved her family, and the Montforto family being warm and joyful, spontaneous and real—what is?

July 15

From early childhood most of us are taught to stay in line. Some elementary schools have a red line that children have to walk on from the classroom to the cafeteria and back.

There are times as we mature when staying in line translates into "stuck in a rut" and gets us in trouble or closes off desirable possibilities. Consider the caterpillar. French naturalist Jean Henri Fabre conducted an experiment with processionary caterpillars. They travel in long lines, one behind another. He took a flowerpot and placed a number of the caterpillars in single file around the rim, each caterpillar's head close to the caterpillar in front of it, making a circle without beginning or end.

Then Fabre placed the caterpillars' favorite food six inches away from the circle and very visible. But each caterpillar followed the caterpillar in front of it, apparently believing that it was heading for food. Round and round they went for seven days, until they all died from exhaustion and starvation.[17] Their favorite food was close by but they missed it because it was off the beaten path. Cause of death on the death certificate could read: "Stuck in a vicious circle."

A part of us hates to protrude, so we toe the line. The original meaning of "toe the line" referred to people in a sporting event positioning their toes on a marked line to start a race. It came to mean to conform. Last century a whole nation including most of its churches uncritically toed the line and bought what leaders of The Third Reich were selling.

Occasionally as adults we need to step out of line and see where the line is going. Or would you rather be a caterpillar?

July 16

I am an inveterate berry picker, having logged hundreds of hours as a little boy gathering wild blackberries and huckleberries, getting eaten up by chiggers, hearing snakes rustling in the brush (once I dropped an almost full bucket and ran for my life), getting sunburned, getting thirsty, getting lost, getting punctured by thorns, and going home with clothes and hands stained a purplish-black, lugging two two-gallon buckets overflowing with berries. Mother's hot blackberry cobbler was my reward. These days I grow red and black raspberries and thornless blackberries in my backyard. Now I wear rubber boots when I pick, still hearing a slick serpent hissing: "Don't tread on me."

I think I learned a life-lesson or two from picking wild berries as a child.

Take a bigger bucket. It is disheartening to come upon a berry patch laden with fat berries that you could pick by the fistful but have no place left to put them. As a novice berry picker, one day I stuffed all four pockets of my jeans with berries. Mother was not pleased. What we seek in life often affects what and how much we find. So, think bigger. Take a bigger bucket than you think you'll need.

Two, stand still until you have harvested every berry within reach. One time a grownup took me berry picking. While I was spotting a pretty berry here and a giant berry there, enthusiastically flitting from here to there gathering treasures, he stood still and plucked every ripe berry within reach. His bucket was full before mine was half full. The man was my father. Some traverse land and sea looking for something more, and ultimately, like Ulysses, find that what they were seeking was all that time waiting back home.

That is some of the gospel according to one of the berry pickers.

July 17

"We wondered if something had happened to you." That was the initially-unsettling greeting from a stranger who approached me on the beach. He explained that he had watched me photographing the sunrise at 6:30 a.m. every morning the second week of July for the last twelve years. When he missed seeing me he remarked to his wife: "I wonder if something's happened to him?" You never know who may be watching.

And is that not an interesting euphemism we use for something catastrophic, like a death or a serious accident or illness? We say to loved ones before a trip: "If something happens, all my important papers are in the shoe box under the bed." "Something happens" is easier to say than the dreaded "d" word—that inevitable date with destiny we would rather deny.

I had another interesting conversation with a retired kindergarten teacher on the beach one morning. Walking away from the beach, we exchanged some comments on different kinds of sunrises. She had been trying to capture the beauty of the sunrise with her iPad and asked for some helpful photography tips. After offering some of my amateurish thoughts, I went on to describe my favorite sunrises: "I hope each morning to see a perfect sphere of orange breaking the horizon, with reddening and pinkening clouds wide around and high above it, with maybe the silhouette of a child holding a sand bucket in the foreground."

The next morning when I saw her again she asked, "And how would you rate the sunrise we had today?" I, the wannabe expert on photographing dawn, pontificated: "Oh, on a ten-point scale I would give it a six or a seven." With a knowing smile, the old woman offered me a sermon I deserved: "I give every one of them a perfect ten."

July 18

One thing troubling me these days is how public schools are so fixated on test scores. Teachers feel pressured to "teach to the test"; principals' job security is tied to rising or falling scores at their schools; state and federal funds follow the numbers. Is testing the goal of it all, the ultimate judge of the quality of an education? Is anything more important?

Dr. Sheldon Berman, former superintendent of Jefferson County (Kentucky) Public Schools, wrote something that I found substantial and visionary:

> With the national educational agenda focused on testing and accountability, schools and districts have begun to define themselves and their mission in terms of improving test scores . . . We often forget that public education serves a larger purpose. That larger mission is to help young people develop the convictions and skills to shape a safe, sustainable, and just world.[18]

I think the same holds true for religious education. Is knowing religious information, memorizing Bible verses, and making a perfect score on a test over Bible content the goal?

Or is that a means to some other end, like shaping a more "safe, sustainable and just world?"

Late in life, humorist Sam Levinson wrote: "To my grandchildren and to children everywhere. I am leaving you everything I have had in my lifetime: a good family, respect for learning, compassion for my fellowman, and some four-letter words for all occasions—help, give, care, feel, love."[19]

More important than getting the answer right on a test is gaining more understanding and wisdom. More important than being a "straight A" student is developing informed convictions, convictions that will help us together build a safer, more sustainable, more merciful, more just and peaceful world.

July 19

I never took physics, but I do remember reading somewhere about Sir Isaac Newton's third law of motion that for every action in nature there is an equal and opposite reaction. For example, the good luck of the early bird that gets the worm means that the early worm had bad luck. Or take lottery winners. Many have said years later that the day they won the lottery was the worst day of their lives because the win translated into a trail of lost families, lost friendships, and lost lives.

Take the escalation of gas prices. As infuriating as it is for most all of us when the prices soar, it undeniably brings some positive reactions. As people drive less, highway fatalities may drop. Neighborhood stores get more customers. Some consumers apparently think: "How intelligent is it for me to hop in my car and burn $10 of gas to find a deal halfway across town instead of going to my neighborhood store and paying a little more?"

Neighbors interact with neighbors more, some for the first time. Ride-sharing goes up. More people walk. People buy smaller or hybrid or electric cars, resulting in fewer total emissions and a cleaner environment. Could the high price of driving affect therapeutically the country's obesity epidemic?

Library usage probably goes up. With almost everything else going up in cost, reading books, thanks to our country's public library system, does not go up—it is still free. In those books people may come across wisdom like the sentence from Sir Francis Bacon: "Prosperity best discovers vice; adversity best discovers virtue." Some of those old British sirs like Newton and Bacon knew a thing or two about turning a phrase.

July 20

A retired scientist invited me to a butterfly count. The expedition wound through a waist-high-with-grass, teeming-with-life meadow. The leader was a retired biology professor who has been organizing the region's butterfly census for over twenty years.

I photographed stunningly gorgeous *lepidoptera* that I would not have seen had we not been intentionally looking for them. What I enjoyed most was seeing retirees thrill to spot and count and call the creatures by name: "I've got two cabbage whites over here!" "Here's our first junonia coenia!" I thought of a Joseph Campbell quotation: "If you follow your bliss, you put yourself on a kind of track that has been there the whole while, waiting for you."

Retirees, like butterflies, are free to follow their bliss. I love what attorney Clarence Darrow, at age sixty-one, said about retirement:

> I have always yearned for peace, but have lived a life of war. I do not know why, excepting that it is the law of my being. I have lived a life in the front trenches, looking for trouble. The front trenches are disagreeable; they are hard; they are dangerous; it is only a question of days or hours when you are killed or wounded and taken back. But it is exciting. You are living; and if now and then you go back to rest, you think of your comrades in the fight; you hear the drum; you hear the cannon's voice; you hear the bugle call; and you rush back to the trenches and to the thick of the fight. There, for a short time, you really live. It is hard, but it is life. Activity is life. Peace is death; and there is no complete peace excepting death.[20]

Joseph Campbell called it bliss. Emily Dickinson called it glee. Longinus, the Greek rhetorician, called it the sublime. Whether you prefer to call it bliss, glee, or the sublime, I hope that, retired or employed, you succeed at staying focused on it.

July 21

Some go to the beach to show or to see skin. I went to the beach last week determined to do some serious skin-watching. I concentrated on flesh like mine—the paleface variety.

One man sported a splotchy red-and-white chest. I asked him about it and laughingly he explained that the day before in his hurry to hit the beach he had been careless in his application of sunscreen. Some on the beach were lobster pink. I know from personal experience that even though they might have absorbed a six-month supply of vitamin D, they also might live to regret it that night as they try to sleep, or thirty years later when they develop a melanoma.

Some people have to stay out of the sun the rest of a vacation because they get so blistered the first day of vacation. I had to do that once on a vacation as a child. Two young men, brothers, were as white at the end of the week as at the beginning. Daily they had slathered their skin with forty-five-proof sunscreen. So what if they went home with their skin not looking like leather?

Then there was the freak on the beach. His only skin showing was the lower half of his face that was caked with sunscreen. The upper half was hidden by a wide-brimmed, cream-colored hemp hat and sunglasses. His arms were covered with a green shirt; his legs with jeans. He turned as many heads as those in teeny bikinis. He looked as out of place on a beach as a girl in a bikini in Northern Siberia.

I was that freak on the beach. When I was young, I soaked up the rays, believing sunshine was good for you and that a suntan made you look good. Sunscreen had not been invented yet. I have lost count of how many squamous and basal cell carcinomas I have had burned off or cut out of my face, chest, shoulders, arms, and back. Only my dermatologist knows. Paleface, take this tip from a world-class authority: Love the skin you are in. It is the only one you are going to have. The life you save may be your own.

July 22

Last century's mythology authority, Joseph Campbell, plaintively pointed out that modern American culture lacks heroes. We have swapped heroes for celebrities.

The difference? Real-life heroes like Gandhi, Schweitzer, Malala, and Mandela, or fictional ones like Luke Skywalker and Princess Leia, rise above selfishness to champion causes bigger than self. They behave with courage, sacrifice, and nobility of spirit, like the firefighters who died in the World Trade Center on 9/11 trying to save lives. Celebrities, by contrast, celebrate self. Whether an actor, politician, rock star, or preacher, for the celebrity it is all about self—my career, my image, my popularity, my pleasure, my fans, my net worth. It is all about marketing me, re-inventing me, doing whatever it takes to grow my fan base.[21]

A fire trapped a mother and her six children in their third-floor Indianapolis apartment. Neighbors and strangers spontaneously gathered below the apartment window, formed a tight circle, extended their arms toward the center of the circle, and begged the mother to drop her children. All six children were caught and taken to safety. The last child, a teenager, jumped, knocking the rescuers down, but no one was injured. "We were his cushions," one of the catchers told the *Indianapolis Star*. Firefighters arrived soon and got the mother down by ladder.

That image—of ordinary people forming a human cushion, putting their lives in jeopardy to rescue the perishing—is what Campbell meant by heroism. Only one of the rescuers' names made the newspaper. The story was buried in section C with no pictures. The rescuers went home or on to work that morning with smoked clothing and hair and a bruise or two, but no standing ovation. I hope they took with them the satisfaction that they had suspended their looking out for self long enough to give perishable children a safe place to jump and a second chance to live.

July 23

A friend e-mailed me a photo album titled "The Day that Albert Einstein Feared May Have Finally Arrived." What followed was a scroll of eight photographs: students seated around a table drinking coffee; two fans standing at a Michigan-Michigan State ballgame; four teenagers spending a day at the beach; several friends having dinner at a restaurant; a couple on a dinner date; two young women conversing with friends; three visitors at a museum; four friends in a moving convertible.

All those individuals had one thing in common: each was text messaging. Not one was looking at real, live human beings close enough to reach out and touch. The slide show ends with a quote from Einstein: "I fear the day that technology will surpass our human interaction. The world will have a generation of idiots."

Einstein used the word "idiot" not in reference to intelligence. "Idiot" comes from the Greek *idios* which means "one's own self." The Greeks applied it to the individual who, instead of participating in democracy and being concerned about the good of the city as a whole, was looking out only for self. Today the idiots, as defined by the old Greeks, are those who never get beyond their own selfish interests to be concerned about the public good.

Henri Nouwen ruminated:

> When we honestly ask ourselves which person in our lives means the most to us, we often find that it is those who, instead of giving advice, solutions, or cures, have chosen rather to share our pain and touch our wounds with a warm and tender hand. The friend who can be silent with us in a moment of despair or confusion, who can stay with us in an hour of grief and bereavement, who can tolerate not knowing, not curing, not healing and face with us the reality of our powerlessness, that is a friend who cares.[22]

The danger, as Einstein said, is that high-tech overwhelms and replaces high-touch. Do a thousand text messages—acquaintances a mile wide and an inch deep—equal one warm and caring touch?

July 24

My church serves me well at this stage of life by providing inspirational role models for aging. One man who died at age 101 had poor health the last year of his life, but his mind was sharp until the end. For four years before he died he went grocery shopping with me the first Wednesday of every month. I would love to reach the century mark if I could have his physical and mental stamina. Another man at ninety-eight has not lost a step mentally or physically. He centers much of his life now on caring for his beloved mate-for-life. Both men have become living saints in my life. I have no earthly idea what they were like fifty or seventy-five years ago, but for decades I have not known kinder, wiser, more admirable men.

Now, sadly, I have added another, a close personal friend only a few years older than I. His physical health has plummeted the last few months. Three things come to mind as I try to unpack why he, through his suffering, has become a paragon of virtue for me.

He does not dabble in denial. He faces his situation squarely. He truthfully tells when you ask whether he is feeling bad, sad, glad, or afraid.

He does everything the rehabilitation team asks of him, giving his all to enhance opportunities for his body to rebound.

He seeks no sympathy. After one big setback he calmly said: "Plan B didn't work, so now it's on to Plan C, and D, E, and F." He apologizes to no one for his appearance or his new limitations and dependency.

What is great about the *living* saints is that they model for us up close and personal how it is possible to behave nobly in the crucible of extreme suffering.

July 25

I read about an unemployed financial manager who wrote a suicidal note about his financial troubles and then killed his wife and four children and himself. We know that an economic downturn in a country will bring out the worst in some people. Crime, suicides, and shooting sprees may go up. "Adversity builds character," the coach tells his team after they lose the big game. The advice comes off so cold, hard, and uncaring—not very helpful when you are going home to lick wounds.

Years after Kentucky's poet laureate, Jesse Stuart, suffered a coronary, he came to see it as a blessing in disguise for his overcrowded life. The journal he kept for a year after that almost-fatal event Stuart turned into a book that he titled *The Year of My Rebirth*. Demosthenes as a child was teased by the other kids for stuttering. He cured his stuttering by speaking with pebbles in his mouth. He cured his shortness of breath by reciting poetry while running uphill. He made our history books as one of humankind's most polished and persuasive speakers.

An inebriated man was down on all fours under a streetlight. A policeman asked him what he was doing. The drunk said he had lost his keys. The policeman joined the search. After a while, finding no keys, the policeman asked him if he was sure he had lost them in that spot. "No," the drunk admitted, "not here, but over there."

"Then why, pray tell, are we looking here?" snapped the exasperated policeman.

The drunk calmly explained, "Because it's way too dark over there."

We dare not tell Jesse Stuart and Demosthenes, when they are feeling lower than a snake's belly, that adversity builds character. Nevertheless, it often is in those dark spaces of life—in circumstances we want to avoid like the plague—where we come to understand years later that character was forged.

July 26

I had a favorite college professor who wrote a quotation on the blackboard at the beginning of every class. One I remember: "Hypocrisy is the tribute that vice pays to virtue." I didn't understand it at the time, but I did sense that there was something profound in it.

Hypocrisy is on my mind these days. Some of it relates to this being an election year when self-righteous pronouncements come from politicians who will say almost anything to get elected. The poster boy as I write is Congressman Tim Mahoney of Florida. He campaigned pledging to restore morality to the seat vacated by Congressman Mark Foley after Foley was caught in a sex scandal involving teenage pages. Now Mahoney, a husband and father, is embroiled in charges that he cheated on his wife with two women.

Ministers who preach lofty ideals set themselves up for charges of "not practicing what they preach." Martin Luther, who taught that the responsibility of every Christian is to be "a little Christ" to neighbors, was anti-semitic. Nazis frequently quoted Luther to justify the Holocaust. Luther wrote a book *On the Jews and Their Lies* where he called Jews a "base, whoring people" who are full of "the devil's feces which they wallow in like swine." Luther even wrote that Jews should be shown no mercy and that their synagogues and schools should be set on fire.[23] So much for being a little Christ to your neighbor.

Thomas Jefferson drafted the Declaration of Independence with its soaring "all men are created equal" affirmation, but he himself owned 150 slaves. Some think he owed his victory in the 1800 presidential election to the clause in the Constitution that allowed masters to count their slaves as three-fifths of a person.

Hypocrisy, Forrest Gump would say, is as hypocrisy does. Where is the hope for a hypocritical culture? "This above all: to thine own self be true, / And it must follow, as the night the day, / Thou canst not then be false to any man."[24]

July 27

A friend was admitted to the hospital last week. It was her first time to be hospitalized in twenty- eight years. Twenty-eight years earlier to the day she had been admitted to the same hospital to deliver her third child.

This time, because of a colon problem, a tube was put through her nose into her stomach to suction out stomach contents. She was denied food and water for four days. Morphine handled much but not all of the abdominal pain. When a colonoscopy was performed on the fourth day, the pain abated. Reflecting back on the preceding three days, my friend cited three highlights.

One was the first time her parched lips got swabbed by a wet sponge. The sponge, about the size of a small marble on the end of a lollipop stick, looked so refreshing that she lunged at it the way a bass rises to a fisherman's fly. She instinctively tried to grasp it with her mouth and suck out the water.

The next time was when she was spoon-fed a few ice chips. You would have thought from her sounds of delight that she was savoring a succulent strawberry. Last was her first taste of food. It was thin chicken broth. After the nasogastric tube was removed and she tasted the broth she exclaimed: "This may be the best food I've ever tasted."

After she was allowed to drink fluids again, an aide observed that she was drinking only cranberry juice. When the aide asked, the patient told her that was because no other juice was stocked on the unit. The aide assertively went from unit to unit and floor to floor until she found the patient some apple juice.

Stripped of almost all human comforts like clothes and food, hospital patients often learn to be more grateful for the simple things of life—little things like ice chips, chicken broth, and aides who seek until they find apple juice.

July 28

Robert Frost, who never graduated from college, was awarded more than forty honorary doctorates. Four times he was awarded the Pulitzer Prize for poetry.

Frost acquired the reputation of a maverick when he taught at Amherst and Dartmouth. He might say at the first class meeting: "Why do we have classes anyway?" He preferred dialogues with students at his house. "What we do in college is to get over our little-mindedness . . . I want everyone to be carried away by something . . . Suggest things to me I never thought of." Frost played the bard and gadfly. A student's only unforgivable sin was not to think.

He trained his Pinkerton Academy debaters to attribute any good ideas they had to Daniel Webster or George Washington, because the judges would think any thought the student spoke was convincing only when masquerading as some great person's thought.

For one final examination Frost gave at Amherst, he wrote on the blackboard: "Do something." Then he left the room. Some students thought that he was expressing his contempt for the grading system, so they took "do something" to mean going back to the fraternity house for beer and games. Some regurgitated into the examination book everything they could remember that Frost had ever said during classes. Others walked upstairs to Frost's office and told him how much they enjoyed his class. But two students thought about insights into life they had made in his class and wrote a few paragraphs about them. To the bard of Amherst, those two "did something."[25]

Life hands each of us a final exam with a similar injunction: "Do something!" I imagine God on judgment day asking each of us, one at a time: "What did you do? Show me your slides. Show me your scars. Where did you go? What did you see? How did you spend the one coin I entrusted to you?"

I like to think Frost would approve of that metaphor.

July 29

One of several fantasies little boys shared when I was growing up was how we would spend a million dollars if we had it. Early black-and-white television came out about that time with *The Millionaire*, a weekly drama exploring what people given a million dollars did with it. My memory is that most of them squandered the gift. I reckon that children in these days, like the adults, speculate over what they would do, not with one million but with six hundred million dollars; that is, if they won the lottery.

Neal Wanless, twenty-three, living with his parents in a poor region of South Dakota, won a $232 million lottery. He said upon winning that he would buy himself some "room to roam" and pay back people in his hometown who had been kind to his family.[26] Wanless could not appreciate that, after winning the lottery, few people would see him in the same light again; indeed, they would find it next to impossible to see beyond the green neon dollar signs blinking on his forehead.

Jack Whittaker of West Virginia won a $315 million lottery on Christmas Day, 2002. Five years later he blamed that day for causing his granddaughter's fatal drug overdose, his divorce, and his inability to trust others. "I don't have any friends," he told The Associated Press in 2007. "Every friend that I've had, practically, has wanted to borrow money or something and of course once they borrow money from you, you can't be friends anymore."[27]

Most of us have lots of acquaintances but few true-blue friends. If we have some real friends, friends who accept us for better or worse, for richer or poorer, in sickness and in health, through thick and through thin—we have won life's lottery. All the money of Donald Trump and Jack Whittaker combined cannot purchase that.

July 30

"What if?" Who of us has not played that game? What if, when we came to a fork in the road, we had gone the other way?

I had two job offers in 1969, one in Memphis and one in Atlanta. What if I had taken the one in Atlanta? In 1970, when I was choosing between the Presbyterians and the Disciples of Christ, what if I had cast my lot with the Disciples? I will never know how different my life would have been.

Shopping the bargain book bin earlier this year, I purchased for a pittance an eight-hundred-page book by Robert Cowley titled *What If?* One of the chapters makes the case that if Pizarro had not discovered potatoes in Peru in 1531 and introduced them to Europe, the history of Ireland and England for the next five centuries would have looked very different. If Alexander the Great had made it to old age, instead of dying at thirty two, or if he had died at twenty-two, which he almost did from a mighty blow to the head from an ax-wielding Persian, how different the history of the world would read. If Charles Martel had not defeated the Arabs in the battle of Tours, Western Europe might have gone Muslim. If Cristobal de Olea had not saved Cortez from the four Aztecs who were getting ready to sacrifice him to their god of war, Central America might not have gone Catholic.

It is human nature to look back and wonder "what might have been" had we zigged instead of zagged. But the past is, as Sandburg said, "a bucket of ashes." An appropriate response is to pray, borrowing the words of Reinhold Niebuhr: "God, give us grace to accept with serenity the things that cannot be changed, courage to change the things which should be changed, and the wisdom to distinguish the one from the other."[28]

July 31

On the day a little girl went home from the hospital following successful heart surgery, her mother left a prayer of thanksgiving on an index card in the hospital chapel. The final sentence of her prayer read: "We are drinking from the saucer because our cup overflows!"

Younger people may not know about that old custom of serving coffee in a cup instead of a mug or a Styrofoam container. The cup of coffee came atop a saucer. If the cup was too full and some coffee spilled out, the saucer caught it. Or, if the coffee was too hot to drink, ill-mannered people intentionally sloshed a little into the saucer, set the cup down on the table, blew on the coffee in the saucer to cool it off, and audibly slurped coffee from the saucer. "Drinking from the saucer" came to refer to something as *mm-mm-good* as that first sip of hot coffee on a frosty morning.

I once wrote a series of articles for a publication and titled one of the articles "Drinking from the Saucer." In response, a letter arrived in my mailbox from a lady in Michigan named Ruby, handwritten in cursive on a yellow, lined sheet of paper torn from a pad. She wrote: "I am an 88-year-old lady confined to my recliner for several weeks while recovering from corrected hammer-toes." Then, referring to my article, she added: "So many of my days are filled with exclamation points!"

What grabbed me most was that she did not say "were" filled but "are" filled. I can almost see her smiling face and the twinkle in her eye, even though she is recovering from surgery and confined to a recliner. Should I make it into my eighties, however physically limited I may be, I hope to have my mind and Ruby's spirit.

July Notes

1. Safire, *Lend Me Your Ears*, 133.
2. *Bartleby*, "Carl Schurz," no pages.
3. Zinn, *A Power Governments Cannot Suppress*, 267–269.
4. *Biography*, "Nellie Bly," 1–3.
5. *Celebration of Women Writers*, "Around the World," Chapter I.
6. Goodman, *Nellie Bly*, 294.
7. Erling, *A Reader's Guide*, 266.
8. Hunter, *Tab Hunter*, 354.
9. Lewis, *The Four Loves*, 169–170.
10. *ABC News*, "Fast-Food Ice," no pages.
11. Allen, "My Speech," no pages.
12. Stuart, *Beyond Dark Hills*, 307–308.
13. Matthew 4:4.
14. Ogbozer, "Love and Forgiveness," no pages.
15. McMahon, "Rwanda," no pages.
16. Cellzik, "Girl, 3," no pages.
17. Ambrose, *Leadership*, 80–81.
18. *Gheens Institute for Innovation Insights,* "From the Superintendent," no pages.
19. McNees, "What Is an Ethical Will?" no pages.
20. Darrow, "Reflections," no pages.
21. Drucker, *American Heroes*, 3–6.
22. Nouwen, *Out of Solitude*, 34.
23. *Jewish Virtual Library*, "Martin Luther," no pages.
24. Shakespeare, *Hamlet*. Act 1. Scene 3.
25. Cox, *Swinger of Birches*, 66.
26. Brokaw, "Neal Wanless," no pages.
27. Mohajer, "Life Not All Wine and Roses," no pages.
28. Lemert, *Why Niebuhr Matters*, 195.

August

August 1

I asked a group of senior citizens: "When you feel defeated, what do you say to yourself?" An eighty-year-old man said instantly and emphatically: "Look for Plan B!" Later I asked the same group: "What advice would you give someone who is feeling hopeless?" the same optimist smiled and chirped: "Look for Plan B!"

That struck me as typical of those Americans I know who survived the Great Depression and World War II. They do not expect life to be easy. They do not assume that they will get their first choice. They do not believe that life owes them anything. Instead of feeling sorry for themselves they get busy crafting Plan B.

James McNeill Whistler's most famous painting, commonly known as "Whistler's Mother," is a portrait of a woman in a black dress seated against a gray wall. One legend is that when his scheduled model didn't show up he painted his mother instead. Another is that he wanted to paint his mother standing but standing for a long period was too uncomfortable for her at her age so he seated her. Regardless of which story is true, the iconic finished product—Whistler's Plan B—is today considered by many as the Victorian Mona Lisa.[1]

Aldous Huxley, grandson of Thomas Huxley who became known as "Darwin's Bulldog" because of his advocacy of Charles Darwin's teachings on evolution, was destined to become a scientist. At age seventeen he came down with an eye disease that left him virtually blind. Blindness making scientific research impossible, Huxley became a writer. *Brave New World*, one of the top ten novels of the twentieth century, was one result. His brother Julian commented on Aldous's bad eyesight: "I believe his blindness was a blessing in disguise."[2]

Plan B often works out just fine. Sometimes Plan B even turns out to have been a blessing in disguise.

August 2

Some of us were taught as children that being religious primarily meant refraining from behaviors that the authorities deemed bad like smoking, drinking, cussing, dancing, and going to movies on Sunday. Because the world was a lost cause, little importance was placed on making it a better place. Either we will blow ourselves up with nuclear weapons, or Jesus will return. So, religious individuals should more or less withdraw from the world and keep themselves pure.

Another religious tradition promotes involvement in the world. Leaving the world "better than you found it" is central in this tradition to being faithful. An ambitious portrait of that lifestyle is The Shakertown (Kentucky) Pledge drafted in 1973. The path portrayed here is positive, progressive, simple, visionary, and revolutionary:

1. I declare myself a world citizen.

2. I commit myself to lead an ecologically sound life.

3. I commit myself to lead a life of creative simplicity and to share my personal wealth with the world's poor.

4. I commit myself to join with others in the reshaping of institutions in order to bring about a more just global society in which all people have full access to the needed resources for their physical, emotional, intellectual and spiritual growth.

5. I commit myself to occupational accountability, and so doing I will seek to avoid the creation of products which cause harm to others.

6. I affirm the gift of my body and commit myself to its proper nourishment and physical well-being.

7. I commit myself to examine continually my relations with others and to attempt to relate honestly, morally and lovingly to those around me.

8. I commit myself to personal renewal through prayer, meditation and study.

9. I commit myself to responsible participation in a community of faith.[3]

What a wonderful world that would be.

August 3

A common cliché in the business world—"To do good we must do well"— means that without a healthy bottom line there will not be enough money in the budget to give to charitable causes.

A popular application of that business principle is to give rich people and corporations more tax breaks so they will have more money to invest and thus help the whole economy. Plus, the argument goes, the rich will use some of that money to hire more workers. For several generations we have called this the "trickle-down" theory. It is summed up in the line immortalized by President Kennedy: "A rising tide lifts all boats." The catch is that corporations may use their tax breaks to buy newer, bigger corporate jets or add another layer of vice presidents or hand out bigger executive bonuses so that very little, if any, trickles down to us peons. William Sloan Coffin amended the "rising tide" quote to read: "A rising tide, instead of lifting all boats, lifts all yachts."

Another model for business is represented by Henry McKoy Jr. When McKoy was twelve, he competed in a national track meet in Hershey, Pennsylvania. On a tour of the chocolate factory he learned that Hershey had built a school for orphaned boys. He later learned that Hershey had donated most of his fortune to the care and schooling of orphans. "That colored my vision from then on that businesses could be used for the greater good," McKoy said. Formerly an All-American track star, McKoy is now CEO of Fourth Sector Financial. His company helps businesses focus on the triple bottom line of sustainable businesses: people, the planet, and profits.[4] Notice what he places first and what comes last.

Maybe the principle applies to all of us, the rich and the peons as well. How well off do we need to be to do good, to intentionally share a portion of what we have acquired with those who have much less? Some in our society live by Robert Ringer's rule: "The one who dies with the most toys wins." The catch is that having more toys— even all the toys—may not bring contentment.

August 4

"The root of all superstition is that people observe when a thing hits, but not when it misses"—Francis Bacon

In my childhood, Jeane Dixon was America's prophetess, mystic, astrologer, psychic, and crystal ball gazer. Tabloid headlines emblazoned her latest forecast. She became famous for predicting that the winner of the 1960 presidential race would be assassinated or die in office. She confessed long after Kennedy's assassination that she had expected the winner of that contest to be Richard Nixon.

John Paulos coined the term "the Jeane Dixon effect" for our tendency to observe when a thing hits but not when it misses—to get dazzled by someone's few correct predictions, but ignore or downplay those that turn out wrong. For example, most of Dixon's followers overlooked her predictions that World War III would begin in 1958 and that Russians would win the race to the moon.[5]

We teach our children to be critical thinkers, not critical in the sense of negative or cynical, but to examine and weigh—instead of swallowing whole and undigested—what authorities try to feed them. Examples of the danger of uncritical thinking abound. Think Branch Davidians or 9/11 terrorists or the lemmings that in a Disney movie follow their leader over a cliff. Bertrand Russell wrote: "In all affairs it's a healthy thing now and then to hang a question mark on the things you have long taken for granted."

Recognizing that most lies are subtle and have some particles of truth mixed in, PolitiFact, a Pulitzer Prize-winning website, features a truth-a-meter that differentiates six levels of veracity. A politician's comment is compared with the facts and shown to be true, mostly true, half true, barely true, false, or pants-on-fire ridiculous.

I take my stand for less superstition, less "truthiness," and more critical thinking.

August 5

"It isn't what they take away from you that counts. It's what you do with what you have left."

Those were some of the last words from "the happy warrior," Vice President Hubert Humphrey, spoken in the last stages of his battle with cancer. As we age and joints hurt, skin goes south and grows strange spots, hair and muscles and bladders forsake us, and memory oftener fails, we need new heroes who model for us how to behave in irreversible, terminal conditions—like growing old.

One such hero for me is Jean-Dominique Bauby. He was editor of the French fashion magazine *ELLE* when he suffered a massive stroke in 1995 at the age of forty-three. When he awoke twenty days later he found himself a victim of "locked-in syndrome." His mind was not damaged, but his body was paralyzed—except for his left eyelid. Bauby wrote a book with his left eyelid. His right eye had to be sewn shut because of an irrigation issue. He dictated the book one letter at a time by blinking his left eye. An average word took two minutes to dictate. The book required over two hundred thousand blinks and over ten months to complete.

Bauby titled the book *The Diving Bell and the Butterfly*. He wrote:

> My diving bell becomes less oppressive, and my mind takes flight like a butterfly. There is so much to do. You can wander off in space or in time, set out for Tierra del Fuego or for King Midas's court. You can build castles in Spain, steal the Golden Fleece, discover Atlantis, realize your childhood dreams and adult ambitions.[6]

Bauby died of pneumonia three days after the book was published. A 2008 film made from the book and with the same name was nominated for four Academy Awards.

August 6

"Have you ever had an epiphany?" I defined epiphany as a deeply significant experience that affects the way you live your life. One person volunteered this story of H.B., his fourth grade Sunday school teacher:

> As a child I really didn't enjoy attending Sunday school. I just wanted to stay at home and watch cartoons. However, this all changed when I entered the fourth grade. The fourth grade Sunday school class was taught by a short, humorous man named H.B. He was unlike any Sunday school teacher I had ever had. H.B. realized that most, if not all of us in the class, would much rather be doing just about anything but attend Sunday school. He addressed our disinterest in two ways. On the first day of class he got us to fill out a form on which we named our favorite soda and our favorite candy. Starting with the very next class, he brought a cooler full of our favorite sodas and a basket full of our favorite candy to every class. All of us loved this since most of our parents still tried to restrict our intake of sweets. On top of this bribe, H.B. had us watch an episode of Garfield at the end of each class. We didn't just watch the cartoons for the sole purpose of entertainment. He selected episodes that he could relate to the religious lesson he had taught during that class. H.B. paid for all of this out of his own pocket. I ended up with perfect attendance throughout the entire year of his class.

The unselfish, creative, caring, unsung individuals of this world like "short, humorous" H.B. put flesh on images like "salt of the earth" and "light of the world."

August 7

You wonder what ongoing effect the publication of Mother Teresa's private letters will have on her admirers and her legacy. Hundreds of millions of people throughout the world have held her in highest esteem for many years. In those letters (that she had asked to be destroyed after her death) she confesses that for the last several decades of her life she experienced the absence of God. In correspondence with her spiritual confidants she wrote of "dryness," "loneliness" and "torture" in her soul, comparing it to the experience of hell. She confessed to doubting the existence of heaven and God. She wrote: "There is such terrible darkness within me, as if everything was dead."[7]

Time magazine deemed this bombshell the top religious story of 2007.

Having always admired her, I now admire her more. She persevered at serving the poor even when warm feelings of religious fervor were missing. She got up every day at 4:30 a.m. to say prayers even when she felt sick-unto-death spiritually. Beset by questions and doubts, she persevered and did the magnanimous thing—embracing and comforting the teeming masses of Calcutta poor.

What if we only got up and went to school or work or church on days when we felt like it? What if we only treated other people right when we felt like it? What if we sat up all night with a sick child only when we felt like it? How common the "dark night of the soul" experience of St. John of the Cross is; how real for us mortals the cry of abandonment from Jesus, "My God, my God, why have you forsaken me?" How human, how like us, Mother Teresa turns out to be.

Mother Teresa is a saint in my book, not just of the poor, but of doubters and assorted other tortured souls.

August 8

At the time of the American Revolution, it took weeks for news to cross the Atlantic. The Boston Tea Party happened on December 16. By the time a British ship, in record time, delivered the breaking news to Londoners it was January 20. That "breaking" news was five weeks old. Andrew Jackson defeated the British at New Orleans on January 8, 1815. But the war had been ended at The Treaty of Ghent that was signed in Belgium on December 24. No one on this side of the Atlantic had any way to know that.

Contrast those time lags with the instantaneous fomenting of revolution all over northern Africa in the Arab Spring of 2011. Without the internet and cell phones and young people who manned and womanned them, the revolutionary spirit would not have spread like wildfire.

Social media educates and connects. It empowers freedom lovers to organize and protest. Any regime today that depends on ignorance and isolation is ultimately doomed, thanks largely to technophiles—bloggers, twitterers, text messagers, and hackers.

But hold the cell phone! Technology, which in itself is neutral, in many hands has a huge downside. Nothing prevents worldwide broadcasting of lies, not to mention inane, vile, half-baked or un-baked thoughts that any individual chooses to disseminate. Gone are the days when you wrote a letter in anger or love and had enough sense to wait three days to mail it—just to make sure you should send it—and then opted to destroy it. Nowadays we get on our cyberspace soapbox and spew unedited chatter into the ether. What we spew today may go viral and tomorrow appear on the evening news.

There is one other downside to instant messaging: the dumbing down of relationships. Some unconsciously are busy as a bee substituting a host of superficial connections for a few true friends, the kind who hold us or sit with us in silence and choose not to check their iPhones, however long their friending of us in person takes.

August 9

"BLOW, BLOW, THOU WINTER WIND / THOU ART NOT SO UNKIND / AS MAN'S INGRATITUDE, AS MAN'S INGRATITUDE"—William Shakespeare[8]

Back when travelers in the Middle East wore sandals on dusty roads, washing the feet of strangers epitomized hospitality. It was an early version of the Golden Rule—welcome strangers the way you, a traveler needing to rest and cool your heels at the end of a long day's journey, would want to be welcomed. Some churches in modern times practice foot washing as an article of faith: "The Bible says do it so we just do it." Some churches practice foot washing once a year on Maundy Thursday, commemorating Jesus's washing his disciples' feet. What might a modern equivalent of the menial, humble act of ancient foot washing look like?

Part of my mother's identity for two decades was that of a volunteer in charge of a nursing home beauty parlor. Beauty parlor was a fancy name for the area where every Wednesday women residents, many of whom did not know their names or where they were, had their hair washed by my mother and her squad.

My mother had to move out of her house because she became unable to care for herself there. She has taken residence in an institution. Now members of her volunteer squad come to visit her every Wednesday. They help her into a car and transport her back to the nursing home where she once shampooed hair. Instead of giving, now she receives a shampoo. Shampooed, she gets taken to lunch by her friends, after which they return her to her new residence. Wednesday has become mother's favorite day of the week. What her friends do for her has a name: gratitude. Sometimes, like bread cast on the waters, what you do comes back to you.

August 10

Tony Conigliaro came away from a field hospital in Vietnam convinced that there are some things in life more important than facts.

When he was twenty years old, back in the late 1960s, Conigliaro became the youngest baseball player ever to hit one hundred home runs. But his promising career came to an abrupt halt at age twenty-two when he was beaned by a bad pitch that left him blind in one eye. It was the height of the Vietnam War, and as he convalesced he decided to participate in one of those celebrity handshaking tours of hospitals.

He came across one soldier in a field hospital who changed his life. The man's body had been blown apart by an explosion. He was in traction with his shirt open, revealing an incision from neck to navel. His head was completely bandaged, except for holes for his nose and ears and mouth. Tony Conigliaro introduced himself, wished the soldier well, patted him on the arm, and as he began moving on to the next bed heard that soldier call out in the strongest whisper he could muster, "To-nee." Conigliaro went back, knelt down, put his ear to the hole in the man's bandage where his mouth should be, and heard him ask, "How's your eye?"

I heard this story on a television talk show in the 1970s. I do not know that soldier's name or even if he survived his injuries. But I think of him when the facts would get me down—when I can't find where I parked my car, or I have a pesky head cold, or the coffee maker goes kaput. Every time I remember his saying, "How's your eye?" I am reminded of the truth psychiatrist Karl Menninger wrote: "Attitude is more important than fact," and that helps me put the facts in their place.

August 11

He could not have been a day past three. I watched as he, hand in hand with great-grandmother, stepped out of the kiddie pool. "Where are we going?" he asked. "Honey, it's time to go home," she gently explained.

Next I watched the equivalent of Bill Bixby turning into the Incredible Hulk. I watched a cute, angelic little boy turn into a scowling stone statue. He instantly stopped, folded his arms, and stiffened his body. Every cell from face to heels proclaimed: "Not ready to go." Great-grandmother tried to lift the stone statue and could not. She signaled a lifeguard to come help. Last I saw him, being toted out by two adults, the boy remained still as a log in Petrified Forest National Park. When her peripheral vision caught onlookers grinning, great-grandmother flashed us an angry frown.

Later that same day I was reading customer reviews of a restaurant. Most reviews of that restaurant were filled with superlatives. One diner, however, reported ordering a steak that came full of fat and gristle. Not wanting to embarrass her friends, she said nothing. Her review went on to indulge in some self-flagellating introspection: "I should have said something and I have been told since that they would have gladly replaced it." She ends with new resolve: "Again it was my fault for not bringing it to their attention. I will not hold it against them and will try them again on another day and if I get a bad steak from them again, I will say something."

Some people are, as my parents used to say, "stubborn as a mule." They are the no-reasoning, no-compromise, no-surrender people. But for every one of them, I know that somewhere is their opposite, like the disappointed diner who lacked sufficient steel in her spine to ask to speak to the manager and say to him, "My steak is full of fat and gristle."

August 12

A friend asked me to visit her dying father. For the thirty minutes I was there, he coughed and sputtered and spit and wiped his nose and shook his head and lamented his wretched state. I left feeling thoroughly spent and, worse, fearing that my time there did him no good and even some harm. I went away feeling profound pity for an inconsolable, miserable, old, dying man.

When I read his obituary a few days later, I was dumbfounded. The pitiable old man I had known only in his death throes had once been an honorable, mighty man. He served for three years in World War II, even fighting on D-Day, even fighting in the Battle of the Bulge, earning the Combat Infantry Badge and four battle stars.

He came home from the war and started a family, founded a successful business that expanded to five offices, taught in a university, was elected chairman of the board for two hospitals, and served as treasurer and chief fund raiser for several charities. He was a charter member of his church where he served as elder, deacon, teacher, and Sunday school superintendent. He served without pay as a director on the board of several organizations. He was Tom Brokaw's quintessential "greatest generation" man who through intelligence, love for community, and Calvinistic work ethic moved heaven and earth to improve things. But all I could see—to my discredit—was a decrepit old man.

Shakespeare grimly proclaimed that life's last of seven stages "Is second childishness and mere oblivion / Sans teeth, sans eyes, sans taste, sans everything."[9]

Because of this visit with this man, I hope I am beginning to learn that well-disguised inside an aged, sputtering, dying man's body may be a noble, exemplary biography.

August 13

American novelist E. L. Doctorow says he has no idea when beginning a book how it will end. He compares writing to driving at night in the fog: "You can only see as far as your headlights, but you can make the whole trip that way."

That headlights-in-fog metaphor stands for the way many of us live. Oh, I know there are some who make twenty-year plans and fulfill them and credit good goal-setting for their success. One friend of mine when he and I were both twenty-five had elaborate plans that would allow him to retire at age forty-five and then write books and travel the country visiting his grandchildren. But the unpredictability of life intervened and none of those things happened. Several marriages failed and he has yet to publish a book.

Some say that the millennial generation (those born 1980-2000) will be more comfortable driving in the fog than their parents and grandparents were. They will change jobs and careers often and easily. They are not interested in getting the gold watch for having done the same thing thirty years.

I like the way David Mitchell, young English novelist, describes life:

> I've got kids, I've got a wife, we're stuck with each other for a while. And suddenly there's an understanding that this is what life is—it's actually the mess, it's the mud, it's the tangle. It's not the clean, hygienic fireworks. It's the little invisible novels that get written between two people every day of their lives. It's the subtle power shifts. It's the love, it's the less-noble sentiments that make every single day either good or bad or not so good or wonderful . . . This is interesting stuff. Why go out there in search of extraterrestrial life when it's already here?[10]

Life, as most of us know it, is trudging through mess, mud, tangle, and fog—interesting stuff.

August 14

"I'm Spending My Children's Inheritance." That bumper sticker from the 1980s celebrated unbridled consumption and self-indulgence. These days the same words are taking on a different meaning. More and more baby boomers are deciding not to pass on the lion's share of their estate to their children, but not because they are heaping up luxuries on themselves.

Warren Buffett, for example, who loves his three children and their children, is donating about 85 percent of his enormous wealth to causes, including more than $30 billion to the Bill and Melinda Gates Foundation, which focuses on finding cures for diseases in the developing world. He believes wealthy parents should leave their children some money but not so much that they are spoiled, or act privileged, or have no sense of accomplishing things on their own, or spend their time shopping and partying. When Buffett's daughter in her fifties asked him for a home-improvement loan, he told her to go to a bank.[11]

Richard Cohen's grandfather was Ben Eisenstadt, who developed the formula for Sweet'N Low. Cohen's book *Sweet and Low* describes how money rent the family fabric, permanently ruining relationships between Ben and his daughter (Richard's mother) as well as uncles, aunts, and cousins. "Money messes you up," Richard writes. "It is like a funhouse mirror. It distorts things and enables the worst."[12]

Peter Munk, chairman of the world's largest gold-mining corporation, is investing much of his largess in Canadian medical and educational institutions. Monk says his five children will not be getting much money when he dies, explaining that he's already passed along the two things they need for success in life—good values and a fully paid education.[13]

It seems that more and more parents with an inheritance to pass along desire not to enable a primrose path for offspring who just might feel entitled to one.

August 15

"Being an Optimist Lowers Risk of Heart Disease" proclaimed the headline in the *New York Daily News*. A massive research project studied over ninety-seven thousand women older than fifty over many years. The research found that optimists are 9 percent less likely to develop heart disease and 14 percent less likely to die from any cause in that time period than their less positive counterparts.

Attitude, researchers have repeatedly found, directly affects blood pressure and heart rate and leads to better or worse heart health. Hilary A. Tindle, assistant professor of medicine at the University of Pittsburgh and lead researcher for the study, said that those with hopeful attitudes are more likely to engage in healthy behaviors such as eating well, exercising more, and smoking less. They are also likely to have better relationships; after all, they are more desirable to be around than those who are cynical or hostile. They also tend to adhere more strictly to medical advice and treatment plans. Tindle concludes: "Sustained negativity is toxic to health, and I would absolutely say that it's important for people to try to reduce the amount of it in their lives."[14]

But how much of attitude is determined by our nature—set in stone at birth? We enter the world with a certain temperament for sure, long before our handlers have opportunity to nurture and mold our attitude. Is it really within our power to choose our outlook, or are we fated to go with whatever heredity and upbringing gave us?

Marcus Aurelius, Stoic philosopher, insisted: "If you are distressed by anything external, the pain is not due to the thing itself but to your interpretation of it; and this you have the power to revoke at any moment." Our glory is that we are the only animal that gets to make a conscious choice—either to ratify, or to revoke, or to revise—the script our parents hand us.

August 16

Cogito, ergo sum. However brilliant the insight of Descartes—"I think, therefore I am"—some of us develop our own variations on it that bring us pain.

Some of us are "I *regret*, therefore I am" people. Much of life revolves around events from the past that still have power to haunt us and weigh us down: the death of a child, an abusive relationship, a bad marriage choice, or the loss of a job. I have never experienced the death of a child but I know people who have and who went on to live relatively happy, fulfilling lives.

My favorite reading material is a biography. I marvel time and again at how many great people in history grew up orphans, or in dire poverty, or handicapped, or disinherited, or abused, sickly, or all of the above. I suspect they had to suppress a pool of pain within them for life; nevertheless, they somehow managed not to let their lives be suffocated or dominated by their most painful memories.

Then there are the "I *worry*, therefore I am" people. Worry is a response to something that has not happened, is not happening now, but could possibly happen someday. A relative could be killed in a home invasion. The economy could tank and wipe out our investments. I could fall on my face when I get up to speak. I could fall on the ice and break my crown. A terrorist could strike any minute. Some of us become immobilized by undesirable possibilities.

I like the way Albert Schweitzer framed life's past, present, and future menaces. Asked whether he was an optimist or a pessimist he said: "My knowledge is pessimistic, but my willing and hoping are optimistic."

We thinkers, like Rene Descartes, have a choice. We can allow ourselves to be ruled by bad things past or future. Or, we can boldly affirm with Schweitzer and his ilk: "I *will* and I *hope*; therefore, I am."

August 17

There is hope for those of us who were not born geniuses. Malcolm Gladwell in his book *Outliers* devotes a whole chapter to "The 10,000-Hour Rule." He quotes neurologist Daniel Levitin who quotes scientific studies proving it takes ten-thousand hours to become an expert in anything. Gladwell argues that natural talent is highly overrated. Intentional, dogged practice—whether playing chess or writing fiction or becoming an excellent neurologist or a virtuoso violinist—is the key to success.

One example Gladwell cites is Bill Gates. Gates did not one day get lucky. He had spent thousands of hours perfecting his computer programming skills as a high school student. Another example is the Beatles. They practiced for eight hours a day, seven days a week, for 270 days over eighteen months. By the time they had their first commercial success they had performed twelve hundred times. The common denominator of other examples Gladwell gives is not innate talent, but the amount of time spent practicing. Gladwell's book reminded me of the words of Joseph Lister, the father of antiseptic surgery, who wrote in a letter to his father: "As to brilliant talent, I know I do not possess it, but I must try to make up for that as far as I can by perseverance."

I thought of Rosa Parks. A common misconception is that one day she was tired and made a spur-of-the-moment decision to refuse to go to the back of the bus and give her seat to a white person. Most people do not know that before that day she had been active for twelve years in the local NAACP serving as its Montgomery secretary.[15]

Maybe stick-to-it-ness is more important that IQ. As young Abe Lincoln said, "I will prepare, and some day my chance will come."

August 18

The death of public figures like Senator Edward Kennedy, Jacqueline Onassis, and President Richard Nixon could motivate us to think seriously about how we prefer to die. All three died at home, relatively pain-free, and surrounded not by technology but by family. Unfortunately, not all of us will be so fortunate. Up to 75 percent of us will die in a hospital or nursing home or some other institution. Some of us will die a sudden and unexpected death, with no opportunity for final farewells. Many of us will have left no instructions on what we want or do not want at the end of life.

One thing for sure—deny it however we may—is that we will die. The good news is that many of us will have some control over how well we die.

For more than thirty years working in a hospital, I witnessed hundreds of patients dying a death they never envisioned in their worst nightmares. They were kept alive by invasive procedures, ventilators, renal dialysis, and other treatments for weeks and months after any reasonable hope for recovery was left. Sometimes the futile treatment liquidated the patient's estate or bankrupted the family or both. Often it happened because the patient had left no verbal or written instructions with family members or physicians on how they hoped to die.

What to do? Discuss your feelings about your death with those near and dear to you. Select someone to be your durable power of attorney, some family member or friend or attorney you trust to make your medical decisions should you ever become unable to speak for yourself. Enact both a Living Will (stating your wishes) and a Durable Power of Attorney (the person you authorize to speak for you). Hospitals have the forms and a notary who can make them legal for free. The ignominious death you dodge may be your own.

August 19

After the preceding article on dying was published in the *Corydon Democrat*, a local nurse wrote this letter to the editor:

> As a certified registered hospice and palliative nurse, I completely agree with this article. Many patients and families are caught off guard by an illness and are not prepared. Many people think that you have to spend a lot of money having these documents drawn up by lawyers. That is not the case. As well as hospitals having the documents, hospice can also assist patients and families with these legal documents. Hospice provides care for patients diagnosed with a terminal or life limiting illness. Many people are not aware that Medicare has a Hospice Benefit that will cover 100 percent of the care provided related to the diagnosis. This includes nursing care, home health aides, social workers, chaplains, volunteers, bereavement counselors, medications, treatments, and medical equipment. Feel free to contact me with any questions.

My wife and children know precisely how I feel about prolonging my dying process. In a two-page, single-spaced manuscript I have spelled out my wishes. Here is an excerpt:

> When I am no longer able to *ooh* and *aah* at spring redbud and autumn orange; when I can no longer greet and hug and hold and kiss and know my grandchildren; when I am totally dependent on others to dress and change and bathe me—my desire is to depart. Please allow no heroics or extraordinary measures that the medical-industrial complex could take to save my biological self. Two of my highest pleasures in life have been reading and writing. When I am no longer able to enjoy reading and when I am no longer able to write coherent sentences, then I charge you to stand in my stead and say no to any stretching out of my natural dying process.

Please think about your own wishes and then communicate them clearly to your next of kin.

August 20

The summer of 2010 made history over much of the country as one of the hottest ever. I would have thought little about the heat that summer had I not worked one day a week on an organic vegetable farm with five other volunteers setting plants, pulling weeds, mashing bugs, and harvesting tomatoes. The heat index was often over one hundred degrees with nary a breeze.

While fighting delirium one day, I found my mind flashing back to childhood when our houses, schools, and churches were not air-conditioned, and air-conditioned cars were something we heard a few rich people off somewhere drove. On the hottest days we opened wide the screened-in windows. We sweltered through hot nights. We installed fans in our attics to draw hot air out of the house or cooler air in. In church, we used hand fans supplied by the local funeral home (with their commercial printed on them) to move hot air around.

As I weeded beans and wrestled garlic out of the ground, my mind turned to slaves in Egypt who built pyramids and to slaves down south who picked cotton all day, with few if any rest breaks and without so much as a vessel of cold water to sip or pour over their heads and necks. I thought about my grandfather who plowed eighty acres with a mule.

Edward Kohn's book *Hot Time in the Old Town* also popped into my simmering mind. Kohn describes New York City's brutal summer of 1896 when for ten straight August days the temperature reached around one hundred degrees. "No wind," Kohn said in an interview, "so at night there was absolutely no relief whatsoever."[16] Over thirteen hundred perished. Countless others were driven to bizarre acts of despair. Most who died were the hard-working poor who lived in tenement houses where they did piece work like rolling cigarettes or sewing. Their brick houses functioned as brick ovens, raising temperatures inside to 120 degrees and cooking the inhabitants.

Bring back the good ole' days? I sure would hate to give up air conditioning in August.

August 21

Another football season is upon us.

Vince Lombardi, whose Green Bay Packer teams won the first two Super Bowls, was a world-class authority on everything about football. Lombardi opened the first practice by huddling the team around him, kneeling down with a pigskin, and saying something like this: "This is a football. It can be kicked, carried, passed, handed off, intercepted, or fumbled. I am the coach. You are the players."[17] He continued talking about the field's dimensions, its shape, the yard markers, and the goal posts. The philosophy was clear—don't assume anything; begin at the beginning; master the fundamentals if you want to succeed. He ate, drank, and lived the old adage: "Well begun is half done."

Barbara Kingsolver seems to take an alternative "begin with the end in mind" approach. She writes: "The very least you can do in your life is to figure out what you hope for." Then she adds: "The most you can do is live inside that hope, running down its hallways, touching the walls on both sides."[18]

Maybe it is not an either-or. Maybe Lombardi and Kingsolver are both right. Which is worse, to have roots without wings, or wings without roots? Either is like trying to clap with one hand. The goal, it seems to me, for us and our children and perhaps for the human race, is to be people who are both grounded in strong values and virtues *and* have a reach that exceeds our grasp. I aspire to conform to that Lombardi philosophy of building the house on rock instead of sand. I also want to conform to that beautiful Kingsolver image of "living inside hope, running down its hallways, touching the walls on both sides."

August 22

The faith healer invited: "Anyone with special needs please come forward for healing prayer." One man in the line that formed, when his turn came, requested, "Please pray for help with my hearing." The preacher placed his hands over the man's ears, applied pressure, and fervently prayed for more than a minute that the man's hearing would be restored. Removing his hands, the preacher stepped back and asked, "Sir, now how is your hearing?" The man told him, "I don't know yet. It's not till next week."

We fail people when we assume, like the preacher, that we understand them instead of making sure by asking, "How do you mean . . . please tell me more . . . help me understand."

A blogger posted a video clip of a speech made by Shirley Sherrod who worked for the Department of Agriculture under Barack Obama. The clip made her look like a racial bigot. When Agriculture Secretary Tom Vilsack heard about it he promptly had her fired, only to learn later that the speech's theme was transcending racism. The blogger had carefully edited out that part of the speech.[19] Ignoring the context of Sherrod's words was a tremendous embarrassment to the White House that could have been easily averted. If Vilsack or his staff had cared enough to understand Sherrod's comments in context by giving her a call and asking, "What were you thinking when you made that comment?" she could have explained. If they had watched the whole speech before jumping to a conclusion, that would have prevented a debacle.

How often we take a snippet of someone's life and let it stand for the whole, instead of trying to understand. Harper Lee wrote: "You never really understand people until you consider things from their point of view." Or to paraphrase Alexander Pope: "To hear is human; to understand, divine."

August 23

Perhaps most of us at some point have fantasized being filthy rich and how glorious that would be. Some multi-millionaires and multi-billionaires are very charitable but many are not. You and I, of course, given the chance would give all our billions (but one) away to help the less fortunate.

Karl Rabeder, an Austrian millionaire, wants to send a message about riches. Rabeder, who came from a very poor family "where the rules were to work more and harder to achieve more material things," wants others to know that the rich lifestyle is not all it is cracked up to be. Rabeder is giving his fortune away. He first got the idea while he was on a three-week holiday with his wife in the islands of Hawaii:

> It was the biggest shock in my life, when I realized how horrible, soul-less and without feeling the five-star lifestyle is. In those three weeks, we spent all the money you could possibly spend. But in all that time, we had the feeling we hadn't met a single real person—that we were all just actors. The staff played the role of being friendly and the guests played the role of being important, and nobody was real.[20]

The sale of his Alpine estate and all the proceeds from selling the rest of his belongings will go to microcredit charities in El Salvador, Honduras, Bolivia, Peru, Argentina, and Chile that help poor people begin a small business. "I had the feeling I was working as a slave for things that I did not wish for or need," Rabeder said. "I have the feeling that there are a lot of people doing the same thing."

May those of us who envy the rich have ears to hear.

August 24

Julie Andrews's book *The Very Fairy Princess*, written in collaboration with daughter Emma Hamilton, is a treasure partly because of its development of the concept "sparkle." *The Very Fairy Princess* is about an ordinary little girl named Geraldine who is sure that deep inside her exists a princess wanting to get out. Geraldine goes through the ordinary events of each day expressing her "inner princess," practicing what adults call the virtues of self-esteem, courage, and excellence. The story terms those behaviors "letting her sparkle out."

This sounds much like the ancient Hebrew idea that inside each person is the image of God, or the Stoic idea that each of us has a spark of divinity within us, or the Christian idea that God has given each person a talent that needs to be expressed for the greater good.

Take Mimi Hughes, a schoolteacher from Taft, Tennessee, who in her fifty-fourth year swam 981 miles down the Ohio River. She used her summer break from school to raise awareness of the need for education, especially for young girls, especially in remote regions of Pakistan and Afghanistan. "I don't have political clout and I don't have money," Hughes explained, "but my arms and legs seem to work for me, so I started using them for positive social environmental change."[21]

Julie Andrews would say Mimi Hughes found her sparkle. Instead of dwelling on all the things she cannot do and envying those who can, Hughes identified a gift she does have—she is a good swimmer. She spends instead of buries her one talent.

Some of us are princes or princesses but still think we are a frog. Before night falls there is time to seek and find and release our sparkle.

August 25

It was my privilege to sit at the feet of four persons older than I in a life-review session and hear them respond to the question: "How do you expect to be remembered? What one personality trait do you think will be your legacy?"

The first to speak said: "I think I'll be remembered as a friend. I genuinely like people. From childhood on I've had a gift of welcoming people and making them feel comfortable around me. I think the people who know me well will remember most my friendliness."

Another said: "I'm enthusiastic. Whenever I tackle something I give it all I've got. I get involved in many causes. I genuinely expect things to go well and they usually do. 'Enthusiastic activism' will probably be the theme of whatever they say about me at my memorial service."

Another said: "I'm a joyful person. I don't let things get me down. Some call it denial; I call it cheerfulness. When people remember me I think they'll see a smiley face."

The last to speak said: "I'm a gardener. I love to have my hands in the soil and dirt under my fingernails. Who am I? Well, I grow things. I hope I'll be remembered for gifts of flowers, berries, plants, and vegetables."

Their summation of how they think others will remember them caused me to go home and wonder (and worry some) about my legacy. I hope I will be remembered as someone who loved words and loved stories and aspired to be a hope-prompter for others. If you are reading this, you too are an unfinished piece of work. There is still time to craft a reputation. There is still time for us to prove that we did more, after dropping in, than just drop out of the world.

August 26

Nothing fosters a sense of helplessness or hopelessness like isolation—a feeling that there is no one to turn to or lean on or confide in.

A young man was, in his words, "just one buffet shy of four hundred pounds." He discovered aerobics and lost two hundred pounds. He has kept the weight off for many years and works in a fitness center. What turned his life around, he says, were the people in that aerobics class: "I found myself in a culture of kindness."

Novelist Barbara Kingsolver, native of Carlisle, Kentucky, gave a great commencement speech to Duke University graduates in 2008. Her theme was the loss of community in America. Over the last thirty years, she pointed out, material wealth has greatly increased, but a sense of happiness, according to the social scientists who study happiness, has steadily declined. Researchers have found that the happiest people in the world are not in either the poorest countries or the richest countries. The happiest are found in places like Ireland, Greece, or Puerto Rico, where people live in extended families and in noisy villages with lots of music, conversation, and dancing. "The happiest people," she concludes, "are the ones with the most community."[22]

Those are the people who discuss problems with a neighbor across the fence or an uncle down the street and not as much over the phone with some stranger in India. They eat food grown by area farmers whose faces they know instead of by strangers in who-knows-where thousands of miles away. They celebrate good times with live music in groups and churches. Only time will tell whether the culture created by text messages, e-mails, and the iPhone will be able to build genuine community and usher individuals into a culture of kindness.

August 27

At this point in life are you more a camel, a lion, or a child? German philosopher Friedrich Nietzsche wrote that the human spirit must travel through three metamorphoses, or stages, on its way to fullness.

Stage one is the camel. The camel represents submission. "Lay your burdens on me. Load me down—I can take it" youth say as they take on old traditions and precepts and absorb the "thou shalts" and "thou shalt nots" of their culture. Some never progress out of this submissive, passive stage.

When we go forth into the desert of life, tired of being a weighed-down beast of burden, our spirit rebels. We morph into a lion and roar at all those authoritative voices in our head: "Get off my back. Leave me alone. I've got to find me and become what I'm destined to be." Some get stuck in this angry, rebellious stage.

The final metamorphosis of the spirit is the child who, according to Zarathustra, is "innocence and forgetting, a new beginning, a game, a self-propelled wheel, a first movement, a sacred 'Yes!'" Having successfully completed the first two metamorphoses, we are free to say "Yes" to life and bring forth a one-of-a-kind creature who is creative, beautiful, and new.[23]

We have six grandchildren age eight and under. One room in our house we have designated the "Sacred Yes!" playroom. We have stocked it with games, toys, books, and family pictures. It is strictly for play. In there, (almost) anything goes. It may well be the grandparents who benefit most from the Sacred Yes room. As we observe kids in their unselfconscious frivolity, something old and sentimental stirs within us. We sit and smile and remember when.

August 28

"God tempers the wind to the shorn lamb." The first time I heard that saying I cynically dismissed it. What about the shorn victims of the Holocaust? What about the children of South Sudan who know nothing but war and violence and starvation, whose suffering never abates? What about the drunk driver's victims, their chronically grieving loved ones shorn for the remainder of their days?

But that phrase kept periodically resurfacing in my brain; it wouldn't leave me alone. Then one day I acknowledged to myself that regardless of all the exceptions there are to it, the proverb has proven true in my life. How many times when I have been down on myself, down in a pit, the phone rang or something came in the mail or something I read in a book grabbed me or I came across an inspirational "triumph of the human spirit" piece on television or I had a conversation with someone that lifted my spirits.

Clarence Darrow gave a speech in which he turned the phrase around. He said six decades had taught him that God tempers the shorn lamb to the wind.

Maybe both are true. Winds of circumstance do change. "The only sure thing about luck," Bret Harte said, "is that it will change." That is the mistake suicidal people make. They convince themselves that the present state of things is permanent when actually it is not. Things absolutely *will* change.

No less than circumstances, we change. We can learn new things. We can acquire new coping skills. We can bless ourselves more and curse ourselves less. We can develop a thicker skin. We can become more discriminating in our selection of friends. We can, with God's help, temper our shorn selves to the wind.

August 29

"We Don't Do Fear."

I heard about a woman in her sixties—out of work for over a year, her resume rejected more than one hundred times—who read that headline in a Harley-Davidson commercial and was moved by it to get up and do something. She re-thought her tactics. She followed up one rejection letter with a response that explained why they had made a big mistake in not hiring her and specified ten things she would do with the job. Conquering her fears, refusing to take no for an answer, she landed the job, thanks indirectly to that Harley-Davidson commercial.

There is a wonderful story in the Midrash of "not doing fear" when the children of Israel were trapped between the Egyptian army and the Red Sea. God told Moses to tell the Israelites who were staring hopelessly at the ocean before them: "Go forward." No one moved until Nachshon from the tribe of Judah waded in. He walked forward until the waters reached his waist and then his neck. When the waters reached his nostrils he plunged headlong into the waves. The waters parted. The Israelites, led by Nachshon and the tribe of Judah, followed a dry path through the midst of the sea to safety on the other side. Because of Nachshon's fearless faith, according to the Midrash, God bestowed a gift of leadership and royalty on the tribe of Judah.[24] The greatest king, King David, descended from the tribe of Judah. The one whom Christians would call Messiah also descended from Nachshon's tribe.

Nachshon's glory was his capacity to act when all others were paralyzed in a state of inaction. The moral for us is to refuse to "do fear," to refuse to sit passively and wait for a miracle like the sea to part or the phone to ring with a nice job offer.

Nicolas Chamfort wrote that "we should swallow a toad every morning in order to fortify ourselves against the disgust of the rest of the day when we have to spend it in society."[25]

Don't do fear! Swallow that toad!

August 30

A five-year-old boy climbed aboard the big yellow school bus. It was his first day of kindergarten. On the second row of seats sat a little girl alone, looking sad or scared or both. He did not know her name, but he took the seat next to her and spontaneously took her hand. They held hands all the way to school.

Several days later the little boy brought home a note the teacher had sent to his parents. The note was from the girl's parents, inviting him to popcorn and a movie at their house. The little boy was and is our oldest grandchild.

My heart flooded with pride and joy when I heard what my sensitive, outgoing grandson had done. I thought of my favorite movie. In one of the early scenes little Forrest Gump, ugly braces on both legs, slowly boarded the school bus on the first day of school. Kids looked the other way as he searched for a seat, hoping the weird-looking new kid would not sit next to them. Finally Jenny, who didn't know Forrest, broke the silence with the sweetest words Forrest later said he had ever heard: "You can sit here if you want." Jenny was the daughter of an alcoholic who sexually abused her. Understanding cruelty, she treated Forrest the way she wished to be treated.

Most of us can resonate to "first day at school" and "new kid on the bus" anxieties. They are useful metaphors for all those times in life we feel existentially alone as we enter a new world, be it a diagnosis of cancer, a divorce, or a pink slip. Then we can identify with the plea of Albert Camus: "Don't walk behind me; I may not lead. Don't walk in front of me; I may not follow. Just walk [or sit] beside me and be my friend."

August 31

She is the world's first billionaire to make her fortune writing books. Twenty years ago J. K. Rowling was a single mother living off welfare, depressed to the point of contemplating suicide. Today she is mega-rich from the sale of half a billion books. Because of her rags-to-riches story, I find fascinating what she said recently about her three children: "I will be extremely disappointed and feel I failed if I turn out individuals who think their only contribution to society is simply to consume."[26]

David Wann, expert on sustainable lifestyles, and Thomas Naylor, Duke University Professor Emeritus in economics, termed the insatiable appetite for more things "affluenza," by which they mean "a painful, contagious, socially-transmitted condition of overload, debt, anxiety, and waste resulting from the dogged pursuit of more."[27]

The pursuit of happiness, commonly defined as chasing the most extravagant lifestyle one can buy, is so pervasive that we may be unaware that it has become our addiction. A research project studied the world's richest and the world's poorest people. On a scale of one meaning "not at all satisfied" and seven meaning "completely satisfied," people on Forbes' list of richest Americans averaged 5.8. That is almost exactly the same number scored by the Pennsylvania Amish, the Inuit people of Greenland who have no electricity or running water, and the Masai of Kenya who live in dung huts.[28]

Some say our country's greatest idolatry is unbridled consumption. President Calvin Coolidge's most famous line was: "The chief business of the American people is business." On the eve of the Great Recession, mired in expensive wars in Iraq and Afghanistan, our president's solution was to encourage the American people to "go shopping more." Let us hope with J.K. Rowling that when our moral fiber is tested, it is not found to be made of straw.

August Notes

1. *Totally History*, "Whistler's Mother," no pages.
2. *Political Philosophy*, "Aldous Huxley," no pages.
3. *Presbytery of Newtown Blog*, "The Shakertown Pledge," no pages.
4. Ranii, "Mission to Do Well," no pages.
5. *Macrohistory and World Timeline*, "Jeane Dixon," no pages.
6. Cleaveland, "The Diving Bell," no pages.
7. Martin, "A Saint's Dark Night," no pages.
8. Shakespeare. *As You Like It*. Act 2. Scene 7.
9. Ibid.
10. Bland, "A Thousand Autumns," no pages.
11. Breitman, "Should Kids Be Left Fortunes?" no pages.
12. Ibid.
13. Intini, "Giving Away Fortune," no pages.
14. *New York Daily News*, "Being an Optimist," no pages.
15. *National Park Service*, "Rosa Parks," no pages.
16. *NPR*, "The Heat Wave," no pages.
17. Ortberg, *Groups*, 15.
18. Kingsolver, "2008 Commencement Address," no pages.
19. Shahid, "Shirley Sherrod," no pages.
20. Samuel, "Millionaire," no pages.
21. McCloskey, "River Swimmer," no pages.
22. *Duke Today*, "2008 Commencement Address," no pages.
23. Nietzsche, *Thus Spoke Zarathustra*, 13–15.
24. Hoffman, "Taste of Torah," no pages.
25. *Quote Investigator*, "Eat a Live Frog," no pages.
26. Ellis, "J.K. Rowling," no pages.
27. Wann, "Affluenza," no pages.
28. Begley, "Wealth and Happiness," no pages.

September

September 1

In September, this aging man's fancy lightly turns to thoughts of school. September takes me back to dusty roads, shorter days, and cooler nights of yesteryear. I hear again nature's melancholic whisper: "Summer's almost gone."

After our children leave home, we parents are largely done, so far as sculpting them goes. We formed them, for better or worse in those impressionable years, wondering and worrying all the way how they would turn out. We need wonder no more. We still may be able to help with some mid-course corrections, but they are missiles launched. Now it is our turn to learn from them—to become their students, to sit at their feet and be instructed by them, to receive their gifts as we approach what Shakespeare called second childhood.

Our first son continues to teach me unconditional forgiveness. After all my fumbles as a first-time father desperately trying to figure out how to corral a strong-willed first child, our oldest son has somehow found it within himself to forgive me. His example impresses on me how we only harm ourselves when we nurse and cling to painful, dated emotions.

Our second son continues to teach me what Sir William Osler termed *aequanimitas*: Keep the steady keel; Cultivate imperturbability; Keep your head, as Kipling wrote, when others are losing theirs.

Our third son continues to teach me contrarianism: Question conventional wisdom; Color outside the lines; Instead of going down someone else's path, as Emerson said, go where there is no path and leave a trail.

Black Elk said to the lucky journalist who got to interview him: "Grown men can learn from little children, for the hearts of little children are pure. Therefore The Great Spirit may show them many things which older people miss."

What Black Elk said about little children holds true for grown children as well.

September 2

Maybe I was a little odd—the exception, not the rule—but I liked school. I never once dreaded the start of school. I do not remember any of our children dragging their feet on opening day—"the whining schoolboy, with his satchel and shining morning face, creeping like snail unwillingly to school," as Shakespeare depicted life's second stage. What I remember about beginning a new school year is wearing new shoes and sporting a new satchel and suntan on day one. I do not remember caring much which teacher I got, but I do remember hoping like crazy that some of my best friends and some of the prettiest girls would be in whatever class they assigned me.

Now what I value most about school days is the poetry some of my teachers made me memorize. I hated doing the work of memorization, but I cherish what is now indelibly etched in my mind. I can still quote chunks of Edgar Allan Poe, Alfred Lord Tennyson, William Cullen Bryant, Thomas Gray, Matthew Arnold, and William Ernest Henley. How often their beautifully-crafted lines still make my soul clap hands.

I agree with what Merlin in Terence H. White's *The Once and Future King* said:

> The best thing for being sad is to learn something. That is the only thing that never fails. You may grow old and trembling in your anatomies; you may see the world about you devastated by evil lunatics. There is only one thing for it then, to learn. Learn why the world wags and what wags it. That is the only thing which the mind can never exhaust, never alienate, never be tortured by, never fear or distrust, and never dream of regretting. Learning is the thing for you.

I wish I had written that. The wizard was right. Thanks, good English teachers.

September 3

"A world turned for me in Mrs. Burrows Smith's English class." Little David Brinkley, like many people, got little affirmation at home. When David was eight, his father died. David was from birth, according to himself, an embarrassment to his mother. David's older sisters told him their mother cried uncontrollably after his birth. She was forty-two when he was born, and among her Presbyterian women friends in the small-town South of 1920, it was thought to be scandalous for a married woman to be having babies that late in life.

Brinkley writes in his autobiography *David Brinkley: A Memoir*: "I now believe that for every day of my life at home with her, every time she looked at me, when she could not avoid looking at me, I reminded her of the agony and suffering that came with me when I was born." One day David, budding writer, wrote something and walked upstairs to show it to his mother. She glanced at it briefly, threw it in his face, and said: "Why are you wasting your time on this foolishness?"

What Mrs. Burrows Smith did in her English class gave David Brinkley the shot of confidence in himself as a writer that he needed to evolve into a world-class journalist. After months of reading and grading his compositions, Mrs. Smith said these words: "David, I think you ought to be a journalist."

Many children like little David Brinkley, for whatever reason, are not going to get "the blessing" at home. It will have to come from a neighbor, a grandparent, an aunt or uncle, a church leader, a scout leader, a school teacher, a coach, or some other adult who seizes the opportunity to bless. What a stem-winding thought for teachers—that one word of praise or affirmation may "turn the world" for some child.

Sir William Osler wrote: "No bubble is so iridescent or floats longer than that blown by the successful teacher."

September 4

The only birthdays that have been difficult for me are the ones that end in a zero or a five, as in thirty and forty and sixty-five. I have now entered a new era, having attained the Biblical "three score and ten." I hope to discover a smidgen of truth in Robert Browning's claim that this new frontier will be "the last of life for which the first was made."

Grandma Moses, forced into retirement from her embroidery job because of arthritis, began painting in her late seventies and continued painting into her nineties. Frank McCourt did not publish his first book, Pulitzer Prize-winning *Angela's Ashes*, until he was sixty-six. Colonel Sanders did not start franchising his fried chicken until he was sixty-six. Roget invented the thesaurus at age seventy-three.

I have found inspiration for beginning this new decade of my life not so much in a person but in, of all places, a plant. For thirteen years our family has gone to the same South Carolina beach the second week in July. There was a stately plant outside our condominium, about eight feet wide and tall, that served as a favorite backdrop for family pictures—until this year. This year the gorgeous plant's leaves were curling up and browning. It was dying of old age.

According to the resort, the plant was at least thirty years old. The good news for us was that we got to see what the century plant does only once in its lifetime, just before it dies. It shoots forth a huge stalk, thick and hard as a small tree trunk, that grows at the rate of six inches a day. Atop this mast thirty-feet-tall was a cauliflower-like, bigger-than-a-basketball bouquet of hundreds of little white flowers.

Approaching my final frontier, like the century plant, I hope to hoist another flower or two.

September 5

Graeme Wood, contributing editor to the *Atlantic*, concluded his article on lives of the wealthy with this comment: "Appetites for material indulgence are rarely sated. No yacht is so super, nor any wine so expensive that it can soothe the soul or guarantee one's children won't grow up to be creeps."[1]

One reader agreed, offering this story to illustrate:

> Working provides structure and meaning for your life. Your family can see the effort you make for them and understand it as a token of your love for them. I spent about five years renovating a house, stripping the dilapidated building down to the beams and rebuilding it as a genuinely pleasant and stately home where my wife and I raised our children. It was a source of real pride and pleasure for me. After a financial reverse, I was forced to sell it. The buyer was the stereotypical Texas zillionaire, who gave it to his twenty-five-year-old single daughter. I still drive by the place once in a while. I enjoy seeing the bay windows I had put in and the elegant columns . . . and curving brick plinths, on either side of the sturdy carved-oak door. If the lights are on, I imagine the girl stuck inside, sitting alone in what to her is just an over-sized hotel suite. Her parents could only give her a house; my parents gave me a life in which I could build houses.

May this Labor Day, with millions of our fellow citizens seeking work or having given up hope of finding it, prompt us who are employed to lift up grateful hearts for the gift of labor—for the opportunity, health, and strength to do it, and for the satisfaction of getting paid a little or a lot for it.

September 6

I love my job. I am the fulltime interim minister for a lively Presbyterian church. One thing I like most is the location of my office. It is across the hall from the toddler room of the church's child development center. I thrill to look through the window several times a day and wave to the tykes and have them smile and wave back, or see them in their high chairs trying to get food on their spoons and then transport the food from their plates to their mouths, succeeding about half the time.

Today the teacher apologized to me: "I'm sorry we've been so noisy today." I smiled and explained that a baby's strong cry is one of the most beautiful sounds I've ever heard. Then I forced on her my reason why.

Most all my professional life I worked in a children's hospital. There were times when I stood with parents in the delivery room, at the end of a problem pregnancy, and their baby presented blue and lifeless. But after a minute or two of intensive intervention by dedicated staff, the limp baby yielded a thin cry. That whimper was the grandest sound those parents, if they live to be one hundred, will ever hear.

Many times I stood in the emergency room with parents whose toddler had drowned in the neighbor's swimming pool or whose crib death got interrupted. After what seemed like an eternity of CPR, suddenly from the lifeless body came a strong, guttural squall, and the parents and grandparents and siblings and I, waiting outside the trauma room, dissolved in tears of joy.

That is how I became conditioned like Pavlov's dogs to smile when I hear a baby's cry. And yes, I feel that way when it is my grandchild at 3:00 a.m.

There is no more beautiful sound than the sound of life that wants to live.

September 7

If you had been blind for forty-three years, do you not think you would jump at the chance to see? It was not that easy a decision for Mike May. Blinded from a chemical accident at age three, he adapted remarkably well. He even set a world record in 1981 in downhill speed skiing. He became a successful inventor and businessman. He married and had two sons.

Blind, he was living a full, rich life. When presented with the possibility of a stem cell transplant that might restore his sight, he initially said no. His life was complete as it was. He did some research and learned of other people, blind from birth, who became terribly depressed, even suicidal, after their sight was restored. The shock of integrating a whole new sense overwhelmed them. Things like spouses and children turned out not to be as beautiful as imagined.

Mike May ultimately chose to have the transplant, primarily out of his sense of curiosity—he wanted the chance to see what vision was like. The surgery was successful. The bestselling biography *Crashing Through* chronicles his remarkable, inspiring journey.

The summer before his senior year in college, Mike May was the first-ever blind counselor at a summer camp. He led his charges that summer on long hikes—around poison ivy and rattlesnakes, through streams and rivers, over rugged terrain. On one excursion the boys asked him how he had achieved such a good, productive life while blind. Mike May told them that if they would remember four things, they would do okay at navigating their way through the world: Have adventures. Speak to your curiosity. Be willing to fall down or get lost. There's always a way.

That is the advice of a blind man—with 20/20 vision.

September 8

"You can become anything you want to be." The proverb is as American as apple pie but patently false. Need proof? Look at the number of children who, when asked what they want to be when they grow up, say pro basketball player or pro football player or president of the United States or the doctor who finds the cure for cancer.

Nevertheless, I do love to sit at the feet of those who realize their dreams against overwhelming odds. Benjamin Carson is one of those. Carson, Director of Pediatric Neurosurgeon at Johns Hopkins Hospital, made history in 1987 by successfully separating Siamese twins joined at the back of the head.

His mother dropped out of school in the third grade and married when she was thirteen. She became a domestic worker, raising Benjamin and his older brother by working several jobs at a time. She made a seminal observation in her life as a domestic. She noticed that successful people had a lot of books in their homes and spent more time reading than watching television. So she restricted her children to two or three preselected television programs a week and required them to check out two books each week from the library and submit to her written book reports. She used a red pen to mark them up with check marks. She was able to conceal from her sons that she was illiterate.

Carson credits his mother and books for his success: "Although we had no money, between the covers of those books I could go anywhere, do anything, and be anybody." Carson grew up poor and black in Detroit. He advises a No-Child-Left-Behind generation: "Learn for the sake of knowledge and understanding, rather than for the sake of impressing people or taking a test."[2]

"By words," the playwright of Athens, Aristophanes, wrote long ago, "the mind is winged."

September 9

"Thank goodness for TiVo," the television viewer wrote. "This wonderful entertainment tool has totally changed the way I watch TV. I never see commercials anymore. If a fire occurred, TiVo would be one of the rescued items going out the door with me."

What? That declaration of values I find astonishing. But it did make me wonder: if my house is on fire, and I am the only one in it, and I estimate I have less than a minute to get out alive, what possessions would I take with me? One would not be a TiVo. I do not have one. Furthermore, I do not want one—I am not crazy about anything on television.

Two highly-prized possessions would leave the house with me because they are always on my person. One is my wedding band, inscribed on the inside *una anima e duae*, Latin for "one spirit out of two." My wife's band is inscribed *aionios makarios*, Greek for "eternal happiness." Both inscriptions have turned out to be—for the most part—true.

The other possession on my person is the ring our middle son gave me when he was in college in New Mexico. I average having a person a week comment on its beauty and ask me about it. Infants and toddlers are drawn to it. It is sterling silver, inset with turquoise, coral and lapis. I dearly love the American Southwest, especially New Mexico. That ring symbolizes the special trips out West I made with our boys when they were teenagers, one at a time.

With whatever seconds are left, I would grab some discs on which are stored my favorite photographs, and with the other hand as many decades-old photo albums as I could get under my arms. I will not be taking the remote control. What would you take?

September 10

Probably all those who make it into their nineties get asked for the secret of their longevity. "No left turns" is the most bizarre answer I have yet heard. Michael Gartner, who won the Pulitzer Prize for editorial writing, heard his father at age ninety-five give that reason for living so long.

His father had quit driving in 1927. He walked everywhere, or his wife—until she turned ninety—drove him. The two were married for seventy-five years and, according to son Michael, were deeply in love the entire time.

No left turns? They had read an article that said most automobile accidents old people have occur when they are turning left in front of oncoming traffic. They decided then that they would never again make a left turn. They figured that three right turns (around the block) would be the same as a left turn and much safer. If they lost count, they made seven rights. If they missed again, they went home and chalked it up as a bad day.

The couple died in a bungalow they purchased in 1937 for $3000. She died at age ninety-four, he at 102. His last lucid words to the family from the bungalow bed: "I want you to know that I am in no pain. I am very comfortable. And I have had as happy a life as anyone on this earth could ever have."

Son Michael's summation:

> Life is too short to wake up with regrets. So love the people who treat you right. Forget about the ones who don't. Believe everything happens for a reason. If you get a chance, take it. If it changes your life, let it. Nobody said life would be easy, they just promised it would most likely be worth it.[3]

And, Michael declined to add—no left turns.

September 11

Is the sky falling? Four times in my life I seriously wondered.

First was the Cuban missile crisis in October, 1962, when for a week or so we feared that all-out thermonuclear war between the United States and the Soviet Union was imminent. I wrote my parents from college to tell them my plans on how I would try to get home to them should Armageddon come.

Second was the year 1968, when it felt like the world was convulsing. It was a year of assassinations and an escalating war in Vietnam. There was close to zero confidence that government officials were telling the truth or doing the right thing or knew what they were doing. That year for many of us marked the end of America as we knew it. I published an article in 1968 that began with a line from the 1936 Broadway play *The Green Pastures*: "Everything nailed down is coming loose!"

Third was September 11, 2001, and its aftermath when we had no idea whether or when the terrorism that had come to America would cease. I remember wondering that afternoon if nuclear weapons carried in suitcases would start going off next in Manhattan. I filled both our cars with gas, without a thought on where we might be traveling.

Fourth was the year 2008. Deceit, swindling, avarice, and ineptitude at the highest and wealthiest levels threw national and global markets into chaos. Many lost their lifetime investments, their jobs, or their homes. Many more lost faith that those in power cared about anything other than feathering their own nests.

What if Armageddon does come? What if the economy tanks again and we enter a second Great Depression? What is better, to wring our hands and run around crying with Chicken Little: "The sky is falling! The sky is falling!" or to nurture our relationships with family and friends and defiantly affirm that we will get through this together? What is better, to pull the shades and turn out the lights and curse the gods that be, or believe that this too shall pass and together we shall overcome?

September 12

The barbed wire held hundreds of photographs, fastened like so many shirts and sheets and socks by wooden pins to a clothes line. I was viewing our public library's exhibit of New York City photographs made on September 11, 2001.

The images—many of them in black and white—were riveting: people jumping to their death from ninety floors up; twisted steel and concrete; living people blanketed with grey soot; faces etched with pathos.

And there were the words that people in shock had scribbled on walls or on paper taped to a lamppost or written with their fingers in the dust on car hoods. "This is hell," one wrote. "Have you seen my daddy?" one child wrote, followed by dad's name and home phone number.

Some messages stoked vengeance: "Nuke them all!" "You will pay, Ben Laden." "The Yanks are Coming—Ben Laden Kiss your Butt Goodbye." Who at such a time is unable to understand primal rage, a victim's visceral urge to even the score? Marcus Aurelius understood the instinct to retaliate, but advised: "The best revenge is to be unlike the one who performed the injury."

Alongside voices for retaliation were other voices of reason. One read: "Our Grief is not a Cry for War." Someone had scribbled on a John Wayne poster: "What we need now is not a cowboy." Another simply read: "Peace."

A handful of peacemakers at various points in history may alone have saved the human race from devouring itself. Gandhi reportedly said: "If we practice an eye for an eye and a tooth for a tooth, soon the whole world will be blind and toothless." Confucius taught long ago: "If you devote your life to seeking revenge, first dig two graves."

September 13

They had a hunch, so they designed an experiment to test it. One group was instructed to journal daily three or four experiences for which they were grateful. Another group was instructed to keep a journal, but to jot down three or four experiences daily that were neutral or negative.

Professor Robert Emmons at the University of California at Davis conducted the research. He found that those who kept the gratitude journals slept better, exercised more, got sick less, had more energy, and felt more upbeat about the coming week than those who recorded neutral events or hassles. He calls it practicing "gratitude lite." "If you want to sleep more soundly," he advises, "count blessings, not sheep."[4]

At Wake Forest University, fifty students were instructed to act like extroverts for fifteen minutes even if they didn't feel like it. The more assertive, energetic, and extroverted the students behaved, the happier they reported feeling afterward.[5]

Albert Schweitzer in his *Memoirs of Childhood and Youth* wrote: "Grow into your ideals so that life can never rob you of them." The idea seems to be that if we want to become better, acting that way—even though it may feel unnatural and contrived at first—helps us to become better. Alcoholics Anonymous has popularized the slogan "Fake it till you make it." The phrase is not encouraging phoniness, lying, or deception. The genius of the phrase is in recognizing that the best way to "grow into our ideals" is to rehearse behaving the way we aspire to be, however awkward it may feel at first.

Do you, like me, ever feel guilty of ingratitude? Philosopher Immanuel Kant called ingratitude "the essence of vileness." Screw up enough courage to write a note or make an "I just wanted you to know how much I appreciated your kindness" or "I just called to say I love you" phone call. Try acting the way a grateful person would act should one someday take up residence in your body.

September 14

In 1991, Michael Weisser became the cantor and spiritual leader of a synagogue in Lincoln, Nebraska. Shortly after he and his family moved in, the phone rang. The caller told Rabbi Weisser that he would soon regret having moved there. He called Weisser "Jew Boy." Several days later a package arrived at the Weisser house containing neo-Nazi propaganda and a card that read: "The KKK is watching you, scum."

The hate-filled phone calls continued coming from a Larry Trapp, the grand dragon of the White Knights of the Ku Klux Klan in Nebraska and a neo-Nazi. Trapp was also a paraplegic, a double amputee confined to a wheelchair, and nearly blind. In one of their phone conversations, Weisser said to Trapp: "Larry, given your physical disabilities, you would have been one of the first people the Nazis would have killed."

Something powerful began to happen. The two men agreed to meet. The whole Weisser family began to develop a relationship with Trapp. Sometimes they even did his grocery shopping for him. Trapp eventually decided to join the people he had so despised. He became a Jew.

When Trapp's health began to fail, the Weissers took him into their home. Julia Weisser quit her nursing job to take care of him. Shortly before he died in 1992, Trapp ordered flowers for Mrs. Weisser with this message attached: "Thank you for changing me from a dragon to a butterfly."

At Trapp's funeral, an African-American man Trapp had persecuted delivered a eulogy praising the Weissers' ability "to sift through the ashes of a very mean world and find the spark of the truly human."[6]

It *is* a very mean world out there. Our moral task is to sift through the ashes and find the spark of the truly human.

September 15

One hundred years ago naturalist John Muir wrote: "When we try to pick out anything by itself, we find it hitched to everything else in the Universe." El Nino, a slight warming of the ocean off Ecuador, causes high tides and record rains on the Pacific west coast and drought in Australia and India. Cells in our bodies communicate with each other. Healthy cells cooperate. A cancer cell, by contrast, goes off and does its own thing and destroys the host on which it lives.

As a teenager in the 1950s, I was slow to see that "every litter bit hurts" (a slogan that became popular then). We did not think twice before throwing candy wrappers and cigarette butts out car windows. Then one day we looked around and found our fruited plains and purple mountains blighted with garbage.

Percy Shelley wrote: "Nothing in this world is single; all things by a law divine in each other's being mingle." John Donne saw the same truth in these famous words: "No man is an island entire of itself; every man is a piece of the continent, a part of the main."

Journalist Tom Friedman illustrates this interconnectedness of the planet in *Hot, Flat, and Crowded*: "The palm oil that fried up your French fries today may have come from a chopped-down tropical forest in Indonesia which in turn helped to contribute to climate change that is intensifying the drought in your backyard."

Poet Francis Thompson caught the vision: "All things by immortal power, / near or far, / hiddenly, / to each other linked are, / that thou canst not stir a flower / without troubling a star."

Our question becomes: am I more an exploiter or a trustee, one who fleeces or one who preserves our precious web of life? Should we not make the Native American prayer our own: "With all people and all things, let us be as relatives."

September 16

One of the most fascinating studies on health, happiness, and longevity in our time is being conducted by Dan Buettner. *National Geographic* sent him around the globe to study "blue zones," places where people not only have more years in their life but more life in their years. Buettner's travels have taken him to the Italian island of Sardinia, the Japanese island of Okinawa, and the Nicovan Peninsula on the Pacific coast of Costa Rica. Four times as many men in Nicova make it to age one hundred than men in the United States even though their medical bills are only about 7 percent as much.

We are not surprised by his findings that the people in these "blue zones" are physically active throughout life, eat plenty of fruits and vegetables and little meat, and drink a glass or two of red wine every day. We have been hearing for fifty years now that poor eating habits and too little exercise are killing us.

Buettner has observed two other things that are not so widely known. One is that people who live both long and large place a high premium on family, friends, and religion. A bottle of diet pills or vitamins probably does not contribute as much to longevity as having a caring, supportive community around us. A second is that those who live long and large talk freely about purpose in life. In Okinawa, for example, there is no word for "retirement." There is another word that roughly translates to "that which makes life worth living." Instead of living to retire, the emphasis is on purposeful living. Men there have one-fifth as much cancer as Americans and one-quarter as much heart disease.[7]

Buettner's book from *National Geographic* is titled *The Blue Zone: Lessons for Living Longer From the People Who've Lived the Longest*. You can take his "vitality compass" at www.bluezones.com and learn how long you are likely to live, given your current habits.

September 17

I deliberately avoid obituaries. Probably they are too big a threat to my denial system. But this morning her sweet smile and her name caught my eye, and because we share a last name, I read on.

She died at ninety-nine, having lived her last nineteen years in a retirement home.

Hemingway said the only people who live life "all the way" are big game hunters, boxers, and bullfighters. Here was not a boxer or bullfighter or big game hunter, but a retirement home resident who, according to those who wrote her obituary, lived life all the way.

She was a twenty-nine-year breast cancer survivor. Of people like her Hemingway wrote: "The world breaks everyone, and afterward many are strong at the broken places." She was president of the resident council, chaired numerous committees, was an emergency floor monitor, made daily dining room announcements "accompanied by her famous jokes," was chairperson of the campus store, acted in many theatrical productions at the retirement home, and served as craft expert at two other homes for the elderly. Before she entered the retirement home she volunteered with "countless organizations" including the Association for Widowed Persons, women stricken with breast cancer, and Meals on Wheels.

She successfully bequeathed her spirit to her children. In the obituary they graciously thanked the staff for "their loving care over the past months." The tribute ended with the family's wish that, in lieu of flowers, memorial gifts be made in their loved one's honor to the Benevolent Fund of the retirement home. Ruth Dowell Willis, when she found herself planted in a retirement home, bloomed. According to those who knew her best, hers was a life lived large.

September 18

I once heard Hans Selye, twentieth-century expert on stress—the man who coined the term—deliver an enthusiastic lecture. He began his speech with this declaration: "There are racehorses, and there are turtles, and I'm a racehorse."

Sometimes we refer to that type personality as obsessive, workaholic, or Type A (turtles are Type B). Other times we call them driven, wired, fanatical, or addicted. When we are feeling charitable, we call them focused.

Sir Isaac Newton often forgot to eat. He would rise from his desk at dawn and eat the congealed remains of the dinner that had been brought to him the day before that he had forgotten to touch. When asked how he discovered the laws governing the universe, Newton answered: "By thinking of them continually. I keep the subject constantly before me and wait till the first dawnings open slowly, by little and little, into a full and clear light."[8]

Aristotle was focused. He spent most of his honeymoon collecting specimens of marine life.

"Pistol" Pete Maravich, thought by some to be the greatest basketball player ever, was focused. As a pre-teen he accepted a $5 bet that he could not spin a basketball on his finger for an hour. After several minutes, when his index finger started to bleed, he switched fingers. He moved the spinning ball from each finger on his right hand to each finger on his left and then he spun the ball on his knuckles and thumbs until an hour was up and he had won the bet.[9]

Great rewards accrue to racehorses, to those addicted to their skill. They get praise, respect, power, success, control—and some make much money. Workaholics sometimes become CEOs and Hall of Fame coaches. They sometimes become our best ministers, physicians, and teachers—shining stars in whatever field they choose. Unfortunately, there is a price to be paid. The cost is often failed or frayed relationships, particularly at home. Blessed are workaholics who can re-direct a portion of their passion to be "the best" to an intimate inner circle of family plus a friend or two.

September 19

I searched the internet for the origin of this fable. One site assumed it was C. S. Lewis; another credited Rabbi Haim of Romshishok. Preachers love it. I have heard it and read it several times over the years, every time in a slightly different version. We may never know who first told it; we only know that it has been preserved and repeated so much because it speaks something true.

A man was offered a tour of heaven and hell. First he was allowed a peak into hell. What stood out was how emaciated the residents were. They looked like scrawny prisoners awaiting death in a concentration camp. Their faces looked very angry; their eyes were filled with rage. The irony was that there were tables laden with fine foods set before them. Within arms' reach was an all-you-can-eat buffet. The residents of hell had one physical anomaly in common—they had no elbows. Their arms were rigid, and as they tried unsuccessfully to get food from their hands to their mouths they spilled food everywhere, knocked the daylights out of each other, and starved.

On his trip to heaven, the tourist found conditions there much the same. There was food galore and the people had no elbows. But they were healthy and happy. Peace and joy reigned, because they were feeding each other.

The tourist rushed back to hell, pulled a skinny guy aside, and tried to make him understand: "Sir, it doesn't have to be this way. Just feed the fellow across the table from you." The starving man cursed and said: "I won't give that #%@$& the pleasure until hell freezes over."

The difference between heaven and hell, in this world and in the next, is the way we relate to others.

September 20

"The more things change, the more they stay the same." Autumn arrives. The temperature is up in the nineties today, but I would bet a Popsicle that there will be a frost in a month. We know the very second that dawn will break every day in the year 2099. Astronomers can predict eclipses and planet alignments hundreds of years off. Mother Nature is in so many ways perfectly predictable.

Even so, everything is transitioning. Physicists tell us the universe is expanding. Mountains, given millennia, crumble to the sea. Beaches erode. Continents shift. Stars fall. Cells divide. Bodies wear out and die. Pluto loses its planet status.

I witnessed a little parable on transitioning while visiting a nursing home. I watched as one of the few residents who could walk unaided by a cane or walker got up from breakfast and wobbled outside. In her eighties, a large bald spot atop her long, white mane, she made her way to a section of sidewalk that I was told she visits every morning after breakfast. With one foot she cleared away the freshly-cut grass, leaving a clean circle into which she dumped a crumbled biscuit held in a napkin. She continued to her room with the napkin, never looking back. Waiting sparrows, knowing her routine, descended immediately for breakfast. Then the lawn keeper came with his blower and blew away the grass—along with the crumbs and the birds—from the sidewalk. One minute later the birds returned in spades and resumed the feast, eagerly extracting bread from grass the hard way: one crumb at a time.

Thomas Merton wrote: "There is in all visible things an invisible fecundity, a dimmed light, a meek namelessness, a hidden wholeness."[10] Autumn's browning unleashes a prodigious seeding, what Merton called "invisible fecundity." Visible things like nursing homes and woodlands host invisible beginnings and endings, dyings and resurrections—Merton's "hidden wholeness."

Death comes, and life goes on.

September 21

Arthur Gordon, in his book *A Touch of Wonder*, writes of a bleak period in his life. Zest for life gone, he visited his family doctor. The wise old physician, after listening to him describe depression, asked, "Where were you happiest as a child?" Gordon answered, without a moment's hesitation, "At the beach."

The physician ordered: "Tomorrow I want you to take the day off. Arrive at the beach by 9:00 a.m. I'll write you four prescriptions. I want you to take one every three hours." He tore four sheets off his prescription pad, wrote something on each, folded them, and numbered them 1–4.

The next morning, expectations lower than the floorboard, Gordon drove to the beach. At 9:00 a.m. he read the first prescription: "Listen Carefully." He discovered over the next three hours that when you become really aware of things outside you, for a while you silence the clamorous, worrisome voices within; for a while you contemplate something bigger than yourself, and the mind finds some rest.

Noon prescription: "Try Reaching Back." Over the next three hours he discovered a treasure trove of half-forgotten people and relationships and positive events that he had not thought about, much less enjoyed, for years.

Three o'clock prescription: "Re-examine Your Motives." After six hours of clearing his mind of negatives, he found himself ready to ponder big matters like: "What is it really all about? What am I living for?"

Six o'clock prescription: "Write Your Worries on the Sand." He took a broken shell, kneeled, and wrote several things one beneath the other. Then he stood up, threw the shell out to sea, turned, walked away, and didn't look back. The tide was coming in.

We have to find creative ways to transport our sagging spirits to the beach.

September 22

I met him our first week of college. He was from Texas and I was from Tennessee. We lived on the same dormitory floor. We were good friends for the next four years. He was gregarious, made good grades, and was athletic—a well-rounded high achiever. Our senior year he married one of the prettiest girls on campus. We went our separate ways. I lost track of him. Years later I read that he had earned a doctorate in the counseling field. Then a few years later I was mildly shocked to learn that he had become president of our alma mater.

Royce Money served twenty years as president. He took the private school of 4,800 students to new heights.

Today I learned something from an article titled "My Brother's Keeper" in the university's quarterly magazine that I have not been able to get off my mind. My college friend has one brother, nine years younger. His brother suffered severe brain damage at birth. His mental functioning is that of a two-year-old. The two brothers' parents both died a few years ago, and my old college friend now has sole responsibility for his little brother. He visits him regularly, as he did ever since our first week of college. I always knew he had a younger brother, but I never knew the rest of the story.

I think of all the quiet saints out there who carry heavy loads over the long haul without calling attention to themselves. They refuse to sell duty to buy sympathy or acclaim. They do it simply because their conscience tells them it is the right thing and their heart tells them that love is the greatest thing.

September 23

I hope to come across something every day that inspires me a little. Any day it might come from geese honking overhead, or from seeing a child pluck and gaze at a leaf, or, most regularly, from reading poetry. Yesterday it came from a radio interview with one of baseball's great catchers.

Dave Davies interviewed all-star veteran catcher of eighteen seasons, Brad Ausmus, who earned the reputation of being the best in the sport at massaging a pitcher's psyche to get the pitcher out of a bad inning. Davies asked Ausmus what he said when he jumped up after a pitch and walked out to the mound to have a heart-to-heart conversation with the pitcher.

Ausmus said:

> The one general rule I have is that, when I leave the pitcher's mound, I want him to feel he can get out of the situation. Even if it's the bottom of the ninth and there are no outs and the bases are loaded and we're one run ahead, I want to leave that pitcher thinking he's got a chance to get out of this. I stay calm to convey to him that it's not an impossible situation.[11]

In my experience, that is an effective strategy for all of us who mean to be helpful with troubled people, whether they have been diagnosed with Parkinson's or are having to face a huge, gut-wrenching decision. First, take initiative. Instead of being a sympathetic bystander, be a stand-up, walk-out-to-the mound advocate for the person coming apart. Second, be reasonably positive. There truly are good possibilities ahead that a person attempting to function in the fog of fear cannot see. Three, stay calm. Someday when you are coming unglued, that is the rational, reassuring kind of presence you hope walks out to your mound and talks—or sits—with you.

September 24

He asked his family to engrave four little words on his tombstone.

Buckminster Fuller was one of the most innovative architects of the twentieth century. He invented among other things the geodesic dome. The four little words he wanted on his tombstone: "Call Me Trim Tab."

A trim tab is a little rudder on the back of the big rudder of a ship or plane. To change direction, a large ship or plane needs a large rudder. But the strong currents of air or water make it almost impossible to move a large rudder without breaking it.

Engineers learned that the solution was to put a tiny rudder—a trim tab—on the back of the large rudder. It moves easily because it is small. When it moves it causes the currents of air or water to shift and move the large rudder which in turn turns the ocean liner or the jumbo jet. Even though it is the big rudder that turns the vessel, it is the little trim tab that gives the rudder its needed nudge.[12]

Fuller understood his place in the great scheme of things. He knew that in life there are few rudders, giants who change the course of history. It was enough for Fuller to think of himself as a trim tab that nudges the rudder that turns the ship.

One thought that inspires me to write comes from playwright Tom Stoppard: "Words are sacred. If you can get the right ones in the right order, you can nudge the world a little."

Most all of us are trim tabs instead of rudders. We are probably not going to move the world. Accepting that, we can move on and give a few people the little push they need.

September 25

Just as there are no perfect mates, there are no perfect strategies for finding the right companion for life's voyage. Most of us find our mate the free-enterprise way. We shop around until we negotiate the best deal we think we are going to be able to get. In other parts of the world marriages are pre-arranged. Parents in their wisdom and according to family values choose a partner for their child.

Charles Darwin went about it differently. According to Quammen's *The Reluctant Mr. Darwin,* Darwin returned home after five years sailing on The Beagle wondering whether he should marry. He had no particular person in mind. He merely wondered whether the state of marriage could be compatible—have "goodness of fit"—with his scientific pursuits. He took out a piece of paper, wrote "If Not Marry" at the top, and listed the advantages of not marrying. They included freedom to travel and freedom from the need to work to support a family. "If Marry" he wrote atop another page and listed mainly disadvantages, like owning few books, having little time for reading, and needing to live like a poor man.

After his wealthy father, a physician, assured Charles that he would never have to worry about money, Charles made lists again. This time the "If Marry" list came out looking better, including the advantage of having a constant companion and a friend in old age.

Shortly after making the second list, Charles visited his cousin Emma and asked for her hand in marriage. They had ten children and, by all accounts, a loving, respectful relationship that lasted over forty years.

I wish for you what Charles Darwin found and the one greatest thing I have found in my life—a lifelong companion and friend.

September 26

Pulitzer Prize-winning playwright Arthur Miller wrote a little story he called "Please Don't Kill Anything." Some think Marilyn Monroe, his tenderhearted wife, was his inspiration for the story. A husband and wife are walking along the beach at sundown when they see fishermen drawing in their nets. A weather-beaten fisherman is throwing the keepers into the back of a pickup truck, and the little or inedible ones onto the sand where they gasp and flop until they die. The woman, looking at the live fish jerking and gasping, asked the fisherman, "Don't you take these?"

He explained, "No ma'am, they're no good." Soon the couple began picking up the worthless, castaway fish and pitching them back into the sea and watching them flit off home. The grizzled old fisherman watched and smiled and shook his head.

As the couple walked away hand in hand, she smiled and said to her husband, "Now some of them may live till they're old."

He replied, "And then they'll die."

His wife continued the banter, "Yes, but at least they'll live as long as they can."

"Yeah," he agreed, "now they'll live long and prosper and see their children grown up."

She said with tears in her eyes, "I love you" and kissed him, and they walked home together.

Miller ends the story with these words: "And that day fifty particular fish swam home."

Love in general is easy, and pretty worthless, but the price is right—it costs nothing. Love in particular, for those fortunate enough to be on the receiving end, is what life-giving water is to a beached fish.

September 27

A stranger on the phone, pretending to be a policeman, told an assistant manager in a restaurant to take one of the teenage employees into the back office and strip-search her. The manager obeyed the voice on the phone. When the assistant manager ordered the girl to remove all her clothes, she complied. The assistant manager called in her boyfriend to help in the investigation. He continued taking orders from the voice on the phone, orders that included having the teenager perform sex acts.

The boyfriend's defense at his trial was: "I just did what the caller told me to do . . . I've always been the type of person that's very easygoing and I've always followed authority, always."[13]

We teach our children to honor boundaries as they relate to authority. We teach them not to believe everything just because some adult says it. We teach them not to be sheep. Many people have found themselves way down the road to destruction because they trusted without reservation a minister, a teacher, a relative, a boss, a commanding officer, or a president.

Adolf Eichmann and other Nazis who were put on trial at Nuremburg unsuccessfully used the "I was only obeying orders" defense, as did William Calley after the My Lai massacre in Vietnam, as did those involved in Abu Ghraib tortures.

To be moral means, among other things, to think critically. Refuse to check your brains at the door when you enter a church; never mistreat certain people even though the culture may condone it; never blindly swallow teachings; never thoughtlessly follow orders. As my dad would say when I tried the I-was-only-doing-what-they-told-me-to-do Nuremburg defense: "Would you jump off a cliff if they told you to?"

September 28

Namaste! A friend of mine had just returned from a trip to Asheville, North Carolina, and handed me a bumper sticker he found in a shop that displayed that solitary word. He knew I would like it. It is now the first bumper sticker ever to adorn a car of mine.

Namaste is an ancient Sanskrit word that probably originated in India. Before yoga practitioners begin their exercises and when they end them, they bow and say *namaste* to each other. When Hindu or Buddhist people meet each other, they place their palms together in front of their hearts, slightly dip their heads, smile, and say *namaste*. The word means: "The image of God in me recognizes the image of God in you."

It is a gesture of deep respect for the other person. It acknowledges and honors the spark of divinity within the other. It attests to the interconnectedness and sameness of us all. I propose that we substitute it for hello, our meaningless telephone or face-to-face greeting. Does anyone really know what "hello" means? I guess it roughly means the same as "hey" or "hi."

Imagine a day when political opponents, out to prove the other a dirty rotten scoundrel, instead of trashing and slashing, slicing and dicing each other, bow to each other first, smile, and say: *namaste*. Imagine them politely proceeding to exchange big ideas, deep thoughts, respecting—and respectfully disagreeing with—the other's position. Imagine parents and children, husbands and wives, beginning a summit meeting in the den with a bow of respect and the word *namaste*. Might that help head off a name-calling free-for-all? Might that help remind us that we are not God Almighty and the other person a no-count piece of garbage?

Would you prefer "Hey" on your bumper sticker?

September 29

My favorite documentary on educational television so far has been the Civil War series produced by Ken Burns.

In one segment the narrator described a remarkable scene that occurred on the fiftieth anniversary of the battle of Gettysburg. In 1913, what was left of the two armies, mostly men in their eighties, staged a re-enactment of Pickett's charge up Cemetery Ridge. Old Union veterans assembled in their blue uniforms, taking positions approximately where they had stood on July 3, 1863. Old Confederate veterans in gray marched across the open field, where fifty years earlier cannonballs had shredded their ranks. As the octogenarian Yankees in blue toddled down the hill to meet the octogenarian Rebels in gray, a loud war cry went up from both groups.

Then, suddenly, something extraordinary happened. When the two forces collided, instead of shooting and bayoneting each other as they had half a century earlier, or even pretending to do so, the old soldiers spontaneously threw down their weapons and threw their arms around each other. Formerly mortal enemies embraced, held on to each other, and wept.[14]

What was the meaning of that unplanned, unrehearsed ending? In mellow old age the veterans apparently shared the sentiments of another warrior, William Tecumseh Sherman: "I am sick and tired of war. Its glory is all moonshine. It is only those who have neither fired a shot nor heard the shrieks and groans of the wounded who cry aloud for blood, more vengeance, more desolation. War is hell." Or Thomas Paine: "He that is the author of a war lets loose the whole contagion of hell and opens a vein that bleeds a nation to death."

Today kids from different racial, religious, economic, and cultural backgrounds, like the civil war vets in their blue and grey, express that same hope when they stand in a circle, lock arms, and sing a prayer: "Let there be peace on earth."

September 30

Jay Winuk had a brother who died trying to rescue people out of the World Trade Center. To honor Glenn Winuk's heroism, Jay and his friend David Paine founded MyGoodDeed.org.

The two men launched an online campaign to turn the anniversary of 9/11 into a day of volunteerism, charity, kindness, and service. They invite those who visit their website to pledge to do a single good deed to help balance the bad of 9/11 with something positive. Hundreds of thousands of deeds have been posted on their website.

Sharyn Jenkins every year bakes a cake for the third-shift crew at her local sheriff's office in Stafford, Virginia. In Greensboro, North Carolina, a Girl Scout troop cooks dinner for a local fire station Sunday night after spending the weekend helping elderly neighbors get their homes ready for winter. In Cincinnati, one elementary school holds a day of car washes, bake sales, and contests to raise money to feed children in Africa.

New Yorkers, forty in number, including twenty firefighters, traveled all the way to Evansville, Indiana, to help rebuild a church destroyed by a tornado. "It's our small way of saying 'thanks' to all the people from small towns and big cities across America who came to help us," said New Yorker Jeff Parness.

Of this cornucopia of good deeds, Jay Winuk reflects: "Sometimes from great tragedy, hope emerges."[15] How sweet would it be if you, or your bridge club, or your Sunday school class, or your soccer team, like the people of MyGoodDeed.org, chose to champion some constructive project and so counter the destructive forces hard at work in the world.

September Notes

1. Wood, "Secret Fears," 1–4.
2. *University of Delaware*, "Commencement 2000," no pages.
3. *HCFA/CMS*, "Gartner's Views on Life," 13–14.
4. Tierney, "A Serving of Gratitude," no pages.
5. *The Wall Street Journal*, "How an Introvert Can Be Happier," no pages.
6. Mann, "True Tale," no pages.
7. *Singularity Hub*, "Blue Zones," no pages.
8. *The Critical Thinking Community*, "Newton," no pages.
9. Kriegel, *Pistol*, 66.
10. Merton, *In the Dark*, 65.
11. *NPR*, "Covering the Plate," no pages.
12. *The Flying Change*, "Trim Tabs," no pages.
13. Wolfson, "A Hoax Most Cruel," 1–4.
14. *Order of the Arrow*, "50th Anniversary Gettysburg," no pages.
15. *PR Newswire*, "Americans," no pages.

October

October 1

It was no ordinary wedding. The setting was a black barn perched high on a hill. The day was sunless, blustery, and cold. A dozen sheep grazed near the orchard.

The ceremony began with the co-mingling of soils. A representative from each of four sets of grandparents came forward and caringly poured a cup of soil from their home into a common clay pot—McClanahan soil from Maysville, Kentucky; Meade soil from Lexington, Kentucky; Jones soil from Nashville, Tennessee; Willis soil from Manchester, Tennessee. The co-mingling of the soils symbolized the co-mingling of the paths and lives and clans of organic-farmer bride and organic-farmer groom.

The officiant explained that the whole human story began in dirt, with the Lord God molding the first human from red clay. He quoted a scripture about all humans coming from, and one day returning to, dirt. The Lord God, he added, gave Adam and Eve, the first couple, a piece of dirt—not to use, abuse, and exploit, but to love and tend, to be its stewards, to leave it better than they found it.

He charged the groom, after reading William Butler Yeats's verse "Brown Penny," to "stay looped in the loops of her hair." He charged the bride, after reading George Eliot's most loved paragraph, to "keep the grain, and with the breath of kindness blow the chaff away." One of the groom's brothers sang unaccompanied Marc Cohn's "True Companion." The groom's other brother and his wife played guitars and sang "You Are Mine" by David Haas.

Bride and groom tenderly spoke vows they had painstakingly crafted and memorized. They exchanged gold wedding bands, one from a great-great-grandmother and one from a great-great-uncle. I pronounced them husband and wife. They kissed, and seventy cheerleaders—already standing—burst into applause. Our son got the girl of his dreams. Ours too.

October 2

Loren Eiseley overcame a lot on his way to becoming one of the leading environmentalist writers of last century. His mother was deaf and mentally unstable. When his father died, Loren dropped out of high school. "I was loved," he later wrote of his years at home, "but I was also a changeling, an autumn child surrounded by falling leaves. My brother . . . was the one true son, not I."[1] Later he enrolled in college, only to have to drop out when diagnosed with tuberculosis. A child of the Depression, he became a hobo, hopping freight trains and traveling the country.

Adversity, plus riding the rails, plus the doctorate he eventually earned, all helped mold him into a stellar anthropologist and writer. One story from "The Star Thrower," written in the last year of his life, is my favorite. Loren Eiseley is walking along a sandy beach littered with starfish that have been washed up on the shore. He sees a boy picking them up one by one and throwing them back. When he asks the boy what he is doing, the boy tells him that if he didn't throw them back they would surely die. But why save a few, Eiseley asked, when so many are doomed? What difference do you think you can make? As he threw another one back, the boy replied, "It's going to make a lot of difference to this one." Eiseley returned home that day to continue writing his book, but found that he could not write one word. He put down his pen, returned to the beach, and spent the rest of the day helping that boy. Eiseley wrote, "Call me another thrower."

The enormity of need out there overwhelms us. We think, "What's the use? How much change can one person make? What difference does anything we do make anyhow?" If you are a starfish stranded on the beach, getting thrown back into the water makes *all* the difference.

October 3

Never underestimate the power of a dated emotion.

In Pennsylvania, in October, 2006, Charles Carl Roberts IV lined ten little Amish girls against the blackboard and began shooting them. Why? Explanations range from guilt over child abuse he committed years earlier to grief over his own daughter who died years earlier to anger at God over many years.

Early in my career a woman in her eighties imprinted on my mind the power of a dated emotion. In the course of our conversation she made a cryptic reference to something painful that had happened to her when she was young. When I gently probed, a gusher of tears came. After pulling herself together, she spoke with great difficulty about a miscarriage known only to her mother and her. Mother advised her at the time to pull herself together, not tell anyone, and look only to the future, assuring her: "You can have other babies." Neither of them ever referred to the miscarriage again. The patient added, through tears, "I did have other babies, but they weren't the one I lost."

For half a century that lady had bourn her grief all alone. Her only advisor, her mother, whom she trusted, had assured her she was handling it the right way.

If you have some old bitterness or grief or guilt that has festered in your soul, please love yourself enough to seek out a professional or a friend you can trust to accept you as you are, gently hear you out, help you separate the wheat from the chaff, and understand you. Then let it spill. Honest confession can improve your health—body and soul. It might even spare those around you from becoming collateral damage caused by your impacted hurt.

October 4

"What would the school of life have me learn from this that will make me wiser?" Maybe that is the most important question this side of Hurricane Ike. Ike knocked out power in much of Louisville for almost a week in September, 2008. It was Louisville's worst power outage in thirty years.

Winston Churchill reportedly said about Stanley Baldwin, who was the prime minister of England when Edward VIII abdicated: "Stanley Baldwin occasionally stumbles over the truth, but he always picks himself up and hurries on as if nothing had happened." Is this not what separates the mature from the immature, the deep from the superficial—a receptivity to learning something from experiences, especially the hard ones?

Following a weather crisis, an introspective pause is in order. If we do not pause, like Stanley Baldwin we just pick ourselves up and rush headlong into our next experience and nothing is gained. We are the hamster in the wheel, running hard but making no progress.

I heard many references to a precious learning experience, courtesy of Hurricane Ike:

"It's all relative. Relative to the devastation of a tsunami or Katrina in New Orleans or Ike in Galveston, our week-long power outage was a little firecracker pop."

"With no television or lights, my family and I communicated more than we have in a long time."

"We keep too much food in our refrigerators and freezers and need to clean them out more often, instead of waiting for a power failure to clean them out for us."

"Most people are good. My neighbor limited his own power by running cords from his generator to five other homes."

Back when I was a schoolboy, when a child said to parents, "That teacher's not learning me anything," our parents quickly corrected us: "The teacher can't learn you anything. She does the teaching; you have to do the learning." Life offers many teachable moments. What have winds of adversity taught you?

October 5

What is the meaning of life? On the last morning of a two-week seminar he was conducting on the island of Crete, Greek philosopher Alexander Papaderos wrapped up by asking, "Are there any final questions?" One of the participants, Robert Fulghum, noted Unitarian minister and author of *All I Really Need to Know I Learned in Kindergarten*, hearing no one else speak, asked, "Dr. Papaderos, what is the meaning of life?"

Papaderos took out his wallet and removed a small, round mirror. He told how as a child he had found the piece of mirror on a wrecked German motorcycle. He soon learned how he could make it reflect light into dark places—into deep holes and crevices and dark closets. It became a favorite childhood pastime to use his little mirror to reflect light into inaccessible places.

As an adult, it dawned on him one day that the little mirror he carried in his wallet was telling him what he should do with his life. He came to believe that he was meant to be a mirror, that light would only shine in some dark places of the world and in some peoples' hearts if he reflected it there. "This," Papaderos concluded, "is the meaning of life." Then he took his little mirror and caught the bright rays of daylight streaming through the window and reflected them onto Robert Fulghum's face and hands.[2]

Occasionally life presents us opportunity to bring a ray of understanding where prejudice reigns or a ray of information where ignorance is king. None of us is light, or the source of light, but we can, as mirrors, dispel a little darkness now and then.

October 6

"Put a little something back in the pot." I overheard my parents and other adults say that as I was growing up, sometimes in a card game, sometimes when money was being raised for a cause. I sensed what the words meant—"It's your turn now to ante up, to make a contribution"—but I did not know the origin of the expression until I became an adult.

Apparently in the frontier days of our nation when pioneers headed west they came upon settlements or groups of other travelers who would hospitably take them in and feed them and allow them to spend the night. Next morning the grateful guests would go hunting before they continued their journey so they could leave behind a rabbit or a squirrel or a turkey in the pot to make up for what they had consumed.

I have heard of little cabins scattered throughout the Alpine mountains that have a similar history and function. They provide safety and refuge for skiers and hikers who get lost or who need a reprieve from the wind and cold. Each unlocked cabin has a fireplace, and all the finder has to do upon entering is strike a match and light the logs that someone else placed there. Before they leave, they are expected to return the favor and leave the fireplace ready to be lit by the next person seeking shelter.

We too are burning wood that others have chopped. Our foremothers and fore-fathers bequeathed to us communities and parks and churches that they built and maintained. Now the time has come for us to chop some wood for those coming after us. Or, to keep mixing the metaphors: it's time to put a little something back in the pot.

October 7

I have been a door-to-door salesman twice. One summer I sold enough books to pay for my next year of college. In a one-week career as an aluminum siding salesman, I made one sale and quit. I hated it. I would rather walk on red-hot coals than sell door-to-door.

One man's poison is another's meat, and Bill Porter is the proof. Born with cerebral palsy, Bill Porter had to learn to sling himself along to walk. His speech was terribly slurred and difficult to understand. The state of Oregon declared him unemployable.

But Porter believed his mother who believed in him. She told him he could do anything he set his mind to do. He finally persuaded Watkins Products to give him a job as, of all things, a door-to-door salesman. But they agreed only after Porter asked them to assign him to the most undesirable section of town. For the next forty years, Bill Porter walked eight to ten miles a day, knocking on doors peddling Watkins Products. He became their top-selling employee in the nation. In 1997, his door-to-door career ended when he fell and broke a hip while trying to get out of the way of a car.

Bill Porter continued to sell Watkins Products over the telephone—one syllable at a time—until he died in 2013 at age eighty-one.[3]

William Macy plays Porter in a movie. *Door to Door* captures Bill Porter's indomitable spirit and determination. It won six Emmy Awards and is one of the most inspiring films I have seen.

October 8

What do you think of the Supplementary Nutritional Assistance Program (SNAP), formerly known as the Food Stamp Program? It is a polarizing issue in this country. One college student shared with me his struggle:

> I could easily benefit from the SNAP program. I don't have a meal plan, I live off-campus and I can only work on weekends on a tip-based wage, meaning that I sometimes make no money at all. A lot of the time I can buy meals with cash I make from valet, but sometimes I'm not so lucky. Sometimes, a friend will grant me one of their meals. Sometimes, I'll eat a single bowl of Ramen noodles and sometimes I will elect to not eat at all. By the middle of the month, I hardly have any money to spend on anything, barely paying the bills I owe. I cannot remember the last time I had more than two six-packs of Top Ramen in my cupboard, and that is not at all nutritious. I've been thinking of signing up for SNAP, but I have chosen not to. I do not wish to contribute to alleged 'student abuse.' There are too many students and hungry children who need and deserve it more than I.

Three things I find admirable about this student. One, his conscience moves him to struggle over doing what is moral. Two, he identifies with and feels deeply for poor people, especially hungry children. Three, he is driven by a value higher than whether he can legally milk or manipulate the system. Sometimes things that are legal (think slavery) are not right.

I know: there is nothing wrong with looking for loopholes in the law. But that is precisely how moral weaklings who were Wall Street millionaires plunged us into a Great Recession and, instead of going to jail, made themselves millions more.

October 9

In August, 1994, we deposited our middle son thirteen hundred miles from home in Albuquerque, New Mexico. Justin enrolled as a freshman at the University of New Mexico.

One key to adjustment in the freshman year of college for most students is the roommate. Justin's assigned roommate was named Shariff. He was not Native American, like many students at the University of New Mexico. Neither was he Hispanic, as are many students there. Shariff was an Egyptian Muslim. Shariff's parents lived across town. Occasionally Shariff took Justin home with him for a meal. On holidays or between semesters, when our son was too far away or it was too expensive to come home, they moved him into their house. When I flew out once to visit Justin, they insisted I come to their house. They proceeded to feed me a sumptuous meal, served with generous helpings of warm, Muslim hospitality. The summer after Justin's freshman year, while he was working as a counselor at Philmont Scout Ranch, Shariff's family stored all of our son's earthly belongings in their house.

Justin had an excellent freshman year, thanks largely to his roommate and his roommate's family. Our son was the stranger, knowing not one person when he landed there, and a Muslim family took him in. That made all the difference. Ever since, I have not been able to lump all Muslims into a stereotype. I want to assume, unless they can prove me wrong, that they are like Shariff and his family. I want to believe that beyond a label such as Muslim or Mormon, ex-con or congressman, atheist or attorney, garbage man or gay, may be a good human being.

October 10

With only my camera and the clothes on my back, I had two hours to spend in downtown Lexington, Kentucky. When I learned that Lexington National Cemetery, where Henry Clay is buried, was only a one-mile walk, I headed toward the 120-feet-tall Corinthian column marking his grave.

In colonial America, the tallest structure in a town was almost invariably the church with its steeple. Next to it was the town's cemetery. Every day people passed the cemetery and saw a reminder that death is a part of life. In hiding our cemeteries, we may have lost something important, as in "out of sight, out of mind."

My favorite tombstone epitaph that day read like this: "William (King) Solomon. 1775–1854. Hero of 1833 Cholera Plague. For Had He Not a Royal Heart? King Solomon."

Plagues have been around forever. From the biblical ten plagues to the Black Death in 1348 killing more than one-third of the population of Western Europe to the flu pandemic of 1918 killing 675,000 Americans to the AIDS epidemic still with us, plague puts everyone to the test.

Albert Camus, in his novel *The Plague*, after 250 pages of describing in unforgettable detail and imagery a twentieth-century plague, concludes: "On this earth there are pestilences and there are victims, and it's up to us, so far as possible, not to join forces with the pestilences." Following strong character development, Camus sorted the plague-ravaged population into three types: the victims; those who joined forces with the pestilence by profiting off of it or doing nothing to "rise above themselves" to help care for victims; and "true healers who take, in every predicament, the victim's side, so as to reduce the damage done."

One of the true healers in the Lexington cholera plague of 1833 was William (King) Solomon.

As his survivors carved on his headstone: "Had he not a royal heart?"

October 1

I asked a group of teenagers if they had ever had an epiphany, explaining that an epiphany does not have to be a supernatural event like talking with an angel or a burning bush. An epiphany is any experience that becomes insightful enough to provoke a positive change of heart and behavior.

A young man volunteered an experience he had one day years ago when he was riding his bike. One tire was nearly flat, so he took it to the nearest gas station to fill it with air. Then he realized that he was one quarter shy of enough money to feed the air compressor. Because he did not have his cell phone to ask a friend to bring him a quarter or pick him up and transport him and his bike home, he decided to ask around the gas station to see if anyone could spare him a quarter. Several people told him they had no money on them. Others told him they were in a hurry. His last option was an old woman walking by who appeared to be very poor. He asked her anyway. She told him she did not have a quarter, but that she did have a dollar. He thanked her, but then she asked if he needed anything to eat or drink. He politely declined her offer but thanked her again for the dollar.

On his bicycle ride home that day this young man processed within himself what had happened. It dawned on him that he had just experienced two epiphanies:

"People are more than just wealthy or poor. What is more important is whether they are good-hearted or not."

"Anytime someone asks me for something, starting today, I must go out of my way to try to help."

Naïve? Gullible? Bound to get exploited? Yes, but he says so far he has enjoyed being this self "instead of a Grinch."

October 12

A century and a half ago there was a popular sport in America named pedestrianism. People speed-walked over long distances. The all-time champion was Edward Weston. In 1874 he walked five hundred miles in six days. When he turned seventy, to celebrate his birthday he walked from New York City to San Francisco—3900 miles—in 105 days. When he turned seventy-one he walked from Los Angeles to New York City—3300 miles—in seventy-seven days.[4]

Imagine the storms, the stinging sleet, the parching heat, the mountains and the deserts that Edward Weston negotiated. Imagine him putting his feet on the floor in the morning for the one- hundredth straight day, knowing what those feet were going to be going through all that day.

Weston died at age ninety in New York City after being run over by a taxi.

"Pedestrian" is a pejorative term in our day. We call something pedestrian if it is common, boring, or repetitive. Putting one foot in front of the other a zillion times lacks the pizzazz, the sex appeal of a sprinter blazing across the finish line in 9.2 seconds. But if what you need most is endurance, the stamina to keep on keeping on is the greatest of all gifts.

In Samuel Beckett's play *Waiting for Godot* two tramps wait beside a tree for a Mr. Godot whom they do not know and who does not show for many days. One day one of the tramps asked a blind man named Pozzo who was passing by, "Where do you go from here?"

Pozzo replied: "On."

It is hope's nature to march on—like tired Edward Weston or blind Pozzo—whether Godot comes or not.

October 13

On April 19, 1989, a group of over thirty teenagers gathered on 110th Street, at the northern end of Central Park in New York City, for a night of "wilding." They later defined "wilding" as senseless violence performed because it is "fun and something to do." Unfortunately, at that same hour Trisha Meili, a twenty-eight-year-old investment banker, was jogging through Central Park.

Early on, it was believed that the "wilding" teenagers had bludgeoned her, stripped her, raped her, and left her for dead. However, after they were convicted, an older loner who was not one of the teenagers was linked by DNA to her brutal attack.

By the time she was found, her body temperature was eighty-five degrees. Every inch of her body was bruised except the soles of her feet. One eye socket was fractured in twenty-one places. She had lost eighty percent of her blood. She could not breathe on her own. A priest administered last rites.[5]

Meili's identity was kept secret until the publication of her 2005 book *I Am the Central Park Jogger*. She reveals among other things that she was unconscious for twelve days, then in and out of delirium for the next five weeks. She describes how, during her years of rehabilitation, she "always felt an envelope of support and love" from family and friends and hospital staff as well as from countless strangers who wrote to wish her well.[6] That support, she maintains, enables her now to think of herself as a *survivor* instead of a *victim*.

Educator Henry van Dyke wrote: "There is a loftier ambition than merely to stand high in the world. It is to stoop down and lift humankind a little higher." The only thing as important as having an "envelope of support and love" is to *be* one of those envelopes for someone else.

October 14

I grew up singing an old gospel song that began: "I'm pressing on the upward way; new heights I'm gaining every day." Every verse ended: "Lord, plant my feet on higher ground." The take-home message for me was that to be a good person you have to make of your life an odyssey of personal improvement.

A Somalian college student who survived tribal wars, famine, and disease that killed more than one million Somalians, escaped in 1999 with his family to India. Now he lives in America and is helping me appreciate some of the deeper meanings of the "plant my feet on higher ground" prayer. Well on his way to realizing his American dream of finishing a degree, he will be entering one of our helping professions. When I marveled at his journey of self-discovery and individuation and asked him to help me understand what makes him tick, he quoted a sentence from *Poor Richard's Almanac*: "The sleeping fox catches no poultry. Up! Up!"

He explained:

> I have learned that you must not sit down and wait for the poultry to come to you. If you're going to catch the chicken, you've got to get to your feet. Working hard to get a college degree is that poultry to me. I'll always know I *catched* that chicken the fair way and deserve to eat the white meat I *catched*.

Another quote got him through the worst years in Somalia when he was very young. Daily his mother assured him, "We'll live to see a brighter day." That promise, he knows now, she might not have been able to keep, but her promise was enough at that stage of his life to keep him from losing hope.

Victory or defeat lies in the sentences we take to heart. "In the middle of my journey," Dante wrote, "I came upon a dark wood." The sentences we have memorized will be the ones that spring to mind when we come upon a dark wood.

October 15

We sometimes call them "aha!" moments. They are the ordinary events that become extraordinarily significant, even transformative, in a life. While reading some of Frank McCourt's writings, I was struck by how two common experiences changed the direction of his life. McCourt grew up extremely poor. His father was an alcoholic. Most meals were tea and bread. His saintly mother explained to the kids that they were having a balanced meal because it contained a solid and a liquid.

At age ten McCourt got typhoid fever and was hospitalized. Forced to spend a week in the hospital, he found the hospital to be a virtual Eden—three meals a day, sheets on the bed, and books lying around. His lifelong love for literature, especially Shakespeare, began then. Later he became an English and creative writing teacher and taught in New York public schools for thirty years.

Determined to become a published author after he retired, he tried describing his miserable years growing up in Ireland. The right words for a long time would not come. Then one day as he was playing with his granddaughter, he noticed the way she used language, and a light bulb came on. He saw that the right way to write his book was in the voice of a child.[7] He picked up a notebook and wrote these words: "I'm in a playground on Classon Avenue in Brooklyn with my brother, Malachy. He's two, I'm three. We're on the seesaw." It was his earliest memory. He placed it near the beginning of his memoir *Angela's Ashes*. The story was published when he was sixty-six, won him a Pulitzer Prize, and sold more than ten million copies.

Few things are better for seeing things clearly than being admitted to a hospital or playing with a grandchild.

October 16

Franz Stigler and Charlie Brown both died of old age in 2008. They first met as enemies in the skies over Europe on December 20, 1943. Stigler was a fighter pilot for the Luftwaffe, with twenty-two kills; Brown was piloting an American B-17 Flying Fortress. Captain Charlie Brown was on his first mission. Having successfully dropped all his bombs on Bremen, Germany, he was lost and trying to get his crippled bomber back to England. Two of his four engines were dead. Four of his crewmen were badly injured and one was dead. Stigler, instead of shooting down the enemy plane, pulled alongside and gestured to its pilot to follow him. After escorting the Flying Fortress to the North Sea and pointing toward England, Stigler saluted Brown and pulled away.

Neither knew the other had survived the war until they met again in 1990, after much searching by Brown. They hugged and cried. Stigler said, "I love you." Instantly they were fast friends. They regarded each other as brothers for the rest of their lives. Their story is now being told by Adam Makos in a non-fiction thriller titled *A Higher Call*.

Why that title? Stigler had been taught by his commanding officer always to fight by the rules of war in order to save his soul: "If you see an enemy airman dangling from a parachute, don't shoot him down, or I'll shoot you down. I want you to have a clear conscience for the rest of your life. This is what separates men from animals."

Makos, who spent eight years researching and writing *A Higher Call*, explains the book's title as the triumph of one man's humanity over his nationality. "Good men," Makos testified in his interview with Diane Rehm, "can be found on both sides of a bad war."[8]

October 17

What kind of a person writes children's books like *Goodnight Moon* and *The Runaway Bunny*, two of the most popular bedtime stories ever for little ones? We might guess that it would be someone like Lewis Carroll (*Alice's Adventures in Wonderland*) or Theodor Seuss Geisel (*Green Eggs and Ham*) or J.M. Barrie (*Peter Pan)*—someone just a little eccentric and childlike.

Margaret Wise Brown, to celebrate her first royalty check for *Goodnight Moon*, bought a street vendor's entire cart of flowers and threw a party to celebrate with her best friends. Her best friends, like her, were members of the Bird Brain Society, where any member could declare any day Christmas and the other bird brains would come over to celebrate.[9]

We who are rigid and controlled to a fault protest "What a waste!" at such extravagance. We might, in addition, feel a smidge of envy. We wish we could loosen up and be more spontaneous and joyful and generous on singular occasions, like the little boy who was so moved by a homeless man that he broke open his piggy bank and gave him all he had saved.

Brown, who died at forty-two, unmarried and childless, left a will bequeathing royalties from her books to Albert Clarke, a cute, blond, eight-year-old son of a friend. After Albert came of age, the squandering of millions of dollars in royalties from Brown's books ensued. He bought and sold cars and houses on whims. Instead of cleaning his clothes when they got dirty, he threw them away and bought new ones.[10] Poor-little-rich-boy Albert knew the price of everything and the value of nothing.

Is there not a heaven and hell degree of separation between giving ourselves permission occasionally to celebrate a special event with a splurge and frivolously running through a fortune earned by someone else?

October 18

It was the perfect football season. We went 11–0, capping the year with a 13–0 victory over Carthage in the Tobacco Bowl. The Red Raider football team of Manchester, Tennessee, would not go undefeated again over the next half century. I received an announcement in the mail that our team will re-assemble in October to celebrate what we achieved 50 years ago.

What has being a part of that championship season meant to my life? In almost every way, it has been positive. Some moments are as vivid as if they happened yesterday. I still chuckle when I relive my best plays; I still grimace when I remember my worst plays.

As a team, we experienced the thrill of being underdogs who took down a giant, of having grateful strangers press fistfuls of dollars into our hands after we won a big one (money I, of course, humbly refused!), of having our pictures printed in the *Manchester Times* and even the *Nashville Tennessean*. We were—for one season—simply the best. On the other hand, a torn cartilage in my right knee reminds me every day of a high and painful price I am still paying for several years of high school glory.

A letter to the editor in another newspaper, written by a grandfather, criticized the awards ceremony at an elementary school. After the soccer and softball teams and cheerleaders were presented their awards, the parents of those kids got up and took their kids home before the chess teams received their awards.

What is more important in the long run, physical or mental achievement? Both can be invaluable, even for a lifetime. When I think about our grandchildren, if I were making the call, I just might nudge them toward the chess players.

October 19

"IF I HAVE A GOOD TRAIT, IT'S PROBABLY RELENTLESSNESS. I'M A HOUND DOG ON THE PROWL. I CAN'T BE SHOOK!"—Bruce Springsteen

It has many different names: relentlessness, persistence, tenacity, perseverance, doggedness, determination, and steadfastness. It describes that uncanny ability of some individuals to keep on when others quit. One exemplar for me will always be the scrambling quarterback for the Minnesota Vikings, Fran Tarkenton. Even though he never won a Super Bowl, his "scrambling" to make something happen, especially in the jaws of defeat, gives him credentials to speak about winning in the game of life. Tarkenton said:

> I have come to really believe that the people who make it in the world aren't the most talented ones or the smartest or the luckiest or necessarily the bravest. The ones who make it are the dogged ones; it's just plain tenacity. Those are the ones who take the jolts and get up and look at the sky.[11]

Another is H.L. Mencken. He graduated at the head of his class at the age of fifteen. He wanted to become a journalist, but out of loyalty to his father he did what his father wanted: he took a job in a cigar factory. Mencken was bored silly. The day after his father's funeral, he shaved his face, combed his hair, put on his best suit, and went down to the *Baltimore Morning Herald* and applied for a job. Turned down, Mencken kept going back every day for four weeks. The editor, worn down, finally let him write two articles of less than fifty words each.[12] Mencken went on to become one of America's most influential and loved newspapermen, exposing con artists and hypocrisy wherever he found it.

Sometimes it takes stubbornness, bordering on obstinacy, to achieve our dreams.

October 20

I stumbled across a blog dedicated to men giving each other advice on how to treat wives on big romantic days like anniversaries and Valentine's Day. One man wrote that he and his wife do nothing special: "We both look at it as just another Hallmark moment to get you to part with your hard-earned money."

Another man, smarting from earlier failed attempts to be romantic, indexed a time sixteen years earlier when he asked his wife what she wanted and she said, "Nothing." He wrote about what happened when the big day arrived:

> She handed me a card and some chocolate, then stared at me with them big ole green eyes waiting on her gift. Well, needless to say she forgot that she didn't want anything. She cried all day. I went out and bought her a bunch of stuff to make up for it, but it didn't make her any happier. Moral of the story: Men, if your lady says she don't want anything, she's lying. Ladies, if you ask for nothing, don't be surprised if this is what you get.

By way of contrast, this ad appeared in the Personals section of the *Nashville Tennessean* decades ago. I tore it out and saved it:

> Happy Anniversary Betty Sue from your Husband Billy Frey! Thanks for loving me another year. Twenty years ago today it was cold and snow on the ground did lay . . . Twenty years from now I hope to say, forty years ago today I took you to be my bride, now I have nothing to hide . . . Your courage is strong, your spirit high, may we live forever some day in the sky. May your smiles be plenty and your tears be few, Happy Anniversary, I love you Betty Sue.

Shakespeare or Wordsworth, it is not. However, for tenderheartedness, this is a masterpiece. A bunch of stuff is good, but for the affectionate it will always be a distant runner-up to little loving words and little loving gestures.

October 21

When I was a high school senior, one of my responsibilities every Monday was to change the Quote of the Week in the school's lobby. In that lobby was hatched my lifelong love for pithy quotations. My recollection is that many of those quotations came from Ralph Waldo Emerson:

"The only way to have a friend is to be one"

"Who you are speaks so loudly I can't hear what you say"

"Hitch your wagon to a star"

"To be yourself in a world that is constantly trying to make you something else is the greatest accomplishment"

It was years later before I learned what an intellectual and ethical giant Emerson was in nineteenth-century America. Only recently I learned the rest of the story. When Emerson was seven he lost his father to stomach cancer. Three of his siblings died in childhood. One of his brothers, Edward, graduated at the top of his Harvard class but later was committed to an insane asylum and died shortly thereafter. Another brother, Charles, died in his twenties of tuberculosis. Two years after they married, Emerson's wife Ellen, age twenty, died of tuberculosis.

We have to wonder how people whose losses are so great sometimes rise above the gloom to become spiritual models and teachers for the rest of us. Here is Emerson's explanation and advice:

> Finish every day and be done with it; you have done what you could. Some
> blunders and absurdities no doubt crept in; forget them as soon as you can.
> Tomorrow is a new day; you shall begin it serenely and with too high a spirit
> to be encumbered with your old nonsense.

Emerson bids us to let our personal history enlighten and sensitize but never define us.

October 22

If you ever question whether some story you come across is true or an "urban legend" (false), go to a website like snopes.com. Their job is fact-checking. This story is true.

The *Washington Post* conducted an experiment to test people's priorities. Joshua Bell, world-class violinist, played six Bach pieces on his $3.5 million violin for forty-five minutes at a crowded subway station during rush hour. Bell was incognito, wearing street clothes and a baseball cap, wanting no one to recognize him. Over one thousand people passed by. Almost no one stopped to listen. About twenty passers-by left a total of $32.17 at his feet, assuming he was a beggar or just some musician working to earn a little spending money. Several children wanted to stop, but parents hurried them along. The children turned their heads and continued to look while being hustled away. During the concert no one applauded. When Bell finished, no one noticed.[13]

I know—we are all busy, in a hurry, with places to go and things to do and appointments to keep. I doubt that I would have stopped.

Maybe this staged event is a parable, only seen by those who have eyes to see. If we fail to stop and listen to the world's greatest music played by one regarded by many as America's best classical musician, that failure to listen surely means something. It may just mean that we have an underdeveloped appreciation for classical music. Or it might mean, as Wordsworth wrote: "The world is too much with us; late and soon, getting and spending, we lay waste our powers." It might also mean that little children who pause to pluck and stare at a blade of grass or stop to watch an ant crawl or be mesmerized by beautiful music may be onto something big, something that the big people hustling their children through life have lost.

October 23

In *Salt Fat Sugar*, food critic Michael Moss describes how food giants learned to manipulate food by adding as much salt, fat, or sugar as necessary to reach a "bliss" point, the point at which the food becomes almost irresistible. If they found that it took sixteen spoons of sugar for a carbonated beverage to become irresistible or addictive, that is what they put in.

Baseball players refer to the "sweet" spot on a bat. That is the best place for the bat to meet the ball. That one place minimizes sting to the batter's hand and maximizes force applied to the ball.

We sometimes call a person who is exceptionally kind, considerate, and thoughtful, "sweet."

I came across an article in *McGuffey's Reader* written by Oliver Wendell Holmes Sr. that gave me a new metaphor for human sweetness. Holmes compared humans to pears. Different varieties of pears reach their sweet spot (the brief time between being too hard and bitter to eat and the time they begin to rot) at different times. Some varieties ripen in early summer, some in late summer, and some after frost.

Just so, some humans are the sweetest they will ever be early in life. Few, Holmes observed, become ripe and sweet in the middle years. Why? "At thirty, we are all trying to cut our names in big letters upon the walls." He speaks of "the softening effects of advancing age" and cautions: "Beware of rash criticisms; the rough and stringent fruit you condemn may be an autumn or a winter pear."[14]

Shakespeare wrote: "And so from hour to hour we ripe and ripe, and then from hour to hour we rot and rot, and thereby hangs a tale." Indescribably delicious—in people as in pears—is that brief, sweet, mellow time between ripening and rotting.

October 24

In September, 2001, Richard Wiseman and The British Association for the Advancement of Science embarked on an unusual piece of research. Their aim was to find the world's funniest jokes and, through that process, understand better how humor works.

A study of humor can be significant because we know that people who laugh more and do not take themselves too seriously are healthier. Laughter increases our heart rate, helps us breathe more deeply, and stretches muscles in our face, chest, and abdomen. A good laugh is like a quick visit to the gym. One researcher claims that a good laugh is the aerobic equivalent of fifteen minutes on an exercise bike.

Of the forty thousand jokes studied, this one came in second. Sherlock Holmes and Dr. Watson went camping. They pitched their tent under the stars and went to sleep. Sometime in the middle of the night Holmes woke Watson up and said: "Watson, look up at the stars and tell me what you see."

Watson replied: "I see millions and millions of stars."

Holmes said: "And what do you deduce from that?"

Watson replied: "Well, if there are millions of stars, and if even a few of those have planets, it's quite likely there are some planets like earth out there. And if there are a few planets like earth out there, there might also be life."

Sherlock Holmes said: "Watson, you idiot, it means that somebody stole our tent."

Did you laugh? If not, that proves nothing. We all find different things laughable. That being said, our laughs usually do involve someone doing something stupid or violent or both.

Why did I choose not to share the joke that came in first? It has a violent punchline, and Americans nowadays are overdosed with tragic shootings.

Perhaps the British are not.

October 25

"No gap! No gap!"

That is what the father of the bride in the 1970 movie *Lovers and Other Strangers* declared repeatedly to his daughter and future son-in-law. My wife and I still use that shorthand phrase for older-generation people bending over backward to assure younger-generation people that they understand and accept their ways.

The generation gap most of us probably know best is the one between baby boomers, those born shortly after World War II, and their children and grandchildren, often called millennials. One term that drills down to a primary difference between the two cultures is "work ethic." Baby boomers claim they had it and that is what made America great, while subsequent generations seem to lack it and that is their problem. Millennials resist "selling your soul to the company store." They value vacations and travel, ever seeking a healthier balance between work and play than they saw in their forebears.[15]

A twenty-year-old wrote me that one gift she cherishes from her father, who worked three jobs, is how to dust: "This was one of my weekly chores. I wanted to just dust around all the items on the tables and dressers, but he made me pick everything up to dust the entire surface. He taught me that anything worth doing is not worth doing if you don't do your best."

Steve Jobs remembered his father teaching him the best way to build a fence: "You've got to make the back of the fence that nobody will see just as good looking as the front of the fence. Even though nobody will see it, you will know, and that will show that you're dedicated to making something perfect."[16]

There is no organic, irreconcilable gap between boomers and millennials, between producing a high-quality product and taking time to smell some roses. Both virtues sometimes even merge in the same individual.

October 26

I returned to my hometown and went to church on Sunday morning. I saw people there that I had not seen since I left home half a century earlier. After the benediction, I make my way to a ninety-something-year-old woman in a wheelchair. Among other things I said to her: "Did I ever tell you that you were the best Sunday school teacher I ever had?"

Then I grabbed the arm of a man who had been my scout leader, identified myself, and said: "Did I ever thank you for that backpack you loaned me for my first campout?"

After church I went by to visit a man who was in the last stages of cancer. When I was growing up, he had been like a second father to me. He gave me my first job. Knowing I would never see him again, I said to him: "I'm so grateful to you for teaching me how to meet the public, make change, and wrap gifts."

As I was leaving that house, a little choked up, the dying man's oldest son, who had taken his parents into his home to care for them, walked me outside. He told me on the front porch, with great pain on his face: "You know, as good as my dad has always been to me and to everyone else in this town, he never once told me he loved me or hugged me." I was shocked because his dad had always been so affirming to me. His son went on to relate how his younger brother several days earlier had gone up to their dad, taken him by both arms, and declared: "Dad, I need you to understand how very much I love you." Then he put his arms around his dad, held him tight, and said: "I'm not going to let you go until you tell me you love me and until you hug me back."

A defining moment—good for a lifetime—becomes possible when one person sends and another receives *the* blessing: "You are precious in my sight."

October 27

"BEFORE I PITCH ANY GAME, FROM SPRING TRAINING TO GAME SEVEN OF THE WORLD SERIES, I'M SCARED TO DEATH"—Curt Schilling

Schilling helped the Philadelphia Phillies, Arizona Diamondbacks, and Boston Red Sox win World Series games. He retired with an unbelievable postseason record of 11–2. On the inside scared to death, on the mound in the World Series he was unflappable.

Another person who confessed to feelings of fear was Georgia O'Keeffe. She said: "I've been absolutely terrified every moment of my life and I've never let it keep me from doing a single thing I wanted to do." My love for the great Southwest is inseparable from my love for Georgia O'Keeffe's paintings of it. Who would ever have thought that this independent woman who lived alone for so many years in Abiquiu, New Mexico, who occasionally came upon rattlesnakes that had crawled into her house, who was described by all who knew her as quiet, calm and relaxed, was in her own words "absolutely terrified every moment of my life?"

When Steve Jobs, guiding genius behind Apple Computers and world-class innovator in computer technology, was asked what helped him most in making the big, controversial decisions he said tersely, "Remembering that I'll be dead soon." He elaborated: "All external expectations, all pride, all fear of embarrassment or failure, these things just fall away in the face of death, leaving only what is truly important."[17]

After suffering a heart attack, humanistic psychologist Abraham Maslow wrote:

> The confrontation with death—and the reprieve from it—makes everything look so precious, so sacred, so beautiful, that I feel more strongly than ever the impulse to love it, to embrace it and to let myself be overwhelmed by it. I wonder if we could love passionately, if ecstasy would be possible at all, if we knew we'd never die."[18]

Death is coming. Swallow fear. Embrace life. Let yourself, as Maslow urges, be *overwhelmed* by it.

October 28

I have never been aware of people staring out of pity for me or doing a double-take prompted by pity—until now. It all began with what I thought would be a simple out-patient surgical procedure to remove a small skin cancer on my forehead. It became a two-inch incision closed with nineteen stitches. Two days later two-thirds of my face was swollen black, red, brown, purple, chartreuse, and yellow. One eye was swollen almost shut.

People who saw me guessed that I had been dashed against the windshield in a car crash or had fallen down stairs or had lost in a barroom brawl. The most common quip was, "Well, how bad does the other guy look?"

I kept thinking about people with birthmarks on their face or neck, people with cerebral palsy who have to twist and throw their bodies along when they walk, people bald from chemotherapy, and people with Down syndrome. A big chunk of humanity has to deal with people staring at them or turning their faces away from them because they feel sorry for them and wonder what sad story lies behind their appearance.

The people who helped me most were friends and family who saw me, sometimes from a distance, and with angst on their face or in their voice or both blurted out, "Whatever happened!" and then, after conversation, as we parted gave this leper a hug. I will never forget them. One other thing meant so much to me. Strangers, say in a grocery store, when their eyes were drawn to my traumatized face flashed me a big smile. That smile, without a word spoken, conveyed: "Hang in there, buddy" or, "Been there; it's going to be okay" or, "I admire your courage to be out in public; keep on trucking."

Sometimes body English, in the form of hugs and smiles and winks, reaches a spot down deep in the heart where words cannot go.

October 29

I have submitted several manuscripts for books that got rejected. I have submitted several manuscripts that got accepted. Accepted is far better. Having a manuscript rejected is like having someone look at your baby for the first time, a baby you think belongs in Gerber commercials or on a *Parents* magazine cover, and hearing the comment: "What an ugly baby."

Most successful writers had lots of babies rejected before one was accepted. Robert Pirsig received 121 rejections before *Zen and the Art of Motorcycle Maintenance* got accepted. The book sold five million copies. Beatrix Potter's *Peter Rabbit* books were turned down so many times that Potter finally published them herself. Today 151 million copies from her Peter Rabbit series have sold in thirty-five languages. *Moby Dick*, acclaimed by some as the greatest American novel ever, was not a success in Herman Melville's lifetime. The initial printing of three thousand copies did not sell out. Total earnings paid to Melville by Harper and Brothers, the publisher, amounted to less than $600. J.K. Rowling submitted *Harry Potter* to twelve publishers who rejected it. Her books are now the best-selling series in history, having sold almost half a billion copies.

Rejection hurts. I cannot help but like E. E. Cummings's defiant act of poetic justice. His first work *The Enormous Room*—which turned out to be an enormous success—was rejected by fifteen publishers, so Cummings self-published the book and dedicated it to the fifteen publishers who had rejected him.[19]

Despite smiling at the spite in that dedication, I believe that Sir William Osler and Robert Louis Stevenson were both right. Stevenson advised: "To travel hopefully is a better thing than to arrive." Osler agreed: "To have striven, to have made the effort, to have been true to certain ideals—this alone is worth the struggle."

October 30

Whenever we pass through a room we unwittingly remove something and leave something behind. So said French forensic scientist Edmond Locard who one hundred years ago fathered poreoscopy, the study of pores in fingers and ridgeology, the study of ridges in the skin of fingers. Locard had in mind primarily fingerprints, but that principle came to apply to dust and fibers and now things like DNA that criminologists can study under a microscope. The principle has come to be known as The Locard Exchange.[20]

Naturalist Annie Dillard makes a similar point. She notes that everything in nature is going through an exchange process. Woodpeckers and worms, praying mantises and people nibble and are being nibbled on, feed off others and in turn feed others.[21] We are a society of consummate nibblers. On our pass through this room called life we stuff our backpacks and bellies with all we can.

An obesity epidemic is ravaging our country.

The month that begins with Thanksgiving and goes through Christmas has become a national orgy of consumption. Insatiable nibbling—shopping and spending and gorging—is killing us, body and soul.

Humanitarian and social critic Lewis Mumford noted that six of the seven deadly sins—greed, avarice, envy, gluttony, luxury, and pride—have transmuted in our time to virtues. Self-denial is now out; greed and avarice, envy and gluttony, luxury and pride are in.[22]

Hope calls us to discipline our desires, to think more about important things that we are losing and less about how much more we can acquire in our one brief walk through the room of life.

October 31

"From goulies and ghosties and long-leggedy beasties / And things that go bump in the night / O' Lord, deliver us!"

This old Cornish prayer still resonates with little children. They fear monsters under the bed or in the closet, not so much in broad daylight as at night. A friend told me about an experience she had with her five-year-old granddaughter as they were getting ready for bed. The little girl said, as she closed the bedroom door, "We are not afraid." Grandmother inquired, "We are not afraid of what?" The answer came matter-of-factly, "Monsters!" Grandmother asked if there were any in the room and she said no. Grandmother asked if they came, where they would enter, and the little girl said through the closet (which she probably got from watching a movie in which monsters entered through a closet).

The wise grandmother agreed with "we are not afraid" and then comforted her granddaughter further with these reasons why: "Your grandfather and I do not allow monsters in our house. We live in a strong brick house. You are a brave little girl who could yell, 'Go away, Monsters!' Your dog would protect you. There is no door from the closet to outside the house."

Things are scarier in the dark for us adults too. Juan Gabriel Vasquez wrote in *The Sound of Things Falling*: "Thinking in the darkness is not advisable: things seem bigger or more serious in the darkness, illnesses more destructive, the presence of evil closer, indifference more intense, solitude more profound."[23] I would guess that half the scariness of night relates to solitude. We need somebody to help us make it through the night.

October Notes

1. Eiseley, *All the Strange Hours*, 13
2. Fulghum, *It Was On Fire*, 170–175.
3. Fox, "Bill Porter," no pages.
4. Davis, "Old Time Walk and Run," no pages.
5. McDonough, "Trisha Meili," no pages.
6. *ABC News*, "Central Park Jogger," no pages.
7. Grimes, "Frank McCourt," no pages.
8. *The Diane Rehm Show*, "Adam Makos," no pages.
9. *Virago Modern Classics*, "Margaret Wise Brown," 165.
10. King, "The Life and Times of Goodnight Moon." *Today in Literature*, no pages.
11. Brotman, "People," E, 5.
12. *The Writer's Almanac*, "September 12, 2008," no pages.
13. Weingarten, "Pearls Before Breakfast," no pages.
14. Holmes, "How Men Reason," 407.
15. *The Daily Beast*, "Millennial Workers," no pages.
16. Indvik, "Steve Jobs's Biographer," no pages.
17. *Stanford News*, "You've Got to Find What You Love," no pages.
18. May, *Love and Will*, 99.
19. *Literary Rejections*, "Best-Sellers," no pages.
20. *Forensic Science Central*, "Edmund Locard," no pages.
21. Dillard, *Pilgrim*, 227.
22. *Worldwatch Institute*, "The Virtue of Restraint," no pages.
23. Vasquez, *Sound of Things Falling*, 277–278.

November

November 1

What is rich? Who are the middle class? Are you rich? During a debate, two who aspired to be the country's next president sparred over whether someone making $97,500 should be considered middle class or upper class.[1]

Robert Frank, who writes the Wealth Report column for the *Wall Street Journal*, in his book *Richistan: A Journey Through the American Wealth Boom and the Lives of the New Rich*, claims that these days you need at least $10 million to be considered entry-level rich. His interviews with the new rich—those who made instead of inherited their fortune—found that the new rich are for the most part uncomfortable in upper class skin. Having been middle class before they made their millions, the new rich want their children to have their old middle class work ethic.[2] The new rich are still a little put off when referred to as upper class or rich. One man with a one-hundred-foot yacht, looking at the bigger yachts around him referred to his own boat as "just a dingy."

Earlier studies show that when people are asked how much it takes to be rich, they always give a number twice their current net worth or income. Those worth $500,000 to $1 million said they needed $2.4 million. And those with $10 million or more said $18 million." When it comes to defining rich, Americans of all income levels look up, rather than down.[3]

Who has it right? Forrest Gump's single mother offered her son this philosophy: "Forrest, you only need so much to live on. All the rest is just for show."

Are you rich?

November 2

Perusing obituaries in the Sunday paper, I was struck by the number of photographs. Two-thirds of the death notices were introduced with a picture of the deceased. It made me wonder if I would want a picture of myself included with my obituary, and if so, which picture would I choose? My recollection is that fifty years or so ago only the picture of "important" people appeared in the paper when they died. What changed? Maybe it is that now families pay for the obituary, so if they pay a little more and buy more space, the obituary will include a picture.

Several of the pictures in the obituaries were obviously taken decades—some more than half a century—before death. One obituary that stood out had "before" and "after" photos side by side. The black-and-white one was World War II vintage; the one alongside it was recent and in color. I suspect that says something about modern views of aging. Are we less accepting of the aged face than we were several generations ago? I thought of Coco Chanel's commentary on aging: "Nature gives you your face at twenty. Life shapes your face at thirty. But the face you have at fifty is the face you have earned."

My favorite picture, evoking a smile, was a picture of a woman who died at ninety-six. On her head was a tiara. I imagined that it was presented at her ninetieth-birthday celebration. She could not have looked happier, crowned "queen for a day."

James Baldwin, who overcame poverty, "frog eyes," and an emotionally abusive stepfather to become an inspirational writer, wrote: "Your crown is already bought and paid for. All you have to do is put it on your head."

I am happy for Phoebe Mae that a regal headdress adorned her farewell to this world.

November 3

There was a sweet moment this past weekend when we were in the backyard after I raked the leaves. Our daughter spontaneously lay down on the grass and said "Daddy back" which means, "Daddy get on your back too." We lay on the ground for a while and pointed out trees, clouds, squirrels, and leaves. I can't remember how long ago it must have been that I last lay down in the grass on my back and looked at the sky.

The e-mail was from our son. The little girl is our eighteen-month-old granddaughter.

Their experience brought to my mind Thomas Hood's plaintive lines on lost childhood: "I remember, I remember / The fir trees dark and high; I used to think their slender tops / Were close against the sky: It was a childish ignorance / But now 'tis little joy / To know I'm farther off from Heaven / Than when I was a boy."

As I recently watched the Muppets being interviewed on the fortieth birthday of Sesame Street, the interviewer asked, "What do you plan to do in your next forty years?" I liked their quick answer: "Play! Dance! Sing!" By play, I doubt that they had in mind video games or a DVD.

We hurried, harried adults should occasionally ask ourselves how long it has been since we took the time to lie down in the grass on our back and look up.

Remember the wisdom of Chief Crowfoot, the Blackfoot warrior: "What is life? It is the flash of a firefly in the night. It is the breath of a buffalo in the wintertime. It is the little shadow which runs across the grass and loses itself in the sunset."

Johnny Cash might add, "Times a wastin."

November 4

When one of our sons was about five, he went through a period when he would not clean his plate. My wife and I were brought up on the child-rearing philosophy that you cannot get up from the table until you clean your plate, so we automatically tried to enforce that with our kids. We would make him sit there while we cleaned the table and washed the dishes. Eventually we would look over and he would have a big smile on his face. His plate was empty, so we excused him from the table.

One day more than a month later, after we thought he had outgrown that eating issue, we detected an unpleasant odor coming from somewhere in the kitchen. After much searching we discovered it was coming from under a green cabinet that was close to our son's seat at the table. There we found a stash of partially consumed meals that he had cagily placed there when our heads were turned.

Imagine if instead of taking out the trash in our homes and putting it in the big garbage receptacle that the garbage truck picks up, we hid it—a little in the closet, a little under the bed, a little in the attic, and a little under the green cabinet. Only a person with serious emotional problems would do that. Yet we do something similar with our emotional garbage. We work overtime at hiding our faults so we can come off "cool" and having it all together.

Conventional wisdom tells us that honest confession is good for the soul. What a heavy burden it is to conceal personal garbage. It feels a little like trying to hold a football under water. What a relief it is to have someone trustworthy in our lives who will listen well and facilitate our moving a little or a lot of our personal trash from the inside out.

November 5

Wilma Glodean was born prematurely on June 23, 1940, weighing in at a little over four pounds. Many babies born that small back then did not survive. Much of her childhood was spent in bed. Following bouts with double pneumonia and scarlet fever, at age four she contacted polio. Doctors told her parents she might never walk again. Wilma was fitted with metal leg braces when she was six. Her mother Blanche, who worked as "help" for wealthy white people, heard that there was hope for her daughter at Meharry Hospital, a medical facility for blacks in Nashville. Once a week, Blanche drove one hundred miles roundtrip to get treatment at Meharry for her afflicted daughter. Wilma was the twentieth of twenty-two children in the household. The family was very poor. Every day her brothers and sisters took turns massaging Wilma's crippled leg.

At age twenty, Wilma Glodean Rudolph became the fastest woman in the world. Long before Missy Franklin won four gold medals swimming, Wilma Rudolph won three gold medals running at the 1960 Olympics in Rome. Italians nicknamed her *La Gazzella Negra*, The Black Gazelle.

The governor of Tennessee, Buford Ellington, who was elected as "an old-fashioned segregationist," offered to welcome her home from Rome with a parade. Wilma Rudolph made it clear to him that she would participate only if it was not a segregated event.

Later Wilma Rudolph attended Tennessee State University, receiving her bachelor's degree in elementary education. In July, 1994, shortly after her mother's death, she was diagnosed with brain cancer, and several months later at age fifty-four Wilma Rudolph died.[4] She inspired many athletes, especially African-American females, most notably Florence Griffith Joyner, the next woman to win three gold medals in the Olympics.

Rudolph's most famous sentence may be: "Believe me, the reward is not so great without the struggle."

November 6

Jim Wallis, founder of *Sojourners* magazine, once overheard his four-year-old son Jack, after praying for family members, finish: "And God, there are a lot of poor, hungry, and homeless people—any questions or comments? Amen." At age four, little Jack is interrogating God. Months later, Wallis witnessed his nine-year-old son Luke pray these words after learning that thirty thousand children die every day of hunger or disease: "Dear God, I pray that so many children won't die again tomorrow, but that's unlikely. So, dear God, I pray that it will be their best day ever. But that's stupid. So, dear God, help us to stop this from happening."[5] Luke agonizes over the horrible things that happen to innocent children and then ponders what caring people should do.

Albert Schweitzer at age eight was given a Bible by his father. Albert—future theologian, humanitarian, and Nobel Peace Prize recipient—read it. Some of the stories puzzled him. If the wise men brought gifts of gold, frankincense, and myrrh, Albert wondered, why were Jesus and his parents poor? And when Albert read about a rain that lasted forty days and nights, covering even the mountaintops with water, he found that hard to fathom because it had rained all summer in his hilly hometown and water did not even get up into the houses. His father explained that back then it rained in buckets, not drops. Little Albert was not so sure.[6]

We teach our kids to question and not just swallow whole whatever the authorities tell them. Tennyson wrote: "There lives more faith in honest doubt, believe me, than in half the creeds." Swallow it whole, Spanish writer Jose Bergamin might say, and you have swallowed—unchewed and undigested—a superstition.

November 7

We were taught as children that big things sometimes come in small packages, like a diamond ring or a key to a new car. The same goes for speech. George Washington's inaugural address was barely one thousand words long and was probably delivered in ten minutes. It is considered one of the great speeches in American history. Compare that with inaugural addresses of recent presidents that are more than an hour long and are for the most part boring, partisan, forgettable, self-serving harangues.

Good Morning America once had a little video segment called "Your Week in Three Words." Most often three people would hold up a card, each with one word on it, like these: "It's a girl"; "No more braces"; "I hate shots"; "Thank a farmer"; "Lost my tooth."[7]

Thoreau, who moved to the woods to live simply, packed the values that drove him there into two verbs: "Simplify, Simplify."

One entertaining part of travel by car sixty years ago was coming upon Burma-Shave commercials. A message was broken into words on five small signs spaced a couple hundred feet apart, like these: "If daisies / are your / favorite flower / keep pushin' up those / miles per hour"; "If / you drive / when you're / drunk/ carry a coffin / in your trunk"; "Don't lose / your head / to gain a minute / you need your head / your brains are in it"; "Is he lonesome / or just blind / that guy/ who drives / so close behind?"[8]

A professor received a letter from a student who had been in his class decades earlier. The student, whose name and face the professor could not recall, thanked him for a note the professor appended to the end of a term paper. Sensing the student was deeply depressed, the professor had penned: "Jim, I believe in you." This student wrote to say that those five words saved his life.

Little things can mean a lot.

November 8

Frumpy, dowdy, homely, plump. Those were some of the adjectives journalists applied to Susan Boyle of West Lothian, Scotland, when she appeared on the *Britain's Got Talent* show. The Associated Press commented on "her frizzy gray-tinged hair curling wildly and a gold lace dress clinging unflatteringly to her chubby frame." But when Susan Boyle opened her mouth to sing, the judges' jaws dropped. Before she finished, the audience leaped to give her a standing ovation. In the next two days tens of millions around the globe downloaded her performance on YouTube. Many viewers reported goose bumps, chilly spines, or tears.[9]

How do we account for the Susan Boyle phenomenon? One, she is a gifted singer. Two, she embodies the Ugly Duckling, Cinderella, Rocky Balboa, or Slumdog Millionaire story. More than nine-tenths of us resonate to that story because we, like her, are not straight out of central casting—like the Ken and Barbie "perfect tens" who sat judging Susan Boyle. Real people get to stand up and cheer once in a while when riches and cosmetic surgery and privilege get trumped by talent.

For her five minutes of fame, Susan Boyle—unemployed and living in a row house in a rough neighborhood—fittingly chose to sing "I Dreamed a Dream." The song is from Victor Hugo's *Les Miserables*, a musical about miserable wretches in nineteenth-century French slums struggling to keep their dreams alive.

"Full many a flower is born to blush unseen," wrote Thomas Gray, "and waste its sweetness on the desert air." Susan Boyle is one exception to that rule. She knew she had a gift and seized the opportunity to express it. All of us have some gift. Susan might say to us, "Dream your dream. If the moment comes—grab it with gusto."

November 9

"THE GREATEST COMPLIMENT THAT WAS EVER PAID ME WAS WHEN ONE ASKED ME WHAT I THOUGHT, AND ATTENDED TO MY ANSWER"—Henry David Thoreau

A friend was discharged from the hospital yesterday following successful surgery. From the day of admission, cards and flowers poured in, surrounding her with symbols—reminders of how much she is loved. But a few well-intentioned friends brought more discomfort than pleasure. Here are some of her words of wisdom for family, friends, and clergy who would be comforters.

When you are a hospital patient and sick as a dog, you hope well-wishers will have the good judgment to limit their visit. Ben Franklin said that visitors, like fish, begin to smell after three days. Five minutes over the phone or fifteen minutes in person—enough time to register genuine concern—is usually enough, especially when the patient is in pain or nauseous or sleep-deprived. Polite patients may feel tremendous pressure to be hospitable and friendly, even when they would rather nap or they feel like they are going to throw up.

St. Francis of Assisi said, "Preach the gospel. If necessary, use words." Visitors can sometimes be terrible listeners. One person phoned my friend and after asking "How are you?" proceeded to spend the next fifty-seven minutes talking about her own troubles. That can happen, especially when the patient is a very good listener.

Instead of shooting the breeze about sports and weather, visitors might ask open-ended questions like: "How's it going today?" or "What's been most difficult?" or "How's the hospital been treating you?" or "Would you tell me—a healthy person today—what it's like to be you in that bed?" or "What are you learning from this? Let's say I'm your student; what would you teach me?"

Most of us feel flattered to encounter someone sincerely interested in what we think and how we feel and can hear us out, should we seize the opportunity to pour out our hearts.

November 10

Rheumatic fever at age thirteen struck him down and left him a puny teenager. Nevertheless, he was determined to play baseball on his seventh-grade team. The school was small, so everyone who tried out made the team. He sat on the end of the bench the whole season. Years later he said: "The coach never even looked at me; I might as well have been invisible." The coach never put him in a game—until the last game of the season.

In the ninth inning, with two outs and two strikes on the batter, the coach sent him into right field. Put in for one play, the last pitch of the season, he stood in right field before peers, their parents, and the whole wide world, humiliated. He said, "I just wanted to sink into the ground and disappear."[10]

Dan Rather went on to become a hard-hitting reporter and journalist. He anchored the CBS Evening News for twenty-four years. Rather cites that experience at age thirteen as a formative event in his life, driving him to be successful, to be thought of by himself and others as an okay person.

This true story brings to my mind three truths. One is how many of us, like Dan Rather, have a "not measuring up" event in our adolescent years that makes us grimace whenever we recall it—not making the team, being taken last when sides are chosen on the playground, striking out with the bases loaded. Two is how many people, instead of going through life blaming the coach or parent or teacher for a loser's script, use that bitter memory to fuel a relentless pursuit of excellence, partly to prove the coach wrong and partly to prove themselves adequate. Three is how many little Dan Rathers are out there right now who seek affirmation, a word of encouragement, an "I think you're okay" from a sensitive and savvy adult.

November 11

If we played the word association game, the first word "hope" conjures up might be "dream," "wish," "fantasy," "imagination," or "optimism." But hope (looking forward positively) is anchored in remembering (looking back). Hope draws strength from those times we overcame obstacles that seemed insurmountable. Remember when they told you it could not be done, and you did it? Remember when you doubted you were up to it, but you were? Remember when you could see no way out, but there was one and you found it?

Carol Burnett said, "Those who survive use what they've gone through."

Hope remembers times the naysayers were proved wrong. In Marlo Thomas's *The Right Words at the Right Time*, Muhammed Ali recalls the day one of his teachers warned him, "You ain't never gonna amount to nuthin." After he won the Olympics, he went back to Louisville and walked into that teacher's classroom and showed her his medal.

Hope remembers kind, affirming faces of individuals who encouraged us by conveying in word, deed, or look: "You are a good person and I believe in you." In hard times their faces pop up from our memory bank. We are keenly aware of them sitting on our shoulder and once again mentoring us, once more whispering words of encouragement into our ear. We find ourselves asking what they would do in our situation, or we imagine how they might advise us if they were physically by our side.

Hope remembers strong sentences from the Bible, other literature, or wise advice from family or teachers or friends. How many times when I was growing up and struggling, the little engine that could, that kept on saying "I think I can, I think I can," popped into my mind. Stored, recalled words sometimes give us that little extra nudge that is just what we need to get over the mountain.

We do not venture into the great unknown a blank slate, unequipped. In our backpack are strong, formative memories—manna and medicine and energy enough to get us over the mountain.

November 12

The first time I heard it on the local news several weeks ago I assumed it was just a poor choice of words, the kind of thing a green journalist might do. I chuckled—or was that a groan—when I heard it. Then several days later another journalist said the same thing. Evidently it is becoming the word of choice for the physical, material part of us—what is left—when we die. We used to call it the body, as in, "His body was cremated" or "The body was flown back to the family in Arizona." Now the word "remains" has replaced "body."

"Remains" for me conjures up road kill or the pitifully little that is left of a person who disappears and whose bones and clothing are found in the woods or a lake months or years later. The media could say carcass if they do not want to use the word body, but carcass signifies some decomposition, like a rusty 1970 Volkswagen that has been winched out of a swamp or a cow ravaged by wolves. Cadaver sounds like a donation to a medical school or an autopsy about to be performed. And corpse makes you think foul play is involved.

The increased use of "remains" has, I have to admit, made me think. What *does* remain of us, if anything, after we leave this earth, besides our cremated or buried or missing body? Few of us will have a bridge named for us or a chair endowed at Stanford in our name or even a cul-de-sac named for us.

The best most of us can hope for is that there will be a few people for one generation—two at the most—who will on occasion remember us with a little affection or gratitude or both.

November 13

Is anyone really surprised? Another football coach, one day repeating promises of everlasting love and denying even having a wandering eye, the next day leaves his team for what he hopes will be a better deal. He explained in a letter to his former, angry players: "This decision was not easy but was made in the best interest of me and my family."[11] Who could fault that reasoning? We act in the best interest of ourselves and our family every day. What is wrong with wanting to improve our station in life, to provide better for our hungry young 'uns? What could be wrong with aiming higher?

Successful coaches and politicians running for high office help set the question: are there *any* values that should ever trump self-interest? Should we ignore or discount or trash any principle that would get in the way of gratifying self and getting ahead?

Should integrity and truth-telling and trustworthiness ever get in the way of getting ahead? There is an old saying: "A man's word is his bond." I think of historical examples like Sir Thomas More, trusted advisor to Henry VIII, who refused to countenance the king's divorces and paid for his principles with his life. More's final words on the scaffold before he lost his head were: "The King's good servant, but God's First."

Soldiers who sacrifice life or limb for country, martyrs like Thomas More, common Joes and Janes who drop their change in a Salvation Army kettle—are they fools for marching to a different drummer than self, for being true to principles they believe are greater than greed and self-advancement? Rabbi Hillel asked: "If I am not for myself, who will be for me? But if I am for myself alone, what am I?"

November 14

"Conscience is a dog," wrote Frenchman Nicolas de Chamfort, "that does not stop us from passing but that we cannot prevent from barking." Many of us have a strong conscience. It barks at us, chastening us when we even think about doing wrong. Freud called that voice in our heads our superego. It can make neurotics of us, making us pathologically concerned with doing right.

Evidence keeps coming in that many growing up today do not suffer pangs of conscience. Michael Josephson, founder of the Josephson Institute and one of the most respected ethicists in America, has surveyed thirty thousand American youth every two years since 1992. In a recent survey he found that eight in ten, including those from private religious schools, admitted to lying. And 63 percent of students in religious schools admitted to cheating. Maybe the most significant finding was that 93 percent said they were satisfied with their personal ethics, considering themselves no worse than most other people they know.[12]

Could it be that presidents looking the public in the eye and lying—Nixon: "I am not a crook" or Clinton: "I did not have sex with that woman"—sent a message to our youth about lying that took? Could it be that tobacco executives raising their right hands and swearing that they did not believe nicotine was addictive sent a message to our youth that anything goes so long as you look comfortable doing it and avoid getting caught? Or are poorly-formed consciences determined closer to home, where parents and grandparents and aunts and uncles have done a lousy job modeling integrity and honesty and highly-principled living?

Comedian Henny Youngman said: "When you battle with your conscience and lose, you win." John Leonard, cultural critic wrote: "Honor grows from qualms."

No one wants a dog that barks all the time. However, we do need one that barks loud and long when we flirt with doing something we know is wrong.

November 15

Our church has a new library. It is tiny as libraries go, taking up only about three square feet of space. It is called The Little Free Library. Shaped like a cottage, it sits like a birdhouse atop a post. It stands four feet off the ground and about twenty feet off the heavily-traveled highway in front of the church. The driver-friendly location beckons motorists to pull off the road, look over the twenty or so books from the comfort of their open car window, and take with them a free book of their choice. The idea is to take a book and leave a book, shop and swap, any time, day or night. Best sellers, classics, and children's books have been most exchanged so far, but it is still too early to know whether the trust system will prove to be sustainable.

Swanton Berry Farm, just outside Santa Cruz, California, has thrived for years on the honor system. Customers take the fruit and vegetables they want, calculate on provided scratch paper what they owe, and stuff their cash or check into an unattended honor box. Jim Cochran, who runs the farm stand, reports that through the years most customers have left more money than they owe.[13]

Brain researcher Paul Zax in *The Moral Molecule* says that whenever we trust or feel trusted, the brain releases oxytocin, the same neuropeptide that helps a mother bond with her newborn and that helps people behave hospitably and generously to strangers. The result is that we leave the transaction feeling better and kinder.

What we learn from The Little Free Library experiment may be what Albert Camus, an atheist, concluded on the last page of *The Plague*. He postulated: "What we learn in time of pestilence is that there are more things to admire [in people] than to despise."

November 16

"Teach a Girl, Save the World." That is the title that *Good Housekeeping* gave Judith Stone's article about Amira Mortenson, twelve-year-old daughter of Greg Mortenson. Author of the bestseller *Three Cups of Tea*, Greg Mortenson raised funds for sixteen years to build schools that teach kids, most of them girls, in remote areas of Pakistan and Afghanistan.

Amira, a seventh grader in Boseman, Montana, got herself deeply involved in Pennies for Peace which in one year raised almost one million dollars in pennies for books, pencils, and other supplies for the schools her father built. After an earthquake in Pakistan in 2005 killed seventy-four thousand people, Amira, then eight years old, asked her dad, "Do the kids over there have anything to play with now?" From that penetrating question, she and her dad decided to raise funds to purchase ten thousand jump ropes for the children of Pakistan who lost their toys in the earthquake.[14]

Meanwhile, in Louisville, Kentucky, Michala Riggle, a fifth grader with an autistic brother named Evan, started making bracelets and selling them for $3 to raise money for autism research. To date Michala and a burgeoning team of volunteers have raised four hundred thousand dollars. Her goal now is to raise three hundred million dollars to build the most advanced autism center in the world and name it the "We Believe! International Autism Research and Treatment Center."[15] Who is ready to bet against twelve-year-old Michala as she goes for her impossible dream?

An old African proverb declares: "Educate a boy and you educate an individual; educate a girl and you educate a community." The good-old-boys system, having held the reins of power from time immemorial, is swiftly losing its grip. Little girls like Amira and Michala, as they increasingly assume leadership roles, will be positioned, using the words of Aeschylus, to "tame the savageness of man and make gentle the life of this world."

November 17

This city slicker went to the woods not "because I wished to live deliberately, to front only the essential facts of life" like Thoreau, but to farm-sit for my son and his wife so that they could take a long-delayed four-day honeymoon. My assignment was to care for Tierra, their hardly-dainty, eighty-pound, one-year-old German Shepherd, to feed and water the chickens, throw the chickens "scratch" and gather their eggs, and to keep the fire from going out in their small wood-burning stove that provides the only heat in their modest house.

My thoughtful daughter-in-law left the refrigerator stocked with nutritious and delicious dishes she had created, like butternut squash soup, roasted garlic hummus, winter squash soufflé, and a loaf of oatmeal and sunflower-seed bread. In the refrigerator, one of their few luxuries, she had left a gallon of straight-from-the-cow milk to wash things down.

The first thing you see when you walk in their front door is a hanging on the wall: "The Earth Says Much to Those Who Listen." Over the portal from the living room to the kitchen one word is suspended on a plaque: "Simplify."

Carden and Courtney are organic vegetable farmers who supply fifty Community Supported Agriculture (CSA) subscribers with a box of fresh vegetables twenty-five weeks of the year. They live, like Thoreau, deliberately—loving each other and their plot of earth and their community, eschewing consumerism, and fronting "only the essential facts of life." Their lifestyle is too Spartan for this tenderfoot, but their down-to-earth values make me examine mine.

November 18

I hope you have the words from two song titles in—or will soon add them to—your repertoire. One is the theme song from the hit Disney movie *Frozen*. My granddaughter and I saw the first showing of it on opening day. At an elementary school talent show I attended recently, "Let It Go" from *Frozen* was the song performed most.

Fun words for little children to sing, "Let it go!" can become a strong mantra for adults bent on leading healthy, happy lives. We inevitably fail, flop, and fall many times along the way. After giving ourselves ample time to grieve and lick our wounds, one day we have to say to ourselves: "Self, enough! Let it go!" Neither could we nor should we forget the painful experience. We need to learn from it. But after a while the time comes to dispatch its grip on and power over us.

We are bound to make enemies along the way. Some people are going to hurt and wrong us. But part of being a responsible adult is recognizing that coddling grudges hurts us more than anyone. Some fine day we need to tell ourselves: "Self, enough—let it go!" We may have to say that to ourselves more than once.

A second mantra to consider adding to our playlist of song titles is "Let It Be." Paul McCartney, when he was going through hard times in 1968, had his mum, who had died ten years earlier, appear to him in a dream and say some calming words like, "It's going to be alright. Just let it be."[16] Out of that sweet dream came the classic Beatles' song.

I hope you are unable to put "Let It Go" and "Let It Be" out of your mind. Repeating three words might even change your life.

November 19

When our children were young and relatives came to our house for Thanksgiving, after the feast we played a game. Before they arrived, my wife and I folded sheets of paper accordion-style and wrote a different person's name at the top of each sheet. As our family sat in a circle, we handed the sheets out with the instructions: "Write something you appreciate about the person whose name is at the top, fold it over where no one else can read what you wrote, then pass it to the person on your right who will do the same thing." When we were finished, each person had a sheet full of accolades to take home.

Last week while cleaning out a desk, I came upon three of those sheets that had been yellowing and gathering dust for decades. The names of three different family members were at the top. Here is a sampler of some handwritten endearments:

"You always listen to others and take time to let them know that you care about them."

"I like the way you can tell my feelings just by looking at my face."

"I appreciate the quick way you help when you sense I need it."

"I like the way you camp out and throw darts."

"I like your attitude that you can handle whatever comes."

"You have always been good to me."

"You are a fine reader for your age."

"You are both wise and playful."

We need not wait for a prompt or a contrived exercise to verbalize how we feel, to tell those close to us the respect and affection we have for them. There is a time for all things, a season for every purpose under heaven, including a time to accentuate the positive and eliminate the negative. There is probably not a very good reason to wait until Thanksgiving.

November 20

I drove past Dealey Plaza and the Texas School Book Depository with the Hertz sign and clock above it and grassy knoll below it a dozen times in the early 1960s on my way to and from college in West Texas.

Into my Hebrew class at 1:10 p.m. on that infamous Friday poked a student's head, shouting: "The president's been shot!"

The professor gave a knee-jerk response: "Well Jackie, how did you enjoy your trip to Dallas?" I was underwhelmed by this professor's sensitivity to his young, stunned, captive audience. He clearly did not share the anguish and anger of a nation mortified by the assassination of a president and the end of Camelot on November 20, 1963.

The primary black-and-white images seared into my mind that weekend are of Walter Cronkite removing his glasses and wiping a tear while announcing that the president was dead; live coverage of Jack Ruby shooting Lee Oswald; the horse-drawn caisson bearing the president's flag-draped coffin through the streets of the capital; "John John" on his third birthday saluting his dead daddy.

I carry within me three legacies of JFK. One is captured in the Latin phrase *homo homini lupus est*: "man is wolf to man." Breaking stories on the evening news of the latest mayhem, murder, and meanness daily confirm that hard law. A second is the incomparable wisdom of electing leaders with gravitas. If cool, calm, rational heads had not prevailed during the Cuban missile crisis, thousands of nuclear weapons would have fallen down out of the sky, transporting any survivors back to the Stone Age. Third was that tantalizing call to service over self-aggrandizement that President Kennedy issued at his inauguration. That call set a permanent hook in many young, idealistic imaginations like mine that had no way to foresee the narcissistic era ahead. He said: "Ask not what your country can do for you; ask what you can do for your country."

November 21

Lately I have been the beneficiary of some unusual, thoughtful, and thought-provoking gifts.

I received a letter from a friend in Nashville, Tennessee, stating that a cash donation had been given in my name to Nashville's Table. Nashville's Table collects excess food from restaurants, hotels, hospitals, schools, and grocery stores and distributes the food at no cost to agencies serving the hungry, needy, and homeless.

A couple whose wedding I had performed wrote to say that they had donated money in my name to Heifer International, an organization that helps fight hunger and care for the earth by giving animals to families in need. Part of their donation bought a starter flock of ducklings for a family in Xiang Qian, China. Selling eggs and ducks will in a relatively short time enable that family to triple their income. Another portion of the newlyweds' gift bought a beehive, complete with box and beekeeping training for a family in El Salvador. Income from honey, beeswax, and pollen will give them a good livelihood.

I think of the upcoming Christmas season and the untold billions of dollars that will be spent on obligatory gifts that are unneeded and may be re-gifted. What a waste of resources in a world where a billion human beings are struggling to survive and where the gift of a beehive or a flock of ducks would be the best gift many families will ever get.

It takes courage and conviction and the vision of a saner world for a family to buck the culture, unplug the Christmas machine, and begin a more humanitarian tradition. Those are the kind of people who will, next thing you know, be giving ducklings to a family in China, taking up yoga, protesting a war, or campaigning to save snail darters.

November 22

From what I have seen, attitude is independent of and often does not correlate with circumstances. Take gratitude. Some of the most grateful souls I know have been through hell. Some are cancer survivors, or bereaved parents, or lack two nickels to rub together. Conversely, some of the most self-pitying ingrates I have ever known have had advantages of abundance, health, and opportunities galore.

When the Pilgrims declared the first Thanksgiving in 1621, half their family and friends had perished either on the voyage over or during their first months on the new continent. William Bradford, their governor, wrote: "That which was most sad and lamentable was that in two or three months' time, especially in January and February, being the depth of winter, and wanting houses and other comforts, being infected with the scurvy and other diseases, there died sometimes two or three a day." So what did the Pilgrims do? They held a Thanksgiving service.

When Abraham Lincoln proclaimed the first national day of Thanksgiving, it was 1863, in the middle of a war that would claim half a million lives. Twice as many more died of infection, disease, starvation, and other causes. So what does Lincoln do but proclaim a national day, not of wearing sackcloth and ashes, but of Thanksgiving.

Has this been a lean year or a bounteous year in your life? Regardless, it is good to be grateful. It is healthy to reach down deep inside and scare up some thanks. Epictetus was right: "People are disturbed, not by things, but by the views they take of them." Gratitude is a choice, independent of circumstances, good for the soul.

November 23

"Does anyone ever truly see life while they're living it?" Thus asked Emily, the little girl in Thornton Wilder's *Our Town* who had died and was given one day to go back home and see everything again. She could see everyone but they could not see her. She wandered around for her one day, appreciating the beauty of everything. The stage manager answered Emily's question: "The saints and artists, maybe—they do some."

An experience that helps some of us see life while we live it is a close encounter with death. "The prospect of hanging," as Samuel Johnson said, "concentrates the mind wonderfully." Think of Dostoyevsky's brush with death. Jailed by the Czar for his radical ideas and condemned to death, he was taken out into the bitter cold to face the firing squad several days before Christmas in 1848. At the last minute, the retreat sounded and his death sentence was commuted to eight years hard labor in Siberia.[17] His depth as a writer, expressed so movingly in *Crime and Punishment* and *The Brothers Karamazov*, was rooted in those moments before the firing squad.

Our fourth grandchild was born at 1:30 a.m. on Thanksgiving Day, 2010. Something went wrong at delivery. He was placed on a ventilator and rushed to the neonatal intensive care unit. Medical crepehangers, heads drooping and faces long, dutifully explained to us that, if Clark lived, he would never walk or talk. My wife and I spent Thanksgiving afternoon at home, the rain pouring down outside, weeping for our little grandson whose brain might be severely and irreversibly damaged—if he lived. What irony that he was born on Thanksgiving Day.

Thanks to wonderful caregivers and technology, Clark Willis is now perfectly healthy. His paternal grandparents will never make saint or artist, but we are better at seeing life while we are living it.

November 24

Many today regard Stephen Hawking as the world's greatest living genius. He is probably best known for his work on black holes and for authoring "A Brief History of Time," the most successful popular-science work ever.

At age twenty-one, Hawking was diagnosed with amyotrophic lateral sclerosis (ALS). Medical authorities gave him two years to live.

Hawking has been almost totally paralyzed for decades. Now in his seventies, he still "writes" with his mouth, using a breath synthesizer connected to a computer. He has written books and many scientific papers at the rate of three words a minute.

In his autobiographical materials, Hawking reflects on the impact the prospect of an early death had on his life. It urged him onward, he says, to intellectual breakthroughs. Before the terminal diagnosis, he was bored with life. Shortly after coming out of the hospital, he had a dream that he was about to be executed. "I suddenly realized," he recalls, "that there were a lot of worthwhile things I could do if I was reprieved. If I was going to die anyway, I might as well do some good."

Another earthshaking experience occurred before Hawking's discharge from the hospital. A boy sharing his room died of leukemia. Hawking writes: "It had not been a pretty sight. Clearly there were people who were worse off than me. Whenever I feel inclined to be sorry for myself, I remember that boy."[18]

This is the season in our culture for counting blessings. My thanksgiving resolution this year is to take for granted fewer ordinary things, like being able to breathe unaided by a ventilator, being able to walk, talk, kiss, and hug. Every other good thing in my life is icing on that good cake.

We the living, like Stephen Hawking, have been given a reprieve. Should we not, like Hawking, do something worthwhile with it?

November 25

Albert Schweitzer offers these insights on giving thanks:

> When I look back upon my early days I am stirred by the thought of the number of people whom I have to thank for what they gave me or for what they were to me. I am haunted by an oppressive consciousness of the little gratitude I really showed them while I was young. Many a time have I, with a feeling of shame, said quietly to myself over a grave the words which my mouth ought to have spoken to the departed while he or she was still in the flesh . . . One other thing stirs me when I look back at my youthful days—the fact that so many people gave me something or were something to me without knowing it. Such people, with whom I never perhaps exchanged a word, yes, and others about whom I merely heard things by report, had a decisive influence on me; they entered into my life and became powers within me. Much that I should otherwise not have felt so clearly or done so effectively was felt or done as it was because I stand under the sway of these people . . . I think that we all live, spiritually, by what others have given us in the significant hours of our life. Much that has become our own in gentleness, modesty, kindness, in willingness to forgive, in veracity, loyalty, and resignation under suffering, we owe to people in whom we have seen or experienced these virtues at work, sometimes in a great matter, sometimes in a small . . . If we had before us those who have thus been a blessing to us, and could tell them how it came about, they would be amazed to learn what passed over from their life into ours."[19]

This is the day to thank others for what has passed over from their life into ours. Happy Thanksgiving!

November 26

A young man called to ask if I would visit his mother. She was hospitalized and he feared she was dying.

Three topics of our conversation in her hospital room I will share. They deal with profound issues, issues that need addressing before we are on our death beds. At one point I asked about unfinished business: have you said everything you need to say to your inner circle of family and friends? She smiled and said that she had. The tributes her family delivered at the memorial service corroborated in spades that she had.

I asked about regrets. Grateful to have had a good education and satisfying career, to have birthed and reared two wonderful children who were happily married, she regretted not having had the opportunity to be a grandmother, an experience outside her control. And although widely traveled, she regretted never having made it to the Grand Canyon. She added with a smile, for my benefit: "If you've got a place you want to see, don't delay. Make haste. Go."

When I asked what she expected death to be like she hesitated not one second: "Transition."

"Hard?" I asked.

"No, easy," she said. "This is hard."

A practicing Christian Scientist, she died "like one who wraps the drapery of her couch about her and lies down to pleasant dreams," to borrow William Cullen Bryant's words in *Thanatopsis*. Some of my take-home messages from that visit are the need to say often those three little words to those we love, not to postpone indefinitely the things we most want to do, and to discuss freely with a few significant others how we ideally one day hope to "take our chamber in the silent halls of death."

November 27

On a sultry day in Coleman, Texas, a young couple and her parents were playing dominoes on the porch. At one point the patriarch suggested that they drive into Abilene for a meal at a new restaurant. They loaded into a 1968 Buick with no air conditioning, drove fifty-three sweltering miles, ate a mediocre meal with poor service, and then returned to Coleman in silence—tired, sweaty, and disappointed.

That night one of them admitted that he had never really wanted to go to Abilene in the first place. Then they all, one by one, confessed they had not wanted to go either, but because they thought everyone else did, they just went along.

This story is known as the "Abilene Paradox," after a videotape Jerry B. Harvey produced in 1974.[20] "Going to Abilene" joins "peer pressure, "herd mentality" and "groupthink" as shorthand for those times when we were not comfortable with the direction things were going, but instead of speaking up when it could still make a difference, we, like the lemmings in the Disney film, went with them over the cliff.

I think of times when I sensed things were going wrong but I was W. H. Auden's "unknown citizen" and held my peace, like the day in 1964 when the House voted 416–0 and the Senate 88–2 to war against North Vietnam, or the many times I was in the company of people putting down homosexuals or women or non-Caucasians and said nothing to dissociate myself from those views.

Just this morning one of the members of our book club e-mailed to make a case for canceling our annual retreat scheduled for this weekend. I was overjoyed! We had not wanted to go either, but lacked the chutzpah to say so. It was our perception that everyone else was gung-ho to go.

One sign of personal integrity is that when we really would rather not go to Abilene, we speak up.

November 28

I grew up going to church three times a week. My family was there every time the doors opened because we believed that was what the Bible commanded us to do in order to go to heaven when we die. Now that I am grown I still go to church, but for different reasons. I am not absolutely sure that they are the right reasons, or better reasons, but they are my grown-up reasons.

Let me explain with a couple of quotes from Anne Lamott. In *Traveling Mercies* and *Plan B*, she discusses why she goes to church and why she makes her teenage son Sam go.

Anne Lamott grew up a flower child of the 1960s. Religion was no part of her upbringing. Her parents consistently ridiculed religion. But after years of promiscuity, alcohol abuse, destructive relationships, and suicidal thinking, Lamott found religion in a Presbyterian church. In a chapter from *Traveling Mercies* titled "Why I Make Sam Go to Church" she writes: "I want to give him what I found—a path and a little light to see by." In *Plan B* she adds, "I want him to see the people who loved me when I felt most unlovable. I want him to see their faces. He gets the most valuable things I know through osmosis."

Personally, that is my first and main reason still for going to church. Something about me craves being part of a little band of strugglers who have shared values and are muddling through marriage, divorce, child-rearing, sickness, depression, loss of parents, personal failures, job changes, getting old, and a host of other stressors, together. I love having my own little "second family" who genuinely care about me and my issues. My second reason is related to the first. I go because some Sunday someone there may need me.

November 29

My father-in-law survived the Great Depression, fought World War II and the Korean War, and returned home to build the American dream. He is the definition of a "self-made" man if ever I knew one. For the past quarter century, for example, way up in years, he made a living mowing yards in the summer and cutting and selling firewood in the winter.

At eighty-seven he fell while getting out of bed in the middle of the night, badly breaking his femur. He instantly realized that he faced months of rehabilitation in an institution.

The Greatest Generation does not whine: "It wasn't the fault of the bed frame or the mattress or the floor," he insisted as we speculated over why he fell. "I was light-headed when I sat up and should have waited a minute to get out of bed. It's my responsibility and mine alone."

As we winter-proofed his house, we came across more than forty boxes of family-size Cheerios and Special K and sixty Omaha steaks in the freezer. We stopped counting the soap bars and cake mix boxes and toilet paper rolls stashed in the attic, garage, and car trunk. The Depression had taught him to save and prepare for a rainy day, even a second Great Depression. We found a few $20 and $50 bills hidden in books. He kept a cash stash hidden in his house in case the banks should ever fail again, as they did in 1929. Imagine that.

The Greatest Generation lived by a simple code: Survive. Work as many jobs as it takes to provide for your family. Encourage your kids to go to college—their ticket to a better life than you had. Love your country. Go to church. Save for the hard times. Don't make excuses.

They are a dying breed: a breed apart.

November 30

An acquaintance of mine married a sailor who was away from home months at a time in a nuclear submarine. Sometimes for long months she would have no idea what or how dangerous the submarine's mission was, when she would hear from him again, or even what ocean he was under. Their relationship, extremely stressed, survived, and today they enjoy a satisfying marriage and a beautiful family.

Blind Man's Bluff is a non-fiction thriller about the critical part submarines played during the Cold War. One story tells how a submarine commander and his wife handled long separations. They made a pact that when he was at sea they would both look at the same star at exactly the same time of night and for one minute send each other loving thoughts. Most nights the submarine was not up to periscope depth, so the sailor had no chance to look skyward. But his wife faithfully gazed at their special star every night at the set time, weather permitting, not knowing if he was able to do the same. She knew that maybe once at best, while parted, their eyes and hearts would be fixed on the same star on the same night. That was enough for her to keep the ritual, faithfully and lovingly, until homecoming.[21]

One of our sons and his wife composed wedding vows that included this pledge: "We are a single traveler." When something is so high you can't get over it, so low you can't get under it, and so wide you can't get around it, love has a way of finding—or creating—a way to protect the bond.

According to Shakespeare, true love "bears it out, even to the edge of doom."[22] The edge of doom for some is months overseas; for others it is months under seas.

November Notes

1. Hopkins, "Middle Class," no pages.
2. Watson, "How Rich Is Rich?" no pages.
3. Frank, "A Rich Person's Definition," no pages.
4. Engel, "Wilma Rudolph," no pages.
5. Wallis, "A Calendar," no pages.
6. Schweitzer, *Memoirs*, 26-27.
7. *ABC News*. "Your Three Words," no pages.
8. Rowsome, "The Verse," 1-29.
9. Flynn, "Susan Boyle's Story," no pages.
10. Green, "Cut," 295–296.
11. *ESPN Sports*. "Petrino," no pages.
12. *Character Counts*. "The Ethics of American Youth," no pages.
13. Franklin, "Psychology of Honor System," no pages.
14. Stone, "Teach a Girl," no pages.
15. *Beading to Beat Autism*. "Michala's Story," no pages.
16. Pierce, "Paul McCartney," no pages.
17. *This Day in History*. "Dostoevsky," no pages.
18. Getlen, "Stephen Hawking," no pages.
19. Schweitzer, *Memoirs*, 104–109.
20. *Advanced Knowledge*, "Abilene Paradox," no pages.
21. Sontag, *Blind Man's Bluff*, 273.
22. Shakespeare. *Sonnet 116*.

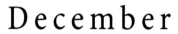

December

December 1

QUESTION: According to polls, what is the fastest growing religious group in the United States?

ANSWER: The Nones. Many Nones consider themselves Christians, although they may attend church only at Christmas or Easter if at all. Most Nones regard themselves as moral or spiritual persons, just not active participants in a particular congregation or denomination.[1]

My spiritual hero and role model for forty-five years has been Albert Schweitzer. With three earned doctorates, he decided to pour out his life serving the sick and dying of Africa. When natives asked the jungle doctor why he had come to them, he declared, "It is the Lord Jesus who has told the doctor and his wife to come to the Ogowe."[2] Schweitzer was considered a heretic by many Christians because of his unorthodox theological views. He had little interest in following the creeds and doctrines developed by councils and denominations over the nineteen centuries since Jesus. Schweitzer believed that following Jesus meant leap-frogging all that history and simply continuing Jesus's work of healing, serving, and loving. He wrote: "A Christian is one who has the spirit of Christ. This is the only theology."[3]

He wrote in a letter to a friend: "The spirit of Jesus commands, and we must obey. Jesus is the master of our lives, our Lord. We do not teach theories about him—that is not the decisive test; rather, we teach the kind of obedience with which we serve him."[4]

Jesus specified "the kind of obedience with which we serve him" as feeding the hungry, welcoming strangers, giving water to the thirsty, clothing the naked, taking care of the sick, and visiting people in prison.[5] You wonder what Jesus would think of what we have made of his plain and simple message and practice.

December 2

Her obituary was exactly two inches—six sentences—long.

Several who attended the funeral had worked alongside her for years. She was the quintessential "round peg in a round hole." Her gift was nurturing, especially young children and old-timers. As a nurse's aide, the only criticism she ever got came from supervisors who occasionally had to warn her to do less for a child so the parents would do more. When she retired in her sixties, she became a professional nanny. Having virtually reared several children from two different families, she was forced to retire from that career by a massive stroke.

A bulletin board on a tripod by the funeral home's podium held some of her favorite things. It displayed mainly ribbons—red, white, and pink ones but mostly blue ribbons awarded over several decades for baked confections at the state fair. A grandson selected and played music for the service. Seated down front facing the assembled, he pushed the start button on his boom box at the appropriate times. The prelude was Elvis Presley's rendition of "How Great Thou Art." Before the eulogies began the boom box played Louis Armstrong's "What a Wonderful World." Mourners filed up to the casket at the end of the service to Israel Kamakawiwoʻole's version of "Somewhere Over the Rainbow." Few eyes were dry.

During the interment, following forty-eight hours of rainy, gray gloom—the sun came shining through. Tears gave way to some smiles as mourners said together Psalm 23, commended her soul to God, and committed her body to the earth.

I heard one friend of the family whisper to someone as he walked away: "Her gift was taking care of others. Plus, she was a great cook. She's wearing a robe and a crown right now—if anybody is."

December 3

Depression feels, according to Henri Nouwen, like you are on the dark side of the moon. Parker Palmer calls depression "the snake pit of the soul." Winston Churchill named his depression "the black dog." Mingling these metaphors, depression feels something like being down in a deep, dark pit full of snakes and unable to find much light or hope.

The first thing to do in dealing with something as debilitating as depression is to name it. Calling it what it is takes a giant first step toward getting some power over it.

My wife and I have a code term for those days when we are feeling blue or down. We say to the other, "I'm feeling low pot today." I got that term decades ago from Virginia Satir, the great family therapist. When she was a girl on a Wisconsin farm there was a huge black pot on her back porch. It held homemade soap at times, stew at other times to feed threshing crews, and manure for flowers at other times. The family called it "the 3-s pot." Anyone who approached the pot had two questions: what is in it today, and how full is it?[6] Satir used that image to help clients describe their feelings: "high pot" for feeling on top of the world, "low pot" for feeling down on self or life.

Down in the dumps? First, name the demon. Admit, "I'm depressed." Next, talk to some wise, caring, trustworthy person about it. Then make yourself do something totally out of character for a depressed person. Take a brisk walk. Play some "up" music and sing and dance along. Break the cycle—act the way you want to feel again.

When your pot is getting low, put something yummy in it.

December 4

"I'm comfortable in the skin I'm in" has become a cliché. It is easy, even fashionable, for celebrities and others to profess how comfortable they are with themselves. But words are easy. Sometimes words conceal more than reveal.

An old story still taught to children in the Middle East is about the need to accept ourselves as we are, "warts and all." It is the story of Abu Kasem's slippers. Abu Kasem was a wealthy merchant known for, among other things, being miserly. He always wore slippers which were old, ragged, and stained. Most people would have been ashamed to wear them in public but Abu wore them everywhere. When asked about them he smiled and said: "I think they still have a few more miles left in them."

The story details several attempts by Abu to part with his slippers. He threw them in the river Tigris but fishermen caught them in their net and returned them to Abu. He buried them in his backyard. A suspicious neighbor was watching, and thinking he was hiding a treasure from tax collectors, reported him to the authorities. They dug up the slippers, scolded Abu, and returned his slippers. Then he drove out to the country and threw them into a deep lake, but the lake fed the town's water supply and the slippers clogged up the pipe. Workers fixing the mess recognized Abu's slippers and returned them to the owner. The slippers just kept coming back.[7]

Abu's slippers represent our whole selves—our family of origin, our culture, our IQ, our faces, our temperament, our heartbreaks, our foibles, our choices, our skin, our scars. Abu's slippers speak to a universal need to embrace and own all our parts. Tweaking Tennyson's words from "Ulysses," we say to ourselves, "All that I have met has become a part of me."

December 5

The story is likely a very old story that could have originated anywhere between Aesop and Mark Twain. I came across a version of it in the October, 1995, issue of "The Hope Health Letter."

Once upon a time there was a man who lived in a tiny hut with his wife, two small children, and his elderly parents. He tried to be patient in the crowded conditions but the noise and absence of privacy wore him down. One day in desperation he consulted the village guru. "Do you have a rooster?" asked the wise man. The man replied that he did. "Well, go home and move the rooster into the hut with your family. Then come back to see me in a week."

The next week the man returned and told the guru that living conditions were deteriorating, with all the rooster's crowing and stinking up the place. "Do you have a cow?" asked the guru. The man reluctantly nodded yes. "Then take your cow into the hut also, and come back to see me in another week."

Over the next several weeks the man—on advice of the guru—made room in his hut to add a goat, two dogs, and his brother's children. Finally he could take it no more. In a fit of anger he kicked all the animals and guests out, leaving only his wife, children, and parents in the hut.

The place suddenly was very spacious and tranquil.

And they lived happily ever after.

This story is an ancient version of: "I complained about my heating bill until I met a person whose hut had no heat." How much of our grousing and whining would stop if we had a smidgeon of an inkling how much worse things are for many others and could be for us?

December 6

We do not know the date of Jesus's birth. For hundreds of years after Jesus was born his followers showed little interest in knowing, much less celebrating, the day he was born. Origen, whom many consider the greatest Christian teacher of the third century, pointed out that it is pagans who celebrate the birthdays of their gods, not the Christians.[8] It was only after the emperor Constantine, three hundred years after Jesus, effectively made Christianity the religion of the Roman Empire that Christians began to talk up a big birthday party for Jesus. But no one knew the date. May 20 and January 6 made the short list. Finally, 350 years after Jesus was born, December 25 won out. But it would be another five hundred years before Christmas—"Christ's mass"—became a major Christian holy day.

Why December 25? Augustine, the great fifth-century theologian, disliked the date. He considered it heresy to identify the birth of Jesus with Saturnalia, for centuries the Roman Empire's most popular festival that partied for a week in mid-December with the lighting of candles, giving of gifts, and much feasting and drinking. Saturnalia concluded with Sol Invictus, Birthday of the Unconquerable Sun, on December 25.[9]

Although the birth date of Jesus is unknowable, I cannot imagine a more appropriate time to locate his birth than in December. Nights are long. The short days contribute to SAD (seasonal affective disorder) and make us long for a turning. In late December, Old Sol does a pivot, adding more light daily until three months later another spring arrives.

Maybe our task is to make Christmas less about drunkenness, gluttony, getting and spending, as in Saturnalia, and more about increasing hope and light in the world. Scripture's interpretation of Jesus's advent agrees: "The light keeps shining in the dark, and darkness has never put it out."[10]

December 7

"We can't go back and make a brand new start, but we can start now to make a brand new end."

Is this a piece of sophomoric, pious drivel? Surely it was written by someone oblivious to the world of suffering, someone hermetically sealed high above the fray in a comfy tower.

Actually the writer survived three years in Auschwitz and Dachau concentration camps where his father, mother, wife, and brother perished, where everything he possessed got taken away and destroyed, where he daily faced hunger, cold, brutality, and the second-to-second possibility of being exterminated like a cockroach.

Following liberation by Americans from the concentration camp on April 27, 1945, Viktor Frankl dedicated the remainder of his days to encouraging people in extreme circumstances to persevere and find enough meaning in life to carry on.[11] Frankl's message is essentially this: "Don't expect happiness as your right. You waste your time asking, 'Why am I unhappy?' or 'What is life's meaning?' Ask rather, 'What is life demanding of me right now?' Then get busy doing it. Do good things, honorable things, responsible things, magnanimous things, and not just as means to some end. Do them just because they are right. In doing the right you forge within yourself the only thing you completely possess, what no one can ever take from you —your attitude."

At ninety, losing his vision, Frankl told interviewer Matthew Scully that with every new physical challenge he draws a deep breath, pauses a second, and then says to himself: "What I would have given then if I could have had no greater problem than I face today."[12]

December 8

There is a program for children ages six to eighteen that a national research organization measured for effectiveness and found the children 46 percent less likely to begin using illegal drugs, 52 percent less likely to skip school, and 33 percent less likely to hit someone. The program is conducted by volunteers.[13]

Big Brothers Big Sisters, now over a century old, is the most effective youth mentoring organization in the nation. Their measurable results testify to the enormous power of one-to-one relationships in inspiring and guiding children, particularly children who lack many or any positive adult role models

Once a week, in a mentoring program called "Every 1 Reads," I tutor two boys who are lagging behind in reading skills. We read books like *Crazy Hair Day* and *The Puppy Who Wanted a Boy*. Instead of feeling embarrassed at being pulled out of a class for tutoring, the boys feel special—singled out for individualized attention. They eagerly look for clues to how each story will end. They innocently compare parts of the book's story to their own story, uninhibitedly commenting on the good, the bad, and the ugly of their life back home.

This mentor gets much from the mentoring. One day the boy who wants to be an artist was eager to draw a picture for me in the little drawing book I had given him. First he drew a giant heart. Then he turned the heart into a man's torso, with arms, legs, and head protruding. The man's hair was kinky and white like mine. I watched as he smiled and printed on the heart-torso, "I Love You." When he smiled and proudly handed the drawing to me, I gulped, and returned the smile.

His mentor savors that moment.

December 9

"Success is counted sweetest for those who ne'er succeed"
—Emily Dickinson

Did Alexander the Great really sit down and cry because he had no more worlds to conquer? We will never know for sure; however, many famous people tell us that achieving success is not all it is cracked up to be. No one expressed this more poignantly than Tennessee Williams. Three years after his smashing success with "The Glass Menagerie" and four days before "A Streetcar Named Desire" opened on Broadway, he submitted an article to the *New York Times* titled "On a Streetcar Named Success."

He spilled over two thousand words on how, "snatched out of virtual oblivion and thrust into sudden prominence," he had come to hate being one of the pampered elite.

> The sort of life that I had previous to this popular success was one that required endurance, a life of clawing and scratching along a sheer surface and holding on tight with raw fingers to every inch of rock higher than the one caught hold of before, but it was a good life because it was the sort of life for which the human organism is created . . . You should not have too many people waiting on you; you should have to do most things for yourself. The sight of an ancient woman, gasping and wheezing as she drags a heavy pail of water down a hotel corridor to mop up the mess of some drunken overprivileged guest, is one that sickens and weighs upon the heart . . . Nobody should have to clean up anybody else's mess."[14]

The one theme of this cry of disillusionment from Tennessee Williams is, in his words, "the vacuity of a life without struggle."

Be careful what you wish for.

December 10

I once had a staff member who was smart, moral, likable, and gifted in many ways. But he had a "follow through" problem. Whenever he was asked to report on a project assigned to him he responded enthusiastically, "Working on it!" or sometimes with this variation, "Getting there!" It took me a while to figure out that those words meant he had not done much. He required regular prodding to pick up the pace.

There is a moment in the movie *Star Wars*, as Yoda is coaching Luke Skywalker on how to actualize his inner resources, when Luke yells out, "I'm trying!" Yoda the Wise rejoins, "Do, or do not. There is no try."

Attorney Lee Rosen, who has practiced family law for decades, writes: "If there's one thing I've learned it's that 'I'll try' means 'probably not.' When I say it myself I'm already figuring out a way to bail. When my employees say it, I know it's never going to happen. There's 'yes' and there's 'no.' When someone says 'yes' I know they might not succeed, but I know they'll do their best. More often than not, an 'I'll try' doesn't even make it onto the to-do list. It's dead on arrival."[15]

Those on the dating circuit tell me that when someone says, "I'll try to give you a call" or "Let's try to stay in touch" that they are just being polite and are not really interested. "Try" is, consciously or subconsciously, a noncommittal, wishy-washy word. Often if we substitute "I'll fail" for "I'll try" we get the true meaning behind the words.

"Just say no," Nancy Reagan once famously said. Jesus taught his students not to swear: "When you make a promise, say only 'Yes' or 'No.' Anything else comes from the devil."[16] Yoda counsels: "Do, or do not. There is no try."

Nike shouts: "Just do it!"

December 11

When I was a boy, people dressed up for church. Men wore suits and women wore hats. I remember being taught that dressing up was a sign of respect toward God—that we should come before God in our finest. Any more I suspect that it was also partly to fool others into thinking that we were the way we looked—together, whole, successful, and contented, as in the old song popularized by Frank Sinatra, "I've Got the World on a String."

Today many preachers, even in some of the mega-churches, no longer wear robes or suits into the pulpit. They wear shirts with the collars open and shirttails out. I think some of it may be strategy to lead with their humanity instead of their divinity, to say with their clothing: "I'm one of you." The congregation is also dressed down.

Occasionally some church, when they can't find anyone else, invites me to preach a sermon. When I stand before them I see things differently than I did years ago. Many years of working in a hospital, seeing people literally and figuratively stripped down to essentials, warped me to think that beyond every scrubbed-up, smartly-dressed, smiling exterior is a wounded soul. Going into imagination mode, I picture a big bandage on her head, him sitting in a wheelchair with one leg elevated in a cast, and you with a plastic tube coming out your nose and emptying into a yellow bag.

Now I think of the church not as some museum for saints, but a hospital for the sick and injured. The preacher's enormous responsibility is to hear the prayers of the wounded. John Milton, blind, worded a prayer for all us wounded supplicants warming a pew: "What in me is dark / Illumine, what is low raise and support."

December 12

In her youth Diana Nyad never dreamed of becoming the world's greatest long-distance swimmer. After three Florida high school championships swimming the backstroke, her ambition was to make the 1968 Olympics team. That dream was crushed by a bout of endocarditis. After three months in bed, Nyad resumed her swimming but quickly became convinced that her days of competitive speed swimming were over.

She decided to switch to marathon swimming. In 2013, at age sixty-four, on her fifth attempt since 1978, Nyad became the first person—male or female, young or old—to swim the 110 miles from Cuba to Florida without a shark cage. She swam all the way not knowing what sharks, storms, jellyfish or other sea creatures might await her, especially at night.[17]

Beyond her age, endurance, and courage, several other things about her historic feat earn my respect. One month after her fifty-three-hour historic swim, she swam back and forth for forty-eight hours in a pool set up at a busy Manhattan intersection. She was parlaying her fame into donations of more than $103,000 for Hurricane Sandy victims.[18]

Nyad credits the mantra "Find A Way!" for much of her success. Through all those years preparing for her historic swim, she says there was never a waking moment without the vision of that other shore and without feeling pressure to tend to every detail that would help make her dream come true.

When the swimming got toughest, Nyad drew strength from writings of the brilliant physicist and quadriplegic Stephen Hawking and from visions of the yellow brick road in *The Wizard of Oz*. Nyad reflects: "We all need to somehow find the courage, the endurance, to find a way to our respective, individual, other shore."[19]

Bloggers who swim competitively now write about being "Nyad-tough" and "kindling their inner Nyad."

May you be Nyad-tough-enough to make it to your other shore.

December 13

I hardly saw it coming. Some are saying that all the problems with this generation can be traced back to Mr. Rogers. Fred Rogers of *Mr. Rogers' Neighborhood* for decades inoculated little ones with a self-esteem message: "There's no one else in the world like you, and I like you just the way you are." Now some say that he single-handedly birthed a generation of kids intoxicated with their own importance.

In the workplace, Mr. Rogers's kids give their Greatest-Generation and Baby-Boomer bosses fits. They expect to be paid more, have more flexible work schedules, have more recognition programs, have more vacation and personal time, and have cell phones and iPads provided. Pampered by Mr. Rogers and coddled by their parents, they are high-maintenance. They do not follow orders well or cotton to authority. They are all about self.

Hmm. Seems I remember hearing how a combination of Elvis shaking his hips and Benjamin Spock teaching permissive parenting in his 1946 blockbuster *Baby and Child Care* ruined my "war babies" generation.

The kids in the neighborhood of Mr. Rogers, now grown up, may be sending a report card back to their seniors that reads something like this: "You people put all your energy into making a living and not enough into making a life. We believe jobs are meant for people, not people for jobs. We are not about to make the mistake you made of gaining the world and losing your souls."

I think of all the "If I had it to do over again I would go barefoot more and pick more flowers" kinds of articles that older people have been writing for the last several decades.

One thing I can promise you hospital chaplains have never heard a dying person say: "My only regret is that I did not give the company a bigger piece of me."

December 14

Publicists declare: "This is the book Santa doesn't want you to read." That book would be Wharton economist Joel Waldfogel's *Scroogenomics: Why You Shouldn't Buy Presents for the Holidays*. It is a rant on how Americans waste over $70 billion a year on Christmas gifts that recipients may not want, need, like, or keep.[20]

If you resonate to that—to the shameful wasting of billions of dollars on obligatory Christmas gifts—I have an idea for you. In an ideal world, a just and compassionate world, we would give gifts at the winter solstice to needy people instead of to those who already have more toys or clothes or sweets than they know what to do with or have enough space in which to store them.

We just bought a water buffalo for $250. Our children will get a card informing them that a share of a water buffalo has been given in their name to help a poor family. Through Heifer International you can give a heifer ($500), a sheep ($120), a flock of geese or ducks or chicks ($20), three rabbits ($60), or a bee hive ($30) to help an impoverished family make a living and begin a business. The recipient family is required to "pass on the gift," to give one of the female offspring to a neighbor who has undergone Heifer International's animal husbandry training. Gifts are passed from recipient to recipient until entire communities are transformed.[21] Heifer International sponsors almost a thousand of these kinds of projects in over fifty countries. The movement is based on the proverb: "Give a man a fish and you feed him for a day; teach a man to fish and you feed him for a lifetime."

I hope our kids will not be too disappointed not to get a chia pet to unwrap this year.

December 15

Once I wrote an article about three words that have lost their meaning in our time due to overuse. One word was "awesome." I contended that it should be used for rare, extraordinary events instead of for tasty peanut butter or an entertaining movie. A second word was "amazing." When everything is amazing, nothing is amazing. The last word was "absolutely." What is so wrong, I argued, with simply saying "yes"?

Two "A" words currently sit atop my favorites list. One is "amateur." The word comes from one of the first words Latin students learn, *amo*—the word for "I love." True amateurs do things because they love doing them, not because it puts food on the table or looks good on a resume. I am an amateur photographer. I know precious little about apertures and I make no money off the pictures I make. I just love looking for beauty in nature and, like the hunter who bags the big buck, bringing it home

"Anonymous" is my other favorite word. Last week I received the kindest card. Somebody wanted me to know how much she (the handwriting looks to me like a woman's) appreciates my work. I wish I knew who sent it. That person did it to affirm me and make me feel special. I have three or four suspects, any of whom might have sent it. I feel warmer and kindlier toward all four.

An unidentified person lavished the city of Erie, Pennsylvania, with $100 million to be divided among local charities.[22] Did the person wish to remain anonymous because the money was obtained unscrupulously or illegally? Did she donate the money because she needed a big tax write-off? I would like to think that people sometimes do kind things not to toot their own horn or for any selfish advantage but simply to make life better for others.

I believe there are a few good people out there who quietly do some things out of love.

December 16

I remember not one parting word of advice from my parents when they deposited me, seventeen years young, at a college in west Texas—a school located one thousand miles from my home that I chose sight unseen. I remember no parting words of wisdom that we offered our three kids when we dropped them off in Lexington and Albuquerque and Chicago respectively for their freshman year. I remember that with quivering lips and chins we said, "I love you" and turned and walked away.

That is why I take my hat off to John Bettis for the poignant charge that he delivered son Jerome when Jerome left home for Notre Dame. Jerome "The Bus" Bettis, unlike many professional athletes, retired in 2006 on top of his game. The NFL's fifth leading all-time rusher and six times Pro Bowl player, after helping his Pittsburgh Steelers win the 2006 Super Bowl, announced his retirement.

On the opening page of his autobiography *Driving Home*, Jerome quotes his father's parting words when he left home: "Son, I don't have much to give you except a name, but it's a clean name. It's never been on any police blotter, and it's never caused any trouble. See that you take care of it."[23] Jerome on the field and off has done his daddy proud.

Many of us cannot say to our kids that we have never caused any trouble or that our name has never been on a police blotter. But we can say: "There is nothing more important than your name. I have had to work hard to improve and redeem mine. Your name is the most important thing you have. Handle it with care."

"A good reputation and respect," Solomon said, "are worth much more than silver and gold."[24] They last longer too.

December 17

In the aftermath of elections, inquiring minds want to know, "Is there no better way?" Most voters deplore the amount of money candidates have to spend to get elected, as expressed in the old saw: "We have the finest government money can buy." And we hate the vicious tactics the money buys, much of it used to slime opponents. The 2012 presidential campaign cost somewhere in the neighborhood of $7 billion.

William Natcher represents an alternative way. Natcher was elected by the second district in Kentucky to the United States House of Representatives in 1953. The second district kept re-electing him until his death in 1994. Natcher cast a record 18,401 consecutive Congressional votes. He did not miss one roll-call vote in forty-one years.

Like Senator William Proxmire of Wisconsin, Natcher refused to accept campaign contributions. He campaigned by placing a few newspaper advertisements, paid for out of his own pocket, and driving from town to town in his own automobile.[25] Few lobbyists ever approached him. He issued one press release each year that summarized his voting record. He took more pride in his daily entries in a diary and the weekly essays on history that he sent to his seven grandchildren than in his eminence in the House.

President Bill Clinton said at Natcher's funeral: "He found a way to live in Washington and work in politics and still be exactly the way he would have been if he'd been here in Bowling Green running a hardware store."[26]

Natcher was asked toward the end of his life what inscription he would like on his tombstone. He said he hoped his family would see fit to engrave six words: "He Tried to Do It Right."

December 18

One of America's favorite children's books for forty years running has been Maurice Sendak's *Where the Wild Things Are*. It is a thriller about how a child sent to his room without supper used imagination to process his anger. The *New York Times* named Sendak "one of the most powerful men in the United States" because of his ability to engage a child's imagination.[27]

Sendak's magic relates directly to his own childhood. A child of immigrant parents, he was frail and sickly. He spent much of his youth homebound. His view of the world was largely fashioned from books and from what he could see looking out his bedroom window. He was scared by movies and the vacuum cleaner. He learned about the concentration camp deaths of most of his extended family. His parents stayed depressed and angry. He was terrified by the Lindbergh baby kidnapping. Age three at the time, he always remembered hearing Mrs. Lindbergh's tearful voice on the radio pleading with the kidnapper.[28]

The impact that his scary childhood had on him as a writer was that he refused to write stories for children about sunshine and rainbows and living happily ever after. His theme became: "Life is full of monsters, little one, and growing up is difficult, but you will survive." What an essential message wee ones need, especially at bedtime—assurance that they can get the better of the monsters in their lives.

Many great works of literature have their origins in sad or sickly childhoods. Charles Dickens believed that the deprivations of his youth brought him great advantage as a writer: "It strongly inclined me," he reflected, "to reading." The Danish theologian Kierkegaard believed his sickly and misshapen body was an asset in preaching, because it helped his audience to keep their ears on his message instead of their eyes on the messenger.

We can use our disadvantaged childhood as an excuse and a crutch, or, like Maurice Sendak, an opportunity to stand in solidarity alongside little ones who are afraid.

December 19

For many of us, the hardest time of the year to keep our spirits up is deep in December when skies are grey and the nights are long and cold. Some hens lay only half as many eggs this time of the year. Their productivity, like ours, goes down. I recall a quote from Nietzsche: "If you gaze for long into an abyss, the abyss gazes also into you."

If we gaze too long at the darkness, the darkness can get in us and to us. We have to find ways to avert our eyes from the darkness. One thing the ancient Romans did was to throw a big party at the time of the winter solstice. They called it Saturnalia. It lasted a week. To counter the darkness they lit candles, gave gifts, and danced in the streets.

Gazing at a television screen is one modern way to bring a numbing darkness to life—any season of the year. I flirt with the thought of giving up local news programs altogether. Looking into the abyss—another automobile accident, another murder, another drug bust, another fire—has to do a spirit harm.

Two hundred years ago Thoreau moved to the woods partly to escape contamination by "news." In *Walden* he wrote: "If we read of one man robbed, or murdered, or killed by accident, or one house burned, or one vessel wrecked, or one steamboat blown up, or one cow run over on the Western Railroad, or one mad dog killed—we never need read of another. One is enough. If you are acquainted with the principle, what do you care for a myriad instances and applications?"[29]

Staring into the abyss is hazardous to health; laying down the remote, getting off the couch, and lighting a candle can do a spirit good.

December 20

"Oh! But he was a tight-fisted hand at the grindstone, a squeezing, wrenching, grasping, scraping, clutching, covetous old sinner. He carried his own low temperature always around with him. No warmth could warm, nor wintry weather chill him. No wind that blew was bitterer than he."

That could be none other than Ebenezer "Humbug" Scrooge, introduced to the world in December, 1843, by Charles Dickens. The Christmas spirit for Dickens is the spirit of hope, even for the materialistic, stingy Scrooges of the world. On Christmas Eve, Scrooge retired to his counting office to count the money he had made fleecing the poor. Suddenly the ghost of his old business partner, Jacob Marley, who had died Christmas Eve seven years earlier and in life had been as greedy and selfish as Scrooge, appeared. From his tortured afterlife, dragging chains, Marley tried to talk some sense into Scrooge about "life's opportunities missed."

Scrooge thought Jacob was referring to business opportunities missed and insisted: "But Jacob, you were a good man of business."

Jacob raised his voice: "Business! Mankind was my business. The common welfare was my business; charity, mercy, forbearance, and benevolence were all my business. The dealings of my trade were but a drop of water in the comprehensive ocean of my business!"

The message for Ebenezer Scrooge, and for those of us whose identity is our work, is that a job should be "a drop in the bucket"—a tiny part of the business of life. Life's primary business for people of good will, according to *A Christmas Carol*, is to see others as "fellow-passengers to the grave, and not another race of creatures bound on other journeys."

December 21

I will never forget. It was during Christmas break and I was probably ten. Mom asked me to help her deliver some food and I agreed. We went to the church and filled the trunk of the car with groceries and proceeded downtown. We delivered bags of groceries to several different families. I remember thinking at the time that I had never seen such poverty and couldn't believe that it existed in the town where we lived. I also remember how grateful each family was. Mom showed me in one afternoon that the people we prayed for were real and that we had an obligation to help. She took me out of my comfort zone to show me something that would stay with me for the rest of my life.

Two days after his mother's death, this young adult e-mailed me the above. He has become an irrepressible voice in a suburban church for serving the downtown poor.

An old, simple prayer before meals in both Catholic and Protestant traditions goes like this: "Bless this food to our use, and us to your service, and keep us ever mindful of the needs of others." Opportunities abound for us to demonstrate to our children what it means to be "mindful of the needs of others" and make the prayer a call to action instead of pious, empty sentiment. I think of Habitat for Humanity where volunteers come together to help build a house for a family in need, or Repair Affair where volunteers spend a Saturday repairing homes and building wheelchair ramps.

Someone said that to get into heaven we will need a letter of recommendation from the poor. What is more important in the grand scheme of things, to give our children another name-brand piece of cloth, or to model for them that those who are strong ought to help those who are weak?

December 22

From a distance on a cold, blustery December day, it looked like another drug trans-action shaping up or maybe one of those teacher-student trysts. The parking lot was empty but for one car. Not long after school let out, two figures, one adult and one youth, moved toward each other, having apparently planned a rendezvous. The teach-er opened her car, took out a coat, and handed it to the student. The student tried it on, embraced the teacher, said something, and walked away. The teacher got in her car and drove off.

Next day the teacher e-mailed a friend, reflecting:

> Yesterday was the best day I've had in so long. I have a student who I've seen walking home from school most days and never wearing a coat. So I asked her if she had one, but she made up an excuse about not having a locker to keep it in. I told her I had a coat I bought at the end of last winter but never wore it and it no longer fits and if she wanted it she could meet me in the teachers' parking lot after school. She did. She told me I was an awesome teacher and started crying. So did I, once I started driving away.

Times are hard. While some of us are anxious about our portfolio shrinkage, oth-ers are cold or hungry or looking at a utility bill they cannot pay. Some are grieving the absence of a loved one this holiday season for the first time. For every person singing about it being the most wonderful time of the year, someone else is muddling through her hardest time of the year.

If we reach out and touch, it may be the best day we and they will have this holiday season.

December 23

It sounds like an urban myth but it actually happened. In 1914 on Christmas Eve, on the battlefields of Flanders in Belgium, with British and French troops in muddy trenches less than sixty yards away from the enemy, German soldiers began putting small Christmas trees lit with candles outside their trenches and began singing *Stille Nacht*. British and French soldiers responded by singing Christmas carols in English and French. Germans who knew some broken English made placards that read: "You No Fight. We No Fight." They were proposing a Christmas truce.[30]

Stanley Weintraub in *Silent Night* describes how by Christmas morning soldiers from both sides were leaving their ditches, meeting and shaking hands in no-man's land, exchanging gifts of cognac, chocolate, coins, sausage, buttons, pipes, and tobacco. Burying of the bodies that had lain for weeks in the land separating the enemies took place. After the dead were buried the two sides kicked around a soccer ball. The truce lasted several days. Commanders on both sides ordered their soldiers to resume hostilities or be court martialed. The soldiers parted "with much handshaking and mutual goodwill." This happened in the fifth month of a war that lasted four more years. Millions more on both sides would die before the armistice of 1918.[31]

Weintraub ends his book with this insight: "A celebration of the human spirit, the Christmas Truce remains a moving manifestation of the absurdities of war."

British survivor Murdoch Wood years later told Parliament: "If we had been left to ourselves, there would never have been another shot fired."[32]

If you think about it, war is easier than peace. One person can make a war, but it takes two to make a peace. Remember the mortal enemies on Christmas Eve, 1914, who gave peace a chance.

December 24

London's *Sunday Telegraph* once referred to Charles Dickens as "the man who invented Christmas." Many of our holiday traditions—sending cards, singing carols, snow, mistletoe and holly, eating turkey—go back 175 years to Charles Dickens. Before Dickens, Christmas was not the major holiday that it has become in America today. Cultural historians checked the December *London Times* for forty-five years (1790–1835) and in twenty of those years Christmas was not mentioned once.[33] Ebenezer Scrooge in *A Christmas Carol* changed all that.

Dickens lived during the Industrial Revolution. He knew firsthand the great disparity between industrial exploiters and industrial exploitees. The second of eight children, young Charles worked in a boot-blacking factory while his daddy served time in a debtors' prison. Christmas represented for Charles Dickens a time-out from humanity's inhumanity—"the only time in the long calendar of the year when men and women seem by one consent to open their shut-up hearts freely."

At the beginning of *A Christmas Carol* Ebenezer Scrooge said: "Every idiot who goes about with Merry Christmas on his lips should be boiled with his own pudding and buried with a stake of holly through his heart." After hearing that some poor people would rather die than go to prisons or workhouses he said: "If they would rather die, they had better do it, and decrease the surplus population."

On Christmas Eve, Scrooge was able to step outside himself and see himself objectively. The good news of *A Christmas Carol* is that when Scrooge saw the light he did not have to change jobs or leave town or go into the ministry. He just had to start treating people differently, beginning with his clerk Bob Cratchit and his sickly little son, Tiny Tim.

May similar epiphanies happen among us this holiday season.

December 25

I met Linda over thirty years ago when she brought her only child, a ten-day-old baby boy, into the emergency room. He had been, inexplicably, attacked by the family pet. He died three days later.

Linda understandably descended into deep, immobilizing depression. Then one day several months later she went out and got her hair styled differently. She began seeing an orthodontist to straighten her teeth. She bought a new wardrobe. She decided not to go back to her job as a supervisor at a fast food restaurant but to enroll in college.

Another change at a deeper level was going on inside Linda—she began seeing other people differently. She began one-day-a-week volunteer work in the chaplains' office in the same children's hospital where her son died. She became a counselor in a support group for bereaved parents. She volunteered to speak to pediatricians on a video about how to help bereaved parents.

Several years later Linda began having balance problems. A large malignant tumor was found in her spinal column. Surgery to remove it left her partially paralyzed. At Christmas she gave the person who would conduct her funeral an audio tape along with these instructions: "I don't care what else you do at my funeral, but play this one song as my final message to the world." It was Barry Manilow's "I Made It through the Rain."

For many years, several days before Christmas, Linda's family, following instructions in her will, delivered a package of gifts to the hospital. The chaplain distributed the stuffed animals and toys, in honor of her son Chris, to the sick boys and girls who had to be in the hospital over Christmas.

Linda proves the truth of Dag Hammerskjold's statement: "We are not permitted to choose the frame of our destiny, but what we put into it is ours."

December 26

Try closing your eyes for a moment and imagining yourself—as Ebenezer Scrooge did with the help of the ghost of Christmas yet to come—running your forefinger over the letters that will one day be engraved on your tombstone. Should you die soon, what would make a fitting epitaph for the life you have sculpted thus far?

Louis Pasteur, with his experiments that had saved a nine-year-old boy from rabies on his mind, asked that three words appear on his headstone: "Joseph Meister Lived."

Abraham Jacobi, the "Dean of Pediatrics," exacted a promise from his family that only two words would go on his grave marker: "I Served."

David Packard, co-founder of Hewlett-Packard and one of Silicon Valley's first self-made billionaires, lived forty years in the same little house that he and his wife built in 1957. For fun Packard would have friends over to string barb wire on his ranch.[34] He had no material symbols of his wealth to trumpet: "I have arrived. I am successful. I am somebody." He bequeathed his $5.6 billion estate to charity. The caption he requested for his tombstone made no reference to his stature as one of the greatest industrialists ever. It reads simply: "David Packard, 1912–1996, Rancher, etc."[35]

I read a scathing obituary that a woman wrote when her mother died. It included these vindictive sentences:

> Dolores had no hobbies, made no contribution to society and rarely shared a kind word or deed in her life. I speak for the majority of her family when I say her presence will not be missed by many, very few tears will be shed and there will be no lamenting over her passing. There will be no service, no prayers and no closure for the family she spent a lifetime tearing apart."[36]

We can only imagine the words she may have engraved on her mother's headstone.

Today, while it is still day, we are composing an epitaph and an obituary. As Mr. Keating whispered to his students in the movie *Dead Poets Society*: "The powerful play goes on. And you may contribute a verse. What will your verse be?"

December 27

There were no gas stations in the little town where I grew up. There were some places where you paid 32.9 cents for every gallon of gas you purchased, but we called them service stations.

When you pulled into the service station, three friendly men (no women need apply back then) ran out to meet you. One opened the hood, pulled up the dipstick, and checked the oil. Then he checked the water in the radiator and the battery and sometimes the brake fluid level. Another man cleaned windows and headlights and checked the air in the tires. The third man put gas in your tank while you waited comfortably, patiently, and trustingly behind the steering wheel.

The emphasis was not on gas, but on service. Gas prices did not vary much from station to station, so each station competed to out-serve and out-friend the others and earn your patronage.

That concept of service at the gas pump is largely gone with the wind, as out of date as a man guiding a '52 Studebaker into an Esso service station and telling the men who ran out: "Fill 'er up and check the tires, please."

Charlie Brown, reading a magazine, shared this with Lucy: "It says here that young people of today don't believe in any causes."

Lucy corrected him: "That's not true at all. I believe in a cause. I believe in me. I'm my own cause."

Since the 1960s, the Church of Service has lost lots of ground to the Church of Self. Staying seated, waiting while someone else pumps my gas, is a distant memory. How ironic that this gluttonous, glitzy, consumption-crazed season is named for one who said that he did not come to be served but to serve, and that the greatest people of all are not the ones who rule but the ones who serve.[37]

December 28

Benjamin Franklin believed in setting aside one week for the perfecting of a new habit. At the beginning of every year he listed thirteen faults he wanted to eliminate or virtues he wanted to cultivate and then worked hard on one a week. He completed four such cycles every year.[38]

To be realistic, perfecting a new habit is going to take most of us longer than one week, but trying on a new behavior, like trying on a new pair of shoes, could become that difficult first step to getting where we want to be.

In Sartre's *No Exit,* when the doors to hell are flung open and the captives are free to leave, no one steps out. Hell's citizens have settled in. What keeps us in our private hells? Often it is a shortage of courage. The word courage comes from *cor,* the Latin word for heart. It takes a lot of heart to take that first step out of our private prisons into the great unknown where we know something even worse could be lurking.

Anne Morrow Lindbergh wrote: "Is there anything as horrible as starting a trip? Once you're off, that's all right, but the last moments are earthquakes and convulsions, and the feeling that you are a snail being pulled off your rock."

Courage, instead of fearlessness, is the ability to go ahead and do something that scares us. Courage is Charlie Brown working up the nerve to walk over to the little red-haired girl's house and deliver the valentine he bought her. Courage is little David going after Goliath with a slingshot and five pebbles. Courage is Moses, the reluctant leader, ordering the most powerful man on Earth: "Let my people go!"

John Wayne said it best: "Courage is being scared to death but saddling up anyway."

December 29

"Life isn't about finding yourself. Life is about creating yourself." Is George Bernard Shaw right? Some of us may spend way too much time gazing at our navels, plumbing the meaning of the whole shebang. Maybe meaning in life is more created than discovered, more made than found. Maybe our task is to sculpt whatever raw materials life throws us into something meaningful.

My favorite example today is William Kamkwamba. His true story is told in a book *The Boy Who Harnessed the Wind*. William grew up in a remote village in Malawi, one of Africa's poorest countries. In 2001 when he was fourteen, ejected from school because his family could not afford the $80 annual tuition, he came across a photo of a windmill in a book and decided he would try to build one. He went to the junkyard. Using strips of PVC pipe, rusty car and bicycle parts, clothes lines, blue gum trees, beer bottle caps, rubber flip flops, and other cast-off items, William fashioned a contraption that eventually was able to generate enough electricity to power a small bulb in his bedroom so that he could read books after sunset.[39] As the village watched the first test of his homemade windmill, some said, "Let's see how crazy this boy really is."[40] Soon he was building windmills that pumped water for the village's fields.

William Kamkwamba has the ambition to build windmills across Malawi that will help Africans pull up deep well water and set his people free from the tyranny of famine. He believes they can solve their problems without reliance on outsiders.

While the crowds worried, or pondered life's meaning, or waited for help to come from afar, a fourteen-year-old boy stayed the course, determined to set his people free from chains of drought and despair.

December 30

Slogging our way through the longest, darkest nights of the year, we seek, as Goethe reportedly exclaimed on his death bed: "More light! More light!" The winter darkness and the end of another calendar year can help us entertain ultimate questions about death and life like: "Who am I? Where am I going? Why am I here?"

Four metaphors call to me as days stay long and dark and another year runs out.

One comes from Francis Bacon who wrote: "The lame man who keeps the right road outstrips the runner who takes a wrong one. The more active and swift the latter is, the further he will go astray." Bacon would have us ask: "Am I on the right path?"

A second is from Albert Schweitzer. Schweitzer invites us to consider the farmer plowing a field: "The plowman does not pull the plow. He does not push it. He only directs it. This is just how events move in our lives. We can do nothing but guide the plow straight." Schweitzer would have us ask: "How concentrated am I on reaching the goal?"

A third is an old story, attributed to a number of different people including Stephen Covey. It is about a person who was climbing the ladder of success and got to the top only to discover that the ladder was leaning against the wrong wall. Whoever said it first would have us ask: "Where are my priorities? Are they worthy of the best years of my life?"

A fourth is the old joke about the pilot who reports over the intercom: "Ladies and gentlemen, I have some good news and some bad news. The good news is that we are making record time. The bad news is that we are lost."

Sitting here in the great darkness could be an opportune time to so some serious navel-gazing and ask ourselves where we are headed, how well we are doing, and what the whole drama, after all is said and done, will have been about.

December 31

As we enter a new year, I share two prayers that are favorites of mine.

First is a Franciscan blessing. It invites us to transcend our individualism and tribalism to see ourselves as citizens of the world:

> May God bless you with discomfort at easy answers, half-truths, and superficial relationships, so that you may live deep within your heart. May God bless you with anger at injustice, oppression, and exploitation of people, so that you may work for justice, freedom, and peace. May God bless you with tears to shed for those who suffer from pain, rejection, starvation, and war, so that you may reach out your hand to comfort them and turn their pain to joy. And may God bless you with enough foolishness to believe that you can make a difference in this world; so that you can do what others claim cannot be done.

The second is from Thomas Merton:

> My Lord God, I have no idea where I am going. I do not see the road ahead of me. I cannot know for certain where it will end. Nor do I really know myself, and the fact that I think that I am following your will does not mean that I am actually doing so. But I believe that the desire to please you does in fact please you. And I hope I have that desire in all that I am doing. I hope that I will never do anything apart from that desire. And I know that if I do this you will lead me by the right road though I may know nothing about it. Therefore will I trust you always though I may seem to be lost and in the shadow of death. I will not fear, for you are ever with me, and you will never leave me to face my perils alone.

Amen and amen.

December Notes

1. *Pew Research Religion and Public Life Project.* "'Nones' on the Rise," no pages.
2. Schweitzer, *On the Edge*, 62.
3. Bahr, *Albert Schweitzer Letters*, 85.
4. Anderson, *Schweitzer Album*, 37.
5. Matthew 25: 34–36.
6. Satir, *New Peoplemaking*, 20–22.
7. Zimmer, "King and Corpse," 9–13.
8. Coffman, "Why December 25?" 1.
9. Forbes, *Christmas Candid*, 25–30
10. John 1:5.
11. Frankl, *Man's Search*, 3–10.
12. Scully, "Victor Frankl at Ninety," 39–40.
13. Tierney, "Making a Difference," 29.
14. Williams, "Catastrophe of Success," no pages.
15. Rosen, "Why I'll Try," no pages.
16. Matthew 5: 37.
17. Maass, "Diane Nyad's Historic," no pages.
18. Levs, "After Cuba-Florida," no pages.
19. Nyad, "Cuba: 3 Weeks Later," no pages.
20. Hilsenrath, "Scroogenomics Author," no pages.
21. *Heifer International.* "Most Important Gift," no pages.
22. *NBC News.* "Anonymous Gift," no pages.
23. Dulac, "Obituary: John Bettis," no pages.
24. Proverbs 22:1.
25. Nash, "For Proxmire," no pages.
26. Wines, "William H. Natcher, no pages.
27. *New York Times.* "Maurice Sendak," no pages.
28. Conradt, "10 Things You Might Not Know," no pages.
29. Thoreau, *Walden*, 94.
30. *Snopes.* "Christmas Truce," no pages.
31. *Indianapolis Public Library.* "Truce," no pages.
32. Lyons, "Christmas Truce," no pages.
33. Forbes, op. cit., 58.
34. Collins, "The Ten Greatest," no pages.
35. Ibid
36. *Snopes.* "Death Penalty," no pages.
37. Mark 10:44–45.
38. Brans, "Twelve Time Management Habits," no pages.
39. Zetter, "Teen's DIY Energy Hacking," no pages.
40. Kamkwamba, *The Boy Who Harnessed*, 2.

Bibliography

"50th Anniversary Gettysburg Reunion." *Order of the Arrow*. No pages. Online: http://history.oa-bsa.org/node/3527

Abbey, Edward. *Postcards from Ed: Dispatches and Salvos from an American Iconoclast*. Minneapolis: Milkweed Editions, 2006.

"Abilene Paradox," *Advanced Knowledge*. No pages. Online: http://www.advancedknowledge.com/item.php?itemId=148&from=client

"Aldous Huxley." *Political Philosophy*. No pages. Online: http://platophilosophy.blog.com/2009/02/26/aldous-huxley/

Allen, Woody. "My Speech to the Graduates." *Aphelis*. No pages. Online: http://aphelis.net/speech-graduates-woody-allen-1979/

Ambrose, Delorese. *Leadership: The Journey Inward*. Reprint, Dubuque: Kendall Hunt, 2007.

"Americans Across the Country Begin to Adopt Idea of Honoring 9/11 Victims Through Community Service and Good Deeds." *PR Newswire*. No pages. Online: http://www.prnewswire.com/news-releases/americans-across-the-country-begin-to-adopt-idea-of-honoring-911-victims-through-community-service-and-good-deeds-55803197.html

"Amish Grandfather: We Must Not Think Evil of This Man." *KLTV*. No pages. http://www.kltv.com/story/5495980/amish-grandfather-we-must-not-think-evil-of-this-man

Anderson, Erica. *The Schweitzer Album: A Portrait in Words and Pictures*. New York: Harper and Row, 1965.

"Anonymous Gift of $100 Million an Erie Mystery." *NBC News*. No pages. Online: http://www.nbcnews.com/id/21772240/ns/us_news-giving/t/anonymous-gift-million-erie-mystery/#.UyDRTPldV8E

"Apple's Steve Jobs: Stanford Commencement Speech Transcript." *Network World*. 1–2. Online: http://www.networkworld.com/community/blog/apples-steve-jobs-stanford-commencement-speech-transcript

"Arthur Meets a Brave Knight . . . and Cuts His Limbs Off." *Monty Python. Holy Grail. Scene 4*. Online: http://montypython.50webs.com/scripts/Holy_Grail/Scene4.htm

Bahr, Hans Walter. *Albert Schweitzer Letters 1905-1965*. Translated by Joachim Neugroschel. New York: Macmillan, 1992.

Barrionuevo, Alexei and Simon Romero. "Stories of Hope and Hardship of 'Los 33.'" *New York Times*. No pages. Online: http://www.nytimes.com/2010/10/25/world/americas/25chile.html?pagewanted=all&_r=0

Bart, Mary. "College Students Unplugged: 24 Hours without Media Brings Feelings of Boredom, Isolation, Anxiety." *Faculty Focus*. No pages. Online: http://www.facultyfocus.com/articles/edtech-news-and-trends/college-students-unplugged-24-hours-without-media-brings-feelings-of-boredom-isolation-anxiety/

Beecher, Henry K. "The Powerful Placebo," *JAMA* 159 (17), December 24, 1955. 1602–1606.

Begley, Sharon. "Wealth and Happiness Don't Necessarily Go Hand in Hand." *Wall Street Journal*. No pages. Online: http://online.wsj.com/news/articles/SB109234085670790101

"Being an Optimist Lowers Risk of Heart Disease, Helps People Live Longer, Says Study of Women." *New York Daily News.* No pages. Online: http://www.nydailynews.com/life-style/health/optimist-lowers-risk-heart-disease-helps-people-live-longer-study-women-article-1.398789

Benjamin, Scott. "Billy Graham: 'Never Say Never.'" No pages. Online: http://www.cbsnews.com/news/billy-graham-never-say-never/

"Best-Sellers Initially Rejected." *Literary Rejections.* No pages. Online: http://www.literaryrejections.com/best-sellers-initially-rejected/

Blanco, John Ignacio. "Charles Carl Roberts IV." *Murderpedia.* No pages. Online: http://murderpedia.org/male.R/r/roberts-charles.htm

"Blue Zones: Places in the World Where People Live to 100 and Stay Healthy." *Singularity Hub.* No pages. Online: http://singularityhub.com/2009/07/20/blue-zones-places-in-the-world-where-people-live-to-100-and-stay-healthy/

Boesak, Allan Aubrey. *Dare We Speak of Hope. Searching for a Language of Life in Faith and Politics.* Grand Rapids: Eerdmans, 2014.

Brans, Pat. "Twelve Time Management Habits to Master in 2013." *Forbes.* No pages. Online: http://www.forbes.com/sites/patbrans/2013/01/01/twelve-time-management-habits-to-master-in-2013/

Breitman, Rachel and Del Jones. "Should Kids Be Left Fortunes, or Left Out?" *USA Today.* No pages. Online: http://usatoday30.usatoday.com/money/2006-07-25-heirs-usat_x.htm

Brinkley, David. *David Brinkley.* New York: Knopf, 1995.

Brody, Jane E. "Secrets of the Centenarians." *New York Times.* No pages. Online: http://query.nytimes.com/gst/fullpage.html?res=9E0DE5DA1639F93AA25753C1A9669D8B63

Brokaw, Chet. "Neal Wanless, SD Rancher, Wins $232 Million Jackpot." No pages. Online: http://www.huffingtonpost.com/2009/06/05/neal-wanless-sd-rancher-w_n_212081.html

Brotman, Barbara. "People in 'Who's Who' Offer Philosophies of Life." *Toledo Blade,* December 21, 1980, Sec. E, 5. Online: http://news.google.com/newspapers?nid=1350&dat=19801220&id=3TBPAAAAIBAJ&sjid=lwIEAAAAIBAJ&pg=6761,1139879

Brown, Robert McAfee. *Spirituality and Liberation. Overcoming the Great Fallacy.* Louisville: Westminster John Knox, 1988.

Buechner, Frederick. *The Seasons' Difference.* New York: Alfred A. Knopf, 1952.

Burns, James McGregor and Susan Dunn. *The Three Roosevelts: Patrician Leaders Who Transformed America.* New York: Grove, 2002.

"Candy Lightner." *Biography,* 1–2. Online: http://www.biography.com/people/candy-lightner-21173669

"Carl Schurz." *Bartleby.* No pages. Online: http://www.bartleby.com/73/1641.html

Carter, Darla. "Program Targets Adolescent Violence." *SPAVA.* No pages. Online: http://www.spava.us/drbanerjee.htm

Cartwright, Heather. "Seeing Is not Always Believing." *Thorn in My Heart.* No pages. Online: http://heathertiger.wordpress.com/2008/02/23/seeing-is-not-always-believing/

Cellzic, Mike. "Girl, 3, Who Tossed Back Foul Gets Phillies Jersey." *Today News.* No pages. Online: http://www.today.com/id/32891414/ns/today-today_news/t/girl-who-tossed-back-foul-gets-phillies-jersey/#.Ux0fM_ldV8E

"Central Park Jogger Helps Others Heal." *ABC News.* No pages. Online: http://abcnews.go.com/GMA/story?id=1051155

"Charles A. Beard." *Encyclopedia Britannica*. No pages. Online: http://www.britannica.com/ EBchecked/topic/57356/Charles-A-Beard

"Christmas Truce." *Snopes*. No pages. Online: http://www.snopes.com/holidays/christmas/ truce.asp

Claypool, John. *Stages: The Art of Living the Expected*. Waco: Word, 1977.

Cleaveland, Clif. "The Diving Bell and the Butterfly." *American College of Physicians*. No pages. Online: http://www.acponline.org/about_acp/chapters/tn/gr_divingbell.htm

"Code of Conduct." *Google*. No pages. Online: http://investor.google.com/corporate/code-of-conduct.html

Coffman, Elesha. "Why December 25?" *Christianity Today*. No pages. Online: http://www. christianitytoday.com/ch/news/2000/dec08.html

Collins, Jim. "The Ten Greatest CEOs of All Time." No pages. Online: http://www.jimcollins. com/article_topics/articles/10-greatest.html

Collins, Paul. "Has Modern Life Killed the Semicolon?" *Slate*, 1. Online: http://www.slate. com/articles/arts/culturebox/2008/06/_.html

"Commencement 2000: Ben Carson Tells of His Journey from Poverty." *University of Delaware*. No pages. Online: http://www.udel.edu/PR/UpDate/00/33/carson.html

Conradt, Stacy. "Ten Things You Might Not Know about Maurice Sendak." *Mental Floss*. No pages. Online: http://mentalfloss.com/article/30618/10-things-you-might-not-know-about-maurice-sendak

Cousins, Norman. *Anatomy of an Illness As Perceived by the Patient*. 1979. Reprint, New York: W.W. Norton, 2005.

————. *Head First: The Biology of Hope*. New York: E.P. Dutton, 1989.

"Covering the Plate: A Baseball Catcher Tells All." *NPR*. No pages. Online: http://www.npr. org/2011/08/18/139649031/covering-the-plate-a-baseball-catcher-tells-all

Cox, Sidney. *A Swinger of Birches*. New York University, 1957. Online: https://archive.org/ details/swingerofbirches000036mbp

Crowe, Jerry. "It Turned out to Be the Biggest Snap of His Career." *Los Angeles Times*. No pages. Online: http://articles.latimes.com/2008/jan/28/sports/sp-crowe28

Currie-Knight, Kevin. Review of *The Righteous Mind. Why Good People Are Divided by Politics and Religion,*" by Jonathan Haidt. No pages. Online: http://www.kevinck.com/ righteousmind

Darrow, Clarence. "Reflections on His Sixty-First Birthday." No pages. Online: http://law2. umkc.edu/faculty/projects/ftrials/DAR_BIRT.HTM

Davidson, Joe. "Augusta Thomas, 87, Sets the Pace at AFGE." *Washington Post*, 1–2. Online: http://www.washingtonpost.com/wp-dyn/content/article/2010/03/30/ AR2010033004341.html

Davis, Don. "Old Time Walk and Run." *Lehigh University*. No pages. Online: http://www. lehigh.edu/~dmd1/kelly.html

"Davy Crockett." *Teach American History*. No pages. Online: http://www.teachamericanhistory. org/File/Davy_Crockett.pdf

Dawkins, Richard. *The Selfish Gene*. 1976. Reprint, Oxford University, 2006.

"Death Penalty." *Snopes*. No pages. Online: http://www.snopes.com/media/iftrue/obituary. asp

"December 22, 1849: Dostoevsky Reprieved at Last Minute." *This Day in History*. No pages. Online: http://www.history.com/this-day-in-history/dostoevsky-reprieved-at-last-minute

Detterman, Paul E. "Worshipping the Triune God: Serve." *Reformed Worship Resources for Planning and Leading Worship.* No pages. Online: http://reformedworship.org/article/june-2012/worshipping-triune-god-serve

Diane Rehm Show. "Interview with Adam Makos. 'A Higher Call: An Incredible True Story of Combat and Chivalry in the War-Torn Skies of World War II.'" *NPR.* Aired December 20, 2012. Online: http://thedianerehmshow.org/shows/2012-12-20/adam-makos-higher-call-incredible-true-story-combat-and-chivalry-war-torn-skies-w-0

Dillard, Annie. *Pilgrim at Tinker Creek.* New York: Harper's Magazine, 1974.

Drucker, Susan J. and Robert S. Cathcart. *American Heroes in a Media Age.* New Jersey: Hampton Press, 1994.

Duhigg, Charles. "The Power of Habit." *Slate,* 1. Online: http://www.slate.com/articles/arts/culturebox/2012/02/an_excerpt_from_charles_duhigg_s_the_power_of_habit_.html

Dulac, Gerry. "Obituary: John Bettis / Father of Ex-Steelers RB." *Pittsburgh Post-Gazette.* No pages. Online: http://www.post-gazette.com/sports/steelers/2006/11/29/Obituary-John-Bettis-Father-of-ex-Steelers-RB/stories/20061129023

"Eat a Live Frog Every Morning, and Nothing Worse Will Happen to You the Rest of the Day." *Quote Investigator.* No pages. Online: http://quoteinvestigator.com/tag/emile-zola/

"Edmund Locard." *Forensic Science Central.* No pages. Online: http://forensicsciencecentral.co.uk/edmondlocard.shtml

Eiseley, Loren. *All the Strange Hours: The Excavation of a Life.* University of Nebraska, 1975.

Ellis, Judy Howard. "J.K. Rowling: 'I Didn't Build This' on My Own." *The Washington Post.* No pages. Online: http://www.washingtonpost.com/blogs/she-the-people/wp/2012/09/27/j-k-rowling-i-didnt-build-this-on-my-own/

Engel, KeriLynn. "Wilma Rudolph, American Gold Medalist and Civil Rights Pioneer." *Amazing Women in History.* No pages. Online: http://www.amazingwomeninhistory.com/wilma-rudolph-olympic-gold-medalist-civil-right-pioneer/

Erling, Bernhard. *A Reader's Guide to Dag Hammarskjold's Waymarks.* Minnesota: Gustavus Adolphus College, 1999.

Everett, Glenn. "Life of Elizabeth Barrett Browning." *The Victorian Web.* No pages. Online: http://www.victorianweb.org/authors/ebb/ebbio.html

"Faith, Hope, and Charity." *The Foundling Museum.* No pages. Online: http://www.foundlingmuseum.org.uk/events/view/fate-hope-and-charity/

Farnham, Alan. "How to Live with a Billion." *CNN Money.* No pages. Online: http://money.cnn.com/magazines/fortune/fortune_archive/1989/09/11/72460/

"Fast-Food Ice Dirtier than Toilet Water." *ABC News.* No pages. Online: http://abcnews.go.com/GMA/OnCall/story?id=1641825&

Flaste, Richard. "Superkids Thrive Despite Lives of Stress." *The Milwaukee Journal,* December 4, 1977, Part 6, p. 12. http://news.google.com/newspapers?nid=1499&dat=19771204&id=1G4aAAAAIBAJ&sjid=fikEAAAAIBAJ&pg=7125,2082857

Flynn, Paul. "Susan Boyle's Story." *Susan Boyle Music.* No pages. Online: http://www.susanboylemusic.com/us/story/

Forbes, Bruce David. *Christmas: A Candid History.* Berkeley: University of California, 2008.

Fox, Margalit. "Bill Porter, an Exceptional Salesman Who Inspired a Film, Dies at 81." *New York Times.* No pages. Online: http://www.nytimes.com/2013/12/10/us/bill-porter-an-exceptional-salesman-who-inspired-a-film-dies-at-81.html?_r=0

Frank, Robert. "A Rich Person's Definition of Wealth." *The Wall Street Journal.* No pages. Online: http://blogs.wsj.com/wealth/2008/01/09/a-rich-persons-definition-of-rich/

———. "How a Secretary Made and Gave Away $7 Million." *The Wall Street Journal Wealth Report*. No pages. Online: http://blogs.wsj.com/wealth/2010/03/08/how-a-secretary-made-and-gave-away-7-million/

Frankl, Viktor E. *Man's Search for Meaning: An Introduction to Logotherapy*. Translated by Ilse Lasch. 1959. Reprint, New York: Washington Square, 1969.

Franklin, Benjamin. *Poor Richard Day by Day: Pithy Paragraphs from the Writings of Benjamin Franklin*. 1732. Reprint, Philadelphia: G. W. Jacobs, 1917.

Franklin, Deborah. "The Psychology of the Honor System at the Farm Stand." *NPR*. No pages. Online: http://www.npr.org/blogs/thesalt/2012/06/11/154750001/the-psychology-of-the-honor-system-at-the-farm-stand

"Frequently Asked Questions." *United States Holocaust Memorial Museum*. No pages. Online: http://www.ushmm.org/research/ask-a-research-question/frequently-asked-questions

"From the Superintendent." *Gheens Institute for Innovation Insights*. No pages. Online: http://www.jefferson.k12.ky.us/Departments/GheensInstitute/images/newsletters/Oct08.pdf

Fulghum, Robert. *It Was On Fire When I Lay Down On It*. New York: Random House, 2010.

"Gartner's Views on Life." *HCFA/CMS Alumni News*. 11–14. Online: http://www.cms.gov/About-CMS/Career-Information/CMSAlumni/Downloads/ALNWS0712.pdf

Gasset, Jose Ortega y. "The Hero." In *Don Quixote - Miguel de Cervantes*. Edited by Harold Bloom. New York: Infobase, 2009.

Getlen, Larry. "Stephen Hawking Became a Thinker—After He Laid off the Beer." *New York Post*, no pages. Online: http://nypost.com/2013/09/14/stephen-hawking-became-one-of-our-finest-thinkers-after-he-laid-off-the-beer/

Gooch, Todd A. *The Numinous and Modernity: An Interpretation of Rudolph Otto's Philosophy of Religion*. Boston: Walter de Gruyter, 2000.

Goodman, Matthew. *Eighty Days: Nellie Bly and Elizabeth Bisland's History-Making Race Around the World*. New York: Random House, 2013.

Gorondi, Pablo. "Csanad Szegedi, Hungary Far-Right Leader, Discovers Jewish Roots." *The World Post*. No pages. Online: http://www.huffingtonpost.com/2012/08/14/csanad-szegedi-jewish_n_1776617.html

Graves, Dan. "Dirk Willem Burned after Rescuing Pursuer." *Christianity*. No pages. Online: http://www.christianity.com/church/church-history/timeline/1501-1600/dirk-willem-burned-after-rescuing-pursuer-11630015.html

Gray, Richard. "Monarch Butterflies Use Internal Compass to Find their Way." *The Telegraph*. No pages. Online: http://www.telegraph.co.uk/earth/wildlife/7855868/Monarch-butterflies-use-internal-compass-to-find-their-way.html

Green, Bob. "Cut." 291-296. Online: http://share.ehs.uen.org/system/files/Cut.pdf

Griffin, Susan. "To Love the Marigold: The Politics of Imagination." *Whole Earth Review*, 89 (Spring 1996), 65–67.

Grimes, William. "Frank McCourt, Whose Irish Childhood Illuminated His Prose, Is Dead at 78." *New York Times*. No pages. Online: http://topics.nytimes.com/top/reference/timestopics/people/m/frank_mccourt/index.html

Gruen, Sara. *Water for Elephants*. New York: Algonquin, 2006

Havel, Vaclav. "An Orientation of the Heart." In *The Impossible Will Take a Little While: a Citizen's Guide to Hope in a Time of Fear*. Edited by Paul Rogat Loeb. New York: Basic Books, 2004.

Hertsgaard, Mark. "The Green Dream." *In The Impossible Will Take a Little While. A Citizen's Guide to Hope in a Time of Fear.* Edited by Paul Rogat Loeb. New York: Basic Books, 2004.

Hilsenrath, Jon. "Scroogenomics Author on the Holidays' 'Orgy of Wealth Destruction.'" *The Wall Street Journal.* No pages. Online: http://blogs.wsj.com/economics/2009/10/16/qa-scroogenomics-author-on-the-holidays-orgy-of-wealth-destruction/

"History of the Devil's Advocate." *Unam Sanctam Catholicam.* No pages. Online: http://www.unamsanctamcatholicam.com/history/historia-ecclesiae/79-history/351-devil-s-advocate.html

Hoffman, Yechiel. "Taste of Torah: Beshaleh." *Temple Beth AM.* No pages. Online: http://www.tbala.org/page.cfm?p=2394

Holguin, Jaime. "Happily Married for 82 Years." *CBS Evening News.* No pages. Online: http://www.cbsnews.com/news/happily-married-for-82-years/

Holmes, Oliver W. "How Men Reason." *McGuffey's Sixth Eclectic Reader.* 1879. Reprint, New York: American Book, 1921.

Hopkins, Andrea. "Middle Class Courted, but Skeptical, in Campaign." *Reuters.* No pages. http://www.reuters.com/article/2007/11/29/us-usa-politics-middleclass-idUSN2864432020071129

"How an Introvert Can Be Happier: Act Like an Extrovert." *Wall Street Journal.* No pages. Online: http://online.wsj.com/news/articles/SB10001424127887324144304578621951399427408

Humphries, Courtney. "Healthy Life Extended in Obese Mice." *Harvard Focus.* No pages. Online: http://archives.focus.hms.harvard.edu/2006/111006/pathology.shtml

Hunter, Tab. *Tab Hunter Confidential: The Making of a Movie Star.* Chapel Hill: Algonquin, 2005.

Hyde, Randy. "Choose Life." *Ethics Daily.* No pages. Online: http://www.ethicsdaily.com/choose-life-cms-21551

Indvik, Lauren. "Steve Jobs's Biographer on '60 Minutes': The Highlights." *Mashable.* No pages. Online: http://mashable.com/2011/10/23/steve-jobs-walter-isaacson-60-minutes/

Intini, John. "Giving Away Fortune Can Benefit Family, Society." *The Canadian Encyclopedia.* No pages. Online: http://www.thecanadianencyclopedia.com/en/article/giving-away-fortune-can-benefit-family-society/

Jackson, Phil. *Sacred Hoops. Spiritual Lessons of a Hardwood Warrior.* New York: Hyperion, 1995.

"Japanese 95-Year-Old Sets Record." *BBC News.* No pages. Online: http://news.bbc.co.uk/2/hi/asia-pacific/4110208.stm

"Jason Alexander Reveals 30-lb Weight Loss (and Much More) in Unique Jenny Craig National Commercial." *Jenny Craig.* No pages. Online: http://www.jennycraig.com/site/content/news-detail.jsp?newsId=2201133

"John Grisham." *Academy of Achievement.* 2–3. Online: http://www.achievement.org/autodoc/page/gri0int-2

Kamkwamba, William, and Bryan Mealer. *The Boy Who Harnessed the Wind.* 2009. Reprint, New York: Harper Collins, 2010.

King, Martin Luther Jr. "Loving Your Enemies." *King Institute Encyclopedia.* No pages. Online: http://mlk-kpp01.stanford.edu/index.php/encyclopedia/documentsentry/doc_loving_your_enemies/

King, Steve. "The Life and Times of *Goodnight Moon.*" *Today in Literature.* No pages. Online: http://www.todayinliterature.com/stories.asp?Event_Date=5/23/1910

Kingsolver, Barbara. "2008 Commencement Address by Barbara Kingsolver." *Duke Today.* No pages. Online: http://today.duke.edu/2008/05/kingsolver.html

Kriegel, Mark. *Pistol. The Life of Pete Maravich.* New York: Free Press, 2007.

Leaf, Munro. *The Story of Ferdinand.* New York: Viking, 1936.

Lemert, Charles C. *Why Niebuhr Matters.* New Haven: Yale University, 2011.

Levs, Josh. "After Cuba-Florida Feat, Diane Nyad to Swim 48-Hours in New York." *CNN.* No pages. Online: http://www.cnn.com/2013/09/03/us/diana-nyad-cuba-florida-swim/

Lewis, C.S. *The Four Loves.* New York: Harcourt, Brace, Jovanovich, 1960.

Lewis, Paul. "Burning the Evidence." *Paul Lewis Writing Archive.* No pages. http://www.web40571.clarahost.co.uk/archive/Wilkie/20041200Dickensian.htm

Lindbeck, George. *The Nature of Doctrine. Religion and Theology in a Postliberal Age.* Louisville: Westminster John Knox, 1984.

"Lion Kings." *CBS 60 Minutes.* Correspondent Lara Logan. Producer Max McClellan. Aired November 25, 2012. Online: http://www.cbsnews.com/news/discovering-the-secrets-of-lions/

Litsky, Frank and John Branch. "John Wooden, Who Built Incomparable Dynasty at U.C.L.A., Dies at 99." *New York Times.* No pages. Online: http://www.nytimes.com/2010/06/05/sports/ncaabasketball/05wooden.html?pagewanted=all&_r=0

Lyons, Matthew N. "Christmas Truce of 1914." *History Matters for Kids.* No pages. Online: http://historymattersforkids.com/tag/christmas/

Maass, Harold. "Diane Nyad's Historic Florida-to-Cuba Swim: a Timeline." *The Week.* No pages. Online: http://theweek.com/article/index/249041/diana-nyads-historic-cuba-to-florida-swim-a-timeline

"Madame X—Plantation to Paris." *Madame Pickwick.* No pages. Online: http://madamepickwickartblog.com/2012/01/madame-x-plantation-to-paris/

Mann, Gil. "A True Tale of Love Destroying Hate." *Being Jewish.* No pages. Online: http://www.beingjewish.org/magazine/fall2003/article1.html

"Margaret Wise Brown." *Virago Modern Classics.* 1–220. Online: http://www.librarything.com/topic/114677

Martin, James. "A Saint's Dark Night." *New York Times.* No pages. Online: http://www.nytimes.com/2007/08/29/opinion/29martin.html?_r=0

"Martin Luther—The Jews and Their Lies." *Jewish Virtual Library.* No pages. Online: http://www.jewishvirtuallibrary.org/jsource/anti-semitism/Luther_on_Jews.html

"Maurice Sendak." *New York Times Topics.* No pages. Online: http://www.nytimes.com/top/reference/timestopics/people/s/maurice_sendak/index.html?s=oldest&

May, Rollo. *Love and Will.* New York: W. W. Norton, 1969.

McCloskey, Scott. "River Swimmer Makes Stop at Pike Island." *The Intelligencer.* No pages. Online: http://www.theintelligencer.net/page/content.detail/id/538202.html?nav=510

McClure, Tori Murden. *A Pearl in the Storm: How I Found My Heart in the Middle of the Ocean.* New York: Harper, 2009.

McCourt, Frank. *Teacher Man. A Memoir.* New York: Scribner, 2006.

McCullough, David. *The Greater Journey. Americans in Paris.* New York: Simon and Schuster, 2011.

McDonough, Victoria T. "Trisha Meili: Going the Distance." *Brainline.* No pages. Online: http://www.brainline.org/content/2009/04/going-the-distance-_pageall.html

McDougall, Christopher. *Born to Run. A Hidden Tribe, Superathletes, and the Greatest Race the World Has Never Seen*. New York: Vintage, 2011.

———. "The Hidden Cost of Heroism." *NBC News*. No pages. http://www.nbcnews.com/id/21902983/ns/health-behavior/t/hidden-cost-heroism/#.UymU-fldV8E

McMahon, Robert. "Rwanda: 10 Years Later, Genocide Survivor Reflects On 'Collective Madness.'" *Radio Free Europe Radio Library*. No pages. Online: http://www.rferl.org/content/article/1052195.html

McNees, Pat. "What Is an Ethical Will?" *A Legacy Letter*. No pages. Online: http://www.patmcnees.com/what_is_an_ethical_will___a_legacy_letter_44837.htm

Meacham, Jon and Sally Quinn. "As Lives and Houses Shattered in Haiti Quake, So Did Some Religious Differences." *Washington Post*. No pages. Online: http://www.washingtonpost.com/wp-dyn/content/article/2010/01/16/AR2010011603140.html

Merton, Thomas. *In the Dark Before Dawn: New Selected Poems of Thomas Merton*. Edited by Lynn R. Szabo. New York: New Directions, 2005.

Meyer, Joyce. *Love Out Loud: 365 Devotions for Loving God, Loving Yourself and Loving Others*. New York: Hachette, 2011.

"Michala's Story." *Beading to Beat Autism*. No pages. Online: http://www.beadingtobeatautism.org/michalas-story/

"Millennial Workers Want Flexibility and Mentorship from Skeptical Managers." *The Daily Beast*. No pages. Online: http://www.thedailybeast.com/articles/2013/09/03/millennial-workers-want-flexibility-and-mentorship-from-skeptical-managers.html

Mohajer, Shaya Tayefe. "Life Not All Wine and Roses for Powerball Winner after Five Years." *USA Today*. No pages. Online: http://usatoday30.usatoday.com/news/nation/2007-09-13-powerballwinner_N.htm

"Most Important Problem." *Gallup*. No pages. Online: http://www.gallup.com/poll/1675/most-important-problem.aspx

"Mother Jones (1837–1930)." *AFL-CIO*. No pages. Online: http://www.aflcio.org/About/Our-History/Key-People-in-Labor-History/Mother-Jones-1837-1930

"Mother Jones, 'Letter to President Theodore Roosevelt,' 1903." *America Catholic History Classroom*. No pages. Online: http://cuomeka.wrlc.org/exhibits/show/industrial/documents/cri-doc7

Nash, Nathaniel. "For Proxmire, The Fleece Goes On." *New York Times*. No pages. Online: http://www.nytimes.com/1987/09/28/us/washington-talk-capitol-hill-for-proxmire-the-fleece-goes-on.html

"Navy Terms and Trivia." *Goatlocker*. No pages. Online: http://goatlocker.org/resources/nav/trivia.htm

"Nellie Bly." *Biography*, 1–3. Online: http://www.biography.com/people/nellie-bly-9216680?page=3

Nemade, Rashmi, et al. "Cognitive Theories of Major Depression: Aaron Beck." *Emergency Health Network*. No pages. Online: http://info.emergencehealthnetwork.org/poc/view_doc.php?type=doc&id=13006&cn=5

Neruda, Pablo. "Childhood and "Poverty." In Neruda and Vallejo, *Selected Poems*. Translated by Robert Bly. Boston: Beacon Press, 1971.

"Newton, Darwin, and Einstein." *Critical Thinking Community*. No pages. Online: http://www.criticalthinking.org/pages/the-questioning-mind-newton-darwin-einstein/505

Nichols, John. "Ensuring the Legacy of Milwaukee's Prime Minister." *The Capital Times*. No pages. Online: http://host.madison.com/news/opinion/column/john_nichols/john-nichols-ensuring-the-legacy-of-milwaukee-s-prime-minister/article_7d1d5681-0ee4-5981-98b7-b8e5fa543cd1.html

Nietzsche, Friedrich. *Thus Spoke Zarathustra*. 1883. Translated by Thomas Common. New York: Courier Dover, 1999.

"'Nones' on the Rise." *Pew Research Religion and Public Life Project*. No pages. Online: http://www.pewforum.org/2012/10/09/nones-on-the-rise/

Nouwen, Henri J. *Out of Solitude: Three Meditations on the Christian Life*. Notre Dame: Ave Maria, 1976.

Ogbozor, Ernest. "Love and Forgiveness in Governance. Exemplars: Immaculée Ilibagiza." *Beyond Intractability*. No pages. Online: http://www.beyondintractability.org/lfg/exemplars/iilibagiza

"On Earth Day, Reflections on the Links between Human & Environmental Health." *The Albert Schweitzer Fellowship*. No pages. Online: http://www.schweitzerfellowship.org/news/category/blog/on-earth-day-reflections-on-the-links-between-human-environmental-health/

Ortberg, John, et al. *Groups: The Life-Giving Power of Community*. Grand Rapids: Zondervan, 2000.

"Our Image Stamped in Dust." *Our Rabbi Jesus*. No pages. Online: http://ourrabbijesus.com/articles/gods-image-stamped-in-dust/

"Pastor Rick Warren is Well Prepared for a Purpose Driven Retirement." *Forbes*. No pages. Online: http://www.forbes.com/sites/robertlaura/2013/03/21/pastor-rick-warren-is-practicing-what-he-preaches-and-getting-ready-for-retirement/

Parini, Jay. *Robert Frost: A Life*. New York: Macmillan, 2000.

Pausch, Randy. "Professor Randy Pausch Graduation Speech." *Gradspeeches*. No pages. Online: http://www.cmu.edu/homepage/beyond/2008/spring/after-commencement-weekend.shtml

Peters, Jason. *Wendell Berry. Life and Work: Culture of the Land*. University of Kentucky, 2007.

Peterson, Eugene H. *Run with the Horses: The Quest for Life at Its Best*. Downers Grove, IL: InterVarsity, 2009.

Peterson, Robert L. *New Life Begins at Forty*. Trident Press, 1967.

"Petrino Resigns Falcon's Post after 13 Games, Goes to Arkansas." *ESPN Sports*. No pages. Online: http://sports.espn.go.com/ncf/news/story?id=3150783

Pierce, Scott D. "Paul McCartney Says 'Let It Be' Came to Him in a Dream." *Salt Lake Tribune*. No pages. Online: http://www.sltrib.com/sltrib/blogstv/52552400-63/dream-song-mccartney-think.html.csp

Popova, Maria. "Kurt Vonnegut on the Secret of Happiness: an Homage to Joseph Heller's Wisdom." *Brain Pickings*. No pages. Online: http://www.brainpickings.org/index.php/2014/01/16/kurt-vonnegut-joe-heller-having-enough/

"Quotes for Oskar Schindler from Schindler's List (1993)." *IMDb*. No pages. Online: http://www.imdb.com/character/ch0002204/quotes

Ranii, David. "A Mission to Do Well and Do Good." *News Observer*. No pages. Online: http://www.newsobserver.com/2010/05/02/463205/a-mission-to-do-well-and-do-good.html

"Reader's Digest Celebrates its 1000th Issue with a Look at Trends that Are Shaping Our Future." *PR Newswire*. No pages. Online: http://www.prnewswire.com/news-releases/readers-digest-celebrates-its-1000th-issue-with-a-look-at-trends-that-are-shaping-our-future-54658472.html

Reed, Sydney. "James Clyburn." *StoryCorps*. No pages. Online: http://storycorps.org/listen/james-clyburn-and-sydney-reed/#

Remen, Naomi. *Kitchen Table Wisdom. Stories that Heal.* New York: Riverhead, 1996.

"Research FAQs." *Gottman Institute.* No pages. Online: http://www.gottman.com/research/research-faqs/

Richardson, H. Edward. *Jesse: The Biography of an American Writer— Jesse Hilton Stuart.* New York: McGraw-Hill, 1984.

"Robert A. Heinlein Quotes." *Odyssey's Homepage.* No pages. Online: http://homepage.eircom.net/~odyssey/Quotes/Popular/SciFi/Heinlein.html

Roc, Dana. "Enough: a Speech delivered by John Bogle." *Danaroc.* No pages. Online: http://www.danaroc.com/guests_johnbogle_102708.html

"Rosa Parks." *National Park Service.* No pages. Online: http://www.nps.gov/features/malu/feat0002/wof/Rosa_Parks.htm

Rosen, Lee. "Why 'I'll Try' Means 'I Won't." *Divorce Discourse.* No pages. Online: http://www.divorcediscourse.com/ill-means-wont/

Rowsome, Frank. "The Verse by the Side of the Road." *Burma-Shave Jingles.* 1–29. Online: http://burma-shave.org/jingles/

"Rules for Teachers—1915." *New Hampshire Historical Society.* 1–2. Online: http://www.nhhistory.org/edu/support/nhgrowingup/teacherrules.pdf

Safire, William. *Lend Me Your Ears: Great Speeches in History.* New York: W. W. Norton, 1997.

Sakya Losal Choe Dzong. "Life of Buddha Shakyamuni." *Tibetan Buddhist Society of Canberra.* No pages. Online: http://www.sakya.com.au/lifeofbuddha/

Samuel, Henry. "Millionaire Gives away Fortune that Made Him Miserable." *The Telegraph.* No pages. Online: http://www.telegraph.co.uk/news/worldnews/europe/austria/7190750/Millionaire-gives-away-fortune-that-made-him-miserable.html

Satir, Virginia. *The New Peoplemaking.* Palo Alto, CA: Science and Behavior Books, 1988.

Schweitzer, Albert. *On the Edge of the Primeval Forest* and *More from the Primeval Forest*: *Experiences and Observations of a Doctor in Equatorial Africa.* 1931. Translated by C. T. Campion. Reprint, New York: Macmillan, 1948.

————.*Out of My Life and Thought. An Autobiography.* 1933. Translated by Antje Bultmann Lemke. Reprint, New York: Henry Holt, 1990.

"Secret Video: Romney Tells Millionaire Donors What He Really Thinks of Obama Voters." *Mother Jones.* No pages. Online: http://www.motherjones.com/politics/2012/09/secret-video-romney-private-fundraiser

Seiden, Richard. "Where Are They Now? A Follow-up Study of Suicide Attempters from the Golden Gate Bridge." *Suicide and Life Threatening Behavior*, Vol. 8 (4), Winter 1978. 1-13.

"Seneca Falls Convention." *Historynet.* No pages. Online: http://www.historynet.com/seneca-falls-convention

Shahid, Aliyah. "Shirley Sherrod, Canned USDA Official, Fired by White House in Rush before All Facts Known: E-mails." *New York Daily News.* No pages. Online: http://www.nydailynews.com/news/politics/shirley-sherrod-canned-usda-official-fired-white-house-rush-facts-e-mails-article-1.188662

Shannon, William. *The Hidden Ground of Love: The Letters of Thomas Merton on Religious Experience and Social Concerns.* New York: Farrar, Straus, Giroux, 1985.

Shearer, Stephen Michael. *Patricia Neal. An Unquiet Life.* University of Kentucky, 2011.

Singh, Anita. "Harper Lee to Disclose Why She Stopped Writing after 'To Kill a Mockingbird.'" *The Telegraph*. No pages. Online: http://www.telegraph.co.uk/culture/culturenews/8463233/Harper-Lee-to-disclose-why-she-stopped-writing-after-To-Kill-A-Mockingbird.html

"Sister, Sister." *Australian Memories of the Holocaust*. No pages. Online: http://www.holocaust.com.au/mm/j_sister.htm

Skully, Matthew. "Viktor Frankl at Ninety: An Interview." *First Things*. 39–43. Online: http://www.firstthings.com/article/2008/08/004-viktor-frankl-at-ninety-an-interview

Solzhenitsyn, Aleksandr I. *The Gulag Archipelago 1918-1956: An Experiment in Literary Investigation I-II*. Translated by Thomas P. Whitney. New York: Harper and Row, 1973.

Sontag, Sherry and Christopher Drew. *Blind Man's Bluff: The Untold Story of American Submarine Espionage*. New York: Public Affairs, 1998.

"Speech and Lashon Ha-Ra." *Judaism 101*. No pages. Online: http://www.jewfaq.org/speech.htm

Stone, Judith. "Teach a Girl, Change the World." *Good Housekeeping*. No pages. Online: http://www.goodhousekeeping.com/family/inspirational-people/education-for-girls

Stuart, Jesse. *Beyond Dark Hills. A Personal Story by Jesse Stuart*. Ashland: Jesse Stuart Foundation, 1996.

Summit, Pat. *Sum It Up*. New York: Crown Archetype, 2013.

Tarr, Herbert. *The Conversion of Chaplain Cohen*. New York: B. Geis Associates, 1963.

The Doctor. Directed by Randa Haines. Produced by Laura Ziskin. Based on Edward Rosenbaum's 1988 book, *A Taste of My Own Medicine*. Touchstone Pictures, 1991.

"The Ethics of American Youth: 2012." *Character Counts*. No pages. Online: http://charactercounts.org/programs/reportcard/2012/installment_report-card_honesty-integrity.html

"The Heat Wave of 1896 and the Rise of Roosevelt." *NPR*. No pages. Online: http://www.npr.org/templates/story/story.php?storyId=129127924

"The Jeane Dixon Phenomenon." *Macrohistory and World Timeline*. No pages. Online: http://www.fsmitha.com/h2/rel09-dixon.htm

"The Man Who Made it Happen—Alfred Nobel." *Trigo*. No pages. Online: http://www.3833.com/wbn_nobel_alfred_bernhard

"The Most Important Gift Catalogue in the World." *Heifer International*. No pages. Online: http://www.heifer.org/gift-catalog/index.html

"The Shakertown Pledge Turns 40." *Presbytery of Newtown Blog*. No pages. Online: http://newtonpresbytery2013.wordpress.com/2013/08/21/the-shakertown-pledge-turns-40/

"The Virtue of Restraint." *Worldwatch Institute*. No pages. Online: http://www.worldwatch.org/node/497

"The Writer's Almanac. September 12, 2008." *Public Radio*. No pages. Online: http://writersalmanac.publicradio.org/index.php?date=2008/09/12

Thoreau, Henry David. *Walden, or, Life in the Woods*. 1845. Reprint, Mineola, NY: Courier Dover, 1995.

Tierney, J.P., et al. *Making a Difference: An Impact Study of Big Brothers Big Sisters*. Philadelphia: Public/Private Ventures, 1995.

Tierney, John. "A Serving of Gratitude May Save the Day." *New York Times*. No pages. Online: http://www.nytimes.com/2011/11/22/science/a-serving-of-gratitude-brings-healthy-dividends.html?_r=0

Toledo Blade, May 15, 1977, E, 3. Online: http://news.google.com/newspapers?nid=1350&dat=19770515&id=JycxAAAAIBAJ&sjid=XgIEAAAAIBAJ&pg=5622,376784

Toobin, Jeffrey. "The Real I.R.S. Scandal." *The New Yorker*. No pages. Online: http://www.newyorker.com/online/blogs/comment/2013/05/irs-scandal-tea-party-oversight.html

"Top Curmudgeon Writers of the Century." *Yahoo Voices*. No pages. Online: http://voices.yahoo.com/top-curmudgeon-writers-century-5895406.html

Tresniowski, Alex. "Not Again." *People*. No pages. Online: http://www.people.com/people/article/0,,20147030,00.html

"Trim Tabs: What They Are and What They Do." *The Flying Change*. No pages. Online: http://www.theflyingchange.com/trim-tabs-what-they-are-and-what-they-do/

Troyat, Henri. *Tolstoy*. New York: Grove, 2001.

"Truce: the Day the Soldiers Stopped Fighting." *Indianapolis Public Library's Kids Blog*. No pages. Online: http://www.imcpl.org/kids/blog/?p=5572

Turnbull, Simon. "How Last Oprah Confession by Marion Jones Hit a Bum Note." *The Independent*. No pages. Online: http://www.independent.co.uk/sport/general/athletics/how-last-oprah-confession-by-marion-jones-hit-a-bum-note-8456568.html

Twain, Mark and Charles Dudley Warner. *The Gilded Age: A Tale of To-day*. Hartford: American Publishing Company, 1874.

"Van Cliburn." *The Economist*. No pages. Online: http://www.economist.com/news/obituary/21573076-pianist-harvey-lavan-van-cliburn-idolised-russians-and-americans-died-february-27th

Vasquez, Juan Gabriel. *The Sound of Things Falling*. Translated by Anne McLean. 2011. New York: Riverhead, 2013.

Vitello, Paul. "William Niehous Survived Three Years in Captivity in Venezuela." *The Globe and Mail*. No pages. Online: http://www.theglobeandmail.com/news/world/william-niehous-survived-three-years-in-captivity-in-venezuela/article14976517/

Wallis, Jim. "A Calendar is a Moral Document." *Sojourners*. No pages. Online: http://sojo.net/sojomail/2009/06/18

Walls, Jeanette. *The Glass Castle*. New York: Scribner, 2003.

Wann, David. "Affluenza." *David Wann Publications*. No pages. Online: http://www.davewann.com/publications/affluenza/

Ward, Mary. *The Literature of Love*. Cambridge: University Press, 2009.

Warner, John. "The Man Behind the Window." *The Morning News*. No pages. http://www.themorningnews.org/article/the-man-behind-the-window

Waskow, Arthur. "The Sukkah of Shalom." In *The Impossible Will Take a Little While: a Citizen's Guide to Hope in a Time of Fear*. Editor Paul Rogat Loeb. New York: Basic Books, 2004.

Watson, Bruce. "How Rich is Rich: Where America Draws the Wealth Line." *Daily Finance*. No pages. Online: http://www.dailyfinance.com/2011/08/23/how-rich-is-rich-where-america-draws-the-wealth-line/

Weingarten, Gene. "Pearls Before Breakfast." *Washington Post*. No pages. Online: http://www.washingtonpost.com/wp-dyn/content/article/2007/04/04/AR2007040401721.html

"What Does It Feel Like to Be an Unattractive Woman?" *Quora Digest*. 145. Online: https://mail.google.com/mail/#inbox/144eb0a015a3b25f

"Whistler's Mother." *Totally History*. No pages. Online: http://totallyhistory.com/whistlers-mother/

Wines, Michael. "William H. Natcher Dies at 84; Held Voting Record in Congress." *New York Times*. No pages. Online: http://www.nytimes.com/1994/03/31/obituaries/william-h-natcher-dies-at-84-held-voting-record-in-congress.html

Witt, Ryan. "Elementary School Student to Michelle Obama: 'But My Mom Doesn't Have Any Immigration Papers.'" *Examiner*. No pages: Online: http://www.examiner.com/article/elementary-school-student-to-michelle-obama-but-my-mom-doesn-t-have-any-immigration-papers

Wolfson, Andrew. "A Hoax Most Cruel: Caller Coaxed McDonald's Managers into Strip-searching a Worker." *Courier-Journal*, October 9, 2005, 1-17. Online: http://www.courier-journal.com/article/20051009/NEWS01/510090392/A-hoax-most-cruel-Caller-coaxed-McDonald-s-managers-into-strip-searching-worker

Wood, Graeme. "Secret Fears of the Super Rich." *The Atlantic*. 1-4. Online: http://www.theatlantic.com/magazine/archive/2011/04/secret-fears-of-the-super-rich/308419/

"Yorba Culture." *Tribe*. No pages. Online: http://tribes.tribe.net/africanspirituality/thread/92f4fde8-0ddf-491a-aa47-47f0c0af0d6e

"Your Three Words." *ABC News*. No pages. Online: http://abcnews.go.com/GMA/Your3Words/

"'You've Got to Find What You Love,' Jobs Says." *Stanford News*. No pages. Online: http://news.stanford.edu/news/2005/june15/jobs-061505.html

Zetter, Kim. "Teen's DIY Energy Hacking Gives African Village New Hope." *Wired Science*. No pages. Online: http://www.wired.com/wiredscience/2009/10/kamwamba-windmill/

Zimmer, Heinrich Robert, and Joseph Campbell: *The King and the Corpse: Tales of the Soul's Conquest of Evil*. New Delhi: Motilal Banarsidass, 1999.

Zinn, Howard. *A Power Governments Cannot Suppress*. San Francisco: City Lights, 2013.

CPSIA information can be obtained at www.ICGtesting.com
Printed in the USA
LVOW09*0728300315

432384LV00002B/2/P

9 781498 206242